THE MANY CONSTITUTIONS OF EUROPE

The Edinburgh Centre for Law and Society
Series Editors: Professor Emilios A. Christodoulidis and Dr Sharon Cowan

Titles in the Series

Law as Institutional Normative Order
Edited by Maksymilian Del Mar and Zenon Bankowski

Law and Agonistic Politics
Edited by Andrew Schaap

Public Law and Politics
The Scope and Limits of Constitutionalism
Edited by Emilios Christodoulidis and Stephen Tierney

Transformations of Policing
Edited by Alistair Henry and David J. Smith

The Universal and the Particular in Legal Reasoning
Edited by Zenon Bankowski and James MacLean

Law and the Politics of Reconciliation
Edited by Scott Veitch

The Many Constitutions of Europe

Edited by

KAARLO TUORI AND SUVI SANKARI
Helsinki University, Finland

Routledge
Taylor & Francis Group
LONDON AND NEW YORK

First published 2010 by Ashgate Publishing

Published 2016 by Routledge
2 Park Square, Milton Park, Abingdon, Oxfordshire OX14 4RN
711 Third Avenue, New York, NY 10017, USA

First issued in paperback 2016

Routledge is an imprint of the Taylor & Francis Group, an informa business

British Library Cataloguing in Publication Data
Tuori, Kaarlo.
The many constitutions of Europe. -- (Edinburgh/Glasgow law and society series)
1. Constitutional law--European Union countries.
2. European Union countries--Politics and government.
I. Title II. Series III. Sankari, Suvi.
342.2'4-dc22

Library of Congress Cataloging-in-Publication Data
The many constitutions of Europe / by Kaarlo Tuori and Suvi Sankari.
p. cm.
Includes bibliographical references and index.
ISBN 978-1-4094-0468-2 (hardback) -- ISBN 978-1-4094-0469-9 (ebook) 1. Constitutional law--Europe. I. Tuori, Kaarlo. II. Sankari, Suvi.
KJC4445.M36 2010
342.402--dc22

2010022189

ISBN 13: 978-1-138-24986-8 (pbk)
ISBN 13: 978-1-4094-0468-2 (hbk)

Contents

PART III ASPECTS OF THE POLITICAL CONSTITUTION

PART IV ASPECTS OF THE SOCIAL CONSTITUTION

List of Contributors

Emilios Christodoulidis is Professor of Legal Theory at the School of Law of the University of Glasgow.

Sabine Frerichs is Post-Doctoral Researcher at the Centre of Excellence in the Foundations of European Law and Polity research, University of Helsinki.

Stefano Giubboni is Professor of Labour Law, University of Perugia.

Sakari Hänninen is Research Professor at the Finnish National Institute for Health and Welfare (THL) and member of the Centre of Excellence in the Foundations of European Law and Polity research, University of Helsinki.

Hans-W. Micklitz is Professor of Economic Law at the European University Institute (EUI) and Professor of Civil Law, University of Bamberg.

Meri Koivusalo is a Senior Researcher at the Finnish National Institute for Health and Welfare (THL).

Inger-Johanne Sand is Professor of Public Law, University of Oslo.

Suvi Sankari is Researcher at the Centre of Excellence in the Foundations of European Law and Polity research, University of Helsinki.

Stijn Smismans is Professor in Law and holder of the Jean Monnet Chair in European Law and Governance at Cardiff Law School.

Kaarlo Tuori is Professor of Jurisprudence, University of Helsinki and Director of the Centre of Excellence in the Foundations of European Law and Polity research, University of Helsinki.

Neil Walker is Professor holding the Regius Chair of Public Law and the Law of Nature and Nations at the University of Edinburgh.

Milène Wegmann, Dr. Phil. (Bern), CIIA, Collaborator to Zentrum für Europäische Wirtschaftsforschung (ZEW), Mannheim.

Editors' Preface

'Le doute n'est pas une condition agréable, mais la certitude est absurde.'

In recent years, European constitutional discourse has been dominated by theoretical debates on constitutional pluralism as a deeper understanding of the co-existence of transnational and national constitutions. This book makes a contribution to the ongoing lively discussion on European constitutionalism by offering a new perspective and a new interpretation of European constitutional plurality. It adopts a different perspective on the many constitutions of Europe, preferring to understand 'constitution' not only as a concept of traditional constitutional law, but as a relational concept, and applies it here to distinguish between the economic constitution, the juridical constitution, the political constitution and the social constitution. This book combines diverse disciplinary approaches (different fields of law, political science, economics and sociology) towards these different aspects of the European constitution, bringing into the constitutional debate even other than merely constitutional scholars. Thus, in addition to providing a general discussion on the European constitution as a relational concept, the book also offers chapters on each specific constitution.

One of the central objectives of this book, and also of the Finnish Centre of Excellence in the Foundations of European Law and Polity Research (Faculty of Law, University of Helsinki) under which this book was assembled, is to facilitate a dialogue between diverse scholarly approaches to European law and to address the legal theoretical implications of Europeanization. In 2009, the main emphasis of the Centre was on the interdependencies between various aspects of the European constitution and constitutional discourse. This multidimensionality of the constitution(s) of Europe inspired the Centre to collect selected contributions by members of the Centre and by its cooperating partners, as well as by its new and old friends, to be first presented, then developed further, and finally published in the form of this book. This cooperation proved that a dialogue across disciplinary boundaries is not only possible, but also fruitful.

We wish to thank Ashgate for agreeing to publish it. Our special thanks go to Alison Kirk and Emilios Christodoulidis and, of course, to all the contributors.

Helsinki, June 2010
Kaarlo Tuori and Suvi Sankari

PART I
Multi-Dimensionality of European Constitutionalism

Chapter 1
The Many Constitutions of Europe

Kaarlo Tuori

The Plurality of Constitutional Pluralities

Europe is living in an era of a plurality of constitutions. But not only that: there exists even a plurality of pluralities of constitutions. There are many constitutions in Europe in at least three senses. Firstly, constitutional concepts, starting from "constitution" itself, are assigned divergent meanings and read through divergent *conceptions*. This variety can be traced back to differences in cultural backgrounds as well as to strategic professional or institutional interests or polito-ideological affiliations of the discussants. Secondly, not only do conceptions of constitution vary but we can also point to different *concepts* of constitution with different connotations and referents. And thirdly, we have the plurality of constitutions in the sense of the co-existence of transnational and national constitutions in Europe.[1]

"Plurality" is not the same as "pluralism". *Constitutional pluralism*, as the term has been used in recent European constitutional debates,[2] is an interpretation of the plurality of constitutions especially in its last sense, as the co-existence of transnational and national constitutions. Emphasis on overlapping, interpenetration and dialogue is common to interventions espousing constitutional pluralism. The term "plurality", in turn, is neutral with regard to the nature of the relationship between the units making up the plurality. Thus, "plurality" should not be confounded with the idea of self-containment and strict boundary-maintenance of the many constitutions either.

The plurality of constitutions is focused on in the second sense of the term, and a distinction at the European level between economic, juridical, political, social and security constitutions is tentatively proposed. The plurality of constitutional conceptions is commented on briefly. However, the interrelations between transnational and national constitutions, the main topic of debates on constitutional pluralism, will largely be left aside. This choice is not due to a wish to downplay the importance of this aspect of plurality but rather reflects the conviction that

1 A terminological clarification: when European constitution is spoken of here, the reference is to the transnational level. By contrast, the expression "constitutions in Europe" covers both the transnational and the national level. Correspondingly, "European law", too, involves the transnational connotation.

2 As a summary, see Avbelj and Komárek 2008.

enriching and deepening debates on constitutional pluralism is not possible without first examining the diversification of the European constitution.

Constitutional Vocabulary in Object-Language and Meta-Language

An integral part of European-level constitutionalization is constitutionalization of the discourse on European law. Constitutional concepts have permeated the vocabulary with which legal actors – such as politicians, as European and nation-state legislators, judges and scholars – express their descriptive and normative views of the past, present and future of European law and polity. Constitutional vocabulary is part and parcel of the object-language employed in the discourse which provides a theorist of European law with source material. By the same token, this vocabulary is – or at least it should be – part and parcel of the meta-language which structures the theorist's own account of European law. The theorist is exposed to the dialectic between object-language and meta-language termed *double hermeneutics*, characteristic of human and social sciences.[3] Through her concepts, the scholar tries to make sense of a piece of social reality which is moulded by the way the social actors themselves conceptualize and try to make sense of their social world. Thus, if a European constitution exists for the relevant actors of European law in the sense of their talking about it, then it should also exist for the theorist. The constitution is brought into existence through the speech acts of the actors of European law.

Due to these inescapable double hermeneutics, a scholar's meta-language cannot drift very far from the object-language of social actors. The scholar shares the culture she is examining; her meta-language draws from the same cultural reservoir as the object-language of social actors. A theorist may strive for, and even attain, a reflexive distance to her culture, but her reflexivity, too, is subject to cultural constraints. However, theorists maintain a two-way relationship with their cultural environment. Not only does the object-language impose constraints on a theorist's meta-language, but a theorist may well contribute to a renewal of object-language. A theorist, too, is a social actor and participant in the discourse through which society's cultural heritage is reproduced and, simultaneously, renovated. In the longer term, even an individual scholar's meta-linguistic innovation may leave its impact on object-language, through a process of cultural sedimentation.

In legal scholarship, the borderline between meta-language and object-language may be even more fluid than in other social and human sciences. Legal scholars are not only actors in the realm of academic science. They are also legal actors, and with the very same speech acts they participate in both scholarly discourse and the discourse shaping the law; a Luhmannian systems theorist would speak here of a structural coupling. Legal scholars constitute the third main group of actors of

3 Neil Walker (2003) has also pointed to the significance of double hermeneutics for a theorist of European law.

modern law, along with legislators and judges. Not only what they say but also how they say it has a potential impact on future law and its cultural underpinnings.

In respect of constitutional vocabulary, the principal choice for a theorist of European law has already been made: quite simply, this vocabulary is by now too ingrained an element of the language of the (other) actors of European law to be ignored. Still, the leeway object-language leaves for a constitutional theorist of European law is wider than is usually granted to a legal scholar. This is due to the existing plurality of both constitutional concepts and conceptions of these concepts; no firmly established and univocal constitutional vocabulary exists at the level of object-language. European law, especially outside the core area of free movement of goods and competition law, is very much law in-the-making, a rather disintegrated body of legal norms with rather underdeveloped and unsteady legal-cultural underpinnings. The process of sedimentation through which a surface-level legal order is furnished with legal-cultural support is still incomplete. In many fields, European law is still in search of its generally accepted language: its conceptual framework as the vocabulary and its characteristic patterns of argumentation as the grammar. This certainly is the case with European constitutional law. For scholars, this state of affairs opens a window of opportunity: the prospects of influencing the ongoing cultural process, of having a say in the evolution of European law and its language, are brighter than in other, more developed fields. This, of course, is a major backdrop to the lively constitutional discussion among European scholars; scholars, too, are moved by their particular professional interests.

Divergent Interests and Cultural Backgrounds

Two main accounts exist for the present polyphony – some would perhaps call it cacophony – of European constitutional discourse: a critical or realist one and a cultural–hermeneutical one.

The first of these is the narrative by critical legal scholars (CLS) and political scientists, especially the so-called neo-functionalists. Conceptual development is explained by the divergent interests stirring legal actors; in terms of speech act theory, the focus is on the perlocutionary aspect of speech acts making up European legal discourse. Conceptual choices are treated, not as pristine intellectual moves, but as motivated by strategic interests which are related to the interlocutors' professional or institutional status or their wider ideological or political affiliations. Conceptual field is examined as a battlefield where individual and collective parties pursue specific strategies, such as introducing new conceptual distinctions or redefining key concepts and hijacking them from adversaries. Thus, the landmark constitutional decisions of the Court of Justice in the 1960s and their acceptance by ordinary national courts, or the invention of fundamental-rights vocabulary by the Court – and its use in the dialogue with national constitutional courts – are traced back to the respective courts' objectives in an inter-institutional power game. Scholarly discourse, too, is seen as engaged in politics of (re-)description and academic turf-fighting; through change of vocabulary, constitutional lawyers aim to recapture the field from international lawyers.[4]

In conceptual contests, concepts with positive value connotations, that is, evaluative-descriptive or persuasive concepts, to use Quentin Skinner's terms,[5] hold a key position. The power of defining the meaning of such concepts and hijacking them from adversaries is crucial for dominance in the conceptual field. The prominent role which constitutional vocabulary played in such foundational moments of legal and political modernity as the French and American revolutions attached to constitutional concepts a highly positive value charge, which they still possess. Constitutional concepts are used in doctrinal expositions of the law in force, and they share the general normativity of legal-doctrinal concepts. But as persuasive, evaluative concepts, constitutional concepts display an even more profound normativity, which relates to the preferred future development of law and its object of regulation.[6] When German ordo-liberals adopted the concept of *Wirtschaftsverfassung* (economic constitution) and endowed it with a meaning decisively different from that propounded by such left-leaning Weimar scholars as Hugo Sinzheimer and Franz L. Neumann, they did not seek merely a cognitive added value in the hermetic realm of legal (and economic) science; they aimed at realizing a specific economic *Ordnungspolitik*, first in post-war Germany and, subsequently, at a transnational European level.

However, the critical or realist account falls short of its objective even as factual description and causal explanation; the truth of this narrative is but a partial truth (perhaps distorted by the hegemonic academic aspirations of CLS and neo-functionalist political scientists!). Conceptual choices are not made in a vacuum; discussants are not offered the luxury of a free choice, but the options available are culturally limited. Legal actors always approach the law and legal problems through a particular hermeneutical pre-understanding, provided by the legal culture which they have acquired and internalized through their education and professional experiences. This entails an intractable perspectivism in law, noticeable even in the nation-state context but still more pronounced in such an emergent and culturally incomplete transnational legal system as the EU.

As has often been noted, transnational constitutional vocabulary still bears evident traces of its original nation-state template. European legal vocabulary inevitably taps the resources of national legal cultures which constitute the only available fount for the legal Esperanto of the emerging legal system. Many of the legal concepts of modern law can be traced back to transnational origins in

4 Martti Koskeniemi's (1999) provocative essay on human rights in the EU provides an excellent illustration of the CLS approach. The classical politological account is Burley and Mattli 1993; see also Alter 2001; and Stone Sweet 2004, from among the continuously expanding literature.

5 See Skinner 2002: 148 and 161.

6 This comes close to the distinction Matej Avbelj (2008) has made between doctrinal and philosophical or visionary use of constitutional concepts.

Roman law. Here constitutional concepts are an exception, so intimately are they – despite their ultimate pre-modern background – linked to the modern nation-state in the worldview of both the general public and legal and political elites. European constitutional law is still in its formative phase, so that differences in national constitutional cultures are bound to influence the way the discussants conceive of the transnational European constitution and its functions. It would be surprising if the fact that the United Kingdom does not possess a unitary written constitution – a constitution in the formal sense of the term – does not colour the view British interlocutors have on the European constitution. Equally surprising would be if divergent national emphases on power-creating and polity-building or power-restricting and controlling functions of political constitutions did not leave their imprint on European-level debates as well. The typical perspectivism of European law affects constitutional law, too.

Indeed, when discussing a European constitution, the level of *constitutional culture – constitutionalism*, we could also say – should always be brought in. Law does not consist merely of surface-level regulations and decisions; it also comprises the legal-cultural underpinnings of such legal speech acts: general legal concepts, legal principles and the like, which inform the pre-understanding of legal actors.[7] This also holds for constitutional law. "Constitution" should not be reduced to a formal constitution, but should include the level of constitutionalism in the sense of constitutional culture, through which constitutional actors approach and read the formal constitution. As long as no uniform European understanding of constitutionalism exists, as long as the European constitution is a constitution without constitutionalism or a constitutional body without a soul,[8] nationally differentiated constitutional traditions are bound to fill the vacuum.

So, the plurality of rival constitutional conceptions has two main sources: institutional, professional, and ideological biases and divergent legal-cultural backgrounds of the discussants. Let us then move from conceptions to concepts, to the second sense of the plurality of constitutions in Europe.

Constitution as a Relational Concept

The polyphony (cacophony?) characteristic of European constitutional debates results not solely from divergent conceptions of one and the same concept. Constitutional object-language also includes different *concepts* of constitution, with different connotations and referents. Thus, the concept of constitution implicit in the ordo-liberal theory of European economic constitution (*Wirtschaftsverfassung*) is not the same as the concept of constitution implicit in the writings of scholars

7 An attempt to expound this view of law is made in *Critical Legal Positivism* (Tuori 2002).

8 These characterisations are by Weiler (1999: 298); and Poiares Maduro (2003: 77), respectively.

detecting a process of constitutionalization running through the landmark decisions of the Court of Justice in the 1960s.

In the face of this plurality, the first task for a theorist of European law – located on a slippery meta-level – is to elaborate a taxonomy of the concepts employed at the object-level, perhaps complemented by the theorist's own conceptual proposals concerning emerging but still un-named European constitutions. Existing discourse, existing linguistic usage provide the theorist with a starting point, but merely a starting point. The theorist may also put forth her own conceptual suggestions, and, if she takes seriously the scholarly obligation to add to the clarity and intelligibility of European law and to give the present polyphony a contrapuntal twist, she should do so. But taxonomy is not all. Obviously, diverse concepts must have something in common, at least in the sense of family resemblances, which accounts for and warrants use of the same term, "constitution". What that something is makes up the general or meta-level concept of (European) constitution. Finding the common denominators of concepts of constitution and (re)constructing a meta-level concept is the second concomitant task facing a constitutional theorist of European law. These two tasks should not be taken in isolation but, rather, as mutually presupposing and supporting each other. To arrive at a taxonomy of putative European constitutions, we have to start from a tentative meta-level notion, which then can be further substantiated after exploring in greater depth the individual instances of constitutions. The Rawlsian term "reflective equilibrium" might be appropriate for describing interaction between the object- and meta-levels. It should be emphasized that this is not engagement in elaborating a universal constitutional theory, applicable as such also to nation-state constitutions. But, undoubtedly, the original nation-state template of constitutional concepts has influenced legal pre-understanding, too, and affects this discussion of European law. Conversely, the possibility that a theory of transnational or European constitution could have more general implications as well is not excluded.

For introducing a tentative taxonomy of European constitutions and, simultaneously, for initiating a (re)construction of a more general concept of (European) constitution, a cue is taken from two – at least at first glance – widely diverse theoretical directions: Niklas Luhmann's systems-theoretically oriented understanding of constitution, and the institutional theory of law already instigated by Carl Friedrich von Savigny and in recent decades expounded by, first of all, Neil MacCormick and Ota Weinberger. What unites these seemingly disparate approaches to constitution or law in general is a relational emphasis. The institutional theory of law has taught us that all law can – and should! – be examined in interaction with its object of regulation: the law generates legal-institutional facts where the social or psychological factual side and the legal normative side are intertwined, and this, arguably, is the very point of law.[9] Correspondingly, Luhmann examines "constitution" as a relational concept. According to him, constitution establishes a *structural coupling* between two differentiated subsystems of modern society: the

9 See MacCormick and Weinberger 1986.

legal and political systems.[10] The idea of the relational character of constitution will be adopted here but it will be detached from its Luhmannian context and given a more general twist.

Through constitution, the law relates to something else (or, in case of the juridical constitution, to itself), to a *constitutional object* and, thus, establishes a *constitutional relation*. The constitutional relation can, but need not, be of a *constitutive* nature. This is the case when a constitution constitutes, helps to bring into existence, the constitutional object as the other pole of the constitutional relation. But it may well be that a constitution constitutionalizes something already existing; something preceding its constitutionalization. In fact, the distinct constitutional features separating the French and the American revolutions have often been examined in light of this variance: in France, the constitutional revolution aimed at constituting a new socio-economic system, whereas in America the emphasis was on reaffirming the traditional "liberties of the Englishman".

Luhmann examines merely a subspecies, albeit a paradigmatic one, of constitution: the political constitution, with the political system as the constitutional object. In addition, his systems-theoretical framework allows for only one particular type of constitutional relation: namely, structural coupling. In Luhmann's auto-poietic systems theory, a structural coupling exists when one and the same social element operates simultaneously in two social subsystems and thereby establishes a bridge over their reciprocal operative closure.

The constitutive significance of the constitutional relation for constitutional theory implies that the taxonomy of constitutions and corresponding concepts should be based on an analysis of constitutional objects, that is, the 'something' to which the law relates through the constitution. The following European-level taxonomy is proposed:

- economic constitution
- juridical constitution
- political constitution
- social constitution and
- security constitution.

Each field appearing as the other pole of the constitutional relation – as constitutional object – has been discussed in constitutional terms; constitutional vocabulary, although perhaps not the very concept of constitution, is already employed in the object-language a constitutional theorist has to reckon with. That is fairly obvious with regard to the first four dimensions of the European constitution. However, even security issues have been discussed in a constitutional framework, although the very term "security constitution" may sound strange.

Let us try to endow these diverse European constitutions or – if you prefer – dimensions of European constitution with brief tentative characterizations. In

10 See Luhmann 2004: 404 *ff.*

respect of the three first dimensions, this should be relatively easy. *Economic constitution* is about the relation of law to the fundamentals of the economic system; *juridical constitution* concerns the fundamental features of the legal system and establishes a reflexive relation of the law with itself; and through *political constitution*, the law regulates the political system or – to use different political vocabulary – the polity, and contributes to both its empowerment and containment. The two last dimensions of European constitution are not equally obvious or uncontroversial. The following definitions are meant to procure merely a starting point. The primary constitutional object of the *social constitution* consists of the members of society, their social life-world. And finally, the *security constitution* addresses the internal and external security risks of society.

In its relational characteristics, the general concept of constitution being sought here bears a resemblance to Gunther Teubner's "societal constitution". Teubner discusses constitutions in the context of global social systems which engender their own law. He argues that the constitution of these systems relates the law to the particular reflexive mechanism of the system at issue.[11] As is the case with Luhmann's analysis of the political constitution, Teubner examines constitutions in terms of a structural coupling between law and another social subsystem. The systems-theoretical ballast of Luhmann's and Teubner's constitutional vocabulary accounts for both its strength and its weakness. The notion of structural coupling may prove fruitful for analysing the constitutive relation of law with those social fields which in general are susceptible to a systems-theoretical examination. This may be the case with law and politics but hardly with the social life-world of the members of society. The systems-theoretical imaginary clearly exhausts its innovatory potential, if not sooner, then at least in front of the social constitution. So let us not burden our constitutional conceptual apparatus with too wide-reaching systems-theoretical pre-assumptions, whilst not categorically rejecting the cognitive potentials of the Luhmannian approach, either.

Constitution as Higher Law

If relational character is not an exclusive speciality of constitutional law, but a feature shared by all law, it seems warranted to ask whether there is something particular in the way a constitution relates to its regulatory object, that is, in the constitutional relation. At least part of the answer may lie in the following: "constitution" invokes a sense of *higher law*. The idea of higher law assigns the constitution a privileged position with respect to other law. The idea can be given either a formal or a substantive reading. The *formal* reading is epitomized by Hans Kelsen's hierarchical *Stufenbau* of legal norms, where constitution occupies the highest level next to the *Grundnorm*. In this model, a constitution as higher law provides the mandate for issuing lower-level norms and, in cases of conflict,

11 See Teubner 2004a and 2004b.

defeats the latter. The requirement of a *qualified procedure* for amending the (formal) constitution or for issuing a new constitution is also related to the formal reading of the idea of higher law. Finally, the formal status of the constitution as higher law implies or at least makes intelligible the need of particular institutional arrangements for guaranteeing its observance. These can range from a constitutional court to bureaucratic or parliamentary forms of ex ante *constitutional review*.

One of the main contributions an examination of the putative European constitution can make to general constitutional theory may lie in the analytical dimension. European constitutional peculiarities compel us to sharpen our analytical precision, to disintegrate "lump concepts": constitutional features which in nation-states go together and whose intertwinement we tend to take for granted may at the European level lead separate lives. Hence either/or questions about the European constitution are often misguided. This also goes for the much-debated issue whether a formal constitution in general exists at the European level. It may turn out that some ideas related to the formal notion of constitution as higher law are applicable, while others are not.

The *substantive* sense of higher law relates to the normative contents of constitution. Here, "higher" means basic or fundamental: a constitution is supposed to give expression to the fundamental normative principles of the polity and its law, as well as society in general. In this sense, the modern constitution has taken over the legacy of pre-modern *lois fondamentaux*. What basics the constitution should affirm are of course debatable. Equally controversial is the extent to which the political legislator, armed with a democratic mandate, is and should be bound by constitutional provisions.

Power-Relations as the Focus of the Constitution

Modern constitutions usually fall into two parts: an *organizational* or institutional one and an individualist, *rights-oriented* one. The main focus of nation-state constitutions lies in the political dimension, where the two-part structure corresponds to the institutional and individual poles of a polity. Institutional provisions organize political power, regulate the interrelations of the bodies wielding this power, and confer on it a legal mandate and form. The rights part of constitutions offers individuals safeguards against abuse of power and protects their private autonomy, provides them with public autonomy (political rights), and may even include guarantees for the factual realization of private and public autonomy (social rights).[12] These typical contents of a nation-state constitution summarize what the main *constitutional topics* are: power and citizenship.

In their various dimensions but perhaps most conspicuously in the political one, constitutions regulate *power relations*, garnishing them with legal attire. At the organizational or institutional pole of a polity, constitutions fulfil both power-

12 The concepts of private and public autonomy derive from Habermas 1996: 118 *ff.*

creating – empowering – and power-constraining functions. The respective weight of these functions varies and, in fact, is one of the main criteria by which diverse types of constitutionalism can be distinguished. From the perspective of the institutional pole of the polity, constitutional rights appear as restrictions on power. Looked at from the other pole, constitutional rights are crucial in the establishment of *citizenship*: through constitutional rights, individuals are transformed from mere objects of political power into citizens of the polity. As citizens, individuals have not only obligations but also rights with regard to the polity. Connected to the power-constraining function of a constitution, citizenship rights, which guarantee the public autonomy of individuals, aim at *democratizing* the exercise of political power. Thus, democratization is to be added to power-generation and power-containment as the third power-related function of modern constitutions.

The rights dimension of modern constitutions alludes to their *individualist* or *individualizing* orientation. This observation provides us with a guideline in the examination of European constitutionalization, too: a central aspect of this process consists of establishing a direct link between European institutions and European individuals, that is, members of "the peoples of Europe", referred to even in the preamble to the Treaty of Rome. This process lends itself to analysis in the framework of *citizenship*: an analysis of the cumulative addition of new layers to European citizenship. But European citizens are citizens of their nation-states as well, and the complicated relations between transnational and nation-state levels also affect the constitutional status of individuals. In present-day Europe, much of constitutional problematics focuses on the *three-part relationship between the EU, nation-states and individuals*.

Constitutional Claims and Promises

Constitutional concepts are typically of a persuasive or evaluative character, evoking positive connotations. This is due to the promises that constitutional speech acts make and the claims they raise. A central claim is that to *autonomy*. Often enough, a constitution equals a Declaration of Independence. Drafting a constitution is the first thing a newly independent nation-state engages in, and in adopting a constitution, it reinforces its claim to autonomous existence. Correspondingly, through its landmark decisions, epitomizing juridical constitutionalization, the Court of Justice raised a claim to independence of the Community legal order with respect to both national legal orders and international law. In the European context, autonomy equals *transnationalization*: as a transnational legal order and polity, the Community (the Union) has asserted its distinctiveness from both nation-state and international legal and political models.

In addition to autonomy, constitutional vocabulary implies a claim to or promise of *unity, order and coherence*. Thus, the political constitution is expected to secure the unity and coherence of political power. The juridical constitution, in turn, indicates the bodies authorized to produce legal norms and, in H.L.A. Hart's terms, determines the rule of recognition of the legal order. It also confirms the principles which define relations between the legal norms identified by the rule of recognition, such as the *lex superior* and the *lex posterior* principles. This is expected to ensure the *logical consistency* of the legal order. In addition, fundamental rights and other constitutional principles, as an integral element of the legal culture, are supposed to bring about *substantive coherence* in law. With respect to individuals and connected to the rights element, the main promise of the constitution, accounting for the positive connotations it provokes or is at least expected to provoke, is that of *autonomy*, *citizenship* and *democracy*. This is closely linked to the claim of *legitimacy*, intractably associated with constitutionalism. The claim of legitimacy, in fact, concerns both poles of the constitutional relation: not only is constitution as a normative entity presumed to be legitimate but it is also expected to transfer its legitimacy to the other pole, the object of constitutional regulation.

The legitimacy of a constitution can be either origin- or contents-based. *Origin-based legitimacy* derives from either or both the circumstances in which a constitution has been enacted or the procedure which was thereby adhered to: the *constitutional moment* which gave birth to the constitution. *Contents-based legitimacy*, in turn, flows from the substance of the constitution, from its correspondence with the basic ethical values and moral principles of society. But it is also possible that the proponents of constitutionalization put their faith in the sheer legitimating force of constitutional concepts – which, in turn, is only explicable against the background of what can be called constitutional normalcy, i.e., origin- or contents-based legitimacy, or both. This is a case of *parasitic legitimacy*.

It is evident that in European constitutional discourse, constitutional concepts are often used in order to enhance the legitimacy of the object pole of constitutional relation, say, European economic order, European legal system or European polity. Accordingly, the claim of constitutionality is often translatable to a claim to legitimacy. But the criteria by which the merits of the claim are assessed or the audience to which the claim is addressed do not necessarily remain the same when constitutionalization advances into new domains. Therefore one issue on the agenda of European constitutional theory is the specificity of the claim to legitimacy attached to diverse European constitutions.

Constitutional Evolution instead of Revolution

Some central concepts which have played a prominent role in recent European debates are lacking from the conceptual toolkit which has been developed for structuring research on the many constitutions of Europe. The missing concepts include the tripartite cluster of *constituent power* (*pouvoir constituant*), *demos* as the subject of this power, and *constitutional moment* as the instance when this power is wielded. The reason for their absence is simple. These concepts, forming an interdependent whole, were coined in a specific branch of constitutional culture: the revolutionary American and French constitutionalism. They are not transferable to an examination of European constitutions, which have not resulted from the exercise of constituent power by a European *demos* at an identifiable, single constitutional moment. Instead of a revolutionary break, the constitutions of Europe are a continuously evolving outcome of an ongoing process which does include such high-profile manifest occasions as treaty amendments but is not exhausted by them.

Should the cluster of revolutionary-tuned concepts of constituent power, *demos*, and constitutional moment find no application at the European level, what is their evolutionary counterpart? It is suggested that it is *constitutionalization*.

"Constitutionalization" is a pivotal concept for European constitutional analysis but of lesser use in many nation-state frameworks. It is no coincidence that European constitutional scholarship focuses so much on the history of the legal aspect of European integration. A European constitution is not a stand-still phenomenon but, rather, an ever-uncompleted series of legal speech acts. It is an evolutionary and, at the same time, a differentiated process: all the putative European constitutions have not developed simultaneously or at the same pace but, rather, successively, following a certain order. Especially in countries with a formal, written constitution, the tacit understanding is that, say, juridical and political constitutions emerge and develop parallel to each other. The very talk of different constitutions, distinguished by their specific regulatory objects, may sound strange in nation-state contexts. By contrast, typical of European constitutionalization is – to borrow Ernst Bloch's expression – *Gleichzeitigkeit des Ungleichzeitigen*. This entails a new task for European constitutional scholars: to track the diverse temporalities of European constitutionalization and to detect the internal logic inherent in its course; provided, of course, that any such logic exists!

According to this (hypo)thesis, European constitutionalization is susceptible to periodization, where each stage receives its colouring from a particular constitution. Reflecting the temporal and functional primacy of economic integration, the first wave proceeded under the auspices of an economic constitution; in the second phase, the emphasis shifted to a juridical constitution; during the third wave, the focus was transferred to a political constitution; and finally, in our time, the pacemaker role appears to have been taken over by a security constitution. This (hypo)thesis guides this version of the narrative of European constitutionalization.

Related to "constitutionalization", even other process-oriented concepts are of particular relevance for European-level constitutional analysis. These include "transnationalization" and "individualization". In important respects, constitutionalization has signified *transnationalization*: superseding nation-state structures and detaching decision-making from member state control. Constitutionalization has also implied *individualization*: establishment of direct links between European institutions and European citizens in their diverse attires. Nevertheless, the tripartite relation between the transnational European level, the nation-state level and the individual also retains its centrality: the direct link established between the transnational and the individual always hints at the potential relevance of the nation-state, too.

In the Beginning There Was an Economic Constitution

Arguably, constitutionalization of Europe started from the economic dimension. The first to employ constitutional vocabulary in the European context were German economists and private lawyers of the ordo-liberal school, who introduced the notion of *Wirtschaftsverfassung* ("economic constitution"). The economic constitution, as the ordo-liberals conceived it, was power-constraining rather than power-constituting in its orientation. What was to be constrained was economic power, and – what is important to note – economic power wielded not only by public but also – and, in a sense, even primarily – by private actors. The ordo-liberals put their faith in the market economy, but they did not trust the market's capacity to ensure the necessary conditions for its functioning through its inherent mechanisms. *Competition law*, which was addressed to private economic actors, constituted an integral part of the European economic constitution. As regards public power, the major threat to a free market was seen to arise from regulatory measures of nation-states and not of the Community itself. The ordo-liberal reading of the European economic constitution was based on a clear division of tasks and competences between transnational and national levels.[13]

The Community was not supposed to assume redistributive or regulatory policies. Indeed, in the original Rome Treaty they were left out; the Community was to focus on establishing and ensuring a European market, while redistribution and market-correcting regulation would be the province of the nation-state.[14] But conflicts between the two orders of competence were more frequent than expected, and the economic constitution also provided for their solution: as a rule, nation-state redistributive or regulative measures were permissible only within limits set by the overriding objective of a common market. Relying on the treaty provisions on the *fundamental freedoms* and *state aid*, the Court of Justice could strike down national legislation and other regulatory measures contradicting this objective, reflecting the constitutional *Gesamtentscheidung*. Thus, especially Article 30 EC (then 28 EC, now 34 TFEU) on free movement of goods developed into an "economic due-process clause".[15] The economic constitution included both a rights element and an institutional-organizational element. The rights element consisted of the four market freedoms which conferred *market citizenship* on European economic actors: they were European citizens, bearers of distinct

13 See also Wegmann's contribution in this volume.

14 Here common agricultural policy was the major exception, constituting a thorn in the eyes of ordo-liberals.

15 Using the term "economic due-process clause" in this context is from Poiares Maduro (1998: 60, 126–31 and 157).

European rights, in their economic roles. If the European constitution(s) embarked on an evolutionary road from the economic dimension, correspondingly, European citizenship was initially instituted as economic citizenship. In the institutional dimension, the key transnational bodies established to monitor observance of the substantive part of the economic constitution were the Commission as the antitrust authority, bearing the main responsibility in supervising the competition rules, and the Court of Justice as the constitutional court.

The European economic constitution included a claim to legitimacy. This claim was addressed to European economic citizens: it was a *promise of economic prosperity*. Indeed, the long post-war period of economic growth, which for its part facilitated the building-up of the welfare state at the national level, seemed to redeem that promise. Such legitimacy is often termed output legitimacy, in contrast to input legitimacy derived from democratic political procedures. In a sense, the emphasis on output legitimacy involved a *negation of a political constitution*, with its democratic implications. Democratic procedures and democratic legitimacy were supposed to be the preserve of nation-states, necessitated by their redistributive and regulatory activities. The expressly defined tasks of the Community flowing from economic *Gesamtentscheidung* were to be the domain of experts, with no need of democratic legitimation; in the ordo-liberal view, transnational democratic procedures would open channels of influence for particular rent-seeking interests and endanger the framework *ordo* required by the transnational free market economy.[16]

The "economic constitution" as propagated by ordo-liberal economic and legal scholars was clearly a normative concept, and not only in the doctrinal but also in the visionary or ideological sense of normativity: it involved a *Gesamtentscheidung* in favour of a free market economy. But the concept can also be used in a more neutral, doctrinal sense, stripped of its ideological connotations. The ordo-liberal understanding of the European economic constitution as a doctrinal account of EC law became more and more contrived, especially after the treaty amendments introduced by the Single European Act of 1986 and the Maastricht Treaty. The objectives of European integration have expanded from establishing a common or single market to socially oriented aims, and the EU has assumed new regulatory competencies within, say, industrial policy and R & D (research and development). The original rather clear-cut division of tasks and competencies between the Community and the nation-states became increasingly blurred with the three-pillar European Union and with the expansion of transnational competences within the Community pillar. Theorists of the European economic constitution were faced with a choice: either to shed the notion of its doctrinal pretensions and retain it as an overtly ideological concept serving as a critical yardstick for assessing the

16 The classic ordo-liberal text, adopting – or rather, hijacking! – the term "*Wirtschaftsverfassung*", is Franz Böhm's *Wettbewerb und Monopolkampf* (1933). The main ordo-liberal theorist of Community law has been Ernst-Joachim Mestmäcker (see especially 1998).

missteps of European integration, or to delete the ideological subtext and employ the concept as a purely doctrinal device for presenting existing European law without any clear commitment to an economic *Gesamtentscheidung*. Both options have been grasped. Orthodox ordo-liberals have adopted a highly critical posture towards the direction taken by European integration after, say, the Single European Act,[17] while others have made their peace with the development and turned the concept into an ideologically neutral doctrinal notion. The non-German authors who starting from the 1990s have adopted the concept of an economic constitution have also prevalently used it in this neutral sense.[18] Thus, diverse conceptions exist of the concept of an economic constitution, too.

The first wave of European constitutionalization was dominated by the economic aspect. During the second wave, the emphasis shifted to the juridical constitution. But this should not be taken as signifying a standstill or an eclipse of the economic constitution; the latent and manifest development of the economic constitution continued, and it retained its functional primacy. The constitutions that followed did not topple or replace the economic one but added new layers to the existing constitution. Yet another phase was inaugurated with the Treaty of Maastricht and its provisions on European monetary union. Entry into force of these provisions brought into existence a new transnational, non-political, expert institution, monitoring the new monetary dimension of the European economic constitution: the European Central Bank.

The Heroic Saga of Juridical Constitutionalization

Of all European constitutional narratives, the one about juridical constitutionalization is perhaps the most familiar and most often recited, frequently with a heroic undertone. It is the story of the great landmark cases of the Court of Justice establishing Community law as an *independent legal order*; the story of *van Gend en Loos* and *Costa v ENEL*,[19] which together make up the declaration of independence of Community law. The aspiration for autonomy was accompanied by a quest for order; in addition to independence, the promise of juridical constitutionalization was the unity of European law.

Influenced by Joseph Weiler's seminal article,[20] the conventional account of juridical constitutionalization points to a deadlock in the political dimension, still dominated by intergovernmental structures and procedures, which left the field to the Court. But another explanation is possible as well, premised on the

17 For a representative summary of the ordo-liberal critique, see Streit and Mussler 1995.

18 See especially Poiares Maduro 1998 and Baquero Cruz 2002.

19 Case 26/62, *Van Gend en Loos*, ECR 1963, 1, and Case 6/64, *Costa v ENEL*, ECR 1964, 585.

20 Weiler 1991.

functional and temporal primacy of the economic constitution. The institutional-organizational element of the economic constitution, as conceived by the ordo-liberals, and its specific quest for legitimacy implied a negation of political transnationalization and constitutionalization. By contrast, this required juridical constitutionalization. Arguably, an internal constitutional logic leads from economic to juridical constitutionalization. The free transnational market economy could not be achieved without assigning the provisions of the economic constitution, such as the competition rules or rules guaranteeing the four freedoms, direct effect in the member states and ensuring their efficacy and uniform application through the constitutional doctrine of supremacy. Indeed, the connection between the economic and the juridical constitution was clearly spelled out in *van Gend en Loos* and *Costa v ENEL*, although not in explicit constitutional terms.

The declaration of independence issued by the Court of Justice was addressed in two directions: towards (general) international law and towards the national legal orders of the member states. While asserting the autonomy of Community law in respect of national legal orders, *van Gend en Loos* still characterized Community law as a "new legal order of international law".[21] By contrast, *Costa v ENEL* dropped this expression and endowed the EEC Treaty with constitutive effects which exceeded those of "ordinary international treaties".[22]

If the tale of juridical constitutionalization is written in terms of a double quest for autonomy and unity, the chapters following *van Gend en Loos* and *Costa v ENEL* should narrate further extension of the principle of supremacy and the effects of Community law on national legal orders as applied by national courts. Central themes would include, say, confirmation by the Court of Justice that Community law was to take precedence even over conflicting national constitutional law and elaboration of the doctrine of direct and indirect effects of directives. A wholly new chapter was initiated by the Maastricht Treaty with its three-pillar structure. The third pillar was originally meant to be a domain of intergovernmentalism, but there, too, a process of juridical transnationalization and constitutionalization occurred which, in a way, reiterated the development already completed within Community law. This development was concluded by entry into force of the Lisbon Treaty, abolition of the pillar structure, and inclusion of Justice and Home Affairs in the legislative competence of the EU. Present-day impetus for juridical constitutionalization has not arisen from the economic constitution but from what may be termed the security constitution.

In line with the economic constitution, the juridical constitution possesses both an institutional-organizational and a rights element. In the former respect, the main beneficiaries were the Court of Justice as the constitutional court of Community law and the ordinary courts of the member states. Juridical constitutionalization created a unique system of judicial constitutional review which combines the German-type centralized model of constitutional court and the US-type diffused

21 Case 26/62, *Van Gend en Loos*, ECR 1963, 1.

22 Case 6/64, *Costa v ENEL*, ECR 1964, 585.

model with ordinary courts monitoring the higher law. In an institutional respect, the juridical constitution meant judicial empowerment, enhancement of the position of both the Court of Justice and the ordinary courts of the member states entrusted with the task of supervising conformity of national legislation with Community law. Through the principle of supremacy, established by *Costa v ENEL*,[23] ordinary courts received norm-controlling powers over Acts of national legislatures even in member states with no domestic system of judicial constitutional review, while instituting a rival form of judicial review in member states that have a constitutional court. If the Court of Justice and the ordinary courts of the member states were the main winners in the institutional power game, the main losers were the national constitutional courts and legislatures.

Juridical constitutionalization did not follow from any decision by the Council as the intergovernmental Community legislature or the member states as the Masters of the Treaties. A juridical constitution is a reflexive phenomenon: the law, as it were, defines its own basic characteristics. This also goes for the juridical constitution of the Community, which defines its relation to national legal orders and international law through such doctrines as direct effect and supremacy. But juridical constitutionalization has been a reflexive process in another sense as well. In the institutional respect, it amounted to judicial auto-empowerment; its primary mechanism consisted of the preliminary ruling procedure, based on the interplay between ordinary national courts and the Court of Justice. National courts and litigants invoking Community law were the immediate addressees of the speech acts by which the Court of Justice introduced and elaborated the doctrines promoting juridical constitutionalization. By the same token, these courts and litigants were also the primary addressees of the legitimacy claims associated with these speech acts. That national courts and private litigants accepted these claims was crucial for the success of juridical constitutionalization.

From the perspective of institutional turf-fighting, it is not surprising that the opposition against juridical constitutionalization did not so much arise from the ordinary courts of member states but from constitutional courts. If the principle of supremacy extended to define Community law's relation to the national constitution and if supervision of Community law as a higher law fell to the exclusive jurisdiction of the Community judiciary (including ordinary courts of member states applying Community law), then the competence of constitutional courts would be notably restricted and their position as guardians of the national constitution threatened in that a significant part of the law applied by national courts would be detached from their scrutiny. As we know, the German and Italian constitutional courts, for instance, did not accept this conclusion without qualifications. After enlargement of the EU in 2004, the constitutional courts of some new member states have adopted positions largely similar to that of the German *solange* and the Italian *controlimiti* doctrine.[24]

23 Case 6/64, *Costa v ENEL*, ECR 1964, 585.

24 See Sadurski 2008.

In the rights respect, juridical constitutionalization confirmed the direct relation between the new legal order and individuals, member state nationals. It established their European economic citizenship and entitlement to economic rights under Community law. By the same token, it added a new *judicial* layer to their rights and their European citizenship by acknowledging their capacity to invoke Community law in national courts.

Like constitutionalization in general, juridical constitutionalization expressed a quest for autonomy and unity, although it actually generated a situation of interlegality[25] and plurality, ripe with potential conflict. As the Court of Justice stated in *van Gend en Loos*,[26] Community law is both an independent legal order and, in the domain of direct effect, part and parcel of the national legal orders of the member states; it is simultaneously something outside and inside national legal orders. As an insider, through the principle of supremacy, it claimed for itself the top echelon of the national hierarchy of legal norms in its field of regulation, as well as the privilege to derogate from the *lex posteriori* rule. In Kelsenian terms, this was a revolutionary claim, implying a change in the national *Grundnorm*. Conceptualized in terms of sovereignty, preferred by the Court of Justice, it was equally revolutionary: it amounted to an assertion that the member states had irrevocably abdicated part of their legislative sovereignty, resulting in divided sovereignty. This being too much for constitutional courts to swallow, they stuck to the old *Grundnorm* and subsumed the Community law applied in national courts under the national constitution. The ensuing stalemate has provided the starting point for the still ongoing debate on constitutional pluralism, whose focus, in the taxonomy of this chapter, is on the juridical constitution. Without going into the details of the debate, one issue concerning the internal logic of European constitutionalization must be pointed out. What especially the German constitutional court was worried about in its *Solange* decisions[27] was the fate of basic rights protection if it was denied the right to review Community law applicable in national courts. In order to accommodate such worries, the Court of Justice introduced the doctrine of basic rights as general principles of Community law, thus extending the process of constitutionalization from a juridical to a political constitution. Here the landmark cases were *Stauder*, *Internationale Handelsgesellschaft* and *Nold*.[28]

Interlegality and plurality are not confined merely to EU law's relation to national legal orders but also characterize its relation to (general) international law, which was the other addressee of the declaration of independence implicit in *Van*

25 "Interlegality" is a term borrowed from Sousa Santos (2002: 437).

26 Case 26/62, *Van Gend en Loos*, ECR 1963, 1.

27 See BVerfGE 37, 271, 1974; and BVerfGE 73, 339, 1986.

28 Case 29/69, *Stauder*, ECR 1969, 419; Case 11/70, *Internationale Handelsgesellschaft mbH*, ECR 1970, 1125; and Case 4/73, *Nold v Commission*, ECR 1974, 491.

Gend en Loos and *Costa v ENEL*.[29] One of the most widely debated recent rulings of the Court of Justice, *Kadi*,[30] concerns not merely the security constitution but has implications for the juridical constitution as well: it can be read as a further step in juridical constitutionalization, as an assertion of European law's supremacy in respect of international law. It remains to be seen what will be the reaction to this claim by the actors of international law, scholars of international law included.

Political Constitutionalization as a Reaction to Economic and Juridical Constitutionalization

Analogically to juridical constitutionalization, political constitutionalization involves a quest for autonomy and unity. In this process, the Union has defined itself as a *transnational polity* beyond the dichotomy of international and national law, distinct from both intergovernmental organizations of international law and nation-states. In the original institutional architecture, the transnational element was manifest by the Court and the Commission. But these were meant to be non-political expert bodies, and their main function was to promote realisation of the economic constitution; they did not represent political but economic constitutionalization. By contrast, the Community legislature adhered to intergovernmental principles, familiar from international organizations subject to international law. The main legislative body was the Council, where the veto power of every member state was the rule. The position of the European Parliament was peripheral; moreover, until 1979 it was not a transnational, but an interparliamentary body, with members elected by national parliaments. Reforms weakening intergovernmentalism within the legislature can be interpreted as steps in political constitutionalization. This applies to, for instance, gradual extension of the majority principle in the Council and increasing involvement of the now directly elected European Parliament. It represents the power-constituting aspect in political constitutionalization, polity-building at the pole of authority or sovereignty.

But, according to modern constitutionalism, polity-making does not proceed merely through power-constituting or through the assertion of sovereignty; it also requires a direct political relationship to be established between the poles of authority and individual members of the polity. Political constitutionalization implies claims of democracy and *democratic legitimacy*; it is not about transnationalization as such but transnationalization with a promise of democratization. Hence the famous deficits of democracy and legitimacy form a central backdrop to European political constitutionalization.

---

29 Case 26/62, *Van Gend en Loos*, ECR 1963, 1, and Case 6/64, *Costa v ENEL*, ECR 1964, 585.

30 Joined cases C-402/05 P and C-415/05 P, *Kadi and Al Barakaat*, ECR 2008, I-6351.

We have noted that both economic and juridical constitutionalization relied on specific claims and mechanisms of legitimacy. Nevertheless, their insufficiency for securing the overall legitimacy of European integration among not only the economic, legal and political elites but the populace at large – the "peoples of Europe" evoked in the preamble to the Treaty of Rome – became more and more apparent. Community competences were extended through treaty amendments and the Court of Justice's integration-friendly case law. At the same time, the Court's constitutional review, in particular under what is now Article 34 TFEU (free movement of goods), imposed constraints on member states' regulatory and redistributive measures, creating a need for compensatory transnational regulation. Outcome-based legitimacy, promised by economic constitutionalization and negating the search for direct democratic legitimacy through political constitutionalization, might have been adequate for negative market integration but could not support the increasing tasks of positive integration. Had the Community taken over regulatory and redistributive functions, this would have evoked similar requirements of input-based, democratic legitimacy as they did at nation-state level.[31] Furthermore, the juridical constitution's auto-legitimation did not reach beyond legal elites. In the rights respect, juridical constitutionalization merely added a judicial layer to European citizenship, which could hardly engender wider social legitimacy.

Besides outcome-based and direct democratic legitimacy, a third alternative exists to meet the legitimacy requirement of European integration; indirect democratic legitimacy channelled through nation-state governments. It is the intergovernmental alternative relied on by international organizations under international law. However, in order to guarantee efficient decision-making and output-based legitimacy, the majority principle was introduced to the Council, the central European legislative body, and coverage of this principle was gradually extended. By the same token, indirect democratic legitimacy lost significance. Direct European democratic mechanisms also tend to diminish possible indirect democratic legitimacy attained through intergovernmental structures. This is a general problem of legitimacy-enhancing reforms in the EU: attempts to strengthen one type of legitimacy easily lead to contrary overall results. Furthermore, as the failure of the Constitutional Treaty suggests, the general public still connects the expectation of democratic legitimacy to the nation-state rather than to a transnational polity. Use of constitutional vocabulary is perceived as hinting at strengthening the transnational polity and, consequently, as a threat to the nation-state as the primary object of political allegiance and loyalty.

One can also raise critical questions challenging the very possibility of democratic legitimacy at European level, whether indirect or direct. Europeanization of politics seems to have enhanced the position of the nation-state executive and the judiciary at the expense of the parliamentary legislature. EU politics belongs

31 Scharpf (1999) is a justly renowned analysis of the EU's dilemmas in terms of the dialectics of negative and positive integration, and output- and input-based legitimacy.

typically to the domain of governments, where formal supervisory powers of the parliament are in general more limited – not to speak of real chances to influence the government's behaviour in the European bargaining processes – than in the continuously diminishing policy areas left to the care of the nation-state. So, arguably, instead of national democratic procedures legitimating the European level, Europeanization has contributed to an overall deterioration of parliamentary democracy. Here, of course, the situation in member states varies; some countries, including Finland, have been able to develop relatively pungent parliamentary mechanisms for deliberating EU issues. At the European level, in turn, the main impediment to the functioning of direct democratic legitimizing mechanisms remains the lack of a European *demos*, in the sense of a politically active citizenry, sufficiently committed to a common European project and unfolding its influence through Europe-wide networks of civil society and the public sphere. It is evident that because of blockages in the channels of both direct and indirect democratic legitimacy, outcome-based legitimacy will retain its importance for support of the European project among the "peoples of Europe".

The rights element in political constitutionalization provides a link between the European polity and its individual members. It is also crucial for the power-constraining functions of the political constitution. Fundamental rights (civil and political rights) were introduced into Community law by the Court of Justice as a response to the German constitutional court's reaction to juridical constitutionalization; the Maastricht Treaty confirmed their status as general legal principles of Community law; in 2000 the EU Fundamental Rights Charter was adopted as a solemn declaration; and, finally, the Lisbon Treaty made the Charter legally binding. As a result of this development, the EU's political constitution includes a full-blown Bill of Rights addressing its power-constraining effects to EU institutions and bodies, as well as to member state authorities when these are implementing EU law. By the same token, constitutional plurality and interlegality have received a new aspect. In present-day Europe, protection of basic rights results from the interplay among three normative sources: the two transnational Bills of Rights of the Council of Europe and the EU, as well as national constitutions.

Through the Maastricht Treaty, the term "citizenship" found its way into European law. The rights explicitly attached to European citizenship in the TEC were quite meagre and did not add very much to those already existing. Yet, in particular the new participatory rights of EU citizens – the rights to vote and stand as a candidate in municipal elections and in elections to the European Parliament in other member states – did reflect the idea of a European-wide citizenry engaged in common democratic practices. Still, arguably, the main significance of the Title on Citizenship lay on a symbolic level: it was intended to manifest a new type of direct relationship between the European polity and its individual members; a relationship where individuals are no longer treated exclusively in their economic roles or as litigants promoting their economic interests by judicial means.

The creation of a European citizenry reflected the quest for unity typical of constitutionalization. But the Treaty of Maastricht and subsequent developments have resulted in a rather chaotic institutional structure; a "Europe of bits and pieces".[32] This is largely due to adoption of the pillar structure and the expansive but by no means unilinear advance of what the Treaty of Amsterdam (1998) termed the Area of Freedom, Security and Justice. This launched a novel process of constitutionalization: the emergence of a security constitution, with unity-disturbing consequences within both the political and the juridical constitution.

Interlude: The Weak Social Constitution

What, then, about the social constitution? "Social constitution" is a tricky concept; it may even appear questionable whether we can speak of a social constitution in the same relational sense as of economic, juridical or political constitutions – as a higher law relating to a distinct extra-legal action field – or, as is the case with juridical constitution, to law itself. What is the social as the other pole of the constitutional relation? It is evident that it cannot be conceived of by means of systems theory and that the Luhmannian concept of structural coupling is of no help in specifying the constitutional relation. Rather, debates on a social constitution concern a policy function, its status among the tasks of the European polity and the means by which it is pursued. Constitutional discourse in this dimension is premised on social values, reflecting the need to guarantee the factual presuppositions of a meaningful and satisfactory life for individual members of society and their families. Due to this value basis, constitutional vocabulary often implies a strong normative message, in the visionary or philosophical sense. But a more doctrinally oriented discourse is possible, too, for example on the division of tasks and competences between the EU and the member states or on the status of social rights with regard to other fundamental rights or market freedoms.

So let us speak of social constitutionalization but with qualifications. Both the institutional-organizational and rights elements of this putative form of European constitutionalization are still in quite a rudimentary state if compared with, for instance, the economic constitution. Again, the rights element is related to European citizenship, adding to it a new, social ingredient. Social rights are so-called second-generation fundamental rights whose realization requires active measures on the part of the polity. This particular character of social rights affects the respective emphasis of power-constituting and power-restricting aspects of constitutionalization: social constitutionalization aims mainly at creating powers and obligations at the pole of authority, while the power-restraining task is relegated to the background.

Social constitutionalization can hardly be deemed to have ever been the pacemaker in or the primary form of European constitutionalization and European constitutional discourse; there has been no era of predominantly social constitutionalization. Rather, the social constitution has been the constitutional

32 Curtin 1993.

underdog, capable of asserting itself merely in the limits and on the terms of the more robust aspects of constitutionalization, chiefly the economic one. The plurality of European constitutions is not a plurality of equals; there are stronger and weaker constitutions, and the social constitution undoubtedly falls among the latter. This is manifest even by the fact that, despite the Maastricht and Amsterdam amendments, treaty provisions alluding to a social constitution remain remarkably vague; to a large extent, they epitomize treaty-level soft law. Thus, they do not really resolve the basic constitutional issue of division of functions and competences between the EU and the member states. No explicit choice has been made between the three models of social Europe, distinguished by Miguel Poiares Maduro: the market integration model, relying on the social effects of the economic constitution; the model of social policy harmonization furthering market integration by equalizing competition conditions and preventing the race to the bottom; and the third model where harmonization pursues European social values and is complemented by EU-level instruments of social justice.[33] In practice, the remaining dominance of the economic constitution, as well as ideological and institutional differences between member states in the field of social policy, tend to tip the balance in favour of the first two options.

The Security Constitution as an Anti-Constitution

Despite the efforts in the dimension of a social constitution, the main contender for the pacemaker in European constitutionalization in the post-Constitutional Treaty interregnum – and, arguably, even earlier – comes from an emergent security constitution. Security is not merely one policy function among others. At treaty level, it was given prominence by the Maastricht Treaty's provisions on the second and third pillars: the second pillar focusing on external and the third pillar on internal security. However, as these pillars were based on intergovernmental premises, the provisions provided but a starting point for subsequent constitutionalization in terms of transnationalization and detachment from the orbit of both international and national law. Emphasis in constitutionalization has lain on internal security, which is at least partly explicable by the relatively minor significance of legal instruments within common foreign and security policy. Determining the other pole of the constitutional relation raises difficulties analogous to those discussed above in connection with the social constitution. Let us tentatively determine it as internal and external security risk, noting that a particular network of internal security seems to be arising whose institutional core consists of nation-state and transnational police, border control, and immigration agencies, interrelated through various informational and communicative links.

At the national level, the security network maintains a curiously ambivalent relation to the constitution. On the one hand, according to traditional liberal rule-

33 See Poiares Maduro 2006.

of-law and *Rechtsstaat* constitutionalism, agencies of internal security are the main addressees of the constitution's power-constraining function. In continental Europe, this function came to be viewed through the opposition of *Rechtsstaat* and police state. A central claim of constitutionalism was to subordinate the latter to the former; the police state was the Other of a *Rechtsstaat* constitution, something pre-existent which was supposed to be negated rather than constituted by the constitution. But security considerations are making a (re-)entry into the constitutional sphere as a public interest justifying limitations to constitutionally guaranteed rights: what originally was supposed to be constrained through the constitution is turned into a ground for restricting the protective effects of the constitution. The same logic applies to transnational human-rights protection, as can be read from the limitation clauses included in the rights provisions of the ECHR. By contrast, the EU security system did not precede constitutionalization, but has largely been brought into existence through it. At least in the initial stage, the focus has been on the power-constituting and not on the power-constraining functions of constitutionalization. Before "9/11", most of the constitutional impetus came from internal constitutional logic, from spillover effects of the economic constitution, in particular free movement of workers. Removal of internal border controls for the sake of a transnational market economy led to a perceived need to coordinate external border controls, as well as other action fields of security authorities. Even in the wording of Article 2 EU (now 3 TEU), the Area of Freedom, Security and Justice was defined through the overreaching aim of assuring free movement of persons.

As is the case with earlier waves of constitutionalization, constitutionalizing the security network has proceeded as a gradual transition from intergovernmentalism with its strong international law traits towards transnationalization. Here the Amsterdam Treaty was the milestone. It transferred visa, asylum, immigration and other policies related to free movement of persons from intergovernmental cooperation under the third pillar to the Community pillar. It also subsumed the Schengen Agreement regime under Community law and thus detached it from its international law moorings. Furthermore, Court of Justice jurisdiction was extended, not only to issues transferred to the Community pillar, but also to legal instruments related to police and judicial cooperation established under Title VI of the EU Treaty. However, even under the Lisbon Treaty, Court of Justice jurisdiction remains limited. Nor has the transnationalization of political and legislative decision-making been taken as far as in other policy fields.

The particular character of the security constitution is perhaps most salient in the link it establishes with individuals. Earlier waves of constitutionalization gradually enriched European citizenship by adding new layers of rights: from economic, through judicial and political, to social citizenship. By contrast, within the ambit of a security constitution the individual is not primarily conceived of as a bearer of rights but as a *security risk*. Security talk is not rights talk; rights are neither the aim nor the means of constitutionalization but rather its putative limit. A security constitution hints at boundaries and the obverse of citizenship. From the perspective of the authority, individuals are not only subjects of rights but also potential risks; moreover, they may be risks exactly as subjects of rights.[34] In Michel Foucault's account, the edifice of constitutional rights was erected upon a disciplinary infrastructure, which was instrumental to producing a subject which could be endowed with rights.[35] A security constitution recalls the limits of citizenship in another sense, too. Citizenship both includes and excludes: it defines membership of the polity through exclusion, by defining and maintaining the boundary towards non-citizens. The security system governs this boundary through external border controls as well as visa, asylum, immigration, and other policies.

Appraised in light of general constitutional aspirations for unity and coherence, the emerging security constitution does not fare very well. Actually, including internal and external security in the objectives of the EU led to increasing fragmentation in the domains of political and juridical constitution, manifest by, for example, the pillar structure and opt-outs allowed to member states. In the juridical dimension, this contributed to fragmentation by introducing new second- and third-pillar instruments whose exact legal effects and relationship to Community law instruments were far from clear. In practice, a new round of juridical constitutionalization was launched especially within the third pillar. The Amsterdam Treaty removed a significant part of former third-pillar issues to the Community pillar, entailing their subsumption under the constitutional principles developed within Community law. Neither were issues that remained under the third pillar spared from mounting juridical transnationalization and constitutionalization. The ongoing process as to third-pillar issues bears striking similarities to what a few decades ago took place within Community law. Again, the key actor is the Court of Justice, who could initiate a new wave of juridical auto-constitutionalization by extending the reach of general principles that have defined Community law's relationship to national legal orders, such as direct effect and supremacy, as well as the overarching and legitimating loyalty principle. What is interesting as well is that during this new round of juridical constitutionalization, member state constitutional and supreme courts have raised similarly motivated objections as during the constitutionalization of Community law. National controversies surrounding implementation of the Framework Decision on the European Arrest Warrant provided them the opportunity to (re)declare their qualifications in respect of the principle of supremacy and to (re)affirm the national *solange* or *controlimiti* doctrines.

34 For example, see Hurri 2009.
35 See especially Foucault 1979.

Intertwined but not Equal

The above summary of European constitutionalization reveals at least some rudiments of an internal logic, accounting for shifts of emphasis from one dimension to another. But, of course, we have to bear in mind that the ultimate causes of legal change always lie outside the law, in extra-legal circumstances. Still, as even Max Weber reminds us, intra-legal mechanisms may have a great impact in channelling and moulding the course and influence of external factors.

The developmental logic sketched here grasps only some of the different kinds of relations the diverse European constitutions maintain with each other. In some connections, what are treated as different constitutions might be more appropriately conceived of as aspects of or perspectives on one and the same process; thus, to take one example, constitutionalization along the security axis involves or implies a new phase in juridical constitutionalization. A black-box model, with mutually impenetrable constitutional compartments, should be avoided, not only in analysis of the interrelations between national and transnational constitutions, but in examination of European constitutions as well. Here, too, interlegality reigns: European constitutions overlap, interpenetrate, and communicate with each other. Still, not all the discursive or contrapuntal guidelines elaborated in the debate on constitutional pluralism are transferable to the past or present plurality of European constitutions. The constitutions do converse with each other, but this is rarely a conversation among equals, and the conversation may be brought to an end by a conflict calling for a legal solution.

The principal forum for conflict resolution is the Court of Justice. Accordingly, Court jurisprudence can tell us much about relations between diverse European constitutions and their respective strength. Often enough, controversies assume the guise of a conflict between, on the one hand, market freedoms (the economic constitution) and, on the other hand, civil and political rights (the political constitution) or social rights (the social constitution). The methodology followed by the Court of Justice bears a clear sign of the primacy of economic integration. The Court has tended to frame issues as concerning potential justification for derogating from market freedom. The legal problem, as defined by the Court, has been whether respect for human rights – mandated by EU law, the national constitution, and the ECHR – constitutes a sufficiently weighty public interest for a member state to warrant exemption from a market freedom. The conclusion in the (fairly) recent *Omega Spielhallen*[36] and *Schmidberger*[37] rulings was in favour of the human rights side, but it would be overhasty to declare a reversal in relations between the economic constitution and civil and political rights. Framing of the legal issue still implied primacy of the economic constitution as the default presumption: even now, the problem was whether respect for a civil or political right justified derogating from a market freedom, not whether an economic

36 Case C-36/02, *Omega Spielhallen*, ECR 2004, I-9609.

37 Case C-112/00, *Schmidberger*, ECR 2003, I-5659.

consideration warranted limiting a right. The approach is fundamentally different from that of the European Court of Human Rights or national constitutional courts; in Ronald Dworkin's terms, we might talk of an inverse relationship between rights-related principles and economic policy factors.

A corresponding analysis could be made of tensions between the economic and social constitutions. The rather weak position of social rights in comparison with market freedoms – and of the social constitution in general in comparison with the economic constitution – comes conspicuously to the fore in *Laval*[38] and *Viking*,[39] both as regards posing the legal issue and the conclusions of the Court. What, of course, is worrying from a Nordic perspective is that what the Court of Justice as a constitutional court struck down was national law epitomizing the Nordic welfare state model.

References

Alter, K.J. 2001. *Establishing the Supremacy of European Law – The Making of an International Rule of Law in Europe*. Oxford: Oxford University Press.

Avbelj, M. 2008. Questioning EU constitutionalisms. *German Law Journal*, 10, 1–26.

Avbelj, M. and Komárek, J. 2008. Four Visions of Constitutional Pluralism. EUI Working Paper Law, No. 2008/21. Florence: EUI.

Baquero Cruz, J. 2002. *Between Competition and Free Movement. The Economic Constitutional Law of the European Community*. Oxford: Hart Publishing.

Böhm, F. 1933. *Wettbewerb und Monopolkampf. Eine Untersuchung zur Frage des wirtschaftlichen Kampfrechts und zur Frage der rechtlichen Struktur der geltenden Wirtschaftsordnung*. Berlin: Carl Heymanns Verlag.

Burley, A.-M. and Mattli, W. 1993. Europe before the court. *International Organization*, 47, 41–76.

Curtin, D. 1993. The constitutional structure of the union: A Europe of bits and pieces. *Common Market Law Review*, 30, 17–69.

Foucault, M. 1979. *Discipline and Punish*. Harmondsworth: Penguin.

Habermas, J. 1996. *Between Facts and Norms*. Cambridge: Polity Press.

Hurri, S. 2009. A legal space for the representation of danger. *NO FOUNDATIONS Journal of Extreme Legal Positivism*, 6, 39–69. Available at: <www.helsinki.fi/nofo> (accessed: 3 February 2010).

Koskenniemi, M. 1999. The effect of rights on political culture, in *The EU and Human Rights*, edited by P. Alston. Oxford: Oxford University Press, 99–116.

Luhmann, N. 2004. *Law as a Social System*. Oxford: Oxford University Press, 2004.

---

38 Case C-341/05, *Laval un Partneri Ltd*, ECR 2007, I-11767.

39 Case C-438/05, *International Transport Workers' Federation and Finnish Seamen's Union v Viking Line ABP and OÜ Viking Line Eesti*, ECR 2007, I-10779.

MacCormick, N. and Weinberger, O. 1986. *An Institutional Theory of Law*. Dordrecht: Kluwer.

Mestmäcker, E.-J. 1998. *Wirtschaft und Verfassung in der Europäischen Union. Beiträge zu Recht, Theorie und Politik der europäischen Integration*. Baden-Baden: Nomos.

Poiares Maduro, M. 1998. *We the Court. The European Court of Justice and the European Economic Constitution*. Oxford: Hart Publishing.

Poiares Maduro, M. 2003. Europe and the constitution: What if this is as good as it gets? in *European Constitutionalism Beyond the State*, edited by J.H.H. Weiler and M. Wind. Cambridge: Cambridge University Press, 74–102.

Poiares Maduro, M. 2006. Three models of a social Europe, in *The Politics of a European Civil Code*, edited by M. Hesselink. The Hague: Kluwer Law International, 126–40.

Sadurski, W. 2008. "Solange, Chapter 3": Constitutional courts in Central Europe – Democracy – European Union. *European Law Journal*, 14:1, 1–35.

Scharpf, F. 1999. *Governing in Europe: Effective and Democratic?* Oxford: Oxford University Press.

Skinner, Q. 2002. *Visions of Politics. Volume I. Regarding Method*. Cambridge: Cambridge University Press.

Sousa Santos, B. 2002. *Toward a New Legal Common Sense*. 2nd ed. London: Butterworths.

Stone Sweet, A. 2000. *Governing with Judges. Constitutional Politics in Europe*. Oxford: Oxford University Press.

Stone Sweet, A. 2004. *The Judicial Construction of Europe*. Oxford: Oxford University Press.

Streit, M.E. and Mussler, W. 1995. The economic constitution of the European Community: From "Rome" to "Maastricht". *European Law Journal*, 1:1, 5–30.

Teubner, G. 2004a. Global private regimes: Neo-spontaneous law and dual constitution of autonomous sectors? in *Public Governance in the Age of Globalization*, edited by K.-H. Ladeur. Aldershot: Ashgate, 71–87.

Teubner, G. 2004b. Societal constitutionalism: Alternatives to state-centred constitutional theory? in *Constitutionalism and Transnational Governance*, edited by C. Joerges, I.-J. Sand and G. Teubner. Oxford: Hart Publishing, 3–28.

Tuori, K. 2002. *Critical Legal Positivism*. Aldershot: Ashgate.

Walker, N. 2003. Late sovereignty in the European Union, in *Sovereignty in Transition*, edited by N. Walker. Oxford: Hart Publishing, 3–32.

Weiler, J.H.H. 1991. Transformation of Europe. *Yale Law Journal*, 100:8, 2403–83.

Weiler, J.H.H. 1999. *The Constitution of Europe*. Cambridge: Cambridge University Press.

Chapter 2
A Default Constitutionalism? A Disquieting Note on Europe's Many Constitutions

Emilios Christodoulidis[1]

Constitution-Shopping?

The title itself of this collection, and of the colloquium from which it emerged, confronts us straight away with a problem: how to think *plurality* when it comes to the *unitary* constitutional order of a *single* entity – Europe? We may of course bypass the problem through a certain – temporary – 'unfolding' of either of the key terms: constitutional order or Europe. 'Pluralizing' either of these comes with the promise that the initial unpacking will allow a later convergence, more fruitful for having taken us through the attendant complexities. If one opts for pluralising the first term, constitutional order, one might talk for example of the proliferation of economic, social, political and other constitutions, or identify constitutionalism across the split of national and supra-national, as the *form* of their distinction. Alternatively, to pluralize the other term, Europe, is to see it as under-determined, whatever form that under-determination might take: whether as a system of overlapping orders or as contested signifier. In either case Europe stands as the name of a plurality that resists singular designation; in the second case – as 'essentially contested' – crucially in the *remainder* of whatever designations instantiate it, for whatever purpose at hand. These are all names for suggestions offered in the burgeoning literature on European constitutionalism. But what they offer comes at the price, it seems, of undoing what is constitutive of constitutionalism, namely its function *vis-à-vis* a political order, in the sense of an order*ing*, or rational *gathering of* (rather than of a splintering off), and thus by definition a moment of *unity* and not of entropy. This is of course not to deny that unity and plurality are both operative in the story of European constitutionalization. But it is to insist that unity is conceptually fundamental; and that plurality, to the extent that it is possible and desirable, builds on the back of unity.

There are interesting questions to ask about what the purported holding together – in its various modalities – of unity and plurality achieves. On the one hand we have a certain promise of unity: of a Europe and of a constitution *for* it. On the other hand we have plurality: the many constitutions, which may or may not eventually

1 With many thanks for their valuable comments to Ruth Dukes, Suvi Sankari and Scott Veitch.

fuse into one, as enabling the multiple logics of action; a constitutional pluralism as reflecting the plurality of *demoi*; and the important distinction of levels sub-national, national, and supra-national as enabling subsidiarity. Every one of these invitations to the 'plural' is about enabling the exercise of constituent power at *appropriate* levels. The judgement over appropriateness allows the introduction of a final dimension of the new constitutionalisms: the promise of *reflexivity*.

This will all be returned to later. In the meantime this threshold objection to a certain version of constitutional pluralism may be renewed: a plurality of pluralisms is arguably not sustainable conceptually (and not just because all human thinking strives to coherence) and certainly not institutionally. If pluralism is to mean anything at all institutionally, variety can only be sustained on the back of something that remains invariable. Otherwise there is no pivot for *scope*. Constitutional pluralism thus must fix, at some level, what is constitutional about the plurality it introduces. And even if this commonality is reconfigured to some extent from within the plurality of its instantiations, some common reference to the constitutional must reduce the 'double hermeneutic' at level and meta-level – for constitutional actors and constitutional theorists.[2] This is a sine qua non for the 'improbable' achievement[3] of constitutional communication. In any case a *reduction* needs to be imported and deployed to get any communication off the ground in any sustainable way.

In the midst of all this reconfiguring of the 'constitutional' across plural axes, it is suggested that a disquieting suspicion arises about which reduction is operative in gathering together Europe's 'many Constitutions', and the variety *it* permits. This may be asked in a stark form. Could it be that the proliferation of constitutions confronts us with a form of *constitution-shopping*, in the way we have become accustomed to talking of law- or forum-shopping? The 'shopping' component of this formulation, in marked opposition to the varieties of its object ('constitutions'), is the term for what remains *entrenched*. What remains entrenched is the logic of the market. Through a series of slippages it elevates itself to the epistemological premise of constitutional thinking: the market – as discovery process – invites cognitive adjustments, social learning as a self-correcting process. And with this it introduces a *default constitutionalism* whereby the drawing of distinctions that pluralism requires and celebrates becomes exercises of internal differentiation, in a way that leaves intact the market meta-structure as providing the pivot and the leverage, constitutionally unchallengeable, politically non-negotiable and socially devastating. Or so it will be argued.

In his very interesting taxonomy of constitution-making at a European level, Kaarlo Tuori, in his contribution to this volume, differentiates between at least five concepts of the constitution: *economic*, *juridical*, *political*, *social* and

2 See Tuori in this volume.

3 Luhmann would identify this as a reduction of the double contingency of the 'double hermeneutic'.

security.[4] Departing from the inextricably relational character of the constitution, the particularity of each of its specific couplings draws attention to the particular exigencies that the regulation of the economy, of security, of the 'lifeworld', and so on, places on its constitutional containment. The narrative Tuori offers is one of internal shifts, reactions and competition: a fascinating account of how successive understandings of European constitutionalism with their alternate emphases came to dominate the trajectory of European integration, as well as the challenge they pose to current understandings of European constitutionalism.

Issue will be taken with the constitutional trajectory in the following sections, with particular reference to the 'economic' constitution. But before then, a methodological caveat with regard to this taxonomy will be briefly introduced. The term 'juridical' constitution warrants separate treatment only in the sense that it, perhaps, marks a special moment of self-reference. Notwithstanding this, what is both politically crucial and theoretically interesting is that each 'constitution' – economic, political, social, etc. – involves first of all a 'relationship' with the legal idiom in that each *finds expression* in the law. So every constitution *is at once also* a juridical constitution. But this is perhaps more complex than is at first apparent. The economic constitution, like each of the others, is always mediated by a relationship of the law to itself (which is the constitutional moment) as register or expression of the economic. A self-understanding always mediates law's reach into other fields. We could call this moment of introspection reflexivity or we could call it something else. But either way it is what allows a legal/constitutional expression of economic and other relations in terms of a particular deployment of self- and other-reference.

Incidentally only, this repeats the crux of Eugeny Pashukanis's important insight regarding the legal form. If (capitalist) production is dependent on a dialectic of content and form, it is the latter that determines the possibilities of the former in terms of providing coinage for the circulation of productive forces within the exchange circuits of capitalist production.

In a methodological vein, there is a worry that the 'political constitution', the 'economic constitution', and the 'social constitution' (*Sozialverfassung*) are now regularly distinguished and increasingly receive separate treatment as a matter of course in constitutional law and theory. This classificatory departure reflects a dangerous disjunction between three domains when it comes to comprehending the 'democratic' and 'social' deficits of Europe *as separate questions*. These theoretical developments reflect and consolidate real processes. In the next section will look at how this separation arose and became constitutionally entrenched in the trajectory of European integration. The final section will reflect on what this separation means for European constitutionalism and how it contrasts with the traditional view that saw tension where currently we see disconnection. It will be argued that the disconnection allows the circulation of constitutional values *as* constitutional commodities, disarticulating the framework that might have

4 See also Frerichs, this volume, for an elaboration of these concepts.

allowed political control of such circulation and undercutting society's ability to react to the logic and processes of capitalist accumulation.

The Staggered Trajectory of a Disembedding

The story of the European economic constitution is well documented and extensively analysed. A number of eloquent contributions to this volume track its trajectory.[5] Two moments in particular matter as far as my 'disquieting' suggestion goes. The first is the split between market integration and social protection, and with it the constitutional disconnection of the processes of production of value from their effects on Europe's producers. The second is the hollowing out of the meaning of the economic constitution in the sense of its collapse into market terms. Let us take each of these in turn.

The first has to do with the progressive decoupling of social policy from the European project. European integration was conceptualized from the beginning along *ordo-liberal* lines. Pitted against discretionary politics, ordo-liberalism underwrote the framing conditions of market order with a rule-of-law like commitment to upholding and guaranteeing economic freedoms, guarantees of property and sanctity of contract. At the European level it promised the opening up of national economies and a commitment to undistorted competition. The ordo-liberal emphasis on what is properly the function of the economic constitution, as Christian Joerges puts it, 'that [it] should respect the interdependence of a system of undistorted competition, individual freedoms and the rule of law – and protect this precious balance against discretionary political influence',[6] further achieves two things. Firstly it delineates what is properly legal, economic, and political; and secondly it unburdens the European project from the political tasks of meeting the social costs of integration. At the same time the national systems of employment regulation are undercut, their viability threatened by the unblinking focus on freedom of goods and services, capital and labour. As a direct result of the separating off of the economic from the means to redress political and social deficits, legitimation questions are divorced from the effects of economic performance and its distributional outcomes. They become – categorially – cut off from political deliberation or negotiation. Questions of redistribution and social protection remain a question for national constitutional orders, which are thereafter burdened with an impossible compensatory task, the means for the performance of which are no longer at their disposal. And yet in a viciously ironic, circuitous way the very inability at national level to compensate the costs of capitalist integration at the supra-national level feeds the momentum of that integration. An answer that can no longer be guaranteed at the level of the state's political distributions

5 See Giubboni and Tuori in this volume; more generally Joerges 2005; and Streit and Mussler 1995.

6 Joerges 2005: 468.

can only be offered in terms of further growth and trickle-down. With the initial constitutive decoupling of the economic from the political, the social question becomes categorially distinct: a matter that can and should be dealt with at an appropriate level, even if the disarticulation is precisely what so substantially undercuts the possibilities of redress, offering too little, too late.

This is a very particular mutation of the concept of the 'economic constitution'. We can see this by returning to the origin of the 'economic' constitution in the writings of that key figure of the Weimar period, Hugo Sinzheimer. For Sinzheimer the economic constitution was seen in terms of a partnership between employers and workers,[7] mandating participation of the latter 'on an equal footing and in cooperation with employers in the regulation of wages and working conditions as well as in the economic development of productive forces'.[8] It should perhaps be noted that Sinzheimer aimed at the empowerment of workers nationally *and* internationally ('[in] safeguard[ing] a minimum of social rights for humanity's working class'[9]). In any case the economic constitution was conceived along the lines of a genuinely constitutional dialogue and in the context of a *political economy*, relationships between producers and owners understood along political lines and in terms of asymmetries of power between corporate actors rather than contractual equality and freedom amongst individuals, where what was at stake was the democratic organization of production and where the objective was co-determination. It is this marked emphasis on the irreducibly political nature of the economic constitution that underlies and drives its interpretation and realization.

In stark contrast, the ordo-liberal economic constitution is economic in that it is not political, economic rationality for the ordo-liberals of the Freiburg school being *sui generis* and categorially distinct. This separation is inscribed in the genesis of the European community and justifies the separation of economics from social policy as a foundational premise. It is with some regret that Fritz Scharpf, once leading strategist of the German SDP, reflects on the road not taken. He asks: 'Where would we be now if in the 1956 negotiations leading to the treaties of Rome and the creation of the EEC [the French line had prevailed] making the harmonisation of social regulations and fiscal burdens a precondition for the integration of industrial markets?'[10] The point is not to labour on foregone alternatives, but to put into perspective the supposedly inexorable march of the market system, at each turn a contingent political decision that could have been decided otherwise, the cumulative effect of which, nonetheless, has been to make it increasingly difficult to envisage and sustain alternatives. Elsewhere Scharpf says: 'There is now no economically plausible Keynesian strategy that would

7 On this see Dukes 2008.

8 Weimar Constitution, Art. 165.

9 Weimar Constitution, Art. 162.

10 Scharpf 2002: 645–6.

permit the full realisation of social democratic goals within a national context without violating the functional imperatives of a capitalist economy.'[11]

This brings us to a second important shift in the understanding of what is economic about the economic constitution. This involves what some have identified as a shift within liberalism itself, from an ordo- to a neoliberal paradigm. The significant theoretical shift within the tradition can be tracked as a move from the 'authoritarian [ordo-] liberalism' of Walter Eucken to the rampant neoliberalism of Friedrich Hayek. The latter's extraordinarily influential 'Competition as process of Discovery' (*Wettbewerb als Entdeckungsverfahren*) in effect turns the market from contested mechanism to uncontested meta-criterion of questions of social justice.

Let us pause here before what is nothing short of a paradigm shift. For the ordo-liberals there was an important role for the state to play in the economy, in providing opportunity structures and incentives in pursuit of social goals or in protection against 'proletarianization'. These were difficult balances that concerned the state's input into the institutions of economic governance. What was significant was that for the ordo-liberalism of Eucken, Roepke and Rustow 'economic activity was embedded within a self-organised society which imposed non-negotiable costs concerning democratic participation in economic decision-making and the necessity of negotiation'.[12] It is only the radical turn to the market as an economic, political, and epistemological principle instigated in the mid-1970s by Hayek, that attacked 'social democracy on philosophical, political and empirical grounds as undesirable, unpatriotic and unfeasible. The response was confused. By the 1980s … the institutions of regulation and welfare distribution … were viewed as contingent arrangements and not as necessary elements of social organization in societies characterised by a market economy'.[13] While the extremes of the agenda of the New Right have partly subsided, the paradigm shift it ushered in generated a creeping consensus that the post-war social democratic settlement was not capable of renewing itself and that, even in the face of radical market failure, any ideal of social solidarity no longer constitutes a *rational* response *across* the economic/political divide.

The significance of the mark of the neoliberal turn on the trajectory of European constitutionalism cannot be exaggerated. It justified and facilitated rapid institutional developments, the market system now propelling forward the processes of deregulation and privatization. For Joerges and Rödl the process of integration acquired renewed impetus:

> … the now legendary 1985 Commission White Paper on completion of the Internal Market signalled the advent of a new era. … In conjunction with the strengthening of the four freedoms, this legal background could be interpreted

11 Scharpf 1991: 274.

12 Glasman 1996: 55.

13 Glasman, 1996, xxiii.

> as providing the framework which ... would expose national legislation to economic rationality tests. ... The attention shifted from market failures to regulatory failures, from the control of the anti-competitive practices of private actors to anti-competitive regulation and state aid. ... This framework seeks to institutionalise economic liberties and economic rationality. It does so more flexibly but also more comprehensively than was originally envisaged by the ordo-liberal school.[14]

The trajectory of these developments is fascinating and the object of serious academic scrutiny that exceeds what can be summarized here. Why it matters will be returned to in terms of the general argument. But in the meantime, this section will close with a short note on a much-discussed decision of the German Federal Constitutional Court[15] and Joerges's very interesting, and incongruous, interpretation of its effect.

The FCC's decision over '*kompetenz-kompetenz*' was seen and broadly analysed in terms of the Court's insistence that sovereignty resided in the national *demos* and consequently that the national parliament retained essential competencies. The decision, as is well known, was criticized for relying on 'existential sameness' for the designation of the German people. This, however, is not Joerges' focus. Instead, his contention is that in order to argue against the erosion of statehood the Court relied on strictly ordo-liberal arguments to designate what was properly a state function and in the process (and largely by default) also designated what was properly economic *as independent* of state processes of democratic scrutiny and outwith the domain of sovereign self-determination of a people. 'Economic integration', says Joerges, 'was qualified as a non-political phenomenon occurring autonomously outside the member states'.[16] Of the 'precarious legitimacy of the whole construct' and the 'need' to find 'a non-political supranational answer to a policy area that was once a core area of national sovereignty and parliamentary control', he says this:

> Fiscal policy is economic policy. And if it is nevertheless political, some actors, identifiable to the citizen, should be accountable for it. ... the Maastricht treaty and the Maastricht judgement were a pyrrhic victory for two reasons: 1) Maastricht confirmed the decoupling of the social from the economic constitution thereby deepening Europe's social deficit; 2) rather than establishing the supremacy of law over monetary and fiscal policy, Maastricht has 'de-juridified' the economic constitution – and now it seems that the effort to cure the social deficit has run into the same trap.[17]

14 Joerges and Rödl 2005: 131, 133 and 143–4.

15 See BVerfGE 89, 155 [1994], on the Maastricht Treaty.

16 Joerges 2005: 475.

17 Joerges 2005: 478.

Thus, for Joerges, the Maastricht decision consolidates the separation whereby the economic constitution remains the un-political framework of capital integration at European level, whereas the political and social constitutions remain tied to the national level as prerogative and burden.

So far we have analysed two moments in the trajectory of economic constitutionalization at European level. The first concerned the separation of the economic from the social as a structural feature of the set-up of the European Community. From the very beginning the economic constitution was conceived as supra-national and the social constitution as national. In that sense the states were given the task of providing protection to exposure to the market system run at supra-national level. The second moment concerned the 'internal' understanding itself of the economic. This genealogy of European economic constitutionalism seeks its origins in the school of ordo-liberalism and its conceptualization of the economic constitution in opposition to the understandings of it propounded by Sinzheimer in the Weimar republic (and Otto Kahn-Freund in England). The divergence relates to radically different understandings of the relationship between economics, politics and the role of state law. What we saw along this trajectory was a gradual hollowing out of democratic and political categories from the economy, in terms of the underwriting of the rationality itself of the economy and increasingly the collapse of all aspects of the political economy into its market form. Since the motor of Europeanization that was increasingly picking up speed was understood primarily as 'negative integration', i.e. the removal of obstacles, such as national regulatory systems, to the integration of markets, the national regulation of social protection was not simply too weak to stem the supra-national tide but came increasingly to be seen as an anomaly to the logic of integration. Richard Hyman calls this the logic of actually existing Europeanization;[18] Alain Supiot, drawing on extra-European sources, will later call it 'communist market economy'.[19] The combination of these two trajectories, of entrenching the separation and of the hollowing out of the political, are constitutive moments of the new European Constitutionalism.

The trajectory of the disembedding arguably takes a further twist with the 'soft' European Constitution and the new constitutional device of the Open Method of Coordination (OMC). To address the urgent question of the social deficit – from employment, to social inclusion and pensions – the new constitutionalization becomes increasingly reliant on soft instruments. One receiving much attention is the Open Method of Coordination, which, according to Jonathan Zeitlin, promises to be:

> an attractive model of how a non-coercive form of policy-coordination emphasizing mutual learning and exchange of good practices could be applied to a politically sensitive field such as social protection which is characterised by

18 See Hyman 2005: 29.

19 Supiot 2008.

> wide institutional variations across EU member States, where harmonisation is considered by many to be neither practicable nor desirable.[20]

Graínne de Búrca defines the OMC as:

> a strategy which leaves a considerable amount of policy autonomy to the Member States, and which normally blends the setting of guidelines or objectives at EU level with the elaboration of Member State action plans or strategy reports in an iterative process intended to bring about greater coordination and mutual learning in these policy fields. As yet, there is no one 'open method', but rather a range of different kinds, all broadly sharing a number of characteristics but with variations and distinctive features according to the particular policy area.[21]

For its more enthusiastic proponents, the usefulness of this 'fully decentralised approach' which can be applied 'in line with the principle of subsidiarity' lies in 're-calibrating social policies in a more flexible, participatory, experimental model' coupled with a commitment to 'permanent democratic experimentation'.[22] Scott and Trubek emphasize its greater flexibility, pointing out not just that it engages a broader range of actors, but that it is also less substantively prescriptive and more accommodating of diversity. They list the following features of new governance: participation and power sharing; diversity and decentralization; deliberation; flexibility and revisability; experimentation and knowledge creation.[23]

In less exalted tones and in view of the very real threat that there is no mechanism for checking against the dangers of either 'race to the bottom' policies or the undesirable slippage in protection in respect of certain fundamental values, Búrca makes the important point that soft law (at least) has the potential to encourage unity, in the sense of addressing the tension between statements of fundamental and universal rights on the one hand and limited EU competences on the other. She asks: 'Is there a way for constitutional values to be reflected and protected within soft law (and open method of coordination – OMC) processes, other than as flexible policy standards, capable of being revised in any direction?'[24] Her proposal for the constitutionalization of 'soft law' is that OMC should be combined with the EU Charter of Fundamental Rights and that there are two ways in which this could proceed: (i) OMC processes could be used as a way of giving concrete contextual meaning to the various rights set out in the Charter. OMC could constitute a suitable vehicle through which the general and abstract guarantees of the Charter are given flesh in particular settings and in the context of particular policies; (ii) Charter rights could be used as 'ideal norms' in relation to

20 As quoted by Joerges 2005: 482.

21 Búrca 2003: 824.

22 Sabel, as quoted in Joerges 2005: 105.

23 Scott and Trubek 2002: 5–6.

24 Búrca 2003: 833–4.

which the outcomes of the OMC processes would be appraised, and as means of stimulating reform or revision of the standards which emerge when the outcomes are considered substantively unsatisfactory.[25]

How is one to respond to, and in terms of, constitutional protection as 'soft' law? In an important article on trade union representation and the European Social model, Richard Hyman reminds us of what, in the practice of the British TUC, is called *the composite resolution*, whereby conflicting proposals are pressed into a unitary form that embraces the opposing viewpoints.[26] According to Article 3 TEU, the 'Union ... shall work for ... a highly competitive social market economy'. Is this a case of such a unity of opposites? This is Hyman:

> From the Delors white paper through Essen, Amsterdam, Luxemburg and all subsequent elaborations, the underlying message seems to have been that the prescriptions of Keynesianism and monetarism, of social regulation and deregulation, can somehow be harmonised through a technocratic fix which transcends hard political choices. The Lisbon European Council in March 2000 famously declared that "the Union has today set itself a new strategic goal for the next decade: to become the most competitive and dynamic knowledge-based economy in the world, capable of sustainable economic growth with more and better jobs and greater social cohesion" ... Do such attempts to square the circle risk abandoning the European social model by stealth, through the erosion of the social protections which unions achieved with such difficulty over many decades?[27]

Hyman is surely right in this: modes of governance, whether informal, more flexible, participatory, etc., are still just that, i.e. modes of governance, geared towards effective problem-solving understood at best as modes of steering market forces. And we might add: they lack a political register, in that they are 'coupled with a commitment to permanent democratic experimentation' only in the hollowest understanding of 'democratic', in terms of modes of coordination and the demand for a certain transparency. For Joerges, OMC invokes qualities inherent in the economic sphere as a yardstick that public governance should respect and internalize. But these affinities are limited, he stresses: 'The proposals to institutionalise democratic experimentalism invoke the imagination not just of market entrepreneurs and market participants but also of deliberating political citizens.' He concludes:

> There is nothing wrong with bureaucracies and experts exchanging experiences and learning about new possibilities. There is a great deal that is wrong with building up opaque networks which get entrusted with the task of seeking to

25 See Búrca 2003: 833–4.
26 See Hyman 2005: 25.
27 Hyman 2005: 25–6.

> carry through what they have learnt and agreed upon in democratic societies. Such a model is soft because it no longer relies on mandatory provisions. It is for the same reason strong because it risks … removing the virtues of democratic accountability, rule-bound public governance and its judicial control.[28]

This is eloquent and is thought to reflect something of what Hyman, in a different paper, called the 'flexible rigidities' of market integration[29] and the privileging of market dynamics over social protection. If the justification for the new 'flexibilities' is that we 'increasingly encounter evidence of diversity in terms of local conditions and regulatory needs'[30] then our justification ignores, and by ignoring redeems, the concentrations associated with globalization. It ignores and redeems the asymmetry between capital's flexibility to play and escape the regulatory net on the one hand, and on the other the rigidity inflicted on labour in terms of its capacity to mobilize across national borders and to envisage and pursue alternatives.

Two Constitutional Tales

The first of the two tales is the more familiar, 'modern' story of constitutionalism, as unfinished project, that in its many variations can still be collected into a single narrative. The constitutional theorist begins by drawing a distinction; between politics and law, between will and reason, democracy and rights, or in its more interesting formulation, constituent and constituted power. However the distinction is configured, what is constant is that the poles articulate, and that their articulation is characterized by tension. Constitutionalism is the name for that articulation and that tension. Constitutionalism here also holds the promise that the tension will be productive.

In this more familiar narrative, the constitution has been analysed as giving us the vocabulary to furnish democratic experimentation and as simultaneously delimiting the field of experimentation. If it achieves both imperfectly, then that imperfection itself has been seen as an advantage. In indeterminacy, i.e. the imperfect delimitation, it harboured responsiveness to the dynamism of the political; in the specificity of constitutional language, necessarily reductive of the scope of political meanings, it secured both containment and stability. This 'imperfection' in both directions guarantees that there will always be tension, and constitutionalism straddles this tension with the promise of self-determination on the back of what it sanctions as conditions of that self-determination in terms of relevant constituency, containment in rights and property regimes, what is negotiable and what is fixed. Niklas Luhmann would call this the constitution's selective release of the future in, respectively, social, material and temporal dimensions.

---

28 Joerges 2005: 484.

29 Hyman 2006.

30 Scheuerman as quoted in Joerges 2005: 484.

This traditional take on constitutionalism does not lack dynamism. Some of its more conservative renditions of course do. But at the other end of the spectrum, with the deconstructive turn, for example, a full range of alternatives becomes visible as inherent in a text that could be unpacked in contrasting ways, the unsettledness of its meaning tracking the restlessness of the political. This has in turn allowed constitutional lawyers a claim on *the constituent* in the various modalities that the constituted does not, and could not, exhaust.

Where there is danger of a lapse – of the live spirit of the democratic into the dead letter of the legal text – a 'constitutional moment' animates the spirit anew. At one level the urge to keep the flame alive explains the obsession to grant the status of a moment to any semblance of mobility of the body politic; where there is no mobility to grant it to a constitutional court; where neither of these live up to the task, to read the constitutional momentum into social dialogue; when the crippling poverty of social dialogue in turn proves to have no capacity to carry anything close to the ambition of constitutional creativity then to defer the constitutional to the ideality of a dialogue that would. There is something nostalgic but moribund about these efforts to ground the appeal of the constitutional in some form of rational public discourse in the era where the political finds its outlets thwarted in mass consumption and mass apathy. And Gianfranco Poggi puts it well when he reminds us that

> Marx was not far wrong in his bloody-minded suspicion that the duty imposed on the member of civil society periodically to experience '*ecstasies*' – to sublimate away their mundane, egoistic interests in order to act as citizens – was at best a high-flown idealistic abstraction, at worst a deceitful cover for substantial continuities and congruities between the interests pursued in each [private and public] sphere.[31]

In any case, it is really difficult in the midst of this inertia to find something, anything, to ascribe momentum to, and Luhmann can ask, not without a touch of *Schadenfreude*, 'if there was no demos, would anyone really notice?'[32] In marked contrast, there is a strong temptation to deny the very status of a 'constitutional moment' to the deafening resonance of political events that do not fit the logic of constitutional moments,[33] such as the decisive reaction to the European constitution and the widespread 'anti-establishment' riots in Paris and Athens. Is it perhaps the exhaustion of this paradigm of constitutionalism as paradoxical but productive, this concept-in-tension whose tension no longer registers with any force nor animates political debate, that has led to the rise of a second narrative of constitutionalism?

---

31 Poggi 1978: 118.

32 Luhmann as quoted in Fischer-Lescano 2004: 78

33 For a very interesting interpretation of the constructive failure of this constitutional moment, see Philippopoulos-Mihalopoulos 2008.

Here it is constitutionalism's *plural* explosion on to the European scene that puts the first paradigm to question. If modern constitutionalism finds its coordinates in the articulation-in-tension of politics and law, the new paradigm leaves it without its constitutive tension. Instead we have horizontal proliferation. What coinage precisely sets something in circulation as constitutional is not specified, but then pluralism perhaps tells us it should not be. Against hegemonic understandings, hierarchy-building, privileged political imaginaries and the rest, pluralism invites plurality also at the level of definitions: no privilege to any one of the criteria of the constitutional; constitutionalisms 'from below' carry with them their own self-definitions. At some level this is invigorating; at another it is hugely problematic.

For us, concerned with the dyad economic and political constitution, it is important to remain with what 'circulates' as constitutional goods and with the varieties of common structures that can be acknowledged and received as constitutional. In this we have a combination of elasticity and rigidity. On the side of elasticity we have fragmentation and flattening, a proliferation of values, rights and interests that are (newly) relevant to the constitutional sphere among an expanded plurality of constitutional actors: individuals, governments, corporations, trade unions, and so on. The competition is played out on a constitutional field reconfigured to accommodate this plurality in the only way possible: where constitutional goods circulate as constitutional commodities, crucially by establishing commensurability across the board. It is at this point that the extraordinary rigidity of the contextual conditions begins to become visible. Throughout this, fluidity is tied to and enabled by forms of rigidity: the entrenchment of both the mechanism for the allocation of value and the coinage of value itself.

Karl Polanyi reminds us of the extraordinary effort it took to set in place and entrench the contextual conditions for the creation of a market system in terms of the subsumption of society to the market through the fictitious commodities of land, labour and money. The articulation of markets in the three commodities created the market system whose effect was the 'disembedding' of the economy from society. The institutional separation of the political from the economic sphere as constitutive of market society, Polanyi insisted, was at the root of the 'great transformation' of capitalist modernity. It is this same separation that we witness in the massive strategic intervention in the social field to create and sustain the European market. The point is that it is the same, continuing story of establishing the conditions for the operation of capital. 'Social exposure' is what for Polanyi results from the stripping back from society of all its protective mechanisms, the forms of solidarity that it harbours as constitutive of the social bond.[34]

Polanyi's work is extraordinarily pertinent today, and it is perhaps surprising that it has been so sparingly, or at least so belatedly, engaged with by theorists of European integration. The reason for referring to him in this context, however, is rather more specific. It is to argue that the proliferation of constitutional goods and constitutional orders requires conditions, and fluidity presupposes rigidities

34 See Polanyi 1944.

in terms of the coinage that establishes the conditions of commensurability and thus of circulation. That is why something fundamental is missing in the work, for example, of someone like Zygmunt Bauman, whose influential theory of 'liquid society' (2000) sets the terms for a certain post-modern understanding of society where structures 'dissolve'. Bauman uses Marx's old metaphor from the *Communist Manifesto* ('All that is solid melts into air') to claim (with Richard Sennett here) that techniques of 'speed, escape, passivity' introduce a new 'liquidity' and with it, 'a re-distribution and reallocation of modernity's "melting powers". They affected at first the extant institutions, the frames that circumscribed the realms of possible action-choices, ... Configurations, constellations, patterns of dependency and interaction were all thrown into the melting pot, to be subsequently recast and refashioned'.[35] He says elsewhere:

> Capital can travel fast and can travel light ... counting on brief profitable adventures ... and its lightness and motility have turned it into the paramount source of uncertainty ... This has become the present-day basis for domination and the principal factor of social divisions. ... Brief encounters now replace lasting engagements.[36]

And, as regards labour:

> [C]apital got rid of the task which tied it to the ground and forced it into direct engagement with the agents exploited for the sake of its self-production ... The disembodied labour of the software era no longer ties down capital: it allows capital to be exterritorial, volatile and fickle.[37]

But capital was always 'volatile and fickle', it always 'travelled fast and light'; that is the point that Marx makes consistently when he talks of the *promiscuity* of capital. And it is still the markers of the 'old' solidity, its mainstays and organizing concepts, its gathering orders and logic of commodification, its 'fences, barriers' and anchorage points, that allow the vastly increased flexibility that capitalism possesses in what Bauman characterizes as its fluid, liquid or 'light' phase. And this is a logic that is unapologetic, that does not depend on 'evasion or slippage', on 'speed, escape, passivity'. What it explicitly introduces is a rigid dismantling of a system, an active disarticulation of alternatives which is at the same time the institution of a framework of guarantees for capital. As ever – this is Polanyi's point – the liquid flows of capital require entrenchment and rigidity. What the 'liquidity' argument misses is that conditions for the flow of capital are set down and entrenched in measures that release resources into its flow and secure guarantees for financial returns. 'For power to be free to flow', Bauman had insisted

35 Bauman 2000: 5–6.

36 Bauman 2000: 121.

37 Bauman 2000: 121.

in his definition of 'liquidity', 'the world must be free of fences, barriers, fortified borders and checkpoints'.[38] *But barriers, fortified borders and checkpoints* are exactly what, in these examples, *have allowed the flow*.

And it is precisely this articulation of flexibility and rigidity that we tracked above that came to underpin the trajectory of – to recall Hyman once again – actually existing Europeanization. 'Barriers, fortified borders and checkpoints' are installed by international economic organizations and policed vigilantly at local, regional and global level. From the privatization of public resources, the granting of patents to public knowledge, the commodification of life and labour down to the minutiae of investment rules and withdrawal clauses for corporate investment, economic self-regulation breaks the power of intermediate institutions and solidarities while severing politics from economics through the elevation of private property claims to the level of human rights. The results are devastating. A functionally integrated Europe repeats the logic of the self-regulating market, its promise of the freedoms of movement of capital and labour underlying the enforced flexibilization of labour, the privatization of common resources and liberalization, the performance of partners policed by an ever more complex system of sanctions and guarantees, the rigidity of which makes a mockery of state power and the severity of which devastates the most vulnerable strata of its citizens.

If the lesson about market fluidity is that it is underpinned, sustained and policed by institutional structures that are rigid, massive and violent, what modalities of political exchange does this other constitutionalism, of the many constitutions of Europe, allow us to envisage, to explore as constitutional theorists and to pursue as political actors?

Let us again discuss this with reference to a particular, recent, example. Take the issue of labour standards and the vexed question of transferring the European social model eastward, to environments – like the Baltic states – where massive deterioration of work standards, including 'safety crimes' are institutionally tolerated. Lithuania currently has twice the rate of workplace 'killings' of the EU and four times that of France.[39] Latvia is in the process of suspending occupational health and safety regulation in response to the financial crisis. A small price to pay perhaps for ridding the workplace of the over-protective state-socialist heritage and imbuing it with market discipline. The US-based Cato Institute's advice for the new EU member states is the creation of a dual standard regulatory system for health and safety, where 'excessive regulation' emanating from the EU … [should] not be allowed to hamper growth or reduce labour flexibility'. The same report continues: 'Over-regulation of conditions of employment will diminish the comparative advantage that CEE workers enjoy over their more highly paid western counterparts.'[40] Unfortunately for the legacy of the 'social market', the Court of Justice has – to put it euphemistically – done very little to allay the

38 Bauman 2000: 14.

39 On this see Woolfson's important work, indicatively 2006 and 2010.

40 As quoted in Woolfson 2010: 5.

fears that the price of integration involves precisely this form of distribution of the risks of production in its unequivocal endorsement of social dumping in the *Laval* and *Viking* quartet of cases.[41] And not surprisingly, traditional 'hard' enforcement strategies are being increasingly substituted, across the board, by 'softer' law, forms of self-regulation and corporate responsibility. The tendency to rely on forms of corporate self-constitutionalization is strong, and is seen as a way to extract concessions from corporations not through political routes but through market discipline.[42]

This is no doubt depressing and sobering to those who had perhaps entertained a different vision of social Europe. But what does it say about the many constitutions of Europe?

This is not, of course, to imply that whatever the neoliberal advisers of the Cato Institute or others advocate does directly impinge on our discussions of constitutionalism. This is suggesting something rather different. That the demand and argument for the 'un-protecting' of labour as comparative advantage marks a departure that could not have been possible previously, under a different conception of constitutionalism. *It is the circulation of 'social protection' or the 'dignity of labour' as only one amongst many constitutional goods that makes it possible.* They are circulated alongside and on a par with other constitutional goods like property rights and economic security. The social constitution is 'released' alongside the economic constitution, and the constitutional goods they each protect circulate as other commodities, the coordinates of their competition undone from any overall framework.

But to have 'circulation' *at all* what is required is a principle of circulation and a common measure; and it is at this point that a default constitution installs itself. The common measure is the reduction of *value* to constitutional *good*. The proliferation of constitutions, the collapse of their internal hierarchizations as well as any hierarchization amongst them, in the name of pluralism, contribute to the *undistorted* circulation of constitutional goods as commodities. Preference, unmoored from any of these constitutions or any value system, becomes the principle of choice. This is a free-floating preference that can only become 'rational' under principles of its own choosing which fold value judgement back upon itself in a gesture that is typical to – and in some sense coextensive with – the principles of market competition. This is the default constitutionalism that installs itself behind the 'many constitutions' of Europe.

To borrow from a rather improbable source, we could speak here of a constitutionalism of simulation that defines a political society, ours, 'in which there is no longer any difference between the economic and the political, because the same language reigns in both, from one end to another'. This is 'a public

---

41 Case C-341/05, *Laval un Partneri Ltd*, ECR 2007, I-11767, and Case C-438/05, *International Transport Workers' Federation and Finnish Seamen's Union v Viking Line ABP and OÜ Viking Line Eesti*, ECR 2007, I-10779.

42 See also Teubner 2009.

sphere with no more subject, no more focal point, no more centre or periphery, pure flexion or circular inflexion'.[43]

What of the attempts to hold onto the concept of the '*social market*' inscribed in our (nearly) constitutional treaties and fundamental documents? These attempts are hollow if they are divorced from the *tradition* of social market democracy as inseparable from the organizing ideals of the democratic organization of the economy and the workplace: a tradition that comprehends the principles of social protection, of preservation of skills and the security of people at work, as qualifications to and controls of rather than products of the market, and as irreducible to the logic of price. Unless it is established politically as a limiting condition of the market, the term 'social', as *under-determined*, offers little defence. The market is like a vortex and it does not happily tolerate predicates. It has its own principles of sociality. If we are to acknowledge moral limits to the market and thereby resist the logic that casts social dumping as comparative advantage, if we are to force the logic of price to withdraw selectively from certain fields, in the name of different conceptions of risk-burdening – where those burdened are not the least capable of carrying those risks – then we need to do a lot better than release more and more of what we hold politically valuable, as commodities into Europe's market of its many constitutions.

References

Baudrillard, J. 1994. *Simulacra and Simulation*. Michigan: Michigan Press.

Bauman, Z. 2000. *Liquid Modernity*. Cambridge: Polity.

Búrca, G. de. 2003. The constitutional challenge of new governance in the European Union. *European Law Review*, 28, 814–39.

Dukes, R. 2008. Constitutionalizing employment relations: Sinzheimer, Kahn-Freund and the role of labour law. *Journal of Law and Society*, 25, 341–63.

Fischer-Lescano, A. 2004. Themis sapiens, in *Transitional Governance and Constitutionalism*, edited by C. Joerges, I.-J. Sand and G. Teubner. Oxford: Hart, 67–80.

Glasman, M. 1996. *Unnecessary Suffering: Managing Market Utopia*. London: Verso.

Hyman, R. 2005. Trade unions and the politics of the European social model. *Economic and Industrial Democracy*, 26, 9–40.

Hyman, R. 2006. Flexible rigidities: A model for social Europe? in *Employment Relations in a Changing Society: Assessing the Post-Fordist Paradigm*, edited by L.E. Alonso and M. Martínez Lucio. London: Palgrave Macmillan, 215–22.

Joerges, C. 2005. What is left of the European economic constitution? A melancholic eulogy. *European Law Review*, 30, 461–89.

43 Baudrillard 1994: 88 and 30.

Joerges, C. and Rödl, F. 2005. The 'social market economy' as Europe's social model? in *A European Social Citizenship? Preconditions for Future Policies in Historical Light*, edited by L. Magnusson and B. Stråth. Brussels: Lang, 125–58.

Philippopoulos-Mihalopoulos, A. 2008. When 'no' means 'yes': A constitution for Europe and the limits of ignorance, in *Paradoxes of European Legal Integration*, edited by H. Petersen, A.L. Kjær, H. Krunke and M.R. Madsen. Aldershot: Ashgate, 29–44.

Poggi, G. 1978. *The Development of the Modern State*. London: Hutchinson.

Polanyi, K. 1944. *The Great Transformation*. Boston, MA: Beacon Press.

Scharpf, F.W. 1991. *Crisis and Choice in European Social Democracy*. Ithaca: Cornell.

Scharpf, F.W. 2002. The European social model: Coping with the challenges of diversity. *Journal of Common Market Studies*, 40, 645–70.

Scott, J. and Trubek, D. 2002. Mind the gap: Law and new approaches to governance in the EU. *European Law Journal*, 8, 1–18.

Streit, M.E. and Mussler, W. 1995. The economic constitution of the European Community: From Rome to Maastricht. *European Law Journal*, 15–30.

Supiot, A. 2008. Europe won over to the 'communist market economy'. *Revue Permanente du Mauss*. Available at: <www.journaldumauss.net/spip.php?article283> (accessed: 20 January 2010).

Teubner, G. 2009. The corporate codes of multinationals: Company constitutions beyond corporate governance and co-determination, in *Conflict of Laws and Laws of Conflict in Europe and Beyond: Patterns of Supranational and Transnational Juridification*, edited by R. Nickel. Oxford: Hart, 261–76.

Woolfson, C. 2006. The 'conventionalisation' of safety crimes in post-communist new member states of the European Union. *Critical Criminology*, 14, 339–64.

Woolfson, C. 2010 (forthcoming). The sense of measure and societies without limit. *Social & Legal Studies*.

Chapter 3

Constitutionalism and the Multi-Coded Treaties of the EU: Changing the Concepts of Constitutionality

Inger-Johanne Sand

From Hierarchical National Constitutions to Combinations of Constitutional Texts and Institutions

The sovereignty and the politico-legal power of modern nation-states have been legally defined and delimited by their constitutions and by the concept of constitutionality. While constitutionality is accepted as a vital quality of modern nation-states, different accounts explain its more precise structure, significance and practical effects. This concerns, for example, the relationship between politics and law both in the making of a constitution and in its emergence over time in adjudication and political–constitutional practice. Modern nation-states have emerged as complex interactions and interdependencies between political power, legal constitutions, liberal rights and citizenship, economic and technological development, social structures, and so on, where it may be difficult to distinguish the specific performance of each of these factors. However, constitutionality has been seen as a defining and quintessential characteristic and politico-legal infrastructure of the sovereignty of the nation-state. It has also been part of the paradigmatic difference and duality between national constitutional legal regimes and international law where constitutionality has had no place.

Over some time, particularly since the end of the Second World War and the Universal Declaration of Human Rights, a significant increase has occurred in international treaties and organizations, also in establishing courts or other dispute-settlement bodies. An increasing number of international treaties address and regulate themes which concern both internal domestic matters and cross-boundary dynamics. The distinction between national or domestic and international matters has thus become seriously blurred. In particular, this concerns areas such as regulation of international trade, human rights, environmental protection, climate change, intellectual property rights, bio-safety, and so on.[1] International decision-making, international courts and international dispute-settlement bodies have

1 See Brunkhorst 2010 (forthcoming); and Sand 2004.

contributed to an increasing effectiveness of international law, with impact also for citizens.

The sovereignty, constitutionality and exclusive competences of nation-states have enabled them to be authoritative and operative. A presumption has also been implied that nation-states would possess a general ability to make political priorities and resolve problems within their boundaries. With increasing globalization and cross-boundary factual dynamics, this presumption has changed. Economic, humanitarian, environmental, climatic, health, migration, technological, social and other problems increasingly have to be dealt with on several institutional and territorial levels in combination and interaction. Current European and international law and politics are responses to this. They have unavoidably resulted in combinations of institutions and texts, at times with insufficient and unclear definitions of their interrelationship.[2]

The EU treaties and the adjudication of EU law is the first legal international regime to have such a comprehensive section of supranational law, as in the areas of free movement and the internal market.[3] A vital part of economic legislation and connected areas is prepared and decided within the EU institutions on the basis of EU treaties, is binding on member states, and has direct effect for citizens. Legislation is also reviewed by the Court of Justice in relation to treaties. The Court of Justice's adjudication is also binding on member states in their implementation of EU law. The result is a form of intervention in the constitutional structures of member states by a supranational treaty. Seen from a constitutional law perspective, the implication of this is a form of combined, overlapping or fragmented constitutionalism.[4] Comprehensive supranational competences which overlap or overrule national constitutional competences and the way these are applied in practice will unavoidably involve consequences for member state national constitutions both in practice and as ideas and symbols.[5] They will also affect the configurations of, and the relationships between, law and politics.

The main argument of this chapter is that when the all-comprehensive and self-sufficient structure of nation-state constitutions changes and is replaced with a combination of institutions and constitutional texts on several levels, changes inevitably occur in what we understand as constitutionalism and in the functions, the forms, the configurations and the principles of constitutions. Constitutional structures on several different institutional and territorial levels need to be combined in order to describe and understand the total and functioning constitutionalism of one state, which will change the variety of structures, functions, and principles in constitutions and constitutionalism.[6] However, analysis of changing constitutions and constitutionalism becomes difficult and complex because these still form

2 See Walker 2002; and Sand 2004.

3 See Weiler, 1999a.

4 See Sand 1998.

5 See Joerges 2002: 133 *ff*; 1999: 311 *ff*; and Weiler 1999b.

6 See Habermas 2008.

part of comprehensive and unpredictable processes of continuous change. The following contributions to such an analysis are still preliminary, partial and in progress. The analysis will limit itself to certain examples of the process so far.

EU member states possess modern democratic constitutions where different and historically specific configurations of democracy, human rights and the rule of law form crucial parts of the legitimacy of national constitutional institutions.[7] With increasing cross-border social, technological and economic dynamics, the preconditions of what may be regarded as the most optimal democratic institutions and as legitimate governance may be challenged and changed. These changes will involve implications for the values and principles implied and thus also for the legitimacy of constitutions.[8]

National, Supra-, Trans- and International Forms of Law: Challenges for Constitutionality

Modern nation-states have obviously been defined in a variety of different ways: by the political regimes which have emerged; by the economic resources and dynamics within states; and by social and cultural patterns and organizations in the same areas. However, constitutions and constitutionality have been seen as core parts of the definition of nation-states as sovereign states by territory, people and government. Constitutions are structural couplings between law and politics. They have to express both the political and the legal and cannot be reduced exclusively to either of them.[9] The exact balance between law and politics in the making and in the application of constitutions is always complex and precarious, also due to the fact that the two sides are carriers of different forms of legitimacy.[10] In the era of modern nation-state constitutionality, political practices, economic production, social patterns and other influences are increasingly seen as parallel and intertwined expressions of the state. Socio-economic processes might be given a politico-legal infrastructure by constitutions, but they may in turn change the preconditions of a specific constitution. Paradoxically, the constitutionality of nation-states is often seen at one and the same time as a defining, vital and necessary quality and also as a quality which in everyday life is often not highly visible.

The more *heterogeneous* institutional and textual situation is a challenge to national constitutions and constitutionality as a single unified and primary force wherein all traditional competences are gathered, as the *prima causa* of domestic law, and to domestic law as the primary expression of material law with relevance

---

7 See Habermas 2008.

8 See Teubner 2004.

9 See also Tuori's contribution in this volume.

10 See Willke 1986; and 1992: Ch 2. See also Ashenden and Thornhill 2010 (forthcoming).

for citizens.[11] Parts of this challenge concern the combination of several institutions and institutional levels of different political and territorial regimes, while other parts concern the fragmentation of functioning constitutions into several politico-legal and textual regimes. Different legal regimes such as the EU, the ECHR, and their member states may share basic values, but minor variations may exist in their internal balance and in the procedures and institutions applied. The more *dynamic* situation of inter- and supranational law presents a further challenge to the previously perceived stability of national constitutions and of their modes of change.[12] National constitutions have also been seen as strong *symbols* of both the values and the stability of nation-states. Inter- and supranational constitutional texts may challenge the unity and values of national constitutions.

It will be argued in the following that the Europeanization and globalization of law, and different regimes of inter-, supra- and transnational law, are processes which are challenging and changing the concept of constitutionality and how we use it. Firstly, *factual interdependence* has in a variety of ways made international cooperation increasingly urgent in more stable legal-political and even constitutional-like forms. The evolution of EU treaties is a primary example of this. Secondly, the EU treaties have stood as the most comprehensive example of a *supranational* treaty, thus intervening in the constitutionality of member states with their legislative, executive and judicial competences at the highest level.[13] This has necessitated a new description and analysis of constitutionality as an aggregate of several texts and authoritative institutions. Thirdly, the EC and EU treaties have emerged as supranational in relation to member states in vital parts and at the same time as *asymmetrical* and delimited in their material competences.[14] The economic constitution of the EU enjoys supremacy in relation to member states which stand among the world's most developed economies and welfare states. The parallel social, environmental, health and other areas of politico-legal regulation are less robustly and more unevenly treated by the EU treaties. The constitutionality of the EU emerges as quite powerful, legally and politically, but very differently structured in its material competences than the typical nation-state constitution. The form of constitutionality is, then, changing with its turn to international arenas. Fourthly, this new aggregate or fragmented association of texts and authorities has thus also contributed to *changing the relationships* between the legal, political, economic, social and security aspects of constitutionality.

The economic constitution of the EU is still the most clearly structured. Constitutionality in other regulatory areas has, in most cases, evolved as part of an expansion of the interpretation of economic competences which has clearly influenced how they have evolved. The specific form of constitutionality of the EU has, then, changed the relationships between the different material competences

11 See Minkkinen, 2009: 16 *ff*; and Kelsen 1925: 102.

12 See Habermas 2001.

13 See Weiler 1999a; and Poiares Maduro 2003.

14 See Sand 2008: 96–101.

in law and in politics. This influences the functioning of constitutionality and its relation to other communicative modes. Fifthly, this challenging process of change may be transforming our *concept* of constitutionality as a designation of the primary levels of politics and of law. The hierarchical construction has broken down. A more aggregate, combined, heterogeneous and dynamic construction has appeared. Constitutionality as in the supreme procedural competences is still there, though not necessarily as one whole structure, but rather as an aggregate of combined constitutional texts and as a more dynamic situation. Coherence and consistency may still be seen as general guidelines or ideal goals for law, but in a more global, dynamic and interdependent world they will have to be combined with a greater degree of acceptance of heterogeneity, change, combinations of competences and reflexive processes within and between institutions.

Clearly this raises several questions. One is the democratic legitimacy of more aggregate and fragmented constitutional structures. However, a continuance of legitimacy built on nation-state democracy alone is also insufficient and flawed in a situation of increasing global interdependence. Uneven and differently combined interdependent structures may, at least, be a preliminary response.

The Heritage of Constitutionalism and the Evolution of EU Law

National sovereign constitutions were initially based on an idea of completeness and pre-emption in their distribution of constitutional competences to the constitutional authorities (sovereign, legislative, executive, judicial). With several new supra- and international treaties, organizations and courts, the relationships between national on the one hand and inter- and supranational treaties and competences on the other hand have changed quite significantly. An increasing number of regulatory tasks and themes are now seen also as inter- and transnational in character and in practice. These changes have also led to significant changes in the relationships between legislative, executive and judicial institutions. The number of international courts or other dispute-settlement mechanisms is increasing, and they are increasingly effective and equipped with the remedy of imposable sanctions. However, the present situation of increased factual global and regional interdependence has so far not led to the development of sufficiently democratic processes and institutions on these levels. This is a challenge with consequences both for politics and law.

The EU is probably by far the most comprehensive and effective supra- and international system of treaties and institutions today. Obviously the most comprehensive part of EU supranational competences are its economic competences, in particular the internal market and freedom of movement of goods, services, persons and capital. It is the interpretation and implementation of Article 28 EC (34 TFEU) and other Articles on free movement which created the first expansions of the material competences of the treaties and their supranational character in relation to the domestic legislation of member states.[15] It is here that the material effects of the constitutionality of the EU treaties have emerged. Focus on the internal market, free movement and competition law has led to the emergence of an economic constitution in relation to member states and their constitutionality.[16] This economic constitution has been further developed by the introduction of qualified majority voting, use of harmonization directives, and extension of other regulatory competences after the Maastricht Treaty. This has led to wider material competences and also to elements of a social constitutionality, but with poorly defined boundaries. Schengen and police and security cooperation have later also led to elements of a security constitutionality. The Court of Justice has in several cases referred to international human rights as part of the basis of EU Law, in so far as the member states of the EU have all ratified the main international conventions. The European Convention on Human Rights and its Court have also emerged as vital legal dynamics supplementing adjudication of human rights in domestic courts.

The EU has developed its material competences step-by-step as proactive or reactive responses to political and socio-economic situations. These competences have been extended by treaty amendments, gradually by new regulations and directives, and at times also partially extended by the adjudication of the Court of Justice. The EU treaties possess a constitutionality in their own right as a separate legal regime with supranational competences, as well as forming part of the total functioning constitutions of the member states. Inter- and supranational treaties may then serve as constitutional texts on several levels and in different contexts at the same time. The EU treaties overlap, supplement and combine with the constitutions and legal regimes of the member states in the total description of their *de facto* constitutional competences. What were previously separate and fully comprehensive nation-state constitutions are now in fact a combination of several legal regimes with constitutional qualities. Functioning constitutions no longer consist of just one text or one specific national set of texts, but a combination of national constitutions with elements of supra- and international treaties.

The emerging closer interaction and interdependence between nation-state constitutions and elements of supra- and international treaties has partly been the result of a political desire to create closer factual interaction to avoid war and conflict, and partly a result of acceptance of the fact that an increasing number of social dynamics are transnational and cross-border, thus creating problems which need to be coordinated or resolved correspondingly.[17] Trade has been used to institutionalize and stabilize closer cooperation between nation-states and to avoid violent conflicts. The present qualities of global and regional factual interaction and interdependence have created a change and a challenge to the preconditions of self-sufficient national constitutions. This includes challenges to

15 See Weiler 1999c.

16 See Joerges 2005; and 2006.

17 See Teubner 2004, and Sand 2004.

develop more democratic and legitimate institutions on regional and international levels. International and regional factual dynamics also require legal and political cooperation in legitimate and democratic, as well as in more binding, forms. The result implies a break with some of the ideas of full sovereignty, self-sufficiency, *prima causa* and comprehensiveness in nation-states and their national constitutions.

Due to increasing cross-boundary factual dynamics, we need to develop institutional and constitutional ideas for more comprehensive and binding inter- and supranational treaties. The UN was founded on peace, the principle of non-intervention and international human rights. The EU treaties have been founded, first, on ideas of the necessity for peaceful cooperation among states, and later also on ideas of economic cooperation and growth, common environmental protection and aspects of a common regime of social protection. With the extension of foreign and security policy, and also police cooperation, security and immigration control have been included in the main purposes.

However, increased regional and international cooperation has resulted in intricate and complex combinations and interactions between national constitutions and supra- and international treaties. The legal linkages between the different treaties and constitutions often contain uncertain and unclear elements with gaps between different formal definitions and with a considerable range of discretion. This is often inevitable and is not necessarily problematic, but it does mean that acceptance has to be created for more complex and uncertain constitutional constructions. The result is an aggregate of institutions, competences and values. The different institutions involved also at times express quite different views or interpretations of their mutual relationships.[18] The task of constitutions has been to give some kind of authoritative, politically accepted and legally founded basis for their relative stabilization, including values, institutions and competences. Today, the equivalent constitutional task is also to create a basis for interaction between nation-states and between these and international organizations.

The Economic Constitution of the EU: From Free Movement of Goods to Persons and Services

The EU has primarily emerged as an economic constitution with the internal market and the four freedoms forming the main part of the supranational area of EC competences. With the pronouncement of the EC Treaty as including principles of supremacy and direct effect and thus possessing supranational status in relation to member states and their citizens, a vital intervention was made in the legislative regimes of member states as well as their constitutional basis.[19] Parts

18 See BVerfG, 2 BvE, 2/08, 30 June 2009.

19 See Case C-26/62, *Van Gend en Loos*, ECR 1963, 1; and Case C-6/64, *Costa v ENEL*, ECR 1964, 585; also Weiler 1999c.

of the then EC, later EU, treaties and their adjudication by the Court of Justice were seen as supranational, at first primarily in relation to legislation concerning the internal market and market freedoms. A supranational treaty is by definition an intervention in the constitutional regime of member states, even if it is ratified and signed by the state itself and through its own constitutional rules. Legislation and adjudication in the relevant area may occur both in member states and by the supranational organization, but the latter enjoys supremacy. The *de facto* functioning constitutional regime will then consist of several texts from different regimes.

Adjudication of Article 28 EC (34 TFEU) and free movement of goods evolved over time in a dynamic manner emphasizing the goal of an effectively functioning market. Interpretation of 'measures having an equivalent effect' of quantitative restrictions thus became increasingly sharp, with emphasis on the economic purpose of free movement and a high ambition for economic effectiveness and a functioning market. An ambitious scrutiny evolved first for discriminatory measures and later also for what could be seen as obstacles to trade. In doing so, the Court of Justice developed ambitious economic policies. However, a vital part of defining such ambitious economic policies in practice is to draw inevitable boundaries towards other policies. Some exceptions to free movement are included in Article 30 EC (36 TFEU). Other general criteria which have evolved are public policies which can be seen as necessary or justified. The main and dominant textual distinction here is *free movement* (of goods). However, this inevitably also means having to evaluate and assess various social, environmental and other forms of regulation which could be seen as measures having the equivalent effect of quantitative restrictions, and thus as discriminatory or an obstacle to trade.[20]

High ambitions, and a high level of precision for the trade side of the distinction between trade and social and other forms of protection, inevitably also means intervening in and assessing the other side of the distinction. Free movement being the primary purpose, it has also been the most open and expansive side of the distinction. Regulation and adjudication were asymmetric, but with increasing indirect or direct influence on and scrutiny of various forms of social, environmental and other forms of protection. Economic and market regulation on a high level of ambition in terms of efficiency cannot be done only as negative integration: it also implies and leads to forms of positive integration. Developing criteria for and evaluating what forms of social, environmental and other regulation and protection are either necessary or justified in relation to public policy and in relation to freedom of movement inevitably also means qualitative intervention and evaluation in that side of the distinction. In highly developed economic and knowledge societies, efficient market regulation cannot be done only as technical negative integration without more substantive regulatory and political effects. Positive integration becomes increasingly evident with harmonization directives and other social, environmental, health, consumer and other regulations. EU

20 See Weiler 1999c.

competences are enumerated, but interpretation of treaties, directives and regulations is at times purpose-oriented and dynamic. The economic and legal constitutionalism of the EU forms the main dynamic of the treaties and their main infrastructure. No equivalent regulatory structure exists for protection of social rights, environmental and health protection, and others, at treaty or constitutional level. These areas are legislated on, but without sufficient substantive basis at treaty level and in a more fragmented and contingent way.

The implication is that economic constitutionalization expands into its boundary areas and also evolves into elements of social constitutionalization. Judicial review of directives in relation to the treaties and purposive interpretation of the treaties add to the qualities of a functioning constitutionalization.

Free movement of persons and services has been increasingly implemented over time both in terms of EC legislation and member state adaptation. The processes of implementation have clearly illustrated the many different social, legal and political dimensions as well as the complexity of free movement of persons and services compared to free movement of goods. Social, labour and immigration rights, as well as taxation and company law, are affected. In these areas, member states often have different traditions and patterns of regulation stemming from different economic, political and historical trajectories and, moreover, from different traditions as to the organization of labour and work–life balance. This makes harmonization in these areas a sensitive issue. The enlargement process and inclusion of members from the Baltic, Central and Eastern European states has contributed significantly to the actualization of free movement of both persons and services. Some of the consequences are illustrated by the *Viking*, *Laval* and *Rüffert* cases, discussed in further detail below. Free movement of services has been given further attention in the Services Directive (2006/123/EC). Services of general economic interest have been discussed in relation to Articles 86 and 87 EC (106–107 TFEU), and in White and Green papers.[21]

Several directives and regulations have been adopted to regulate free movement of persons and services more specifically. Regulation 1408/71 on the application of social security schemes to 'employed persons and their families moving within the Community' includes the right to health services of EU citizens. The regulation was enacted primarily with the aim of securing social security rights for migrant workers. Considering the differences between national legislations regarding such rights, it was seen as preferable to establish the principle that the regulation apply to all member state nationals insured under social security for workers.[22] Regulation 1408/71 and its adjudication thus illustrate not only rights necessary for persons who have made use of their freedom to move to other member states, but also how those rights have been extended to those living in their home states,

21 See Commission White Paper on services of general interest (COM(2004) 374 final) and Green Paper on services of general interest (COM(2003) 270 final).

22 Regulation 1408/71, *cf.* the preamble and Articles 1–3; see also Case C-372/04, *Watts*, ECR 2006, I–4325.

albeit on certain conditions. This may be seen as representing a vital intervention in regulation of access to health services in general. The Regulation illustrates how EU legislation, which initially had a more delimited purpose, is given a more extended area of competence. Part of the background for this is probably the difficulty of making highly specific regulations in the area of work, social rights and welfare because the different purposive areas and their instruments are quite closely coupled.

The ECJ has ruled that under Article 49 EC (56 TFEU) citizens are entitled to receive medical services which are available in their home states in other member states also. Not to grant such a right would be an unacceptable restriction of free movement of persons and services. For the home state to remunerate the cost of medical services, member states may impose a prior authorization requirement. If services in demand are available and of sufficient quality in the home state of the citizen, then remuneration may be denied. This is done in order for member states to ensure sufficient and permanent access to a balanced range of high quality medical services and to assist them in controlling the costs of those services. However, the conditions and procedures for granting such prior authorization must satisfy requirements which are reasonable and proportionate. Authorization practices must be based on objective and non-discriminatory criteria, which are known in advance, and which are applied proportionately and within a reasonable time. Free movement of persons and services thus implies EC regulatory action concerning health services and rights, with vital consequences for health planning and budgets in all member states.

Other examples include Directive 96/71/EC concerning the posting of workers in the framework of provision of services – securing work-related rights for these workers in the relevant member states – and Directive 2004/38 EC on the right of citizens of the Union and their family members to move and reside freely within the territory of member states.[23]

These directives also illustrate how actualization of the right to free movement for persons and services easily leads to legislation stretching far into the general fields of social, labour and immigration law. The same directives and regulations again illustrate the problems involved in or the impossibility of strictly delimiting economic legislation to forms of negative integration in advanced and well-regulated welfare states with comprehensive legislation in the area of social, health, labour and other rights. It is also probably next to impossible to secure social and labour law rights in the relevant member state for persons coming from other member states or posted workers without entering into complex dilemmas partly involving division of responsibility between the member states concerned and partly involving division of responsibility between EU and member state levels. Directive 96/71/EC gives posted workers several minimum rights in terms of pay, working hours, conditions, health and others, which are secured by law or

23 See, e.g., Case C-127/08, *Metock and Others*, ECR 2008, I-6241.

collective agreements in the host state.[24] Collective labour law and substantive parts of social and welfare rights are framed in domestic law and not included directly in EU competences. This may create both substantive and more technical legal problems for posted workers. The purpose of the Directive is to secure some basic rights of workers in the host state for posted workers. Defining when the conditions for such rights are met involves drawing a boundary between actualization of two different member state regimes. This is not only a technical task: it may also have political–legal implications. The host state has an interest in treating all workers equally and in avoiding social dumping. The home state may have an interest in keeping wages of posted workers on their own level if this involves a competitive advantage. Directive 2004/38/EC grants leave to enter the territory of the host state to both the Union citizens involved and their family members, including those who are not citizens of a member state. This involves immigration rights for non-member state citizens and well illustrates how different regulatory schemes overlap in complex ways if certain rights are to be secured.

The directives and regulations mentioned here are not constitutional in their own right, but they do form part of the economic constitution of the EU, or rather of its boundary areas. They illustrate the close relations between free movement and internal market rules, competition law, social rights, labour law and health rights. They also illustrate the tendency of the economic constitution of the EU to expand both incrementally as well as qualitatively and by both legislation and adjudication.

Free Movement of Persons and Services: Extending the Economic Constitution to Labour Law and Social Rights

The enlargement to the east has resulted in a union of states with, at this stage, significant economic and social differences among the member states. Free movement of persons and services and the principle of non-discrimination have come to form crucial instruments of economic integration between the different states. Free movement has been interpreted as a right for citizens of all member states to use, with total prohibition of discrimination on the grounds of nationality in a host member state. This is a necessary requirement for liberal markets to function. With implementation of free movement of persons, a variety of questions emerge as to what domestic legislation concerning social, labour and other rights might constitute discrimination. Work–life balance is a multidimensional situation including a variety of social rights and the whole structure of labour law with rights of organization, negotiation, and so on. The EU addresses some of these, but not all, and not systematically. The core of labour law concerning collective agreements falls to the responsibility of member states, operating within the International Labour Organization (ILO) framework, and often through contractual

24 See also Giubboni's contribution on Directive 96/71/EC in this volume.

arrangements with the parties involved. The EU has no harmonized legislation on collective rights in labour law, but several directives concern protection of special groups of workers and other social rights. The result is a legally uneven and complex situation. Legislative and constitutional competences are shared between the EU and its member states.

In Europe, collective labour law traditionally forms a distinct legal regime with a structure historically defined by employer and employee organizations and state authorities, and which thus varies between the various EU member states. Different structures of collective labour law are also related to different structures of social rights, family law and economic law. Collective labour law is not only a technical economic regime. It is also deeply embedded in the different and specific traditions of relations between employer and employee parties and their organizations. These relations have distinct and different social and political qualities which are not easily reconciled or harmonized with new regulations without changing vital social and organizational patterns and values. With the current enumerated material competences of the EU and the more comprehensive competences of member state legal regimes, arguably a constitutionally embedded and secured division of competences is in place. Collective labour law has never formed part of the explicit material competences of EU law. However, employment policy is included in the Treaty, Articles 125–130 EC (145–150 TFEU), and certain social rights and policies are included in Articles 136–145 EC (151–161 TFEU). These Articles include employment strategies along with guidelines and references to the charter of fundamental social rights for workers. These include more specifically the purposes of proper social protection, development of human resources with a view to lasting high employment, combating exclusion and several specific rights.

However, in recent decisions by the Court of Justice concerning free movement of persons and services, collective labour law and the different regimes in charge of this in member states are significantly affected. In *Laval*,[25] a conflict arose between Laval un Partneri Ltd, a company incorporated in Latvia but operating in Sweden, and Swedish construction workers' organizations concerning the understanding of certain collective agreements in Sweden and to what extent the Latvian company and its workers were bound by this. The Latvian company had signed collective agreements with their Latvian employees in Latvia and maintained that in terms of payment they were bound by those agreements. Negotiations concerning the Swedish collective agreements were not successful. The Swedish organizations insisted that minimum pay requirements under the Swedish collective agreements were also binding on the posted Latvian workers. The Swedish construction workers' organization then declared a blockade of the construction site in question, preventing delivery of goods and prohibiting the Latvian workers from entering the site. The conflict was taken to the Swedish labour court for mediation, but Laval refused to sign the Swedish agreements because 'it was not possible to know

25 Case C-341/05, *Laval un Partneri Ltd*, ECR 2007, I-11767.

in advance what conditions would be imposed on it in relation to wages'.[26] In the Court of Justice decision, the relevant main provisions are the general principles of prohibition of discrimination on grounds of nationality (Article 12 EC, now 18 TFEU) and of freedom to provide services (Articles 49 and 50 EC, now 56–57 TFEU). On the one hand, a member state cannot prohibit a person established in another member state from moving freely on its territory to provide services. On the other hand, a member state cannot be precluded from applying its legislation or collective labour law agreements on minimum wages within its own territory.[27] However, the Court argued that application of the rule must be appropriate for securing the objective in question and not go beyond what is necessary to attain that objective. But the Swedish collective agreements in question had not been made universally applicable. The Swedish system was based on decentralized collective negotiations of a nature which were not provided for by Directive 96/71/EC. The Swedish tradition for collective negotiations is not included in the various provisions of the Directive on posting of workers and conditions of employment in the host member state, and is thus not seen as directly protected under the Directive.[28]

In *Laval*, Sweden and Denmark argued that the right to strike and to use other forms of recognized collective action had to be seen as fundamental rights and thus protected as such, therefore falling outside the scope of Article 49 EC and Directive 96/71/EC. Moreover, collective action is also protected under Convention 87 of the ILO.[29] However, the Court of Justice maintained that these fundamental rights did not fall outside the scope of the Treaty, but had to be reconciled with the requirements relating to rights explicitly protected under the Treaty and in accordance with the principle of proportionality. The Court here referred to the previous cases of *Schmidberger* and *Omega Spielhallen*, where protection of fundamental rights was seen as legitimate and thus could possibly justify restrictions on obligations imposed by Community law.[30] However, the collective actions in question had to be specifically examined to see whether these constituted a restriction and, if so, whether this could be justified. On the one hand, freedom to provide services was seen as one of the fundamental principles of the Community. On the other hand, the right to collective action was seen as a measure which could constitute an overriding reason of public interest.[31] The two elements would have to be balanced in relation to each other. In this case the Court decided that the collective action could not be justified in light of a public interest objective because of lack of provisions 'of any kind, which are sufficiently precise and

26 Case C-341/05, *Laval un Partneri Ltd*, ECR 2007, I-11767, para. 36.

27 See Case C-341/05, *Laval un Partneri Ltd*, ECR 2007, I-11767, para. 57.

28 See Case C-341/05, *Laval un Partneri Ltd*, ECR 2007, I-11767, paras 75–7.

29 See Case C-341/05, *Laval un Partneri Ltd*, ECR 2007, I-11767, paras 90–94.

30 See Case C-112/00, *Schmidberger*, ECR 2003, I-5659, para. 74; and Case C-36/02, *Omega Spielhallen*, ECR 2004, I-9609, para. 35.

31 See Case C-341/05, *Laval un Partneri Ltd*, ECR 2007, I-11767, paras 101–104.

accessible that they do not render it impossible or excessively difficult in practice for such an undertaking to determine the obligations with which it is required to comply as regards minimum pay'.[32] Moreover, it was also seen as discriminatory that the Swedish labour market parties had not recognized the obligations which the Latvian company had already entered into in Latvia. Similar patterns of argumentation were applied in *Viking* and *Rüffert*.[33] They further emphasize the points already made above, but do not add qualitatively new arguments.

The remarkable aspects of these cases are the scrutiny of collective agreements and negotiations in relation to Article 49 EC (56 TFEU) and the analyses of what, on the one hand, may constitute a restriction and what, on the other hand, may be justifiable as public policy. Collective labour law is not directly a part of or regulated by EU law. The cases thus illustrate how the case law on Articles 28 and 49 EC (now 34 and 56 TFEU), as it has developed, inevitably leads to evaluation of a variety of legal measures in member states, in terms of possibly being prohibited restrictions under EU law or exceptions to free movement justified by public policy. Even though national measures do not form part of EU law, they will be evaluated and assessed in relation to free movement under EU law. This may lead to the conclusion that member state legal measures are restrictions and not justifiable. Thus EU law overrules elements of member state domestic laws. This assessment is made on a variety of different national legal measures. Collective labour law, however, may be seen as having particular legal and social qualities because it is connected to and embedded in policies and contracts between employer and employee organizations. It is socially embedded in the different work–life and socio-economic traditions and patterns of each state. Hence it may be difficult to assess from the outside and by the European Court of Justice what the exact social and economic qualities are and how exactly they should be assessed in relation to free movement. The right to collective action is also legally secured by the ILO conventions, which do not form part of EU law. The pattern of argumentation by the Court of Justice in relation to Articles 28 and 49 EC (34 and 56 TFEU), especially when it involves vital and socially sensitive areas of member state law, may be said to have constitutional qualities. Free movement and the internal market are seen as overriding principles of European and member state law. All other legal measures, including collective labour law, are scrutinized in relation to these principles also when they are of a quite different legal quality. The Court of Justice clearly intervenes in other areas of member state legal regimes and thus demonstrates the constitutional qualities of EU law in relation to member states.

32 See Case C-341/05, *Laval un Partneri Ltd*, ECR 2007, I-11767, para. 110.

33 Case C-438/05, *Viking Line ABP and OÜ Viking Line Eesti*, ECR 2007, I-10779, and Case C-346/06, *Rüffert*, ECR 2008, I-1989.

Security, Police and Justice Dimensions: Evolving Constitutionalism?

The two last pillars of the EC – foreign and security policy and police and justice cooperation – have not been supranational thus far, but with the Lisbon Treaty they will be included in the scope of qualified majority voting. In both areas, cooperation has significantly increased along with common legislation and decision-making. The Schengen Agreement has been included in the EU treaties, and police and justice cooperation connected to Schengen has expanded. A European Pact on immigration and asylum has been passed, and various directives exist under Schengen information systems and common asylum and immigration policies.[34] Police cooperation has expanded. Suffice it here to mention just the examples of the European arrest warrant and the principle of availability concerning exchange of information between member state police.[35] After '9/11' a UN resolution obliged UN members to secure necessary measures.[36] The EU followed suit and legislation on surveillance, anti-terrorism, and various measures has been prioritized. A Council Framework Decision on combating terrorism was first passed on 13 June 2002.[37] A variety of specific measures have been passed. Most importantly, a data protection directive was passed in 2002 and later in 2006, as part of the fight against terrorism, a data retention directive obliging member states to store data traffic for a minimum of six months and up to two years.[38] The 'freedom, security and justice' area has thus expanded enormously as a result partly of huge immigration challenges, partly the war against organized crime and partly the war against terrorism. This is still an area which in its actual operations are in many ways predominantly national, though a very significant increase has occurred in common policies, pacts, guidelines, directives, registers and factual cooperation (exchange of information), for example. Significant interaction occurs between different institutional levels and different authorities. Vital initiatives come from the Commission and are followed up by decisions and legislation. Security and police work traditionally form part of the core of national sovereignty. With the Schengen Agreement and its various directives, Schengen information systems, enhanced police cooperation, common initiatives in the fight against organized

34 See Council document of 24 September 2008 (13440/08): European Pact on Immigration and Asylum.

35 Council Framework Decision 13 June 2002 on the European arrest warrant and the surrender procedures between Member States (2002/584/JHA).

36 Security Council Resolutions 1368 and 1373, of 12 September 2001 and 28 September 2001; and 1735, of 22 December 2006.

37 Council Framework Decision 2002/475/JHA on combating terrorism, and the Commission proposal for a new Framework Decision (COM(2007) 650 final).

38 Directive 2002/58/EC concerning the processing of personal data and the protection of privacy in the electronic communications sector, and Directive 2006/24/EC on the retention of data generated or processed in connection with the provision of publicly available electronic communications services or of public communications networks and amending Directive 2002/58/EC.

crime, corruption, drugs, terrorism and so on, 'freedom, security and justice' is becoming an area where it is difficult to distinguish between domestic and EU policies, initiatives and legislation, and also the running of control systems. Irrespective of whether this area is formally inter- or supranational, it is clear that constitutionally speaking it is in fact characterized by close interaction, comprehensive EU policies and policy papers – thus, in fact, engendering close interdependence between member states and EU institutions.

Security policy is in many ways balanced by emphasis on protection of fundamental human rights, as is also the case with the Court of Justice. Even if the EU has not included explicit human rights catalogues in the Treaty, until Lisbon for a limited period the Charter of Human Rights has been in existence and, preceding it, the Court of Justice has in several decisions included fundamental human rights as parts of the general principles of law which the Court observes.[39] In *Omega Spielhallen*, the Court ensured that in drawing upon the 'inspiration from the constitutional traditions common to the member states', and from the guidelines of international treaties, fundamental rights 'form an integral part of the general principles of law'.[40] A further expression of this appears in the judgment of the Court in the *Kadi and Al Barakaat* case.[41] This concerned the freezing of funds presumed to be related to terrorist activities and to Osama bin Laden and his groups. The Al Barakaat Foundation and Al-Quadi Yasin (Kadi) were put on lists by the UN on suspicion of such relations, which lists were also accepted by the EU. The Court of Justice found that the provisions involved, EC Regulation 467/2001, with Commission Regulations EC 2062/2001 and 2199/2001, and EC Regulations 881/2002 and 561/2003, did infringe upon certain fundamental rights of the persons concerned, and no authority existed in this case to derogate from 'principles of liberty, democracy and respect for human rights'.[42] The Court made it explicit that even though the measures were based on UN decisions, this could not be binding on the Court in reviewing the legitimacy of an EU Act. Community law is seen as 'an autonomous legal system which is not to be prejudiced by an international agreement'.[43] The Court found that the persons concerned had not been afforded the rights to be informed of the evidence, to be heard, or to an effective legal remedy. The Court found that it was fully entitled to review the case even if the EU regulations involved were based on a resolution by the UN Security Council adopted under the Charter of the UN.

39 Lately Case C-112/00, *Schmidberger*, ECR 2003, I-5659, para. 74.

40 Case C-36/02, *Omega Spielhallen*, ECR 2004, I-9609, para. 33.

41 Joined cases C-402/05 P and C-415/05 P, *Kadi and Al Barakaat*, ECR 2008, I-6351.

42 Joined cases C-402/05 P and C-415/05 P, *Kadi and Al Barakaat*, ECR 2008, paras 25–45, 303.

43 Joined cases C-402/05 P and C-415/05 P, *Kadi and Al Barakaat*, ECR 2008, para. 316.

The decision illustrates how the Court of Justice views the Treaty as an autonomous legal order, and that the Court also enjoys full review of all Community Acts in the light of fundamental rights which form an integral part of the general principles of EU law.

Changes in the Concept and Uses of Constitutionality

What has been seen as the constitutionality of the EU has emerged over time and in different ways than in nation-states. The constitutionality of (democratic) nation-states is often identified in explicit constitutional texts, but has also evolved over time. The E(E)C was first seen as a regional or international treaty and organization. In the first Treaty and its preamble, several elements signalled a more ambitious legality than the international as between states. The ambition was to create a common market which could effectively function economically. Institutions with legislative, executive and judicial competences were already included in the first Treaty and evolved with an increasingly dynamic and open style of interpretation and ambitious implementation. The success of the economic constitution of the EC/EU has probably been due to a combination of legislative, executive and judicial competences and institutions with a high level of ambition focusing on implementation, not only on policy. The supranational competences pertaining to the four freedoms were partly included the Treaty, partly extended by legislation, and partly further developed by the case law of the Court of Justice. No other international organization had previously enjoyed the same combination of political, legal and economic dynamics and institutions. The success and relative stabilization of free movement of goods and implementation of Article 28 EC (34 TFEU) concerning goods formed the core of, and laid the foundation for, a functioning internal market. Over time, free movement of persons, services and capital could follow. As indicated above, a regulated and functioning internal market cannot over time function as an isolated and clearly delimited regulated sector within advanced welfare states that offer high levels of social and other forms of protection. In defining what may be seen as discriminatory measures or restrictions to trade, one must also take into account the other side of the distinction of effective markets or competition, namely the various forms of social, environmental, health and other forms of protection or regulation. In defining an effectively functioning market, 'competition' or 'social market economy', other competing regulatory goals are also defined.

What was first seen as negative integration, limited to economic integration, developed into positive integration by way of drawing the boundaries between the market and various other forms of social and other legislation. The high level of ambition for an effective market, combined with supranational competences, contributed to the economic constitution of the EU. Over time, assessment of various measures which could be seen as discrimination or as restrictions to trade in terms of their justifiability, harmonizing directives and other regulations and directives have also contributed to elements of a social constitution in the EU. More active implementation of free movement of services and persons has also proved to be a much more complex task due to relevant regulatory schemes transcending any easy distinction between trade and other policies. The enlargement process, with the economic and social inequalities implied, enhanced these tendencies further. With free movement of persons and services in an internal market, the many-dimensional and complex character of these forms of regulation was imminently demonstrated. The relationships between various regulatory areas of the market, the environment, social rights, labour law, tax law and corporate law, and so on, were obviously impossible to draw consistently.

Increasing immigration from the less-developed regions of the world and acute measures against international terrorism have led to security, police and justice cooperation being extended relatively rapidly over the last ten years. Hence, aspects of a security and immigration constitution are also evolving.

In the context of the EU, the concept of constitutionality has been used due to the EU's supranational competences, their comprehensive character, their (relatively) effective implementation, and emphasis on the EU as an autonomous legal order. However, the EU and its competences may also be seen as contributors to the total, functioning and also fragmented constitutions of the member states. Nation-states and supra- and international organizations increasingly exist in a state of interaction and interdependence where each is both legally bound to the other and also in other ways more indirectly, but effectively, influenced by the other and in arrangements of cooperation. The EU is a prime example of an international organization existing in close legal, political and economic interdependence with member states – and also on the constitutional level. These are not merely formal arrangements, but responses to factual and increasingly intensive and comprehensive interactions and interdependencies. In focusing on the interdependence between states and inter- and supranational organizations, a different concept and principle of constitutionalism emerges.

References

Ashenden, S. and Thornhill, C. 2010. *Legality and Legitimacy: Normative and Sociological Approaches*. Baden-Baden: Nomos.

Brunkhorst, H. 2010. Cosmopolitanism and democratic freedom, in *Legitimacy and Legality: Normative and Sociological Approaches*, edited by S. Ashenden and C. Thornhill. Baden-Baden: Nomos, 168–92.

Habermas, J. 2001. The postnational constellation and the future of democracy, in *The Postnational Constellation*. Cambridge: Polity, 58–112.

Habermas, J. 2008. The constitutionalization of international law and the legitimation problems of a constitution for world society. *Constellations*, 15:4, 444–55.

Joerges, C. 1999. Good governance through comitology, in *EC Committees: Social Regulation, Law and Politics*, edited by C. Joerges and E. Vos. Oxford: Hart, 311–38.

Joerges, C. 2002. Deliberative supranationalism – Two defences. *European Law Journal*, 8, 133–51.

Joerges, C. 2005. Free trade: The erosion of national and the birth of transnational governance. *European Review*, 13, 93–117.

Joerges, C. 2006. Constitutionalism in postnational constellations: Contrasting social regulation in the EU and the WTO, in *Constitutionalism, Multi-Level Trade, Governance and Social Regulation*, edited by C. Joerges and E.-U. Petersmann. Oxford: Hart, 492–527.

Kelsen, H. 1925. *Allgemeine Staatslehre*. Berlin: Springer.

Minkkinen, P. 2009. *Sovereignty, Knowledge, Law*. Abingdon: Routledge.

Poiares Maduro, M. 2003. Europe and the constitution: What if this is as good as it gets? in *European Constitutionalism beyond the State*, edited by J.H.H. Weiler and M. Wind. Cambridge: Cambridge University Press, 74–102.

Sand, I.-J. 1998. Understanding the new forms of governance. *European Law Journal*, 3:4, 271–93.

Sand, I.-J. 2004. Contextuality as an alternative to constitutionalism, in *Transnational Governance and Constitutionalism*, edited by C. Joerges, I.-J. Sand and G. Teubner. Oxford: Hart, 48–52.

Sand, I.-J. 2008. (Re-)constructing the boundaries of the market, in *Paradoxes of European Legal Integration*, edited by H. Petersen, A.L. Kjær, H. Krunke, and M. Rask Madsen. Aldershot: Ashgate, 89–110.

Teubner, G. 2004. Social constitutionalism: Alternative to a state-centered constitutional theory, in *Transnational Governance and Constitutionalism*, edited by C. Joerges, I.-J. Sand and G. Teubner. Oxford: Hart, 9–18.

Walker, N. 2002. The idea of constitutional pluralism. *Modern Law Review*, 65:3, 317–59.

Weiler, J.H.H. 1999a. The transformation of Europe, in *The Constitution of Europe*. Cambridge: Cambridge University Press, 16–101.

Weiler, J.H.H. 1999b. Epilogue: Comitology as revolution, in *The Constitution of Europe*. Cambridge: Cambridge University Press, 344–9.

Weiler, J.H.H. 1999c. The constitution of the common market place: Text and context in the evolution of the free movement of goods, in *The Evolution of EC Law*, edited by P. Craig and G. de Búrca. Oxford: Oxford University Press, 349–76.

Willke, H. 1986. The tragedy of the state. *Archiv für Recht- und Sozialphilosophie*, 22, 455–67.

Willke, H. 1992. *Die Ironie des Staates*. Frankfurt: Suhrkamp.

Chapter 4

Constitutional Ideal Types in the Global Age: A Sociological Review

Sabine Frerichs

Introduction: 'Law as Culture' and the Sociology of Law

Within jurisprudence, sociologists are commonly considered as outsiders: as outsiders of the normative world of the law. Moreover, sociological knowledge *about* the law is often conceived as a challenge to laymen's or lawyers' belief *in* the law. However, the sociology of law does not necessarily involve ignorance, nihilism, or even cynicism about the values that are intrinsic to and/or cultivated within the legal system – that is, about law's inherent culture. Sociological enlightenment is thus not always destructive or 'deconstructive' of existing normative orders but can also serve constructive and 'reconstructive' purposes.[1]

The notion of 'law as culture'[2] already hints at the contributions of the 'cultural sciences' (as they are defined by Max Weber) to understanding and explaining the development of legal systems: both from the outside and from the inside. This view is based on the specificity of the cultural sciences *vis-à-vis* the natural sciences, namely their social reflexivity and performativity. In this regard, social scientists are products as well as producers of the societies they analyse: modern societies that build, not least, on scientific rationalities. Consequently, they have to include themselves (and science, more generally) in their field of study. Furthermore, they can make sense of the social world only to the extent they are actually taking the perspectives (and, thus, sharing the presumptions) of their 'contemporaries'.[3]

While the problem of 'objectivity in social science' is typically referred to in terms of the freedom from value judgements (according to which empirical statements of the 'Is' are to be separated from normative questions of the 'Ought'), Max Weber also points to the inevitable value-relatedness of any scientific engagement with culture.[4] 'The concept of culture is an evaluative concept [value-

1 See Habermas 1996.

2 See Gephart 2006. For a new research programme under the name, see <www.recht-als-kultur.de> or <www.law-as-culture.com>.

3 See Schütz 1967.

4 See Weber 2004 (original from 1904).

concept]. Empirical reality is for us "cultural" in the sense, and to the extent that, it is related to evaluative ideas [value ideas]; it comprises those elements of reality rendered meaningful by this relationship, no more.'[5] As a cultural science, the sociology of law thus has to start from the 'meaningfulness' or 'cultural significance' of the law – which is, of course, meaningful and significant only to those who are insiders of the normative order it embodies (that is, those who have internalized the basic norms and values of the legal system).

In this sense, objectivity also involves certain '"subjective" presuppositions':[6] it builds on what is considered worthwhile and meaningful by the members of a cultural community. The sociology of law, therefore, includes – and does not exclude – (inter-)subjective value orientations to the (legal) culture studied and shared by social and legal scientists alike. In other words, since the normative orders of modern societies are notably shaped by the law (and rationalized through legal science), the sociology of law also has to take seriously the perspectives of its inhabitants: the 'legal subjects' – be it legal persons, in general, or legal professionals, in particular.

Under these premises, a 'cultural' sociology of law can fulfil constructive as well as critical functions with regard to legal science and legal theory. It can combine the perspectives of insiders and outsiders, participants and observers of 'legal belief systems' and argue from facts to norms (outside-in) as well as from norms to facts (inside-out).

From a sociological point of view, legal culture is part and parcel of the general culture of society. Moreover, as a 'rationalized' culture, law is not only typical of modern society, but modern society can itself largely be considered a legal construction. In fact, many classical as well as contemporary social theorists start from legal categories.[7] At the same time, there is not only one but there are many cultures of law.[8] Legal modernity is thus balanced with long-standing (regional and national) traditions.

In this chapter, an example will be given of a sociology of law that focuses on the cultural significance of legal and constitutional discourse. More specifically, different 'ideal types' of constitutions that can be extracted from the 'empirical reality' of legal and social practices will be explored.

In the methodology of the cultural sciences, ideal types embody 'our ability and need for conceptually ordering empirical reality in such a manner as to lay claim to validity as experiential truth'.[9] This means two things: on the one hand, ideal types are nothing but 'thought constructs' – conceptual artefacts in the mind of scholars. On the other hand, they help to identify and distil 'cultural ideas' that are effective – albeit not necessarily fully realized – in practice. In other words,

5 Weber 2004: 377 (original emphasis omitted).

6 See Weber 2004: 382.

7 See Gephart 1993.

8 See Wilhelmsson, Paunio and Pohjolainen 2007.

9 Weber 2004: 365.

they are 'realistic' inasmuch as they represent the ideas of a certain culture 'on the grounds that the features so characterized are taken from significant parts of our lived culture and rendered into a unified ideal image'.[10]

Law's Social Embeddedness and 'the Many Constitutions'

The leitmotif of this volume is 'the many constitutions of Europe'. Hence, editors and contributors start not from a unitary concept of *the* constitution but from a pluralistic notion of the *many* constitutions. Following Weber, it is possible therefore to 'presuppose' different cultural ideas about constitutions and constitutionalism, which can be assembled and analysed not only from a legal but also from a sociological point of view. However, the focus of this book is not only on constitutions but on European constitutions, or the different constitutions of Europe. The 'presupposition' is here that constitutional pluralism matters most – or is culturally most significant – in so-called 'postnational constellations':[11] constellations that also threaten the constitutional unity of the nation-state.

According to Kaarlo Tuori's keynote to this volume, European 'integration through law' has thus generated at least five different types of constitution (that are here reinterpreted as ideal types): the economic constitution; the juridical constitution; the political constitution; the social constitution; and the security constitution. Whereas the juridical constitution is defined in terms of autonomy of the legal system, the economic, political, social and security constitutions are thought to represent law's relatedness to other social systems.

Drawing on sociological (and socio-legal) systems theory, 'constitution' can thus be understood as a relational concept. In this perspective, formal autonomy and material relatedness of the law (or, in Luhmann's terms, its 'operational closure', on the one hand, and 'cognitive openness', on the other[12]) do not necessarily contradict each other. Rather, it is possible to conceive of the relative autonomy of the law as a basic condition of its functioning in society. This means that law is dependent and independent, at the same time; it is 'characterized by an independence [which is] achieved in and through dependence'.[13]

As regards the juridical constitution, it has been emphasized that the European legal order is distinct both from national and international legal orders. Furthermore, the juridical constitution stands for 'the reflexive relation of the law with itself', that is, for the self-referential aspects of the legal system, or the (secondary) level of 'constitutive' rules and principles. Whereas European law is generally considered as less coherent and complete than the more mature legal systems of the nation-

10 Weber 2004: 388 (original emphasis omitted).

11 Habermas 2001.

12 See Luhmann 1993.

13 Bourdieu 1987.

states, there is also good reason to assume that some functional properties of the law are more recognizable on the trans- or supranational level.

In fact, the rather rigid 'structural coupling' of legal and political systems at national level can easily be considered an anomaly (or anachronism) in a 'functionally differentiated world society'.[14] In this respect, it makes sense also to explore other forms of constitution that emerge from law's interaction with functional systems that are less concerned with national borders. This seems much easier in the case of less integrated, more fragmented trans- and supranational legal orders as they are exemplified by European law, which can still be considered 'work in progress'.

Accordingly, the focus of the present volume is on the economic, political, social, and security constitutions that have successively formed at the European level. Following Tuori, these 'partial' constitutions document law's relations to the economic system, the political system, the social life-world, and the security system. Since all these spheres have themselves become subject to processes of Europeanization and globalization, 'the many constitutions of Europe' also reflect the possibilities and limits, merits and biases of 'integration through law beyond the state'.[15]

In the following, debates on law's autonomy and the formal, juridical constitution of Europe will be left aside and the focus will be on the material constitutions that result from law's relatedness with other social spheres, that is, law's embeddedness in society at large. This also raises the question of what society is being talked about. In order to avoid the 'epistemological obstacles'[16] of social theories that presume a national society and a national culture ('methodological nationalism'[17]), notions of a European society and a world society as well as the respective ideas of a European culture and a world culture will, therefore, be included.[18]

Four Constitutional Ideal Types: A Sociological Synopsis

The ideal types of economic, political, social and security constitutions that are introduced in Tuori's chapter and further discussed in the other contributions to this volume will now be addressed, in turn. Again, the perspective is not a legal but a sociological one. Hence, the four constitutional ideals will be related to alternative conceptions of the social order (namely, *oikos*, *polis*, *nomos* and *physis*) that are relevant both in legal and in social science. These general ideas of the social, which can also be taken as different ideologies or worldviews, will then be specified with

14 Luhmann 1997.

15 Frerichs 2008.

16 Bourdieu et al. 1991.

17 Beck 1997.

18 See Münch 2008; and Meyer 2009.

respect to the model of society, the model of man and the model of law which are implied or, at least, preferred by the respective legal and social theories.

In the perspective of a cultural sociology of law, the four constitutional ideals are thus considered both empirically relevant and culturally significant. Nevertheless, the following synopsis can also be supported by theoretical reflections about the 'essential functions' which all (social) systems have, in principle, to fulfil. This is the idea behind the work of Talcott Parsons, an American sociologist whose 'general theory'[19] also inspired the works of Niklas Luhmann and Jürgen Habermas. In the centre of Parsons' systems theoretical approach is an analytical scheme – the so-called AGIL paradigm[20] – that assembles the functions of 'adaptation' (A), 'goal attainment' (G), 'integration' (I) and 'latent pattern maintenance' (L).

For the present purpose, these ominous four letters will be translated into a quadruple of E's: namely, evolution, enforcement, embeddedness and enlightenment.[21]

The concept of evolution is based on Parsons' adaptation function. The problem here is how a system can open up for change and readapt to a dynamic environment. An appropriate solution is a decentralized, quasi-evolutionary search process which allows the system to constantly renew itself through the variation and innovation of its elements.

In contrast, the concept of enforcement, which is derived from Parsons' notion of goal attainment, stands for the government functions in a system: a system does not only have to decide its specific goals but also the means to attain them. These decisions are typically taken and implemented in a more or less hierarchical manner.

Embeddedness, in turn, is a concept that builds on what Parsons calls the integration function. The question here is how to provide for order and stability and, thus, security of expectations. In order to preserve its identity, a system has to reproduce its structures and also protect its borders. In other words, it has to close itself to a certain extent.

Finally, the concept of enlightenment is inspired by the notion of latent pattern maintenance in Parsons' approach: actions and events only make sense against a background of options (and non-options); they derive their meaning from a larger frame of reference. This cultural repertoire can be explored by way of generalizing from concrete phenomena to abstract principles.

Altogether, the AGIL paradigm helps not only to distinguish analytically between the different functions social systems have to fulfil but also between the different preoccupations of the constitutional conceptions discussed in this volume. In anticipation of the following, it is possible to thus claim that (1) the economic constitution is preoccupied with the adaptation function and the

---

19 For his original ambition, see Parsons et al. 1976. For a reassessment, see Münch 1987.

20 First elaborated in Parsons and Smelser 1984 and *passim* in the rest of his work.

21 See also Frerichs and Münch 2010 (forthcoming).

principle of evolution; (2) the political constitution with the latency function and the idea of enlightenment; (3) the social constitution is primarily concerned with the integration function and the concept of embeddedness; and (4) the security constitution with the goal attainment function and the notion of enforcement.

Basic notions of order

The ideal type of *economic constitution* is connected with a liberal ideal of the social order; its constitutive principle is thus economic liberalism. In economic conceptions of the constitution, 'individual will' plays a pivotal role. This means, on the one hand, that individuals are preferred to collectives – both as an empirical entity and a normative category (methodological individualism). On the other hand, the focus is on individual interests and preferences, which are taken as given and seen as the major driving force of human development. As a shortcut for this ideal type of order, the term *oikos* will be used, which includes, in this sense, all types of economic organization, from ancient households to modern companies, from national economies to the integrated world economy. In today's neoliberal perspective, the entrepreneurial aspect of the economic order is particularly emphasized. Everybody is called on to think in categories of capital and investment, not only business leaders but also workers and consumers, governments and civil associations. The very idea is that all this entrepreneurial activity brings about a maximum of efficiency and innovation for the system as a whole, which grants the best possible evolutionary success.

The ideal type of *political constitution* has at its core a rational concept of order; its ideological basis is rationalism. Accordingly, political conceptions of the constitution centre around the idea of 'individual reason', or, more precisely, communicative reason as an inter-subjective capacity. Again, the ideal of order is thus based on the individual and some form of agency; the main argument is therefore bottom-up. However, in this case, social order is not simply the aggregate of wilful individual action but the result of meaningful interaction. In other words, reasoning – especially moral reasoning – is not a self-centred activity but always related to the other (who can, of course, be 'internalized' and hence be represented in individual minds). Drawing on the history of political ideas and the paradigm case of the ancient Greek city-state, this ideal of order will be referred to as *polis*. Other than the (neutral) notions of polity, politics and policy used in political science, this term indicates a social practice based, more or less, on communicative rationality. Nevertheless, the connotations of the concept, as it is used here, are modern ones. That is, political constitutions nowadays build on the Age of Enlightenment, its immediate achievements and its long-term implications in terms of the universalization of human rights.

The ideal type of *social constitution* evokes notions of a customary order; the worldview behind it is some form of conservatism. An emphasis on the social dimension of constitutions presupposes a clear conception of the collective. In other words, it implies an understanding of the moral bonds that make up society and of the collective identity that arises from living and acting together. The cultural scripts and traditions that emerge from social interaction can also be referred to as a form of 'collective reason'. Integration, on these grounds, therefore involves the minds and memories of the individuals as members of a collective. Since the ideal of a social constitution is thus premised on the ideas and values, norms and customs that are shared by a particular community, the term *nomos* will be used as a shortcut. Originally, this notion refers to man-made order in contrast to natural order – and notably includes the human law. However, the source of order is no abstract morality but the concrete mores and manners of a community. This notion will be transferred into the modern context since it comes closest to an organic understanding of solidarity that is based on ongoing interaction and functional interdependencies. At the same time, it recalls more traditional notions of social embeddedness.

The ideal type of *security constitution* follows the model of a coercive order which is adapted to the realities of politics (*Realpolitik*); it is thus supported by political realism. According to this ideology, the driving force of social – namely international – relations is the vital interests and coercive power of nation-states. Again, the starting point is a collective entity; but this time the focus is not on the inner cohesion of a (national) community but on the external force applied by the (nation-)state. Moreover, security questions are typically dealt with in a hierarchical or exclusive manner by an authority which can be more or less representative of the population encompassed. At the centre of this constitutional conception is thus the will of the respective sovereign which is hypostatized as the 'collective will'. The realist vision of order draws on the state of nature depicted as a 'war of all against all' and leads to the idea of a powerful Leviathan as a peacemaker – not by consensus but by the threat of force. This is, again, very different from the state of culture that is presumed in a moral community. For that reason, the idea of a natural order (here seen from a realist point of view) will be adhered to and *physis* will be used as a symbol. This notion also seems suitable because of its affinity to questions of physical security and biopolitics.

Models of man and society

So far, the basic notions of order (*oikos*, *polis*, *nomos*, *physis*)[22] that are at the core of the four ideal types of constitution (economic, political, social and security constitutions) that emerge at the interface of legal and social systems have thus been identified. In the following, these constitutional ideals will be further elaborated on in terms of their respective conceptions of society (or the collective), of man (or the individual) and of the law (between reason and will). Again, the previous heuristics proves viable.

The ideal type of *economic constitution* was characterized by the primacy of individual will. The social model that corresponds best with this idea is the market

22 See also Frerichs and Münch 2010 (forthcoming).

society: a form of social organization within which self-regulating markets play a dominant role. At first sight, the market society is nothing but a thought experiment: an artefact of economic thinking. However, through economic government – and its legal backdrop: the economic constitution – the vision of a society governed by the invisible hand of markets also gains practical relevance.[23] According to Karl Polanyi, one of the main critics of the market society on the part of economic sociology, this 'means no less than the running of society as an adjunct to the market. Instead of economy being embedded in social relations, social relations are embedded in the economic system'.[24] Consequently, the economic system – a functional system based on the principles of the market economy – is the main point of reference of legal and social theories that are based, more or less explicitly, on an economic concept of order. Its monetary logic easily transgresses national boundaries; hence, it seems only natural also to think and act in terms of a global(ized) market society. The idea of man required and furthered by economic approaches to the constitution is, for obvious reasons, *homo oeconomicus*. This model assumes an individual actor strategically using his/her resources in order to maximize his/her benefits. Social action is thus specified as end-rational action that takes into account the presence of others but does not necessarily rely on meaningful interchange. Economic man is, in this sense, a monadic actor, or a solitary *homo faber*.

For the ideal type of *political constitution*, a primacy of individual reason was asserted. The preferred social model is civil society, that is, a form of social organization that builds on voluntary associations. A society that follows the principle of associationalism, or associative democracy, is clearly a normative project.[25] Yet this is also true for the 'liberal dream' of the market society (which critical voices rather consider as a 'commodified nightmare').[26] Both market society and democracy are thus powerful cultural ideas that have inspired not only liberal philosophies but also policies and practices: economic liberalism, on the one hand, and political liberalism, on the other. However, the ideal types of economic and political constitution clearly differ with respect to the social sphere they rely on and the sort of actor they address. For that purpose, it is possible to build on the distinction between *bourgeois* and *citoyen*.[27] Whereas the former follows his/her private (economic) interests, the latter is committed to public (political) interests. A similar distinction can be drawn between *homo oeconomicus*, the model favoured by economic constitutionalism, and *homo politicus*, the model preferred by political constitutionalism.[28] Hence, political action is more about other-oriented, communicative action than self-centred, strategic action. Nevertheless,

23 See Frerichs 2010 (forthcoming).

24 Polanyi 1957: 57.

25 See Hirst and Bader 2001.

26 See Fourcade and Healy 2007.

27 As introduced by Karl Marx in 1844 (see Marx 1994).

28 See Faber et al. 1997.

the reference system of political constitutionalism is not the political system in the form of a state bureaucracy but the cultural system in the form of a political culture. As part of a rationalized life-world, a democratic political culture is not bound to particularistic national traditions but strives for discursive forms of universalism[29] – and thus a global(ized) civil society.

For the ideal type of *social constitution*, a primacy of collective reason was claimed. The related social model is the legal community: a form of social organization that is based on normative commitments and legal solidarity.[30] Following the classical distinction between community and society, the former is typically equated with pre-modern forms of the social whereas the latter is understood as a distinctive, modern phenomenon.[31] Accordingly, traditional (that is, more concrete) notions of solidarity are connected with the idea of closely integrated, normative communities while modern (that is, more abstract) forms of solidarity are rather seen as characteristic of highly individualized, rationalized and differentiated societies.[32] However, it is also possible to talk of a 'societal community' and thus bring the two notions together.[33] The societal community can be understood as a translation of the community concept into a modern context (namely a nation-state context). For the present purpose, it can be interpreted as a (national) legal community which combines notions of traditional, customary law (community law) and rationalized, positive law (state law). Accordingly, modern society rests on integration through law; its integrative core is the legal community. Hence, social constitutionalism is biased towards the community system, or, in other terms, the social norms and networks of the life-world. The preferred model of man is *homo sociologicus* – an actor which has largely internalized the norms and values of his/her social surroundings and generally complies with them.[34] With his/her conformist style of behaviour, he/she is the embodiment of the social animal (*animal sociale*). Nevertheless, normative behaviour can combine elements of affective, traditional, and value-rational action and thus be more or less reflective.[35]

Finally, the ideal type of *security constitution* was derived from the primacy of collective will. The relevant social model is the control society,[36] that is, a form of social organization which is dominated by the state and its various – blunt or subtle – methods of monitoring and manipulating the behaviour of groups and individuals. At first sight, the top-down logic of this notion of society seems to be at odds with the bottom-up logic of market society as discussed above: whereas

29 See Habermas 1996.
30 See Frerichs 2008.
31 See Tönnies 1957.
32 See Durkheim 1984 (original from 1893).
33 See Parsons 2006.
34 See Dahrendorf 1964.
35 See Weber 1968 (original from 1922).
36 See Deleuze 1992.

the former is based on the executive powers of the state (typically the nation-state), the latter builds on individual freedoms and self-regulating markets. However, collective will and individual will can also be reconciled in the – somewhat paradoxical – concept of (economic) government through self-government. This '(neo-)liberal governmentality' is, according to Michel Foucault, characteristic of the modern 'state of government ... which essentially bears on the population and calls upon and employs political economy as an instrument'. This form of state 'correspond[s] to a society controlled by apparatuses of security'.[37] Accordingly, the reference system of security-based conceptions of the constitution is the government system. By means of physical as well as symbolic violence, it affects the realities which the population – and each individual – have to live with and adapt to.[38] The connected model of man is *homo gubernabilis*, that is, someone who has to be controlled and governed in order to increase collective wealth and security, and, at the same time, 'someone who is eminently governable'.[39] From a political economic point of view, this is the working animal (*animal laborans*); from the perspective of homeland security, it is the migrant animal (*animal migrans*). In both cases, alienation poses a threat that has to be controlled – whether by integration or exclusion.

Table 4.1 The four constitutional ideal types at a glance

	Economic constitution	Political constitution	Social constitution	Security constitution
Main argument	Evolution	Enlightenment	Embeddedness	Enforcement
Notion of order	*Oikos*	*Polis*	*Nomos*	*Physis*
Basic unit	Individual	Individual	Collective	Collective
Basic motive	Will	Reason	Reason	Will
Model of society	Market society	Civil society	Legal community	Control society
Reference system	Economic system	Cultural system	Community system	Government system
Model of man	*Homo oeconomicus*	*Homo politicus*	*Homo sociologicus*	*Homo gubernabilis*

37 Foucault 2007: 108.
38 See Bourdieu 1987; and 1994.
39 Foucault 2008: 270.

Concepts of law (I): Between instrument of will and expression of reason

Having thus specified the notions of society and the views of man that are connected with the different constitutional ideals, attention will now turn, more explicitly, to the concepts of law inherent in these perspectives. This final step will be largely built on the analysis above – the more so as it already deals with questions of social *and* legal order, if only on a very general level. Before proceeding, the previous steps will thus be briefly summarized: the starting point was a relational understanding of constitutions as normative settings that emerge at the interface of law *and* society, that is, at the intersections between the legal system and other social spheres. The four ideal types of material constitutions, as they are given in this volume (namely, the economic, the political, the social and the security constitutions) were then elaborated on.

First, the general functions, or functional preoccupations, of the different approaches (adaptation, latent pattern maintenance, integration, goal attainment) were outlined and their main patterns of argument (evolution, enlightenment, embeddedness, enforcement) were derived therefrom. Second, the concepts of social order that are characteristic of the respective constitutions (*oikos*, *polis*, *nomos*, *physis*) were explored and whether their particular focus is rather on individual or collective actors, on extrinsic or intrinsic motivations (individual will, individual reason, collective reason, collective will) was discussed. Finally, for each constitutional ideal type, the – more or less 'hidden' – models of society (market society, civil society, legal community, control society) were specified, and also their preferred reference systems (economic system, cultural system, community system, government system) was marked. On the micro level, the analysis was completed by highlighting the models of man (*homo oeconomicus*, *homo politicus*, *homo sociologicus*, *homo gubernabilis*)[40] which are integral to the different constitutions (Table 4.1).

This was all deliberately done in a sociological perspective, which, nevertheless, cannot be reduced to an outsider's point of view. As initially stated, the sociology of law is – not least – a cultural science that takes legal values seriously, that is, the 'value-concepts', or cultural ideas, that are at the bottom of the law. Hence, legal theory and legal sociology find themselves on common ground inasmuch as they understand 'law as culture'. In this respect, they share a 'value-related' insider perspective which obviously favours constitutional conceptions that are based on (individual or collective) notions of 'reason', that is, the symbolic dimension of the law, its inner logic and coherence. This is much different in realist or critical approaches that do not start from legal ideas as legitimate cultural expressions but as 'ideologies' that only conceal the material interests of certain political and economic elites. These are classical outsider perspectives that emphasize the instrumental functions of the law and its powerful effects within social relations.

---

40 Alternatively, *homo faber*, *zoon politikon*, *animal sociale*, *animal laborans*; see Arendt 1958.

Accordingly, they resonate with constitutional conceptions that are based on (individual or collective) notions of 'will'.[41]

The ambiguity of the law as an instrument of will and a manifestation of reason is thus also reflected in constitutional discourse: as ideal types, economic and security constitutions stand for an exercise of (individual or collective) will, whereas political and social constitutions represent the realm of (individual or collective) reason. These 'elective affinities' were already hinted at by referring to control society as a natural, or even necessary, counterpart of market society. According to that, individual freedoms and collective security do not contradict each other but can rather be considered as mutually dependent. Private autonomy then appears as a condition of public sovereignty, and vice versa. While this concerns the 'will' pole of the constitutional field, the same applies to its opposite pole of 'reason': in modern democracies, the ideal types of civil society and legal community are no real alternatives; instead they are interdependent forms of social organization. Whereas the former furthers rational discourse and thus provides for a basic openness of the polity, the latter builds on the taken-for-grantedness of the life-world[42] and hence implies a certain degree of social closure. In the end, a universal(ist) culture of critique is thus balanced with a particular(ist) culture of conformity.

However, these pairings are not fixed. In order to shed light on the legal models inherent in the different constitutional conceptions, it is also possible to group them together according to their emphasis on either the micro or the macro level, that is, on individuals or collectives. In this setting, the security constitution is on the same level as the social constitution. Both start from collective entities and thus mainly follow a top-down perspective. At the same time, the economic constitution is on a level with the political constitution. Their common point of departure is what individuals do; social order is mostly explained in a bottom-up manner. That may be interesting in itself; but what is required here is, more specifically, to relate this scheme to questions of Europeanization and globalization. The impression is thus that constitutions that focus on collectives are typically also biased towards national collectives, be it the nation-state that exercises a territorial monopoly of force (security constitution) or the national community that is depicted as a self-contained context of solidarity (social constitution). In contrast, constitutions that emphasize the role of individuals seem to be more flexible with regard to collectives of a national or otherwise localized origin. While competitive markets (economic constitution) and civil networks (political constitution) do need an institutional framework in order to flourish, this does not have to be a national one.

41 On the dichotomy between law's reason (*ratio*) and will (*voluntas*), see Tuori 2007.

42 See Schütz 1967.

Concepts of law (II): Between national collectives and globalized individuals

This issue has already been touched on when the question was initially raised of what society was being talked about in the field of law and society – a national, European, or even world society. Later, the globalization potential of both the market society and the civil society was hinted at, in contrast to the legal community and the control society, which seem to be more bound to a nation-state context.

A closer look at the relations between individualization and globalization yields the following scale: the legal model of the *economic constitution* is the most individualized, and at the same time, the most globalized. It furthers the autonomy and mobility of economic actors all over the world. While the neoliberal – especially the ordo-liberal – ideal of an economic constitution does presume a strong and vigilant state, this is not an interventionist one.[43] The main principle of order is thus bottom-up: rules of just behaviour, or economic fairness, emerge from repeated interaction between economic actors within the market society, which includes cross-national contacts and exchange. In other words, they are the efficient result of a quasi-evolutionary search for a balance between creative destruction[44] and the stability of expectations, which nowadays takes place in a (more or less) globalized context.

The legal model of the *political constitution* is not as individualized as the economic one although the emphasis is still on individual agency (namely in so-called agonistic theories).[45] But actors are considered less self-centred than other-oriented; they engage in rational discourse, thereby striving for a universal morality. Accordingly, norms are in need of justification and enlightenment; they have to be rationally acceptable to all those concerned. What appears possible in theory is, however, not so easy to achieve in practice. The realization of a global civil society thus seems to lag behind the – normatively less demanding – project of a transnational market society. Many theorists of democracy, therefore, stick to the primacy of the national political culture, which is considered the best place to start with the democratic experiment. Supranational organizations are, instead, criticized for their enduring 'democratic deficit' (which is, in a strict bottom-up perspective, not a matter of time but a matter of principle).

The legal model of the *social constitution* is, again, a less individualized and globalized one. In a way, it even seems to be the least 'individualizable' and 'globalizable' of the four constitutional ideal types discussed in this chapter. This appears immediately plausible as long as the social dimension of constitutionalism is defined through customary norms and legal solidarity in a national collective. However, a distinction has already been made above between more traditional and modern types of solidarity. Modern solidarity follows the patterns of social exchange and interdependencies that result from the division of labour; that is,

43 See Hayek 1973; 1976; and 1979.

44 See Schumpeter 1976.

45 See Arendt 1958.

it extends – but also weakens – in more differentiated and dynamic forms of social organization.[46] In contemporary societies, it thus develops towards what has been termed 'network solidarity'; normative commitments are then no longer confined to national collectives but can also take transnational forms.[47] Against this background, it is also possible to conceive of a European or even a global legal community.

Finally, the legal model of the *security constitution* is, obviously, based on collective needs as perceived by the sovereign or the state. Regulation is more centralized and also more formalized than in the previous model and, therefore, exemplary of a classic top-down perspective. Individual rights seem to play only a secondary role. In this perspective, even the 'right to security' (which is emphasized today) is derived from the security needs of a sovereign. On the one hand, there is thus little individualization – although the control society can very well have individualizing effects ('divide and rule'). On the other hand, there are also clear impediments to the globalization – or rather, a further centralization – of enforcement powers, global security threats notwithstanding. Patterns of international hegemony and cooperation are exemplified by 'our common fight' against (transnational forms of) terrorism. Generally speaking, an emphasis on enforcement implies that there is less a transformation of norms into facts than of facts into norms. The juridification of will power (as part of the 'colonization of the life world') is thus prior to its justification through moral reasoning.[48]

In this section, the assumption has been built on that individualization and globalization go well together, whereas a preoccupation with the national community or the nation-state inhibits both. In classical sociology, this idea has been anticipated by Georg Simmel who claimed that the enlargement and intersection of 'social circles' (meaning social groups or collectives) furthers individualization – and vice versa, one could add.[49] Admittedly, modern nations are already rather abstract entities, and as regards the citizens of a nation, individuality is probably more pronounced than ever before. However, with respect to national societies, Europe would still be a new step on this scale, and with respect to the European society, the world as a whole (or rather, their symbolic representations). In order to make sense of 'the many constitutions of Europe' from a sociological – or socio-legal – point of view, it therefore seems advisable to understand Europe as a mediator between 'the national age' and 'the global age'.[50] The observable fragmentation of European constitutionalism is then nothing but a side effect of an ongoing process of modernization (differentiation, individualization, rationalization) that

46 See Durkheim 1984.
47 See Münch and Frerichs 2008.
48 See Habermas 1984; 1987; and 1996.
49 See Simmel 1983 (original from 1908).
50 See Albrow 1996; and Meyer 2009.

also undermines national borders and thereby exploits the globalization potential of the different legal models.[51]

Conclusion: A Cobweb Model of 'the Many Constitutions'

With the notions of individual and collective, will and reason, a two-dimensional account of constitutional ideal types has already been built on. Yet, this can still be done more systematically and also be linked more closely to sociological categories of differentiation and integration.

In a very general sense, all sociology starts from the problem of social order; hence, all sociological theories also have an idea of what makes society hold together (integration) or drift apart (disintegration).[52] Based on a terminology introduced by David Lockwood, it is possible to distinguish between theories of 'systems integration' and theories of 'social integration'. Whereas the former focus on the interplay of different social spheres or subsystems, the latter concentrate on relations and interchange among actors. The emphasis can thus either be on the inner cohesion of collectives, understood as systems, or on the social inclusion of individuals, conceived as actors.[53] System and actor perspectives are not necessarily congruent, since the rationality of systems does not have to build on, or be reducible to, the rationality of actors – the more so as both are idealized scientific constructs that only bring out selected characteristics of an 'undivided' empirical reality.

A similar distinction can be drawn between 'functional differentiation' and 'social differentiation'. Again, the former mainly refers to social systems and their rationalized and specialized principles of organization, while the latter concerns the effects that rationalization and specialization have on individual actors and the roles they play in society. If society is thus something else from a bird's eye and a worm's eye perspective, its constitution is also seen differently from a planner's and a citizen's point of view, that is, from the one who organizes a collective and the one who lives in it. A constitutionalism that deals with questions of functional differentiation and systems integration is, therefore, also different from a constitutionalism that engages with problems of social differentiation and social integration.

---

51 See Münch 2008.

52 For these notions, see Imbusch and Heitmeyer 2008; Heitmeyer 1997a; and 1997b.

53 See Lockwood 1964.

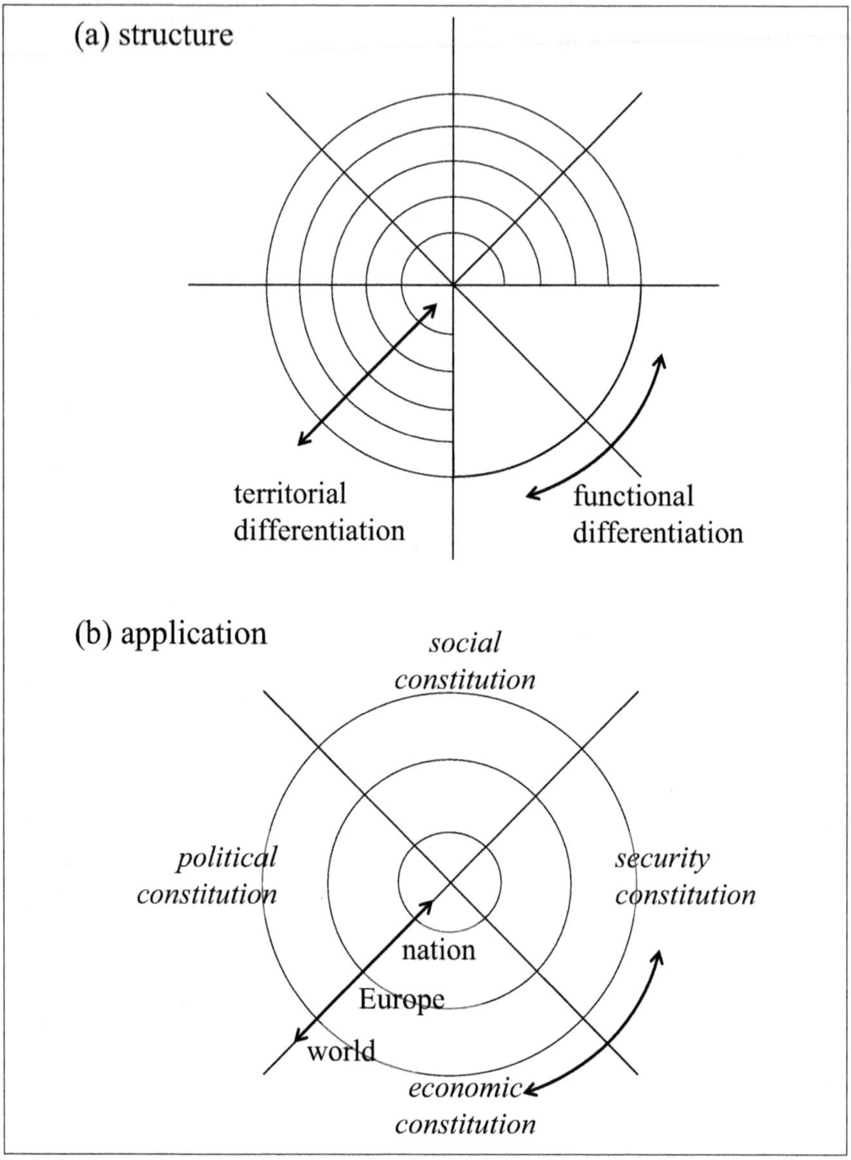

Figure 4.1 The constitutional cobweb

It was stated above that this book is based on a pluralistic notion of constitutionalism: There is not one unitary constitution but there are many interacting ones. However, in order to be able to identify the different constitutions, one already needs to know – or, at least, have a certain pre-understanding of – the principle(s) of constitutional differentiation. Contemporary debates on trans- and supranational forms of constitutionalism seem to cluster around at least two distinct principles: on the one hand, there is an influential discourse with a strong background in normative legal theory that situates constitutional pluralism mostly in the relations between (different) national and supranational constitutional entities.[54] Here, the predominant principle of differentiation is still a territorial one. From a citizen's perspective, territorial collectives act as 'imagined communities' – abstract entities that nonetheless evoke a sense of belonging.[55] In the minds of individuals they are represented as a place or a people one can identify with, thus creating a we-identity.

On the other hand, more sociologically inclined theorists (contributors to this volume included) increasingly take recourse to the principle of functional differentiation in order to make sense of 'the many constitutions' that mix and intermingle in a post-national setting.[56] In this case, the relevant collectives are even more abstract and artificial than the above 'fictions' of nations and regions. Functional systems are not confined to a place or a people; instead, they are only confined to a specific function, medium or code. In this respect, they can then be considered global and all-inclusive. A functional collective hence works more or less behind the backs of individuals. Individuals are included in many different functional systems, but they are not defined by them and, accordingly, cannot identify with them, at least not in an encompassing sense. Each functional system only requires and furthers a specific role. In this context, the perspective of citizens as members of meaningful cultural or constitutional communities seems to fail.

The plea is here to better integrate these two discourses – or to be, at least, more aware of their respective potentials, pre-analytic visions, and blind spots. Analytically speaking, one should thus move towards a cobweb model of constitutionalism: the cobweb is made up by circular threads and radial threads. Seen from its centre, that is, the spider's, lawyer's, or citizen's point of view, there are thus concentric circles, representing territorial collectives of various extension, and centripetal (or rather centrifugal) segments, indicating the different functional systems. The intersections of circles and radii in the cobweb illustrate the compartmentalization of constitutionalism alongside the principles of territorial and functional differentiation and the integration problems that result therefrom. It also visualizes how fragmentation (in the form of the functional segments) might play a bigger role than cohesion (in the form of the territorial circles) the more one walks from the inside of the web to the outside: from a society 'centred' in the nation-state to a 'decentred' world society.

The question is then how the different compartments of the constitutional cobweb combine and interact. In the simplified version, there is merely a web of three – either additive or alternative – territorial affiliations (nation, Europe,

54 See Walker 2002; Avbelj and Komarek 2010 (forthcoming).

55 See Anderson 1991.

56 See Joerges et al. 2004; Fischer-Lescano et al. 2009.

world) intersecting with four functionally differentiated systems (economic system, cultural system, community system, government system). This two-dimensional grid was analysed in terms of individual and collective, on the one hand, and reason and will, on the other hand. In doing so, principles of territorial and functional differentiation have already been referred to, albeit not explicitly. The dichotomy of individual and collective thus anticipated issues of 'nationality' (and globality) in constitutional discourse while the dichotomy of reason and will touched on the 'rationality' of different constitutional fragments, that is, their prevailing social functions. Both are relevant to understanding ongoing developments in constitutional theory and practice. Moreover, they are 'culturally significant' for legal and social theorists alike.

References

Albrow, M. 1996. *The Global Age: State and Society Beyond Modernity*. Cambridge: Polity Press.

Anderson, B. 1991. *Imagined Communities: Reflections on the Origin and Spread of Nationalism*. London: Verso.

Arendt, H. 1958. *The Human Condition*. Chicago: University of Chicago Press.

Avbelj, M. and Komarek, J. 2010 (forthcoming). *Constitutional Pluralism in the European Union and Beyond*. Oxford: Oxford University Press.

Beck, U. 1997. *Was ist Globalisierung? Irrtümer des Globalismus – Antworten auf Globalisierung*. Frankfurt am Main: Suhrkamp.

Bourdieu, P. 1987. The force of law: Toward a sociology of the juridical field. *Hastings Law Journal*, 38:5, 814–53.

Bourdieu, P. 1994. Rethinking the state: Genesis and structure of the bureaucratic field. *Sociological Theory*, 12:1, 1–18.

Bourdieu, P., Chamboredon, J.-C. and Passeron, J.-C. 1991. *The Craft of Sociology: Sociological Preliminaries*. Berlin: Walter de Gruyter.

Dahrendorf, R. 1964. *Homo sociologicus: Ein Versuch zur Geschichte, Bedeutung und Kritik der Kategorie der sozialen Rolle*. Cologne: Westdeutscher Verlag.

Deleuze, G. 1992. Postscript on the societies of control. *October*, 59, 3–7.

Durkheim, É. 1984. *The Division of Labour in Society*. Basingstoke: Macmillan.

Faber, M., Manstetten, R. and Petersen, T. 1997. Homo oeconomicus and homo politicus: Political economy, constitutional interest and ecological interest. *Kyklos*, 50:4, 457–83.

Fischer-Lescano, A., Rödl, F. and Schmid, U. 2009. *Europäische Gesellschaftsverfassung: Zur Konstitutionalisierung sozialer Demokratie in Europa*. Baden-Baden: Nomos.

Foucault, M. 2007. *Security, Territory, Population: Lectures at the Collège de France 1977–1978*. Basingstoke: Palgrave Macmillan.

Foucault, M. 2008. *The Birth of Biopolitics: Lectures at the Collège de France, 1978–1979*. Basingstoke: Palgrave Macmillan.

Fourcade, M. and Healy, K. 2007. Moral views of market society. *Annual Review of Sociology*, 33:1, 285–311.

Frerichs, S. 2008. *Judicial Governance in der europäischen Rechtsgemeinschaft: Integration durch Recht jenseits des Staates*. Baden-Baden: Nomos.

Frerichs, S. 2010 (forthcoming). Re-embedding neo-liberal constitutionalism: A Polanyian case for the economic sociology of law, in *Karl Polanyi, Globalisation and the Potential of Law in Transnational Markets*, edited by C. Joerges and J. Falke. Oxford: Hart Publishing.

Frerichs, S. and Münch, R. 2010 (forthcoming). Morality, modernity, and world society, in *Handbook of the Sociology of Morality*, edited by S. Hitlin and S. Vaisey. New York: Springer.

Gephart, W. 1993. *Gesellschaftstheorie und Recht: Das Recht im soziologischen Diskurs der Moderne*. Frankfurt am Main: Suhrkamp.

Gephart, W. 2006. *Recht als Kultur: Zur kultursoziologischen Analyse des Rechts*. Frankfurt am Main: Vittorio Klostermann.

Habermas, J. 1984. *The Theory of Communicative Action, Volume 1: Reason and the Rationalization of Society*. Boston, MA: Beacon Press.

Habermas, J. 1987. *The Theory of Communicative Action. Volume 2: Lifeworld and System: A Critique of Functionalist Reason*. Boston, MA: Beacon Press.

Habermas, J. 1996. *Between Facts and Norms*. Cambridge, MA: MIT Press.

Habermas, J. 2001. *The Postnational Constellation: Political Essays*. Cambridge, MA: MIT Press.

Hayek, F.A. von. 1973. *Law, Legislation and Liberty, Volume 1: Rules and Order*. London: Routledge and Kegan Paul.

Hayek, F.A. von. 1976. *Law, Legislation and Liberty, Volume 2: The Mirage of Social Justice*. London: Routledge and Kegan Paul.

Hayek, F.A. von. 1979. *Law, Legislation and Liberty, Volume 3: The Political Order of a Free People*. London: Routledge and Kegan Paul.

Heitmeyer, W. 1997a. *Die Bundesrepublik Deutschland auf dem Weg von der Konsens- zur Konfliktgesellschaft. Bd. 1: Was treibt die Gesellschaft auseinander?* Frankfurt am Main: Suhrkamp.

Heitmeyer, W. 1997b. *Die Bundesrepublik Deutschland auf dem Weg von der Konsens- zur Konfliktgesellschaft. Bd. 2: Was hält die Gesellschaft zusammen?* Frankfurt am Main: Suhrkamp.

Hirst, P. and Bader, V.-M. 2001. *Associative Democracy: The Real Third Way.* London: Frank Cass Publishers.

Imbusch, P. and Heitmeyer, W. 2008. *Integration – Desintegration: Ein Reader zur Ordnungsproblematik moderner Gesellschaften*. Wiesbaden: Verlag für Sozialwissenschaften.

Joerges, C., Sand, I.-J. and Teubner, G. 2004. *Transnational Governance and Constitutionalism.* Oxford: Hart Publishing.

Lockwood, D. 1964. Social integration and systems integration, in *Explorations in Social Change*, edited by G.K. Zollschan, W. Hirsch and D. Martindale. Boston, MA: Houghton Mifflin, 244–57.

Luhmann, N. 1993. *Das Recht der Gesellschaft*. Frankfurt am Main: Suhrkamp.
Luhmann, N. 1997. *Die Gesellschaft der Gesellschaft*, Vol. 2. Frankfurt am Main: Suhrkamp.
Marx, K. 1994. On the Jewish question, in *Selected Writings*, edited by L.H. Simon. Indianapolis: Hackett Publishing, 1–26.
Meyer, J.W. 2009. The European Union and the globalization of culture, in *World Society: The Writings of John W. Meyer*, edited by G. Krücken and G.S. Drori. Oxford: Oxford University Press, 344–54.
Münch, R. 1987. *Theory of Action: Towards a New Synthesis Going Beyond Parsons*. New York: Routledge.
Münch, R. 2008. *Die Konstruktion der europäischen Gesellschaft: Zur Dialektik von transnationaler Integration und nationaler Desintegration*. Frankfurt am Main: Campus.
Münch, R. and Frerichs, S. 2008. Markt und Moral: Transnationale Arbeitsteilung und Netzwerksolidarität, in *Handbuch der Wirtschaftssoziologie*, edited by A. Maurer. Wiesbaden: Verlag für Sozialwissenschaften, 394–410.
Parsons, T. 2006. *American Society: A Theory of Societal Community*. Boulder, CO: Paradigm.
Parsons, T. and Smelser, N.J. 1984. *Economy and Society: A Study in the Integration of Economic and Social Theory*. London: Routledge.
Parsons, T., Shils, E.A., Allport, G.W., Kluckhohn, C., Murray, H.A., Sears, R.R., Sheldon, R.C., Stouffer, S.A. and Tolman E.C. 1976. *Toward a General Theory of Action*. Cambridge, MA: Harvard University Press.
Polanyi, K. 1957. *The Great Transformation*. Boston, MA: Beacon Press.
Schumpeter, J.A. 1976. *Capitalism, Socialism and Democracy*. London: Allen & Unwin.
Schütz, A. 1967. *The Phenomenology of the Social World*. Evanston: Northwestern University Press.
Simmel, G. 1983. *Soziologie: Untersuchungen über die Formen der Vergesellschaftung*. Berlin: Duncker & Humblot.
Tönnies, F. 1957. *Community and Society*. East Lansing: Michigan State University Press.
Tuori, K. 2007. *Oikeuden ratio ja voluntas*. Helsinki: WSOY.
Walker, N. 2002. The idea of constitutional pluralism. *Modern Law Review*, 65:3, 317–59.
Weber, M. 1968. *Economy and Society: An Outline of Interpretive Sociology*. New York: Bedminster Press.
Weber, M. 2004. The 'objectivity' of knowledge in social science and social policy, in *Essential Weber: A Reader*, edited by S. Whimster. London: Routledge, 359–404.
Wilhelmsson, T., Paunio, E. and Pohjolainen A. 2007. *Private Law and the Many Cultures of Europe*. The Hague: Kluwer Law International.

PART II
Aspects of the Economic Constitution

Chapter 5
European Competition Law: Catalyst of Integration and Convergence

Milène Wegmann

Integration and Interdependence in Neo- and Ordo-Liberal Thinking

In neo- and ordo-liberal thinking the terms 'integration' and 'interdependence' are characterized by a domestic policy dimension as well as a foreign policy dimension. European integration as conceptualized by neo- and ordo-liberal economists and jurists forms an integral part of a worldwide international order, worldwide integration. Like integration of the national economy, international integration would also be based on a community of market, price and payment.

Since the end of 1949 or early 1950, the term 'integration' has narrowed in the general language of economics and politics and taken on the meaning of 'regionally freer trade with free movement of production factors, workforce and capital'.[1] Neo- and ordo-liberals continued to orient themselves to the original more extensive content of the term integration: integration aimed at worldwide interconnection. 'The integrated system of world economy [is] an interdependent, unified and intercommunicating system of international trade relations.'[2] According to Röpke's definition, integration meant 'interdependence and interconnection between all regions' of a nation, or, respectively, of the world, in the case of international integration.[3] The holistic concept of integration by neo- and ordo-liberals makes itself plain not only in its universal dimension, but also in the internal coherence of social, economic and political interrelation. Neoliberal economics and jurisprudence regard freedom as whole and indivisible. All order based on the principle of liberty has to take into account freedom of individuals in all fields of life equally: political freedom, religious freedom and economic as well as intellectual freedom. Neo- and ordo-liberals deny economic matters to be autonomous.[4] Economic integration in its regional area and intensity presupposes

1 Wegmann 2002b: 354–58.

2 Röpke 1942: 14–16, 59; and 1979: 218.

3 Röpke 1950: 2.

4 See Röpke 1942: 69–71. As stated by Röpke (1961: 665): 'There is no autonomy of the economic sphere' ('Es gibt keine Autonomie des Wirtschaftlichen'). See also Röpke 1957a: 167.

a corresponding meta-economic, social integration.[5] Competition is not capable of giving rise to social integration according to the view of neo- and ordo-liberals and is no principle to build up society as such.[6] In order to preserve society in general and competition in particular from collapsing, sufficient integration outside the competitive market is required.[7] 'Social' integration as a basic condition of economic integration stands for a steadfast law-based order[8] and a code of norms, principles, rules of conduct and moral concepts.[9]

Social and political integration is a precondition for economic integration according to the neoliberal theory of integration.[10] By emphasizing the social and political basis of economic integration, neo- and ordo-liberals were thinking contrary to Walter Hallstein's approach that considered economic integration to be a pacemaker of social and political integration.

From the point of view of neo- and ordo-liberals, European integration is a matter of order-based policies (called '*Ordnungspolitik*' in neo- and ordo-liberal terminology).[11] Only measures being aimed at international freedom and order as well as at the establishment of a meta-economic framework will have a positive effect on integration. 'Order-based policies' in the original conception formulated by Eucken stand for the part of economic policy that is long-term oriented. The core idea of classic liberalism became inverted in the neo- and ordo-liberal conception of order-based policies. Whereas classic liberalism had separated economics from law and politics, neo- and ordo-liberalism regarded a basic decision for the political and legal system as a prerequisite for the economic system. For neo- and ordo-liberal thinkers, the economy needs the state to be protected from private interests that would undermine or abolish competition. Neo- and ordo-liberals trust in the force of law to carry through the power of the state.[12] Any 'diversity of systems'[13] is excluded in the neo- and ordo-liberal ideal of integration on which a European Community would be based. Neoliberals aim at more than an economic system, since the overall context of law, ethics, economics, society and policy is to the fore. Economic policy and social policy are interdependent aspects of an indivisible whole.

5 Röpke used the concept of '*soziale Integration*' in German for 'meta-economic integration', see Röpke 1951: 271. See also Röpke 1979: 106; 1955: 211; and 1957b: 497–8; Hahn 1953: 10; Erhard 1988: 747; Villey 1958: 21–2, 35; Einaudi 1956: 77–81.

6 See Willgerodt 2001; 1989 and Röpke 1942: 6, 21 and 71.

7 See Röpke 1942: 6, 21 and 71.

8 '*Rechtsordnung*' in the specific sense of the neoliberal system

9 See Röpke 1979: 105–6.

10 See Wegmann 2002a: 11–35.

11 See Wegmann 2009: 220–31.

12 See Gerber 1998: 249–250.

13 See Rusk 1965: 75.

The Ordo-Liberal Economic Order

'*Ordo*' is the name given to the economic system of a free market economy within a legal framework of institutional rules. The system was drafted by the ordo-liberals as the ideal form of such an economy, which would prevent concentration of economic power and secure the proper functioning of competition. '*Ordo*' does not refer to an arbitrary, historically occurring order, but to an ideal sort of order: the 'order which corresponds to the essence of mankind and an object, in which proportion and balance persist'.[14] The ordo-liberals do not believe that *ordo/ordre naturel* will materialize on its own, but are instead convinced that to establish '*ordo*' an active policy is needed, one which is supported by coercive measures in accordance with the rule of law in order to enforce and to preserve the economic constitution. The neo- and ordo-liberals go far beyond a purely economic liberalism in that they position their concepts of an economic constitution within the context of all departments of life. Ordo-liberalism also goes far beyond the scope of economic sciences into that of jurisprudence.[15]

Competitive Order as the Axis of Economic Order

Neoliberalism, according to Milton Friedman,[16] replaces the goal of *laissez faire* with the goal of competitive order. In contrast to numerous adherents of the classic liberal school, neoliberals assume that the competitive free-market economy is not sociologically autonomous and that it presupposes a particular state, a particular society, a particular morality, as well as extra-economic forces and ideas. The neoliberal concept distinguishes itself by emphasizing the *interdependence* of order-based policies. It points out the necessity of building up the competitive order in all fields of legislation – from trade policy, to credit policy, tax policy and corporate law up to and including bankruptcy law – in jurisdiction as well as in administration.[17] The entire economic constitution should be shaped by competition as the fundamental principle, on a national as well as on an international level. The neoliberal concept of European economic and social order was aimed at restoring competition in its various dimensions.

The *convertibility of European currencies* and the *liberalization of international trade* were both achieved after multiple transition phases in the framework of the Organisation for European Economic Co-operation or European Payment Union by the end of 1958. The *basic orientation towards a free-market economy* had

14 Eucken 1940: 239: 'Ordnung, die dem Wesen des Menschen und der Sache entspricht, d.h. Ordnung, in der Mass und Gleichgewicht bestehen.'

15 See Wegmann 2002b: 204–14 and 2003: 87.

16 Friedman, 1950–51: 5.

17 See Eucken 1952: 304–8, *cf.* Eucken 1942: 43–4. See also Willgerodt 1991; Willgerodt and Peacock 1989; and Schüller 2002.

been established in Article 2 EEC under the decisive influence of the neoliberal Alfred Müller-Armack, and external pressure from the US government, with some limited concessions to French demands with respect to social and industrial policy. However, the framing, filling out, and continuing development of the Treaty was not followed by a unified, economic–political concept. The Treaty establishing the EEC offered a framework for different economic systems with more or less distinctly free-market oriented principles.

Liberal foreign trade policy stipulated that European integration should form an integral part of a worldwide international order. The EEC initiative to grant the members of GATT a reciprocal linear reduction of 20 per cent in the common external tariff set the course for a liberal foreign trade policy by the EEC in the industrial goods sector. The GATT law was interpreted as an integral component of the foreign trade law of the EEC, which conforms to the neoliberal understanding of European integration as an integral component of a worldwide international order. With the introduction of a common external tariff there was no acceptance of the traditional protectionism of Italy and France by the low-tariff states. On the contrary, the liberal concept was able to assert itself in the foreign trade policy of the EEC under the economic and political conditions of the *Pax Americana*.

As to *macro-economic stabilization policy*, coordination of national economic stabilization policy, aimed at stabilizing employment and the value of currency, could not be achieved in spite of multiple initiatives from Müller-Armack, then acting as Chairman of the EEC Committee on Stabilization Policy. The member states insisted on their own authority to act on economic policy, particularly since the majority of them did not want to abandon Keynesian full employment and demand management in favour of a stabilization policy shaped by neoliberal principles like stable value of currency, balanced budget, or a restrained anti-cyclical economic stabilization policy.[18]

Restoration of a 'freer' economy with worldwide exchange of goods had to be supplemented with a competitive order if the intended liberalization of trade was not to be vitiated by private law restrictions. Competition was in fact the axis of the neo- and ordo-liberal concept of a new free-market economy. Essential freedom of prices and competition on the one hand and private property on the other were the two essential elements of the concept of a free-market economy, which were to form part of an entire civil order. The waging of 'Total War' had widely sharpened awareness of the monopoly problem in the consciousness of European liberalism. Thus, the group of ordo-liberals came to play an important role in the international debate concerning monopolies and cartels, especially since Miksch,[19] Böhm[20] and Eucken[21] had, in the *interbellum* period, already recognized the rise of private monopolies and cartels as *the* danger for the constitutional order and had pushed

18 See Wegmann 2009.

19 See Miksch 1937.

20 See Böhm 1928: 324–6; 1933a; 1933b; and 1937.

21 See Eucken 1932; 1947; and 1940.

for the establishment of an effective competition law system, which would strive to attain 'complete competition'[22] as its ideal.[23]

The overwhelming majority of neoliberals regarded complete competition in broad areas of the economy as a norm which would *not automatically* materialize on its own but which had to be striven for through the following order-based policies: the goal of competition policy is to secure individual freedom of action; a strong law-based state that stands above economic interest groups is a prerequisite for a functional system of competition; competition policy is to be aligned with the principles of the rule of law; and the competitive order has to be embedded in the economic order of a free and open society.

The competition law system has to be the framework for the other parts of the legal system, such as corporate law and labour law. According to Eucken, the 'whole context, that is, the so-called "interdependence" of all economic facts' must be taken into consideration in all decisions concerning economic policy.[24] Improvements in the legal framework must also include corporate law; stock companies must have no voting rights in other companies, even if they hold shares in them.[25] Additionally, neoliberals call for the reduction of patent protection.[26]

Paradigm Shift: Competitive Economic System Instead of International Cartels Promotes Peace, Social Welfare and Integration

Since the 1920s and 1930s, German ordo-liberals and Austrian neoliberals had developed the foundations of competition law. These original core ideas spread from Germany and Austria and already formed part of the common European

---

22 Concerning the limits of the realizsability of 'free competition' ('*freien Konkurrenz*') *cf.* Röpke even in 1937: 132–3. Later on, Röpke (1994: 210–14 and 217) suggested the concept of an 'active' or 'effective' competition ('*aktiver*' *oder 'wirksamer' Wettbewerb*) instead of the 'pure' or 'perfect competition' that was to be considered as unattainable and rather being a model. Eucken (1940: 131) described the 'complete competition' ('*vollständige Konkurrenz*') as well as the 'monopoly' as ideal types ('*Idealtypen*'), where the reality was in between. Both cases were 'unreal'. Röpke (1940) emphasized that to make competition outside the sector of self-sufficiency 'the tone setting principle, but not the only one' is what matters. According to Eucken (1952: 244) 'the market form of complete competition' ('*die Marktform vollständiger Konkurrenz*') is predominant in the system based on competition ('*Wettbewerbsordnung*'), but it is not that this is the only existing 'market form'. Referring to Eucken, Röpke (1953: 1 and 6) underlined that the 'absolutely predominant market form' (die '*absolut vorherrschende Marktform*') in the new market economy had to be that of free competition, and he conceded that a more or less long way with 'conduction loss' ('*Leitungsverluste*') stood between the ideal and its realization.

23 See Wegmann 2008: 20–35.

24 Eucken 1947: 75.

25 See Hayek 1959: 216–17.

26 See Eucken 1946: 3–4.

concept of competition law in the 1920s, a concept which would be enacted into law in the decades following World War II.

In the *interbellum* period, social welfare as well as peacemaking functions were attributed to international cartels. In 1931, the Expert Committee of the European Commission of the League of Nations still asserted that international cartels could contribute to the 'realisation of the European economic unity' by creating an atmosphere of trust.[27] From 1931, the idea kept recurring that international cartels would act as catalysts for integration of the European economy. This was even the case in the debate of the Economic and Social Council of the UN about the Charter for an International Trade Organization, as well as in the discussions of the Council of Europe concerning the European Convention on Control of International Cartels.[28]

Only in the various efforts to find a solution to the cartel question at an international level – at the World Trade Conference in Havana, in the OEEC, in the Council of Europe, and in the Economic and Social Council of the United Nations – did a paradigm shift begin to take hold. The idea that international cartels would promote trust between nations[29] and pave the way for European economic unification made way for the insight into the character of a competitive economic system as a promoter of peace and social welfare, which would bar cartels in cross-national trade inside the common market that was to be created. The instrument for creating a binding competitive order for establishing peaceful economic relations was transferred from the international to the supra-national level with the goal of using the prohibition of cartels and of abusive exploitation of market-dominating positions as a means of fostering understanding and rapprochement between the six nations.[30]

Negotiations on a European Political Community

The German delegation pressed for laying down the rules governing competition and for protecting these institutional laws at the outset of the negotiations for a European Political Community. At this stage, the delegations were not in a position to reach agreement on particular rules governing competition or on general principles as documented in the report by the Commission for the European Political Community to the Foreign Ministers (Paris, 12 December 1953–8 March 1954).[31]

27 See Günther 1952: 244.

28 See Wegmann 2008: 78.

29 See Günther, 1952: 244. Herczec (1952) recommended 'functional integration' by private law means, i.e. through cartels, in order to integrate the European national economies as a unified market.

30 See Wegmann 2008: 76–7.

31 See Wegmann 2008: 74–6.

The First Supra-National Competition Law in the Treaty of the European Coal and Steel Community

In 1951, the Treaty of the European Coal and Steel Community (ECSC) established the first supra-national competition law in Europe. The ECSC Treaty contained the first comprehensive prohibition against discrimination in the legal community of continental Europe, as well as being the only multilateral agreement of any kind that had created a regulatory regime controlling cartels. On the six-member common market for coal and steel, agreements among enterprises which would tend to prevent, restrict or distort competition within the common market were prohibited. Any transaction (or merger) creating a dominant position was generally prohibited. Authority over enforcing these prohibitions and granting exemptions under certain preconditions was transferred to the supra-national High Authority under Articles 65–66 ECSC.[32] The text concerning prohibition of cartels and regulation of mergers is based directly on a formulation of Robert R. Bowie, an expert in antitrust law from Harvard and legal consultant to the Economic Division of the Allied High Commission. As a matter of fact, competition law was to serve to secure political freedom and protection of the democratic system in West Germany and Western Europe.[33]

The US government feared that the ECSC would lead to formation of a single cartel or to an accumulation of cartels with the High Authority acting as their directorate.[34] Prohibition of cartels and regulation of mergers were more stringently formulated in the ECSC Treaty than in US antitrust law, which, in contrast to the Treaty founding the ECSC, was not restricted to a *single* economic sector. But application of these Articles was less strict in the 1950s and 1960s than application of the corresponding US provisions. In particular, the ECSC prohibition of cartels played a subordinate role, and one could not even discuss unleashing the competitive potential of the Ruhr region of West Germany. Now, only the other five Western European nations could exert an influence on the Ruhr industry over the High Authority. Nevertheless, the coal and steel market remained highly concentrated and highly dominated by cartels. Thus, the High Authority's competition policy led to a system of oligopolies, which can be characterized by Galbraith's metaphor of 'Countervailing Power'.[35]

32 See Wegmann 2008: 64–5.
33 See Wegmann 2008: 62.
34 See Hentschel 1988: 103.
35 See Wegmann 2008: 51–73.

Competition Law: The Axis of the Economic Order in the Treaty of the European Economic Community

With the founding of the European Economic Community (EEC) in 1957, a process of integration began in which competition law played a key role. Competition law became a significant factor in decision-making in Europe. In the decades that followed, the founding states of the EEC and those states that wanted to join the Community aligned their national laws governing competition with EEC competition law. Unlike the national competition law systems, which focus primarily on the customer network (keeping prices low), technological innovation and economic efficiency, EEC competition law is mainly understood as part of the process of integration and unification of the European market.[36]

The laws governing competition in the six nations which participated in negotiations on the European Political Community, the Messina Conference, and negotiation of the legal instruments of the EEC were not uniform. Introduction of a unified national competition law in all six member states was abandoned from the start. As yet, Belgium, Luxembourg and Italy had no national legislation against cartels. The cartel laws and cartel law drafts in Germany, France and the Netherlands followed different principles. In the Netherlands, the principle of abuse prevailed for cartels, with the option of applying the prohibition principle in particular cases.[37] The French as well as the German regulatory regimes were based on the principle of prohibition. However, in France vertical agreements were much more strictly prosecuted than cartels while, in the Federal Republic of Germany, exactly the opposite was the case.[38] Export cartels were excluded from national regulations and, on the international level, a general consensus in favour of the moderate American position[39] had emerged, under which only the harmful effects of international cartels were to be combated. International approaches such as the draft by the Council of Europe of a European Convention for the Control of International Cartels (1951) worked to effect the realization of a competition law system for international intra-Community trade. Thus, on a European level,

36 See Gerber 1998: 334.

37 See the Commission's first general report of the activities of the EEC (1 January–17 September 1958), published as: Materialien zum EWG-Kartellrecht, *Wirtschaft und Wettbewerb*, 1959, no. 9, 51. See also Arts 8–10 of the (1951) Dutch proposal for, and Arts 19–21 of the statute (1956), on economic competition, published, respectively, as Niederländischer Gesetzesentwurf über den wirtschaftlichen Wettbewerb vom Februar 1951, *Wirtschaft und Wettbewerb*, 1952, no. 2: 544–8, and Niederländisches Gesetz über den wirtschaftlichen Wettbewerb vom 28. June 1956, *Wirtschaft und Wettbewerb*, 1961, no. 11: 30–38.

38 See Günther 1961: 760.

39 See Document E/2030, of 22 June 1951, UN-ECOSOC of the US-Government on Restrictive Business Practices, published as: Dokumente des UN-Wirtschafts- und Sozialrates zum Wettbewerbs- und Kartellproblem, *Wirtschaft und Wettbewerb*, 1951, no. 1, 75–7.

significantly further-reaching suggestions for a European competition law had already been formulated in the convention draft by the Council of Europe than the UN Commission on Cartels was able to present for a global competition law. In contrast to the UN Commission on Cartels, which only wanted to grant investigative, consulting, recommendatory and publishing authority to an international cartel authority, the proposal of the Council of Europe had provided for registration of all international restrictions of competition and intended to entrust a *European Court* with the task of assessing the harm done by infringements against cartel regulations and the authority to impose penalties. Government members as well as individual persons could file legal complaints.[40]

On 14 November 1956, French approval of the prohibition against abuse of market-dominating positions enabled the delegations to unite on the version of the anti-monopoly law that the German delegation had originally submitted.[41] In negotiations on the Articles concerning competition in the EEC Treaty, the German view, which had arisen under the guiding influence of neoliberal economists, had prevailed. Competition law as presented in the EEC Treaty acknowledged the differentiation between *market-dominating positions* ('principle of prohibiting abuse') and *agreements* ('principle of prohibition with an exception system'). The applicability of these laws was restricted to international, intra-Community trade. Article 86 EC (later 82 EC, now 102 TFEU) prohibits abuse of a dominant position within the common market. Article 85 EC (later 81 EC, now 101 TFEU) prohibits all *agreements and concerted practices that have as their object the restriction of competition within the common market*. The German delegation was also able to ensure that the prohibition against discrimination was removed from the chapter on competition and placed instead at the beginning of the Treaty, in Article 7 EEC (later 6 EC then 12 EC, now 18 TFEU), since it went beyond the scope of competition law in the narrow sense and concerned the foundations of the common market.[42] The delegations agreed on the German proposal to limit themselves to establishing general principles according to which any form of discrimination on the basis of national origin or citizenship is forbidden.[43] The broad interpretation of discrimination, which was preferred by the French delegation, would have run

40 See the memorandum of the Committee of Ministers' Seventh session in Strasbourg, 2 March 1951, on the proposal of the Consultative Assembly for the preparation of a European Convention for the International Cartels, reported in *Wirtschaft und Wettbewerb*, 1952, no 2: 296–302.

41 See Ophüls 1956.

42 See the minutes of 27–29 November 1956, Procès-verbal des réunions du groupe du marché commun de la conférence intergouvernementale pour le marché commun. Les règles de concurrence: Normes applicables aux entreprises (EC Historical Archives, Florence: CM 3/ Nego 236): 1.

43 See coded telex to the German Foreign Ministry of 27 November 1956, concerning the integration conference in Brussels (*Brüsseler Integrationskonferenz: Arbeitsgruppe Gemeinsamer Markt*. Typescript. Reproduction. Politisches Archiv des Auswärtigen Amts: Fiche A9054): 1.

the risk of excluding competition as a system-ordering principle of the common market, since every trade treaty would have to be declared illegal under a too-widely constructed prohibition against discrimination.[44]

With Articles 85 and 86 EEC, competition law entered new territory, since a law governing competition would be applicable to all trade between multiple independent states. In 1960, half of the six member states, namely Belgium, Italy and Luxembourg, still had no national competition laws. For that reason, no chance was available to assert the prohibitions in Articles 85 and 86 EEC with the assistance of national administrative authorities in the early years of the European Economic Community. Furthermore, the principles of equal treatment and mutuality delayed application of the Articles on competition in those three states that had already passed national laws governing competition. Inside the Commission and at the second cartel conference of Governmental Experts in Brussels, the German interpretation of the legal nature of Articles 85 and 86 EEC, shaped by neoliberal thought, prevailed over the French position. According to the German view, Articles 85 and 86 EEC contained legally binding regulations and not just, as the French representatives tried to assert, principles that would have to be developed before they could achieve any practical significance.[45] Both Articles were understood by the Commission as a unified instrument of competition policy. The Commission's view, that the EEC Treaty directly placed it and national authorities in the position of being able to proceed against cartels and misuse of market dominating positions, was eventually accepted by the European Parliament and all member states.[46]

Completely in accordance with the neo- and ordo-liberal concept of economic policy, the report by Groeben on 'Competition Policy in the European Economic Community' of 1961 stated:

> Undistorted, honest competition does not work out automatically on its own. Commonly, its external preconditions have to be established by the mentioned measures directed at an order-based policy and its continuing in existence has to be protected by binding rules. Therefore, the above discussed Articles of the Treaty and the measures of the EEC Commission based on them are neither dirigistic nor geared to a "planned economy". On the contrary they are oriented towards making competition work as an institution for coordinating market economy on a greater scale and keeping its ability to work. The whole

---

44 Wegmann 2008: 84–90.

45 See §84 of the Commission's first general report of the activities of the EEC (1 January–17 September 1958), of 17 September 1958: 65–6. See also Haenlein 1959: 20–21, *Stellungnahme der zweiten Kartellkonferenz der Regierungssachverständigen zur Rechtsnatur der Artikel 85ff des Romvertrages* by the European Commission's Directorate (A) for Competition, of 19 January 1959 (EC Historical Archives, Florence: CEAB 2. 1795/1–3): 1, and Groeben 1960: 2, 5 and 19.

46 Groeben 1960: 19.

ompetition policy of the Commission serves this double purpose. With this aim in view alone, the external conditions of competition are laid down by the Treaty and its implementation.[47]

Referring to the 'interdependence' of all measures concerning economic policy and the alignment of all parts of economic policy towards competition policy – as emphasized by neo- and ordo-Liberals – Groeben pronounced himself in favour of establishing higher competition neutrality in the fields of tax law, corporate law and patent law as well as of determined reduction of external tariffs. These aims geared to an order-based policy were taken up in the Commission memorandum on an action plan for the second stage of the EEC, in 1962, and formulated as a call for establishing higher neutrality of competition in the areas of corporate law, tax law and laws of commercial protection.[48]

The European Competition Law was accepted politically because it was primarily perceived as affecting jurisprudence and not politics. From the 1950s to the 1980s, the Commission concentrated on private restrictions of competition. For political reasons, the Commission avoided dealing with state interventions in the economy which distorted competition, such as state subsidies and public monopolies.

Responsibility of the Commission and the Court of Justice for the Competition Law: A Catalyst of the Process of Integration

A decisive contribution to the integrative effects of European Competition Law can be seen in that European lawmakers developed their own institutions and procedures and did not, as the US had done, build on pre-existing concepts and institutional forms such as ordinary courts.[49]

In 1962, Regulation No. 17[50] established the Commission's responsibility and authority to determine, at the request of participating enterprises and associations of enterprises, if there was a cause for it to intervene under Articles 85 or 86 EEC against an agreement, decision or concerted practices. Agreements, decisions and concerted practices for which the participating parties wished to request an exemption were now to be reported to the *Commission.* This established a

47 Groeben 1961: 12. *Cf.* also Deringer 1961.

48 See Mémorandum de la Commission sur le programme d'action de la Communauté pendant la deuxième étape (Commission memorandum on the Programme of action of the EEC towards the second stage of the period of transition), 24 October 1962, ch. 2.

49 See Gerber 1998: 422.

50 EEC Council Regulation No. 17: First Regulation implementing Articles 85 and 86 of the Treaty, OJ 13, 21 February 1962: 204–11 (English special edition: Series I, Ch. 1959–1962: 87).

Community Competition Law System, not just a coordinated one, and with it the 'first truly supra-national policy'[51] of the EEC.

Regulation No. 17 was of great importance to the process of European integration as it centred the implementation of competition law and the prerogative of policy-making on the Commission, marginalizing the role of national legal systems. National authorities had to transfer their competence to the Commission should it investigate a competition law case. The head of the Committee of the European Parliament that drafted Regulation No. 17 was German attorney Arvid Deringer. The Regulation elaborated by his committee represented the German ordo-liberal concept that attached central value to competition law.[52] Another significant element was Article 9(1) EEC delegating to the Commission sole competence to grant exemptions under Article 85(3) EEC. In addition, Regulation No. 17 guaranteed a high degree of autonomy in decision-making of the Competition Directorate (General Directorate IV).[53] The role of the Commission was enormously enlarged by Regulation No. 17.

The first significant legal cases concerning competition came before the Court of Justice in the 1960s, at exactly the time when the continued existence of the Community was under threat of being thrown into question by the 'empty chair crisis'. At this time, the Court of Justice was the only institution still in a position to preserve the momentum of integration. It further developed competition law as an important means of promoting the process of integration.[54]

With the end of the Cold War, insight into the significance of competition for Europe received additional impetus. Starting in the late 1980s and early 1990s, a transition from the principle of abuse to the principle of prohibition took place in national European competition law systems.[55] The basis for this was insight into the significance of competition in almost all Western and Central European states. Conforming national competition laws with the Competition Law of the European Community, ongoing since the late 1980s, can be spoken of as the 'convergence of national competition laws'.[56] However, this convergence is only indirectly attributable to the (E)EC and its institutions. In accordance with early neoliberal postulates, merger controls were also instituted at national level, and institutions entrusted with application of competition law were granted greater independence from the influences of politics and administrative bureaucracy.[57] Starting in the middle of the 1980s, the Commission began to add emphasis to the application of competition Articles to state subsidies and public monopolies, as contained in Article 90 EEC (then 86 EC, now 106 TFEU). The introduction of

51 Cini and McGowan 1998: 19.
52 See Wegmann 2008: 93–4.
53 See Gerber 1998: 349–52.
54 See Gerber 1998: 352.
55 See Gerber 1998: 402.
56 Gerber 1998: 401.
57 Concerning French, Italian and Swedish legislation, see Gerber 1998: 403–13.

the Merger Control Regulation in 1989, intended to protect competition and not to achieve the goals of structural policy, signified the fulfilment of an early neoliberal postulate. The failed Constitutional Treaty of 2004 was to do justice to the great importance of competition for the integration and 'regional internationalisation' of the Community and to integrate a common market with 'free and undistorted competition' into the EU's catalogue of goals, instead of just making undistorted competition an item on the list of 'Activities of the Community' as in Article 3 EEC (also 3 EC). However, during negotiations on the EU Reform Treaty, this elevation of competition from an instrument of the common market to a very goal of the Community failed, due to the resistance of French President Sarkozy.[58]

Conclusion

Since the founding of the European Economic Community in 1957, European competition law has shown itself to be a decisive catalyst of integration and convergence. The unquestionable success of the European economic order is based mainly on the fact that implementation and ongoing development of competition law were the responsibility of the Commission and the Court of Justice, which are relatively politically independent, and that these were primarily perceived as affecting jurisprudence and not politics.

References

Böhm, F. 1928. Das Problem der privaten Macht. *Die Justiz*, 3, 324–45. Reprint 1960: *Böhm, Franz: Reden und Schriften. = Festschrift für Franz Böhm zum 65. Geburtstag*, edited by E.-J. Mestmäcker. Karlsruhe: C.F. Müller, 25–45.

Böhm, F. 1933a. *Wettbewerb und Monopolkampf. Eine Untersuchung zur Frage des wirtschaftlichen Kampfrechts und zur Frage der rechtlichen Struktur der geltenden Wirtschaftsordnung*. Berlin: Carl Heymann Verlag.

Böhm, F. 1933b. *Kartelle und Koalitionsfreiheit*. Berlin: Carl Heymann Verlag.

Böhm, F. 1937. *Die Ordnung der Wirtschaft als geschichtliche Aufgabe und rechtsschöpferische Leistung*. Stuttgart, Berlin: Kohlhammer.

Cini, M. and McGowan, L. 1998. *Competition Policy in the European Union*. New York: Palgrave Macmillan.

Deringer, A. 1961. Europäisches Parlament: Ausschuss für Fragen des Binnenmarktes der Gemeinschaft: Vorentwurf eines Berichtes zu der Konsultation des Europäischen Parlamentes durch den Rat betreffend eine

58 See *Neue Zürcher Zeitung*, 2 July 2007: 'Brüssel' bricht eine Lanze für den Wettbewerb, 11, and *Neue Zürcher Zeitung*, 21–22 February 2009: Der EU-Binnenmarkt im Rezessionstest, 19. See Art. 3(1)b TFEU listing as exclusive competence of the Union: 'the establishing of the competition rules necessary for the functioning of the internal market'.

erste Durchführungsverordnung zu den Artikeln 85 und 86 des Vertrages. Januar 1961. EC Historical Archives, Florence: CEAB 02 – 2012/1. CCE Commission Archives.

Einaudi, L. 1956. Tipi e connotati della federazione discorrendo di comunità europea di difensa (2 June 1952), in *Luigi Einaudi: Lo scrittoio del presidente (1948–1955). Opere di Luigi Einaudi. Seconda serie. Vol. 1*, edited by G. Einaudi. Rome: Einaudi, 62–84.

Erhard, L. 1988. Lehren der Geschichte. Ansprache auf dem 11. CDU-Bundesparteitag in Dortmund, 4. June 1962, in *Ludwig Erhard: Gedanken aus fünf Jahrzehnten. Reden und Schriften*, edited by K. Hohmann. Düsseldorf, Wien: ECON Verlag, 743–60.

Eucken, W. 1932. Staatliche Strukturwandlungen und die Krisis des Kapitalismus. *Weltwirtschaftliches Archiv*, 36, July–August, 297–321.

Eucken, W. 1940. *Die Grundlagen der Nationalökonomie*. Jena: Gustav Fischer Verlag.

Eucken, W. 1942. Wettbewerb als Grundprinzip der Wirtschaftsverfassung, in *Der Wettbewerb als Mittel volkswirtschaftlicher Leistungssteigerung und Leistungsauslese. Schriften der Akademie für Deutsches Recht 6*, edited by G. Schmölders. Berlin: Günter.

Eucken, W. 1946. *Letter to Friedrich A. von Hayek*. Freiburg i. Br., 12 March 1946. Typescript. Friedrich A. von Hayek Archive. Hoover Institution Archives. Stanford University, CA, USA. Box 18.

Eucken, W. 1947. *Nationalökonomie wozu?* 3rd revised edition. Godesberg: Küpper.

Eucken, W. 1952. *Grundsätze der Wirtschaftspolitik*. Bern, Tübingen: Francke und Mohr Verlag.

Friedman, M. 1950–51. *Neoliberalism and its Prospects*. Typescript. Collection Milton Friedman. 4. Hoover Institution Archives. Stanford University, CA, USA. Box 42. Folder 8.

Gerber, D.J. 1998. *Law and Competition in Twentieth Century Europe: Protecting Prometheus*. Oxford: Oxford University Press.

Groeben, H. von der. 1960. Europäische Wirtschaftsgemeinschaft: Kommission: Kartellpolitik. Mitteilung vorgelegt von Hans von der Groeben. Brüssel, 15 February 1960. Typescript. Reproduction. EC Historical Archives, Florence: CEAB 2. 1795/ 1 – 3. CCE Commission Archives.

Groeben, H. von der. 1961. *Wettbewerbspolitik in der Europäischen Wirtschaftsgemeinschaft*. Brüssel: Sekretariat der Kommission der Europäischen Wirtschaftsgemeinschaft. EC Historical Archives, Florence: CEAB 2 – N2013/2. CCE Commission Archives.

Günther, E. 1952. Europäische Konvention zur Kontrolle internationaler Kartelle. *Wirtschaft und Wettbewerb*, 1, 243–51.

Günther, E. 1961. Vereinheitlichung der Wettbewerbsbedingungen im europäischen Raum. *Wirtschaft und Wettbewerb*, 11, 755–63.

Haenlein, F. 1959. Schreiben betr. Erster Gesamtbericht der Kommission der Europäischen Wirtschaftsgemeinschaft. Adressat: Bundeskanzler. Europäisches Parlament: Ausschuss für Fragen des Binnenmarktes der Gemeinschaft: Mitteilung an die Mitglieder. Luxemburg, 22 September 1958. Reproduction. Historisches Archiv der Europäischen Gemeinschaften, Florenz: CM2. 1959. 741. Cass. 99. Fiche 2.

Hahn, L.A. 1953. *Dächer ohne Häuser*. (Translation of Hahn's article published in *The Freeman*, 23 February 1953.) Typescript. Bundesarchiv Koblenz: B102. 11042.

Hayek, F.A. von. 1959. Strukturpolitik und Wettbewerbswirtschaft. *Die Aussprache*, 9:6, 215–20.

Hentschel, V. 1988. Deutschland und die Gründung der Europäischen Gemeinschaft für Kohle und Stahl. Ein chronologischer Bericht: May 1950 to April 1951. *Scripta Mercaturae*, 22, 77–118.

Herczec, K.L. 1952. Die Vereinheitlichung der europäischen Kartellgesetzgebung im Dienste der wirtschaftlichen Integration. *Wirtschaftsberichte der Creditanstalt-Bankverein*. Wien.

Miksch, L. 1937. Wettbewerb als Aufgabe. Die Grundsätze einer Wettbewerbsordnung, in *Ordnung der Wirtschaft 4*, series editors F. Böhm, W. Eucken, H. Grossmann-Doerth. Stuttgart, Berlin: W. Kohlhammer.

Ophüls, C.F. 1956. Fernschreiben (verschlüsselt) an das Auswärtige Amt betr. *Brüsseler Integrationskonferenz; Arbeitsgruppe Gemeinsamer Markt*. Brüssel, 14 November 1956. Reproduction. Politisches Archiv des Auswärtigen Amts: Fiche A9108.

Röpke, W. 1937. *Die Lehre von der Wirtschaft*. 1st edn. Wien.

Röpke, W. 1940. Grundfragen wirtschaftlicher Neuorientierung. *Neue Zürcher Zeitung*, 25 July 1940. No. 1064.

Röpke, W. 1942. *International Economic Disintegration*. London: William Hodge & Co.

Röpke, W. 1950. *European or International Federation*. Typescript. Centre d'Etudes Industrielles. Genf, 13 November 1950. Nachlass Wilhelm Röpke: Signatur na 72. Institut für Wirtschaftspolitik an der Universität zu Köln.

Röpke, W. 1951. Wirtschaftssystem und internationale Ordnung. *Ordo*, 4, 261–97.

Röpke, W. 1953. *Einige grundsätzliche Bemerkungen zum Monopolproblem. Referat auf der internationalen Konferenz über das Monopolproblem*. Zürich, 3. Juli 1953. Abteilung für Volkswirtschaftliche Studien. Schweizerisches Institut für Auslandforschung. Typescript.

Röpke, W. 1955. Economic Order and International Law, in *Académie de droit international. Recueil des cours 1954. II. Tome 86*. Leiden, 203–70.

Röpke, W. 1957a. Europa als wirtschaftliche Aufgabe, in *Europa – Besinnung und Hoffnung*, edited by A. Hunold. Erlenbach, Stuttgart: Rentsch, 159–84.

Röpke, W. 1957b. Integration und Desintegration der Weltwirtschaft, in *Wirtschaftsfragen der freien Welt. FS für Ludwig Erhard zum 60. Geburtstag*, edited by E. von Beckerath, F.W. Meyer and A. Müller-Armack. Frankfurt am Main: Knapp, 493–501.

Röpke, W. 1961. Die Weltwirtschaft im 19. und 20. Jahrhundert, in *Historia Mundi 10*, edited by F. Valjavec. Bern, München: Francke Verlag, 653–79.

Röpke, W. 1979. *Internationale Ordnung – heute*. 3rd edition. Erlenbach: Verlag Paul Haupt.

Röpke, W. 1994. *Die Lehre von der Wirtschaft*. 13th editon. Stuttgart: Verlag Paul Haupt.

Rusk, D. 1965. The first twenty-five years of the United Nations: San Francisco to the 1970s, in *The Quest for Peace: The Dag Hammarskjöld Memorial Lectures*, edited by A.W. Cordier and W. Foote. New York: Columbia University Press, 67–81.

Schüller, A. 2002. ORDO-Liberalismus – eine Synthese, in *Grundbegriffe zur Ordnungstheorie und Politischen Ökonomik. Arbeitsberichte zu Ordnungsfragen der Wirtschaft Nr. 7*, edited by A. Schüller and H.-G. Krüsselberg. Marburg: Marburger Gesellschaft für Ordnungsfragen der Wirtschaft, 50–55.

Villey, D. 1958. Le marché commun dans l'optique européenne. *Revue d'économie politique*, Janvier/Février, Sonderheft Nr. 1, 11–42.

Wegmann, M. 2002a. Neoliberale Europa-Föderationskonzepte 1918–1945. *Journal of European Integration History*, 8, 11–35.

Wegmann, M. 2002b. *Früher Neoliberalismus und europäische Integration. Interdependenz der nationalen, supranationalen und internationalen Ordnung von Wirtschaft und Gesellschaft (1932–1965)*. Baden-Baden: Nomos.

Wegmann, M. 2003. Für die Bewahrung der Werte einer freien Gesellschaft. Wirtschafts- und gesellschaftspolitische Konzeption des frühen Neoliberalismus. *Neue Zürcher Zeitung* 15/16.3.2003, Nr. 62, 87.

Wegmann, M. 2008. *Der Einfluss des Neoliberalismus auf das Europäische Wettbewerbsrecht 1946–1965. Von den Wirtschaftswissenschaften zur Politik*. Baden-Baden: Nomos.

Wegmann, M. 2009. Das neoliberale Europakonzept, in *Leitbild Europa? Europabilder und ihre Wirkungen in der Neuzeit. Historische Mitteilungen der Ranke-Gesellschaft Beiheft 74*, edited by J. Elvert and J. Nielsen-Sikora. Stuttgart: Steiner-Verlag, 220–31.

Willgerodt, H. 1989. Wertvorstellungen und theoretische Grundlagen des Konzepts der Sozialen Marktwirtschaft, in *Währungsreform und Soziale Marktwirtschaft. Erfahrungen und Perspektiven nach vierzig Jahren. (Jahrestagung des Vereins für Socialpolitik. Freiburg i. Br. 5–7.10.1988)*, Schriffendes Vereins für Socialpolitik NF 190, edited by W. Fischer. Berlin: Verlag Duncker & Humblot, 31–60.

Willgerodt, H. 1991. Wirtschaftspolitische Grundbedingungen der Europäischen Gemeinschaft. Sonderdruck. *Bitburger Gespräche, Jahrbuch 1991/1*, 49–65.

Willgerodt, H. 2001. Christliche Ethik und wirtschaftliche Wirklichkeit, in *Schlesien auf dem Weg in die Europäische Union. Ordnungspolitik der Sozialen Marktwirtschaft und Christliche Gesellschaftslehre. Marktwirtschaftliche*

Reformpolitik NF 6, edited by L. Gerken and J. Starbatty. Stuttgart: Lucius & Lucius, 89–108.

Willgerodt, H. and Peacock, A. 1989. German liberalism and economic revival, in *German Neo-Liberals and the Social Market Economy*, edited by A. Peacock and H. Willgerodt. London: Palgrave Macmillan, 1–14.

Chapter 6
Failures or Ideological Preconceptions? Thoughts on Two Grand Projects: The European Constitution and the European Civil Code

Hans-W. Micklitz[1]

Failures or Ideological Preconceptions

This topic is inspired by three different intellectual environments. First, my home university in Bamberg, where we are running a graduate school on '*Öffnung und Schließung von Märkten und Sozialräumen*' (Markets and Social Systems in Europe – Between Global Orders, European Decision Making and National Traditions).[2] The graduate school is an interdisciplinary project, led by sociologists, political scientists, economists and lawyers. Secondly, my current home, the European University Institute, where constitutional lawyers and human rights lawyers set the agenda. So not only intellectually but also institutionally I am, as a private lawyer, confronted with two broad issues – firstly, the relationship between EU private law and European constitutional law and secondly, between EU private law and human rights. My third inspiration emanates from the Centre of Excellence (CoE) of the University of Helsinki, which asserts that constitutional and private law should be analysed in a joint perspective. The CoE project is very much guided by the idea of multi-constitutionalism, of plurality of private legal orders, and of multiculturalism,[3] which, however, does not exclude development of a genuine European legal order.[4]

The three projects have one thing in common – private law seems to be at the borderline of the agenda. I take this perception as a challenge and an opportunity

1 I would like to thank N. Reich, R. Münch and the participants of the workshop in Helsinki for their extremely helpful comments which helped me to improve my argument. The usual disclaimer applies.

2 See <http://www.uni-bamberg.de/fileadmin/uni/wissenschaft_einricht/gk_mse/Paper/research.pdf>.

3 See Dam 2009.

4 This was the 'result of a conference' which took place in Helsinki in 2006, the results of which are published in Wilhelmsson, Paunio and Pohjolainen 2007.

to maintain the possible contribution of private law to the well-established and widely recognized European constitutionalization process. Agreement seems to be absent on whether and to what extent private law forms an integral part of the constitutionalization process.[5] I am interested in the relationship between constitutional and private law. The two Grand Projects serve as a catalyst to develop my argument. I will first look at the link between the two Grand Projects by placing emphasis on six parameters which may help to explain and to analyse the reasons why both ended or seem to have ended in deadlock. In my oral presentation I used the metaphor of 'failure', meaning political 'failure', the non-realization of the European Constitution which has now been replaced by the Lisbon Treaty and the predictable 'failure' of the European Civil Code project, called the Common Frame of Reference, which obviously does not have the support of the European Commission, the Council or the member states. On further reflection, triggered by Norbert Reich, I think 'failure' may not fully cover the parameters which I intend to analyse as tentative explanations for the deeper reasons lying behind the 'failure'. 'Failure' is too dramatic and too superficial. Too dramatic, since it is conceivable that both projects might survive in one form or another and in fact impact the further European integration process; too superficial since 'failure' suggests that the two Grand Projects were terminated via a formal act, like the French and Dutch vetoes to the constitution. A similar political vote on the European Civil Code project is hard to imagine. Whilst I will not deny that I originally had such a rather formal scenario at least *sotto voce* in mind, I equally wanted to identify the reasons why the projects 'failed'. To this end, 'failure' falls short of realizing my original intentions. The term 'ideological preconceptions' seems to capture my concern more precisely. 'Ideological preconceptions' refers to implicit assumptions which united elaboration of the two Grand Projects despite their conceptual differences. It will have to be shown that the idea of a European Constitution is at least based on a mandate from the member states, whereas no such mandate exists in the European Civil Code project. So an inherent deep difference separates the Grand Projects. However, seeking deeper links via implicit assumptions suggests that the two Grand Projects are politically and legally connected despite their different origins and functions. Only by understanding the linkage may we create an opportunity to put private law into a constitutional perspective.

Six Parameters Linking Ideological Preconceptions

Feasibility of the two Grand Projects

Is it timely, possible and feasible, at the beginning of the twenty-first century, to establish a European identity via a European Constitution and a European Civil

5 See Cherednychenko 2008; Mak 2008; and Grundmann 2008.

Code and to 'develop' a European *demos*?[6] Do the two Grand Projects reflect ninetheenth century ideologies? These issues have indeed been debated with regard to the European Civil Code project.[7] The Grand Projects have their proponents and opponents, both at the political and the academic level, and numerous contributions have been written on the feasibility of the European Constitution as well as on the feasibility of a European Civil Code. From the constitutional law side, emphasis is put on constitutional pluralism[8] against any explicit or implicit attempt to replace the national constitutions via a European Constitution. This corresponds to the plea for private law pluralism – bearing different headings in the private law discourse – 'Private Law and the Many Cultures of Europe'[9] – or 'Private Law Beyond the State'.[10] I have elsewhere expressed my reservations against the need for a European private law codification project superseding national private legal orders, against the chosen methodology which governs the work of the Acquis Group and the Study Group and last but not least against its shaky democratic legitimacy.[11]

Seeking an answer to these questions involves not only investigating the deeper reasons behind the idea of the Grand Projects and their historical, economic, political and social feasibility in a globalized world where the nation-state is on the decline. Constitution-making and private law code-making bear an inherently political dimension. People like Professor Christian von Bar or EP Diana Wallis share a common vision on the role and function of a European Civil Code, a vision which might be inspired by personal experience of the post-war period. A European Constitution and a European Civil Code form an integral part of a harmonic perspective of a United Europe with a common legal order. Sceptics, who favour multi-constitutionalism and a multifaceted European legal order, often find themselves in a more defensive position. However, the 'vision' of a multifaceted European legal order is gaining ground in Europe, particularly bolstered by the current economic crisis which has strengthened the position of the member states[12] and perhaps also due to the fact that the coming political and academic generation is not at all afraid of legal diversity,[13] understanding different legal orders as a useful and helpful level playing field. We lawyers form part of the European elite which works at the forefront of the European integration process with or without the two Grand Projects. I will come back to this aspect later.

6 See in the aftermath of the Maastricht decision of the FCC, Weiler 1995: 4; on the controversy between Habermas and Grimm, see Kraus 2004.

7 See Schulze 2008.

8 See Baquero Cruz 2007; Kumm 2005; Walker 2007; Poiares Maduro 2003.

9 See Wilhelmsson 2004; and Wilhelmsson, Paunio and Pohjolainen 2007.

10 See Michaels and Jansen 2006; and Jansen and Michaels 2008.

11 See Micklitz 2007a; and Micklitz and Cafaggi 2010.

12 See James 2009.

13 To paraphrase the heading of Dam 2009.

The link then could be that the two projects started out with mistaken premises in that they intended to realize a model of a homogeneous European society, united in a European *demos*, and bound together by a European Constitution and a European Civil Code. What has not taken place is a true public debate on European unity and European diversity, on where unity is needed, but also where unity is not needed. This implies that a new round of research should open up on pluralism within the constitutional and the private law frame.[14]

'The Social' in the two Grand Projects

I start from the premise that the current EU legal order is unbalanced in that the economy enjoys primacy over social concerns. The European Community remains a liberal project meant to open up markets with a touch of social oil.[15] The European Court of Justice is testing national social regulations ever more strongly against the four freedoms,[16] a process which was not and is not counterbalanced by corresponding positive European regulation, not even within the European Constitution project. As a matter of fact the European Constitution did not bring about new rules of what Duncan Kennedy[17] termed 'The Social'. This is particularly true with regard to consumer protection where the European Constitution tackled none of the difficult questions which result from the coexistence of the competence rules, Article 95 EC (now 114 TFEU) on the internal market on ensuring a high level of consumer protection and the role and function of Article 153 EC (now Articles 169 and 12 TFEU) which grants the European Community a set of competences reaching beyond Article 95 EC.[18] This is likewise true with regard to social and labour law, where the rules have remained more or less the same since adoption of the Treaty of Amsterdam. The European Constitution did not foresee any major shift in competence away from the member states to the European level. A correlation even exists between the limited scope of EU competence and its societal relevance. The greater the social relevance, the less developed the EU competences. This does not mean that the European Constitution does not deal with 'The Social' at all. Since adoption of the Single European Act, 'The Social' belongs to the European integration project. The gradual shift in competence since 1986 is perceived as either deconstruction or modernization of the national social welfare state via Community law, resulting in quite different perceptions of the role and importance of 'The Social' at the European level.[19]

14 On pluralism see Christodoulidis in this volume.

15 See Fischer-Lescano, Rödl and Schmid 2009.

16 See Reich 2010 (forthcoming), who argues, however, that the Court of Justice restricts the negative impact in its more recent judgments via the proportionality principle.

17 Kennedy 2006.

18 See Micklitz, Reich and Weatherill 2004.

19 See Leibfried and Mau 2008.

Substantial changes, however, may be reported from what Florian Rödl[20] calls overarching standards or guiding principles (*Leitnormen*), which have been proposed in the European Constitution and even elaborated on in the Lisbon Treaty. The latter grant neither rights nor competence but they do yield legal effects in the development of EU social and labour law. Article 3(3)TEU (ex 2 EU) states:

> The Union shall establish an internal market. It shall work for the sustainable development of Europe based on balanced economic growth and price stability, *a highly competitive social market economy*, aiming at full employment and social progress, and a high level of protection and improvement of the quality of the environment. It shall promote scientific and technological advance.
>
> It shall combat social exclusion and discrimination, and shall promote *social justice* and protection, equality between women and men, solidarity between generations and protection of the rights of the child.

The new Article 2 TEU states:

> The Union is founded on the values of respect for human dignity, freedom, democracy, equality, the rule of law and respect for human rights, including the rights of persons belonging to minorities. These values are common to the Member States in a society in which pluralism, non-discrimination, tolerance, justice, *solidarity* and equality between women and men prevail.

Of particular importance might be Article 3(3) TFEU which introduces the concept of a highly competitive *social market economy*. The key question is whether the reference to 'The Social' will have a long-standing impact on the future outlook of the European legal order. Christian Joerges[21] argues that this will not be the case for two reasons: firstly, the concept and the success of the social market economy was due to particular post-war circumstances in Germany which cannot be transposed to the making of a *social* market economy in the EU at the beginning of the twenty-first century; and secondly, that a true change from a market-driven European legal order to a more social outlook would entail a massive shift of competences from the member states to the EU level which is politically inconceivable and, if it did take place, would have to resolve problems of deep complexity.[22] Dragana Damjanovic and Bruno de Witte[23] offer a more optimistic reading of the future of 'The Social', in particular due to the fact that the European Court of Justice is ready to randomly uncouple social rights from the market logic of the integration process. However, the only delegation of competence foreseen in the European

20 Rödl 2009 (will also be published in English in 2010).
21 See Joerges 2009: 42.
22 See Scharpf 2002; and Leibfried, Obinger and Scharpf 2005.
23 See Damjanovic and Witte 2009.

Constitution (Article I-14(4)), where the EU should have competence 'to promote and co-ordinate the economic and employment policies of the Member States', has been repealed.

Solidarity is another *Leitnorm* which has been subject to attempts at legal scrutiny, so far, however, with little consistency.[24] Its upgrading in the European Constitution and the Lisbon Treaty might pave the way for reconsideration of this concept, perhaps in a new light. European solidarity differs from national solidarity. Constructing solidarity in categories of national stagnancy in law simply overlooks the ongoing transformation of national welfare states. European solidarity requires an autonomous interpretation. This in turn requires an understanding of what lies behind the concept of solidarity at the European level and to what extent it complies with the particular national understanding. Solidarity will play a crucial role when I look at the dialectic of European integration and national disintegration.

This rather negative account of the European Social Model is somewhat outbalanced by the massive expansion of *social rights* since the Treaty of Maastricht. Social rights, an idea emanating since the development of the European Social Charter in 1989, were meant to compensate for the competence deficiencies in the European legal order. In *Laval*[25] and *Viking*[26] the Court of Justice contributed to this trend in recognizing the right to strike as a fundamental right, but then restricting it against market freedoms via the proportionality principle. The Lisbon Treaty now cuts back the more ambitious goal of the European Constitution to fully integrate the Charter of Fundamental Rights. This formal shortfall might, though, be outweighed by an activist European Court of Justice which is ready to integrate the Charter of Fundamental Rights into interpretation of EU law.[27] *Kücükdeveci*[28] speaks for itself. However, even full integration of the Charter in the Lisbon Treaty would not and could not have helped to resolve conflicts between market freedoms and social rights. Expansion of social rights does not help to overcome the narrow boundaries of the EU competence rules on 'The Social'.[29] Rights can function as a substitute for missing competences in the European Constitution. Similar experiences result from the missing fourth dimension in the principle of proportionality, which does not allow for shaping competences between the member states and the EU.[30]

The picture is not so different with regard to the European Private Law Codification Project, as enshrined in the Draft Common Frame of Reference

24 See Wunder 2008; and Grimm 1973.

25 Case C-341/05, *Laval un Partneri Ltd*, ECR 2007, I-11767.

26 Case C-438/05, *The International Transport Workers' Federation and The Finnish Seamen's Union*, ECR 2007, I-10779.

27 See Case C-275/06, *Productores de Música de España (Promusicae) v Telefónica de España SAU*, ECR 2008, I-271; and with regard to private law, Kosta 2009.

28 Case C-555/07, *Kücükdeveci*, judgment of 19 January 2010, n.y.r.

29 See Rödl 2009.

30 See Opinion of AG van Gerven in the Sunday Trading cases (C-145/88, *Torfaen BC v B&Q*, ECR 1989, 3851); and in more detail Micklitz 2005.

(DCFR). At first sight, it seems as if the DCFR is meant to realize 'The Social' as it merges the European consumer law *acquis* and European anti-discrimination law with the essence of national private legal orders (of the Western European democracies). Both areas of the law are commonly associated if not equated with the social dimension in the private legal order. Whether or not such an interpretation of the social character of European consumer law is correct, is subject to a controversial debate.[31] What is striking is that the DCFR does not deal with labour law. This side of 'The Social' is entirely left aside.

The key question is whether and to what extent the DCFR meets the requirements of social justice as foreseen in the European Constitution and implemented in the Lisbon Treaty. The social model enshrined in the DCFR might be regarded as a compromise between those who defend private autonomy as the key principle and starting point of the private legal order[32] and those who advocate restriction of party autonomy to the benefit of the weaker party. Martijn Hesselink, in his study commissioned by the European Parliament on the question of whether the DCFR complies with the needs of social justice, concludes:

> [F]rom the point of view of social justice, the DCFR is fairly balanced. ... The level of consumer protection is sufficiently high. However, as an absolute maximum beyond which the member States would not be allowed to go in the case of full harmonisation, it is submitted, the level of protection in the DCFR is insufficient. However, there is certainly room for improvement.[33]

His critique is mainly devoted to the minimum/maximum debate which currently dominates revision of the consumer *acquis*.[34] The DCFR does not, however, meet the standards set in the 'The Social Justice Manifesto'.[35] The whole codification project, asserts the major critique voiced by the authors of the manifesto, is said to be overwhelmingly designed to guarantee the effective functioning of the internal market, without paying tribute to social justice in the meaning of how to protect the weaker party in contractual relationships. It seems as if the worrying scenario of the manifesto is realizing itself, if not in the DCFR then in attempts by the European Commission to implant the consumer shopper as the leading feature in the revised consumer *acquis*, thereby overruling the protective device of consumer law. The social dimension of contract law is then outsourced into the field of universal services, which might contain the nucleus of a 'true' social European private law.[36]

31 See Micklitz 2009a.

32 See Basedow 2008a.

33 Hesselink 2008: 85–6.

34 See Whittaker 2009; Rott and Terryn 2009; Tonner and Tamm 2009; and Micklitz and Reich 2009.

35 See Social Justice Study Group 2004.

36 See Micklitz 2009b.

A conceptual bridge seems to exist which links constitutional and private law and which is built out of a genuine European understanding of 'justice'. The starting point for such a European model is to be found in the concept of anti-discrimination, laid down in the Treaty and forcefully developed by the European Court of Justice in the field of social and labour law. By way of secondary Community law, the anti-discrimination principle has now reached private law. Perhaps the innovative potential of the DCFR lies in the integration of anti-discrimination into the proposed European Civil Code. However, such a paradigm change is far from being commonly accepted. Quite the contrary, resistance is strong against intrusion of such a constitutional principle into private law relations.[37] I have elsewhere developed that the European concept of justice should not be equated with social justice but can best be understood as 'access justice'.[38] It is for the European Community to grant justice to those who are excluded from the market or to those who face difficulties in making use of market freedoms.[39] European private law rules have to ensure that weaker parties enjoy, and can maintain, access to the market – and to European society as far as it exists. In this way 'access justice' corresponds to the *Leitmotif* of European social and labour law which is guided by the paradigm of '*Beschäftigungsfähigkeit*' (the capacity to be qualified for a job).[40]

So the answer then is that the European Constitution and the European Civil Code project do take 'The Social' into account – however, to a limited degree only and guided by a different paradigm of justice. The different concepts of 'The Social' demonstrate the need for an open political discourse over the chances and the limits of the European Social Model. This has not taken place, either in the debate on the European Constitution or amongst the drafters of the European Civil Code project. A European Union, even via a constitution or via a European Civil Code, can and should do no more than establish a general framework led by the paradigm of access justice, whereas it should remain for the member states to decide whether they are ready to go beyond access justice and guarantee social justice. The newly introduced Article 2 TEU of the Lisbon Treaty is very much in line with such a concept of shared responsibility. The Article may not and could not be read in the sense that the EU is obliged to establish 'social justice', but the EU has to recognize social justice as a guiding principle in a multilayered EU legal order. I would read into AG Maduro's conclusions in *Viking*[41] such a coexistence of the internal market paradigm with social concerns, as long as the Court of Justice confirms the wide discretion of member states in balancing market freedoms

37 See Basedow 2008b; and Säcker 2004.

38 Micklitz 2010a (forthcoming).

39 In this sense, see Case C-518/06, *Commission v Italy*, ECR 2009, n.y.r., no cherry-picking in compulsory insurance law.

40 See Salais 2006; and Somek 2005.

41 See the Opinion of AG Maduro in Case C-438/05, *The International Transport Workers' Federation and The Finnish Seamen's Union*, ECR 2007, I-10779.

against social rights.[42] This implies, and here I can only underline Hesselink's argument, that minimum harmonization should be the general standard of any secondary community law intruding into the social dimension of EU law.

Legitimacy of the two Grand Projects

Both grand projects suffer from one major flaw: constitution-building and private law-making appear as a matter of proper governance and EU citizens as mere stakeholders.

The process of elaborating the European Constitution is well documented.[43] The starting point was the *Laeken Council*, which established the European Convention. Under the presidency of Giscard d'Estaing, representatives of the heads of old and new member states, members of national parliaments from the old and now new member states, as well as members of the European Parliament and of the European Commission concluded their work in 2003.[44] This sounds as if the peoples were well represented – via their national parliaments and via their governments. However, what might have worked after the Second World War, when a constitutive assembly drafted the German *Grundgesetz* (Basic Law) and when similar institutions in the new member states drafted their constitutions in the late twentieth century, might not be opportune for development of a European Constitution.

What was missing and what should have been organized by the European Community and the member states is a public process which allows all citizens to participate in the process – and not only via the internet but via local and regional debates. If I may take Germany as a striking example, the whole process since 2001 until formal signature of the Constitution in 2004 remained largely unnoticed. All that German citizens could learn was that the European Community and the member states were planning to draft a constitution for Europe, combined with enlargement of the EU. However, there was literally no public debate. It is characteristic of Germany that the major player in the debate became the German Federal Constitutional Court (FCC), which confirmed the constitutionality of the Lisbon Treaty but set high benchmarks for the further integration process.[45] The major source of information for interested citizens was newspapers, reporting via the media and via the internet. There are, however, more promising experiences to be reported. France initiated a public debate, in preparation for the referendum in which the French rejected the Constitution. No overall survey is available on the degree to which the European Constitution became a subject of public concern.

42 In this direction, see Case C-112/00, *Schmidberger*, ECR 2003, I-5659, paras 79–81, Case C-36/02, *Omega Spielhallen*, ECR 2004, I-9609, para 36; and Reich 2008.

43 Available at: <http://europa.eu/institutional_reform/chronology/index_en.htm>.

44 Available at: <http://european-convention.eu.int/bienvenue.asp?lang=EN>.

45 Available online in English and German at: <http://www.bundesverfassungsgericht.de/entscheidungen/es20090630_2bve000208en.html>.

The majority of citizens might have perceived the process of constitution-building as one where the true decisions were taken in the backyards of governmental agreements and talks behind closed doors.[46]

The process of elaborating the Charter on Fundamental Rights does not fully fit into that scenario.[47] The Convention, which was headed by Roman Herzog, former president of the FRG and of the German Supreme Court, brought together not only governments and parliamentarians, but also representatives from the Court of Justice, from the Committee of the Regions, from the Social and Economic Committee, the Ombudsman, and the Council of Europe. NGOs were invited to comment and their contributions were made accessible via the internet.[48] So the drafting process was definitely more open, although a disclaimer applies as to the degree to which a true public debate was initiated.

If we look into the drafting process of the European Civil Code project, the scenario is completely different. The project was initiated by the European Parliament, which pushed the European Commission for over a decade before the codification process was launched in 2001.[49] The European Commission delegated the law-making into the hands of two academic circles, the Study Group and the Acquis Group. Without having a mandate, the two groups stretched the codification projects beyond contract law and integrated the law of obligations including security interests. Citizens, members of governments and parliamentarians remained widely excluded from the law-making. In fact, the consultation procedure organized by the Study Group and the Acquis Group remained far behind the democratic standards which guided the consultation process of the European Constitution and the European codification process. Even in between the two groups, major differences have to be reported on the accessibility of the codification process. Both worked behind closed doors in working groups which met numerous times at various places in Europe. The Study Group assembled two hundred academics. It made every effort to make elaboration, shaping and resolution of possible conflicts – via the internet (although addressed to lawyers only) – transparent.[50] This was not the case with regard to the Acquis Group, where the process took place in numerous closed meetings where the members of the group assembled. The rather limited accessibility resulted from the fact that the European Commission did not want information to be disclosed before the results of the Acquis Group were officially made public. Once the European Commission recognized the limited political support from member states in the Council, it dropped the codification project like a hot potato and focused its interests on revision of the consumer *acquis*.[51]

---

46 For a deeper analysis in particular of post-failure efforts by the EU to establish a bottom-up political discourse, see Culpepper, Fagatto, Fung and Lee 2010 (forthcoming).

47 Available at: <http://www.europarl.europa.eu/charter/composition_en.htm>.

48 Available at: <http://www.europarl.europa.eu/charter/civil/civil0_en.htm>.

49 Available at: <http://ec.europa.eu/consumers/rights/contract_law_en.htm>.

50 See McGuire 2007.

51 See COM(2006) 744 final.

What matters in our context is the resemblance of the private law-making process to the nineteenth century German '*Professorenmodell*'. The question is whether legal academics at the turn of an era – the shift from the second to the third globalization of law and legal thought[52] – can be and still are the appropriate legal agents to codify the law and if not what their role could and should be in the early twenty-first century. The DCFR will now have been discussed in the European Commission and in the European Parliament. But where are the European citizens? Does it suffice to determine a number of selected stakeholders who are invited to comment on drafts presented to them by professors? Is no more democratic input needed? What should be the role of the European Parliament?[53]

Relying on Fritz Scharpf's[54] distinction between input and output legitimacy, both Grand Projects are highly deficient. The input was organized in a way which restricted access to the law-making process to an elite circle of persons, less in the development of the Constitution, more in the development of the European Civil Code. Both clearly lacked output legitimacy, as is documented in the referenda on the European Constitution[55] and in the reaction in the wider economic and political environment of the Civil Code. This does not mean that the European Constitution or the DCFR will remain without any, even legal, influence. The Court of Justice formally has no jurisdiction to refer to rules which were not taken over in the Lisbon Treaty, but it cannot be excluded that these rules may inspire the Court of Justice in its interpretation. The DCFR has already become the benchmark in academic discourse whenever a particular issue in European private law comes to the fore. It remains to be seen whether the DCFR may gain the same or similar status as the PECL not only before the Court of Justice but also before national courts.

Competence transfer in the two Grand Projects

The Treaty of Maastricht brought the last substantial competence transfer from the member states to the European Community. The treaties of Amsterdam and Nice were much more stamped by the efforts of the member states to set limits to the expansion of EU law rather than active promotion of the development of EU policies via competence transfers. One of the major purposes behind the Grand Project of the European Constitution was to clearly shape the distribution of competences between the EU and the member states – which is, by the way, a typical phenomenon of a federal constitution. Seen this way, it is even more surprising that neither the European Constitution nor the Lisbon Treaty ever openly addressed the constitutional question of whether the European Community needs

---

52 See Kennedy 2003.

53 Hesselink (2004: 694–7) proposed that the Parliament should raise at the very least a set of key questions.

54 See Scharpf 1999.

55 See Glencross and Trechsel 2010 (forthcoming).

a particular competence to adopt a European Civil Code. Raising such a question would have paved the way for a discussion over the function of a Civil Code in the envisaged European Constitution.

These findings correspond in an astonishing way to the silence of all those institutions which have been and still are involved in the European Civil Code project. Neither the European Commission, nor the European Parliament, nor the Study Group nor the Acquis Group has openly addressed the highly sensitive competence issue. It seems as if all parties have deliberately avoided getting to grips with the most important question behind the European Civil Code codification project – the question of competence.[56] It is easy to imagine the reactions, in particular of member states, if a Community organ had brought the question to the fore. So far Article 95 EC (now 114 TFEU) has served as a competence basis in most European regulations and directives dealing with private law issues. The Europeanization of private law took place via the back door, i.e. coupled with completion of the internal market. The competence issue has been left to academia, which is divided.[57] However, the competence question will arise in the European Parliament, even if it advocates only adoption of a recommendation for application of the DCFR on a voluntary basis.

The question remains – which follows what: the European Civil Code the European Constitution, or vice versa? Historically, examples are available at national state level to provide evidence in both directions, although it is not easy to define the decisive juncture.[58] The French Civil Code was adopted after the French Constitution, the German Civil Code before the Weimar Constitution. Europe does not have a homogeneous political identity. If any, Europe has a cultural identity which rests on national identities and which unites different nation-states in Europe. This is the way I understand the results of the 2006 conference in Helsinki on the many cultures of European private law. Whether this suffices to build a constitution is under wide discussion in legal and political science. There is, however, a difference between private law and constitutional law-building. It is much easier to imagine private law as a bottom-up construction which supports development of a common European identity than to build a bottom-up constitution. We might recall Stephan Rodotà:[59] 'we can easily see how the civil codes played an essential role in the development of the nation state, representing the real constitution of social society'. We must not go as far as arguing in the way Franz Böhm did, when he laid down the ground rules for a '*Privatrechtsgesellschaft*'. Hugh Collins[60] and Jan Smits,[61] although from a different angle, favour such a bottom-up approach of

56 See Booys, Hesselink and Rutgers 2007.

57 See Basedow 1996; and Weatherill 2006.

58 See James 1997.

59 See Rodotà 2006.

60 See Collins 2008.

61 See Smits 2010.

European private law-building that might one day yield a common or European cultural identity.

Regulatory character of the two Grand Projects

The European project was designed to establish a common market, later an internal market. The driving force of the EU project was how to find the correct market design which could best guarantee 'peace' and 'prosperity'. The legal tools meant to realize this were either de-regulation = negative integration, or re-regulation = positive integration. The key to understanding the singularity of the European legal order may be found in this objective-related regulatory function. This comes close to the regulatory state in the meaning Giandomenico Majone gave to it.[62]

The core of EU law consists of what I would call from my German legal background *Wirtschaftsverwaltungsrecht* (the law used to administer the economy – economic administrative law). It is from here that the Court of Justice initiated and developed supremacy, direct effect and state liability. Citizenship issues came into play only after the Treaty of Amsterdam. However, the Court of Justice is using, in this new field of EC law, the same instruments and the same methodology as in the field of negative integration.[63] The Court of Justice then developed out of this 'economic administrative law' first a 'genuine European Legal Order' and later a 'European Constitution'. This goes very much hand in hand with a widespread understanding that administrative law at the nation-state level yields those innovate elements which later might gain constitutional status.[64] Similar phenomena may be observed at the EU level, where principles laid down in secondary law were later upgraded to the constitutional level (for instance, affordability). The drafters of the European Constitution went down the same route, in that they presented to the public an extended version of the Treaty as a European Constitution, the basics of which were designed by the various treaty amendments, the case law of the European Court of Justice, and condensed concepts and principles of secondary Community (administrative) law. They did not start from national constitutions in order to find out what the content of a European constitution should be in the light of existing national constitutions. Therefore, preparation of the European Constitution was not preceded by a comparative constitutional analysis.[65] If anything, comparative analysis remained erratic.

EU private law is regulatory law per se. Most European private law rules are mandatory rules. They do leave leeway for deviating member states' laws but only within the boundaries of the still prevailing minimum approach. The respective rules may often combine two different substantial purposes: the first, to open up

62 See Majone 1996.

63 See Azoulai 2008.

64 See, for example, with regard to the right to safety, Micklitz 1991.

65 See Albi and Ziller 2006. This is now at the core of the EuNaCON (The European and National Constitutional) Project at the University of Tilburg.

markets via regulation and the second, to set binding standards for the behaviour of market participants. This is different from national private legal orders, where default rules establish a kind of a reserve order which leaves much room for freedom of contract.[66] The drafters of the European Civil Code, i.e. the DCFR have taken European regulatory law into account only to a very limited extent, or more precisely, consumer law and anti-discrimination law. The major basis of the DCFR is national law, or more precisely, comparative national law (of the old member states). In this sense, the DCFR is diametrically different from the European Constitution. The whole project of the DCFR suffers from not having looked at the different areas in which the EU has set private law standards, either directly or indirectly, in combination with sector-related rules meant to open up regulated markets. Again I feel free to refer to previous research in which I have extensively dealt with the character of European private law and the implications which follow from their genuine regulatory nature.[67]

The differences between the two Grand Projects are clear: the European Constitution might be understood in its substantive parts largely as an attempt to build out of *Wirtschaftsverwaltungsrecht* (administrative economic law) a legal order which is then called 'Constitution'. The European private law codification project, quite to the contrary, more or less neglects the regulatory character of EC law. What would have been needed at the very least is a stocktaking of the private law *acquis* and a proposal on how the European regulatory private law *acquis* could be merged with the comparative findings of the different national legal orders. The link would then be that the Constitution builders put far too much emphasis on *Wirtschaftsverwaltungsrecht*, whereas the private law makers overlooked the importance of EU regulatory private law and instead relied on private autonomy as enshrined in national private legal orders as the starting point.

Misleading labelling and marketing in the two Grand Projects

I never understood the European Constitution as a constitution in the meaning of the French Constitution, the American Constitution, the German *Grundgesetz*, or the constitutions of countries like Portugal, Spain or Greece in the 1980s, or those of the new member states. The emerging European Constitution, if we subscribe to the concept invented by the European Court of Justice, is a singular project whose design cannot easily be compared with nation-state constitutions.[68] By calling the envisaged Grand Project 'Constitution', the European Community and the member states made citizens believe that the project contains a set of rules similar to national constitutions and that it is therefore – at least implicitly – aimed

66 Default rules too might have a regulatory function, see Möslein and Riesenhuber 2009.

67 See Micklitz 2010b (forthcoming).

68 See Walker 2007, Poiares Maduro 1998; and Weiler 1999.

at substituting national constitutions. Is this a 'cosmetic particularity'?[69] But even if it had been possible to make clear to the public at large that the European Constitution complements national constitutions and that it grants rights additional to those already enshrined in national constitutions, one might wonder whether such a project would not have required a referendum of all citizens in all member states on the same day and at the same time. The new clothes of the Constitution project now called the 'Lisbon Treaty' cannot so easily settle disputes which have arisen, not least due to the misleading design.

The situation is somewhat different with regard to the European Civil Code project. The DCFR as elaborated by the Study Group and the Acquis Group is in fact the European Civil Code, which the European Parliament has been asking for since the early nineties. It is much more than the famous or infamous toolbox the European Commission had in mind. So the DCFR is a European Civil Code in disguise. For the peoples of Europe and European citizens it might be much more difficult to grasp the role and function of a European Civil Code for the unity of Europe. They may not even have a clear understanding of what a national private legal order means.

Why is it that Grand Projects at the European level come in disguise? The Lisbon Treaty realized more or less the core of the original European Constitution – will it then turn into a constitution? The DCFR reflects the European Civil Code for which the European Parliament was fighting so strongly: will it become a European Civil Code despite or because of its misleading labelling? The deeper reasons for this widespread opacity belong to a well-settled policy which unites all Community organs and the member states. The European Commission is a master at dressing far-reaching legal concepts in harmless clothes. The member states are using the same strategy, though for a different reason. If the integration process brings about positive results, member states tend to claim ownership, whereas if the result is negative according to the member state in question, then it is the European Commission which is responsible. Only the Court of Justice uses clear language – a genuine European legal order, built on supremacy and direct effect – even a European Constitution. This, however, remained unnoticed between the early sixties and the 'November Revolution' of the Court of Justice.[70] Today the Court of Justice is in the limelight again due to its judicial activism and the Lisbon judgment of the FCC. Even the acceptability of the Court of Justice depends largely on the fact that the member states and their courts did not fully realize what supremacy and direct effect meant until it showed up in the European Constitution. Half-truths might have been the true reason for the 'success' of the European integration process, perhaps not only with regard to the role and function

69 See also Walker in this volume.

70 This is the heading of an article by Reich (1994), where he analyses, inter alia, *Keck*.

of the Court of Justice.[71] In this sense the 'chameleon character'[72] of the DCFR might, in the end, strengthen its legal impact on national private legal orders.

The Dialectic of European Integration and National Disintegration

I would like to come back to the graduate college at the University of Bamberg entitled '*Öffnung und Schließung von Märkten*'. The leading sciences were and are the social sciences, more precisely sociology and political science. Richard Münch, one of the intellectual leaders of the college, just published a book which precisely defines and shapes what I had the pleasure to participate in for quite a number of years. The book is called '*Die Konstruktion der Europäischen Gesellschaft – Zur Dialektik transnationaler Integration und nationaler Desintegration*'[73] (*The Construction of European Society: The Dialectic of Transnational Integration and National Disintegration*).[74] Research on European integration, as is well known, is scientifically speaking in the hands of lawyers and political scientists. Richard Münch is a sociologist and takes a different perspective. As the title indicates, he focuses his research interests on the emerging European society and what it looks like.

I will use the ideas behind the book to try to show that the two Grand Projects, the 'European Constitution' and the 'European Civil Code project', have been overlooking or setting aside the most urgent questions in the further construction of Europe. These questions require an answer from the legal system and I would equate them in a societal perspective with the conflicts resulting from the dialectics of transnational integration and national disintegration. The answer to these questions requires a general look at the further development of the European legal order and European private law. In all modesty, I dare to say that private law – and private lawyers – may provide some useful insights into the new round of academic and political discourse triggered by the two 'failures'. What should be avoided is consideration of the two Grand Projects as separate from each other. They are indeed closely interlinked. What is missing politically and intellectually is to elaborate the ties.

The second part of this chapter is devoted to that task, though from a private law perspective combined with an attempt to demonstrate the constitutional implications. Münch's analysis supports me as he looks into society as a whole and does not care about distinctions between constitutions and private legal orders. He uses two parameters to explain the tensions between transnational integration and European disintegration: the fading away of mechanical solidarity via the international division of labour and the transnational elites which are accelerating

71 See Alter 2001.

72 I have borrowed this expression from Weatherill.

73 Münch 2008.

74 A somewhat shortened version, see Münch 2010 (forthcoming).

that bifurcation to their own benefit. I will use and dwell on these parameters to point to the effects of shrinking mechanical solidarity and the potential power of organic solidarity in the European integration process before I attempt to shape the transnational elites, the moral pioneers as Münch calls them. Neither of the two Grand Projects nor existing primary and secondary Community law takes the distinction between mechanical and organic solidarity fully into account, thereby enhancing the tension between those who benefit and those who suffer from the European integration process. What is needed is a deeper look into the composition of European society, which may be broken down into the transnational elites already mentioned, the average citizen and the vulnerable citizen, and the corresponding legal requirements at the constitutional and private law levels.

Mechanical/organic solidarity (the process) and transnational elites (the actors)

The starting point of Münch's analysis of the European integration process is Adam Smith and David Ricardo and their overall idea that mutual exchange of goods and services between nations may create wealth. We might recall that the original purpose of the European Economic Community was to guarantee peace and prosperity. Münch links Smith and Ricardo to Émile Durkheim, who analysed the effects on societies of the international division of labour. What matters is Durkheim's recognition of the changing function of solidarity, which is transformed from mechanical into organic or network solidarity. Mechanical solidarity may be associated with collective national solidarity rooted in the nation-states whereas organic or network solidarity refers to those new forms of collective (transborder) activity which are made possible by the international division of labour once the individual is freed from the national collective environment. The impact on the law, according to Durkheim, is striking. The rights of individuals are strengthened, he calls it the 'cult of the individual', while the rights of collective national entities are weakened. Durkheim developed his vision of a future European Society 20 years before the First World War. His assertion of the role and function of individual rights looks modern, in particular in light of the making and shaping of the European legal order by the Court of Justice via the extension of subjective rights, thereby indirectly turning down collective rights.[75] However, the cult of the individual is characteristic of the EU as a whole.

The long-term effects of the transformation process which Durkheim foresaw are becoming ever clearer. Somewhat overstated, we may observe that national collective entities, societies, but also groups within societies (trade unions, consumer organizations), are losing their homogeneity and that the sharp differences between former different national cultures are beginning to wane. This complies with the summary findings of Thomas Wilhelmsson's contribution to the conference on Private Law and the Many Cultures of Europe.[76] By way of

75 See Kelemen 2003.

76 See Wilhelmsson 2007.

inner differentiation (migration, foreign workers), national societies are steadily assimilating each other. EC law and the European legal order are enabling this transformation process and they are accelerating it by way of extending the legal position of all those who are willing and able to make use of the new freedoms. The recent case law of the Court of Justice on migrant workers and migrants provides ample evidence for such a development.[77] This process, according to Durkheim, shadowed by Münch, enables the development of transnational ties between individuals, who are freed from their national cultural constraints. The question remains of whether these transnational networks that are the yield of denationalization and deterritorialization may still be associated with the term 'solidarity'. Here more research is needed to disclose the nature of a European concept of solidarity in labour and consumer law.[78]

Not only from a sociological point of view, the question remains: what are the driving forces behind this transformation process. Neither the mere spillover effect of transborder trade nor bilateral or multilateral negotiations between states[79] might explain why transborder trade, division of labour and creation of the European legal order are constantly accelerated. The ongoing transformation process produces negative effects on the average citizen through the changing patterns of solidarity – from mechanical to organic – effects on distributive justice – enlargement of *Leistungsgerechtigkeit* (equity of needs), equality of opportunity, and fairness, in contrast to collective distributive justice guaranteed by the national welfare state[80] – which have so long been protected by a national identity and a national legal order.[81]

Münch offers four factors which help to explain the shift of legitimate power and construction of the legitimate order from the national to the European level:

1. The instauration of a formal European legal power. Institutional procedures for law-making and law-application must present a stable ground which allows *transnational elites* to realise their vision of a transnational project from which they benefit.
2. The orientation of a '*Leitidee*' a guiding idea or leading concept which allows the *transnational elites* to realise their own vision whilst guaranteeing that possible conflicts resulting from social transformation are resolved, which is equated with the fundamental freedoms and anti-discrimination.
3. Emergence of a dominant community of European lawyers and the transformation of politics into a juridical technique. The *transnational elites* can only apply legitimate power which respects procedural rules,

77 See Dougan 2009a.

78 On the concept of solidarity in insurance against accidents at work and occupational diseases, see Case C-350/07, *Kattner Stahlbau GmbH*, judgment of 5 March 2009, n.y.r.

79 See Moravcsik 1993.

80 See Münch 2008: 129.

81 See Münch 2008: 71.

thereby enabling national resistance to be overcome whilst securing output legitimacy.

4. Functional adaptation has to be transformed into construction of a legitimate legal order. The transnational legal order which is the result of conflicts between *transnational elites* and national resistance must gain the status of a new legal order, which makes sense as a whole and which appears to be just and can therefore require legitimacy to justify the transformation of national legal orders and national concepts of justice.

I will focus in my analysis on the role and function of 'the transnational elites' which are at the forefront of those who are building new European, i.e. transnational, ties and thereby uncoupling themselves from their national cultural links. Münch is not advocating a *Verschwörungstheorie*, a theory of conspiracy or complot. He claims to observe and to analyse the current reality, which is the construction of a European society via transnational elites. He identifies transnational elites, also termed 'moral pioneers', in science, art, economics, politics and law as the driving force behind the integration process.[82] Lawyers are said to play a crucial role, in the comitology procedure – in law-making and law-enforcement via the executive (the member states and the European Commission), and in the application and making (judicial governance)[83] of law via the Court of Justice (the European judges and the national judges as European judges). Both areas read together establish a European legal field[84] – Münch calls it a transnational network – composed of academics, judges, public officials, lawyers and NGOs.[85] Genuine European actors such as the European Commission, the European judges or European NGOs are united in a network of which national executives, national judges, national lawyers and national NGOs form an integral part. They are forming and building a new identity, objectively in the meaning that transnational networks are becoming ever more institutionalized, and subjectively as members of transnational networks develop a genuine sense of affiliation with their particular European legal and political environment.[86] However, a clear demarcation line stands between those national courts, national lawyers, national executives and others who form part of the transnational network and those who are excluded from the network. Those excluded from the transnational network, be they national courts, national

82 See Münch 2008: 60.

83 See Frerichs 2008.

84 See Bourdieu 1986.

85 On the role of NGOs in organized law enforcement, with regard to labour and consumer organizations, see Micklitz 2005; with regard to environmental organizations, see Slepcevic 2009a and Slepcevic 2009b.

86 See Culpepper, Fagatto, Fung and Lee 2010 (forthcoming).

governments or national lawyers, are marginalized.[87] They belong to a different, nationally determined, legal field.

Members of transnational legal networks are led by a common *Leitidee*, which is to my mind a widely understood anti-discrimination principle, mainly one where different nationalities do not and should not matter. The *Leitidee* of anti-discrimination so strongly favoured by the Court of Justice enabled the ideal of a collectively shared nationality to gradually lose importance in European society-building. This entails the 'supremacy' of (the politically intended) European organic solidarity over (still existing) national mechanical collective solidarity. Social litigation before the Court of Justice may serve as a prominent and paradigmatic example. Transnational judicial networks intentionally (if the claimants are business organizations and manage to mobilize national courts and the Court of Justice) or unintentionally (if the claimants are public interest groups using the same strategy as business organizations) are accelerating a drift away from national solidarity, thereby deepening the conflict between transnational integration and national disintegration. The ambiguous effects of law-making and law enforcement via transnational judicial and executive networks raise *legitimacy questions* which have featured at the forefront of political and academic discussion for decades and which gain pace the deeper EU law intrudes on and destroys national mechanical solidarity.[88] *Laval* and *Viking*[89] stand as beacons of this type of conflict in the European judicial legal field. They are widely perceived as favouring transnational integration at the expense of national disintegration. Scharpf goes as far as requesting civil disobedience against the Court of Justice, which is said to act beyond its jurisdiction and without a solid legitimatory basis.[90]

Mechanical/organic solidarity and the missing collective dimension

The two Grand Projects do not pay much attention to the tension between transnational integration and national disintegration. This would have required a strong attempt to openly address conflicts and to seek a solution resulting from the falling apart of national mechanical and transnational organic/network solidarity, more precisely to discuss collective rights, collective participation in administrative decision-making within transnational executive networks, and new forms of collective judicial action. Quite the contrary is true. The two Grand Projects largely miss the point in that they oscillate between attempts to strengthen national mechanical solidarity and half-hearted attempts to pave the way for a new

87 See the interesting analysis of Schepel and Wesseling (1997), who analyse the *Common Market Law Review*, *Europarecht* and *Cahiers de Droit Européen*.

88 See, in particular the work of Scharpf 2002 and 2009a; and Joerges 2006.

89 Case C-341/05, *Laval un Partneri Ltd*, ECR 2007, I-11767, and Case C-438/05, *The International Transport Workers' Federation and The Finnish Seamen's Union*, ECR 2007, I-10779.

90 See Scharpf 2008 and 2009b.

European organic solidarity. Existing EU law does not suffice to close that gap. In theory, my hypothesis could be demonstrated in both European legal fields, those governed by the executive (comitology and Lamfalussy) or by the judiciary. For the sake of argument, it might suffice to have a deeper look into collective litigation.

The Treaty does not deal with collective rights, with the exception of Article 230(4) EC (now Article 263(4) TFEU). Whether or not, and under what requirements, these Articles grant NGOs standing to sue has been the subject of major controversy even between the CFI and the Court of Justice. In *UPA*[91] and *Jégo-Quéré*,[92] the Court of Justice held inadmissible – contrary to the opinion of AG Jacobs – two actions for the annulment of Community regulations because the respective applicants did not satisfy the condition of individual concern under Article 230 EC (263 TFEU). The Court of Justice delegated to member states the question of who should have standing. The European Constitution as well as the Lisbon Treaty contains changes which might facilitate access to the Court of Justice. Article 263(4) TFEU now reads as follows: 'a regulatory act which is of direct concern to him or her and does not entail implementing measures'.[93] Whether or not the amendment will enhance modes of organic solidarity remains to be seen. Hans Roland Schwensfeier[94] calls it a shame package as only regulatory Acts may be directly attacked, but not regulations and directives.

Whilst the European Constitution seems inclined to somewhat strengthen the role and function of collective organizations before the Court of Justice, the European Civil Code project has deliberately set aside the collective dimension in private law. The DCFR is based on an individualistic conception of private law, in line with nineteenth century philosophy and in line with the Court of Justice's ability to use individually enforceable rights as a vehicle to promote transborder integration. This does not exclude the possibility of individually enforceable rights in fact standing for collective interests – a recent example is *Janecek*[95] – but such disguised collective conflicts may reach the court only if they can be presented in the form of individual rights.[96] In fact, many preliminary reference procedures bear that strategic touch, be they brought to court by companies or by NGOs.[97]

All in all this is a rather poor record for two Grand Projects which are designed to meet the challenges of ongoing European integration. However, at this stage it

---

91 Case C-50/00 P, *Union de Pequenos Agricultores (UPA) v Council*, ECR 2002, I-6677, affirming Case T-173/98, *Union de Pequenos Agricultores (UPA) v Council*, ECR 1999, II-3357.

92 Case C-263/02 P, *Commission v Jégo-Quéré & Cie SA*, ECR 2004, I-3245, setting aside Case T-177/01, *Commission v Jégo-Quéré & Cie SA*, ECR 2002, II-2365.

93 See amendment to Art. 263 (OJ L 115, 9 May 2008: 47).

94 See Schwensfeier 2009: 362.

95 Case C-237/07, *Janecek v Freistaat Bayern*, ECR 2008, I-622.

96 This complies with Walker's concept of legal formalism which dominates the EU Constitution: see his contribution in this volume.

97 See Cafaggi and Micklitz 2009.

seems necessary to look into current primary and secondary community law, as interpreted by the Court of Justice, in order to provide a somewhat fuller account of the impact of EU law on Durkheim's distinction between mechanical and organic solidarity. I will limit my rough overview to labour, anti-discrimination and consumer law and the degree to which EU law provides guidance on collective rights.

The right for workers to organize themselves is laid down in Article 28 of the constitutional EU Charter of Fundamental Rights. More specific rules on collective rights may be found in recent anti-discrimination directives.[98] They do not grant collectively enforceable rights before national courts.[99] The rules limit the legal position of trade unions and NGOs operating in the field of anti-discrimination law to participate in individual litigation. The collective right is dependent on a pending individual case in which a collective interest group can then provide support to the individual in their litigation. More interesting and more telling are the few judgments of the Court of Justice which deal with the collective dimension of labour law. Neither in *Albany*[100] nor in *Viking*[101] did the Court of Justice provide guidance on how the right to strike could be voiced in the courts.

The situation is slightly more promising in consumer law. Since the Treaty of Amsterdam, Article 169 EC (ex Article 153 EC, now 185 TFEU) grants consumers the right to organize themselves, but neither the Treaty nor the Constitution nor the Charter provide for any collective rights. Secondary Community law on collective consumer rights exists in the form of an action for injunction in the field of unfair terms and unfair commercial practices; however, this right is tailored to national markets, the mechanical side of solidarity. Directive 98/27 provides for rules on transborder litigation on the basis of the principle of mutual recognition. Regulation 2006/2004 sets up a transborder network of enforcement authorities which includes the right to take action for an injunction. Both rules may be read as an attempt to lay down ground rules for fostering organic and network solidarity through collective litigation. In practice, transborder litigation in consumer law does not play a role, either at national or EU level.[102]

In short, EU law is reluctant in protecting mechanical solidarity, which means it does not set clear boundaries for national disintegration. What is likewise missing in EU law, primary, secondary, Treaty and Constitution, is a consistent attempt, perhaps with the exception of consumer law, to mobilize the potential of organic

98 See the identical rules and the identical recitals in Art. 7(2) of Directive 2000/43/EC; Art. 9(2) of Directive 2000/78; Art. 6(3) of Directive 2002/73; Art. 8(3) of Directive 2004/113; and Art. 17(2) of Directive 2006/54.

99 For a different reading, Nickel 2001.

100 Case C-67/96, *Albany*, ECR 1999, I-5751.

101 See again in this context the opinion of AG Maduro in Case C-438/05, *The International Transport Workers' Federation and The Finnish Seamen's Union*, ECR 2007, I-10779; and the comment by Reich 2008.

102 See Micklitz 2007b.

solidarity which results from transborder integration, although Article 65 EC (now Article 81 TFEU) allows regulatory measures to develop organic solidarity. The existing set of rules in the Brussels Regulation and the Rome I and II Regulations are limited to a mere individualistic conception of cross-border enforcement.[103]

What role for transnational elites, average citizens and vulnerable persons in mechanical/organic solidarity?

With Münch we may distinguish between three broad categories: the transnational elites, the average citizen and the weak = vulnerable parties. The European Constitution and the Lisbon Treaty start from citizenship. Vulnerable parties are not directly addressed. If at all, they show up in what Rödl calls *Leitnormen*, such as social justice and solidarity, which leave room for interpretation. The DCFR shows more promising signs in that it distinguishes between the average market citizen and the consumer, who is equated with vulnerable parties.[104] If we break down existing EU law (broadly speaking, treaties and secondary Community law) to the three categories, we shall find that EU law is using the first two groups of persons for fostering transborder integration, whereas the last group suffers from national disintegration. I would like to demonstrate that the questions behind the threefold distinction as well as the possible effects resulting from that decision can only be resolved by Constitutional and Private Law in tandem.

The EU Constitution (including existing primary and secondary Community law) and the European Civil Code project (the DCFR) are designed to meet the needs of the *average* citizen – who is the mobile, active and multilingual worker or the famous circumspect, well-informed consumer. The driving force behind this concept has been the Court of Justice. The abundant case law on the freedom of persons – i.e. workers and consumers – may be translated into an attempt by the Court of Justice to transform the national worker and the national consumer into pioneers of EC law. They are invited by the Court of Justice to make use of their rights to reap the benefits of the markets – to use the language of Presidency Conclusions of the Lisbon European Council, adopted in 2000.[105] These consumers and workers are the spearhead of transnational integration via collective litigation in the judicial legal field and via their input into the various consultation mechanisms in the administrative legal field. They will use their enforceable rights to free themselves from national restrictions which hinder their search for the individual best solution. The whole bunch of secondary EU law on labour, anti-discrimination and consumer law is largely governed by the very same spirit. The recent shift in secondary EU law from minimum to maximum harmonization – which affects not only consumer but also labour law, despite the

103 On this, see Saumier 2009; Rott 2009; and Stadler 2009.

104 See Principles DCFR no. 46.

105 Available at: <http://www.europarl.europa.eu/summits/lis1_en.htm>.

restriction in the Treaty[106] – translates the Court of Justice's *Leitbild* into an ever-denser system of rules which narrows down the leeway for member states to take protective measures for the benefit of the most vulnerable parties. The DCFR fits into that perspective as it is conceptualized as a fully fledged code which does not conceptually distinguish between the average and the vulnerable consumer.[107]

The further construction of Europe will largely depend on whether it is possible and feasible to educate at least the majority of average citizens, workers and consumers so that they comply with the normative requirements of the EU *Leitbild.* Transnational integration via development of appropriate organic networks will largely depend on the – factual, not normative – success or failure of that transformation (education) project whose outcome is hard to predict. It might well be that the average citizen/worker/consumer will not meet the challenge and that the threefold distinction has to be replaced by a new, twofold differentiation: first an enlarged group of transnational elites and moral pioneers who meet the average standards and secondly the then larger group of vulnerable citizens/workers/consumers which would cover not only 'true' vulnerable parties but also the 'average' citizen/worker/consumer who fails the education process.

How will Europe deal with the group of vulnerable parties, be it smaller or larger? Are these the socially excluded who, according to the Lisbon Council of 2000, should be integrated into the 'most competitive economy of the world'? One might argue that protection of the weakest in society is not a task for the European Community but for member states and that at least with regard to this group the old consensus reached between the founding members in 1957 still applies. For good or ill, even in this highly sensitive area of the social domain, the EU Constitution as well as current EU primary and secondary Community law have already set the tone. My hypothesis is that EU law on universal services provides for the nucleus of a set of rules aiming at protection of the socially excluded.[108] This set of rules cuts across primary and secondary community law, public and private law, and provides a fertile ground for studying the interplay between constitutional values and private law issues.

Rethinking the Relationship between European Constitutional and European Private Law

The European Constitution is now part of the history of European integration. The Lisbon Treaty just passed the ratification procedure and will now absorb political and academic attention. The DCFR is still an academic project. Officially, the

106 With regard to labour law and in particular on correct interpretation of the Directive on posted workers, see Deakin 2008; Dougan 2009b: 12–13; with regard to consumer law, company law, capital market law and competition law, see Gsell and Herresthal 2009.

107 Different from Art. 5(3) of Directive 2005/29 on Unfair Commercial Practices.

108 See Micklitz 2009b.

European Civil Code project has not (yet) come to an end. Neither the European Commission, nor the Council, nor the European Parliament has taken a final position on the political future of the DCFR. Whatever the final position of the Community organs, the least that can be said is that its political future is uncertain.

However, a decisive conceptual difference exists between the two Grand Projects. The so-called European Constitution never was a constitution in the sense of the American or the French constitutions. That is why an even greater danger exists in that the promoters of the European Constitution might feel tempted to read into the Lisbon Treaty the original intentions and conceptual ideas which could not be realized and which ended in deadlock. This might indeed be feasible *because* the European Constitution never was meant to be a constitution but a further amendment to the Treaty of Rome. The DCFR is instead conceived as a fully fledged European Civil Code, even though labelled and marketed under a different acronym. The danger here is that the drafters, as well as the Community organs, despite the absence of official political support, will use the DCFR as a kind of a benchmark in the debate on the future development of European private law. The current debate over the European Commission Proposal on a Consumer Rights Directive[109] seems to prove the contrary, as the European Commission did not refer to the DCFR as a reference point for its solutions. However, the European Parliament[110] as well as the Economic and Social Committee[111] have criticised the European Commission exactly for this, for setting aside the DCFR. If the DCFR turns into a benchmark for law reform, the conceptual flaws lying behind the DCFR, the missing analysis of the European Regulatory Private Law, the missing collective dimension, as well as the missing integration of private regulation, would be neglected and set aside.

What is needed instead is to initiate a second round of research[112] which discusses the flaws, the deficiencies of the two Grand Projects and which takes their ideological preconceptions into account. My chapter may be a modest contribution to this debate and it is mainly written with the intention of highlighting the links between the two Grand Projects of a European Constitution and a European Civil Code. Perhaps the European Court of Justice is paving the way for joint research projects beyond merely academic considerations. In *Hamilton*,[113] the Court of Justice referred for the first time, if I am correct, to 'general principles of civil law'. This recalls a similar reference in early Court of Justice judgments some decades ago, when it started to refer to the 'common principles of constitutional

109 COM(2008) 614 final.

110 See the study by Hesselink (Booys, Hesselink and Mak 2009) on behalf of the European Parliament; and Schulte-Nölke 2009.

111 See OJ C 317, 23 December 2009: 54–61, for its opinion on the Commission Proposal for a Consumer Rights Directive.

112 See Micklitz and Cafaggi 2010 where we tried to outline the need for further research.

113 Case C-412/06, *Hamilton*, ECR 2008, I-2383, para 42.

law' mainly to justify the reference to human rights in its judgments. The short reference in *Hamilton* opens up a new horizon for research. What kinds of principles are meant here? Certainly not the ones the DCFR presents, since they do not contain principles but solutions. Why not develop these common principles in constitutional and private law jointly, thereby striving to overcome the boundaries between the two disciplines? However, any further research has to be aware that the role and function of Europe in the world has changed.[114] This is true for the construction of Europe as a federal state[115] as well as for building a European private legal order.[116] The outer boundaries of the two Grand Projects still deserve deeper analysis which reaches beyond the scope of this chapter.

References

Afilalo, A. and Patterson, D. 2008. *The New Global Trading Order – The Evolving State and the Future of Trade*. Cambridge: Cambridge University Press.

Albi, A. and Ziller, J. 2006. *The European Constitution and National Constitutions: Ratification and Beyond*. The Hague: Kluwer Law International.

Alter, K. 2001. *Establishing the Supremacy of European Law: The Making of the International Rule of Law*. Oxford: Oxford University Press.

Azoulai, L. 2008. The Court of Justice and the social market economy: The emergence of an ideal and the conditions for its realization. *Common Market Law Review*, 45:5, 1335–56.

Baquero Cruz, J. 2007. The Legacy of the Maastricht-Urteil and the Pluralist Movement. RSCAS Working Paper 2007/13.

Basedow, J. 1996. A common contract law for a common market. *Common Market Law Review*, 33:6, 1169–95.

Basedow, J. 2008a. Freedom of contract in the European Union. *European Review of Private Law*, 16:6, 901–23.

Basedow, J. 2008b. Der Grundsatz der Nichtdiskriminierung im europäischen Privatrecht. *Zeitschrift für Europäisches Privatrecht*, 2, 230–51.

Booys, T. de, Hesselink, M. and Rutgers, T. de. 2007. The legal basis for an optional instrument on European Contract Law. Centre for the Study of European Contract Law Working Paper No. 2007/04.

Booys, T. de, Hesselink, M. and Mak, C. 2009. *A Comparison between the Draft Common Frame of Reference and the European Commission's Proposal for a Consumer Rights Directive*. Available at: <http://www.europarl.europa.eu/studies> (accessed 2 March 2010).

Bourdieu, P. 1986. La force du droit: Éléments pour une sociologie du champ juridique. *Actes de la recherches en sciences sociales*, 64, 3–19.

114 See Majone 2009.

115 See Afilalo and Patterson 2008.

116 See Michaels and Jansen 2006; and Jansen and Michaels 2008.

Cafaggi, F. and Micklitz, H.-W. 2009. *New Frontiers of Consumer Law*. Mortsel: Intersentia.

Cherednychenko, O.O. 2008. *Fundamental Rights, Contract Law and the Protection of the Weaker Party: A Comparative Analysis of the Constitutionalisation of Contract Law with Emphasis on Risky Financial Transactions*. Münich: Sellier European Law Publishers.

Collins, H. 2008. *The European Civil Code – The Way Forward*. New York: Cambridge University Press.

Culpepper, P., Fagatto, E., Fung, A. and Lee, T. 2010 (forthcoming). *Beyond Elections? Deliberations of Democracy in the European Unio*n (on file with author).

Dam, C. van. 2009. Who is afraid of diversity? Cultural diversity, European co-operation, and European tort law. *King's Law Journal*, 20:2, 281–307.

Damjanovic, D. and Witte, B. de. 2009. Welfare integration through EU law: The overall picture in the light of the Lisbon Treaty, in *Integrating Welfare Functions into EU Law – From Rome to Lisbon*, edited by U. Neergard, R. Nielsen and L.M. Roseberry. Copenhagen: Djoef Publishing, 53–97.

Deakin, S. 2008. Regulatory competition after *Laval*, in *Cambridge Yearbook of European Legal Studies 2007–2008*, edited by C. Barnard. Portland: Hart Publishing, 581–609.

Dougan, M. 2009a. Expanding the frontiers of union citizenship by dismantling the territorial boundaries of the national welfare states? in *The Outer Limits of EU Law*, edited by C. Barnard and O. Odudu. Oxford: Hart Publishing, 119–66.

Dougan, M. 2009b. Minimum harmonisation after *Tobacco Advertising* and *Laval Un Partneri*, in *Views of European Law from the Mountain: Liber Amicorum Piet Jan Slot*, edited by M. Bulterman, L. Hancher, A. McDonnell and H. Sevenster. The Hague: Kluwer Law International, 12–13.

Fischer-Lescano, A., Rödl, F. and Schmid, C. 2009. *Europäische Gesellschaftsverfassung*. Baden-Baden: Nomos Verlag.

Frerichs, S. 2008. *Judicial Governance in der Europäischen Rechtsgemeinschaft, Integration durch Recht jenseits des Staates*. Baden-Baden: Nomos Verlag.

Glencross, A. and Trechsel, A. 2010 (forthcoming). First or second order referendums? Understanding the votes on the EU Constitutional Treaty in four EU member states. *West European Politics*.

Grimm, D. 1973. *Solidarität als Rechtsprinzip*. Frankfurt: Athenäum-Verlag.

Grundmann, S. (ed.) 2008. *Constitutional Values and European Contract Law*. Alphen aan den Rijn: Wolters Kluwer.

Gsell, B. and Herresthal, C. 2009. *Vollharmonisierung im Privatrecht, Die Konzeption der Richtlinie am Scheideweg?* Tübingen: Mohr Siebeck.

Haas, E.B. 1958. *The Uniting of Europe. Political, Social and Economic Forces, 1950–1957*. Stanford: Stanford University Press.

Hesselink, M. 2004. The politics of a European civil code. *European Law Journal*, 10:6, 694–7.

Hesselink, M.W. 2008. *CFR & Social Justice*. Münich: Sellier European Law Publishers.

James, H. 1997. Monetary and fiscal unification in nineteenth-century Germany: What can Kohl learn from Bismarck. *Essays in International Finance*, 202, 15–57.

James, H. 2009. Die Finanzkrise und ihre Herausforderung für Europa. TranState Working Papers, 105/2009.

Jansen, N. and Michaels, R. 2008. *Beyond the State? Rethinking Private Law*. Tübingen: Mohr Siebeeck.

Joerges, C. 2006. 'Deliberative political processes' revisited: What have we learnt about the legitimacy of supranational decision-making. *Journal of Common Market Studies*, 44:4, 779–802.

Joerges, C. 2009. A renaissance of the European eonomic constitution, in *Integrating Welfare Functions into EU Law – From Rome to Lisbon*, edited by U. Neergard, R. Nielsen and L.M. Roseberry. Copenhagen: Djoef Publishing.

Kelemen, D. 2003. The EU rights revolution: Adversial legalism and European integration, in *The State of the European Union*, edited by T.A. Börzel and R.A. Cichowski. Oxford: Oxford University Press, 221–35.

Kennedy, D. 2003. Two globalisations of law and legal thought: 1850–1968, *Suffolk University Law Review*, 36, 632–79.

Kennedy, D. 2006. Three globalisations of law and legal thought: 1850–2000, in *The New Law and Economic Development*, edited by D. Trubek and A. Santos. Cambridge: Cambridge University Press, 19–73.

Kosta, V. 2009. Internal market legislation and the private law of the member states – The impact of fundamental rights, in *The Impact of the Internal Market on Private Law of Member Countries*, edited by S. Gschwandtner, V. Kosta, H. Schebesta and P. Verbruggen, EUI Working Paper Law 2009/22, 17–30.

Kraus, P. 2004. *Europäische Öffentlichkeit und Sprachpolitik. Integration durch Anerkennung*. Frankfurt: Campus.

Kumm, M. 2005. The jurisprudence of constitutional conflict: Constitutional supremacy before and after the constitutional treaty. *European Law Journal*, 11:3, 262–307.

Leibfried, S. and Mau, S. 2008. *Welfare States: Construction, Deconstruction, Reconstruction*. Cheltenham: Edward Elgar Publishing.

Leibfried, S., Obinger, H. and Scharpf, F. 2005. Beipässe für ein soziales Europa: Lehren aus der Geschichte des westlichen Föderalismus. *Der Staat*, 44:4, 505–42.

Majone, G. 1996. *Regulating Europe*. New York: Routledge.

Majone, G. 2009. *Europe as the Would-Be World Power*. Cambridge: Cambridge University Press.

Mak, C. 2008. *Fundamental Rights in European Contract Law: A Comparison of the Impact of Fundamental Rights on Contractual Relationships in Germany, the Netherlands, Italy and England*. Alphen aan den Rijn: Kluwer Law International.

McGuire, M.-R. 2007. Ziel und Methode der Study Group on a European Civil Code, in *Auf halbem Weg – Vertragsrecht und europäische Privatrechtsvereinheitlichung, Deutsch-Polnisch-Ukrainisches Seminar in Krakau*, edited by U. Ernst. Cracow: Wydział Prawa i Administracji Uniwersytetu Jagiellońskiego, 225–46.

Michaels, R. and Jansen N. 2006. Private law beyond the state? Europeanization, globalization, Privatization. *American Journal of Comparative Law*, 54:4, 843–90.

Micklitz, H.-W. 1991. Consumer rights, in *European Union – The Human Rights Challenge, Human Rights and the European Community: The Substantive Law*, edited by A. Cassese, A. Clapham and J.H.H. Weiler. Florence: EUI, 53–110.

Micklitz, H.-W. 2005. *The Politics of Judicial Co-operation in the EU*. Cambridge: Cambridge University Press.

Micklitz, H.-W. 2007a. Review of academic approaches on the European Contract Law Codification Project, in *Liber Amicorum Guido Alpa Private Law Beyond the National Systems*, edited by M. Andenas, S. Diaz Alabart, Sir B. Markesinis, H.-W. Micklitz and N. Pasquino. London: British Institute of International and Comparative Law, 699–728.

Micklitz, H.-W. 2007b. Transborder law enforcement – Does it exist? in *The Regulation of Unfair Commercial Practices under EC Directive, New Rules and New Techniques*, edited by U. Bernitz and S. Weatherill. Oxford: Hart Publishing, 235–54.

Micklitz, H.-W. 2009a. Jack is out of the box – The efficient consumer–shopper. *Tidskrift utgiven av Juridiska Förening i Finland: Festskrift till Thomas Wihelmsson* (special issue edited by N. Bruun, J. Bärlund and F. Nyberg), 145:3–4, 417–36.

Micklitz, H.-W. 2009b. Universal Services: Nucleus for a *Social* European Private Law. EUI Working Paper, Law 2009/12.

Micklitz, H.-W. 2010a (forthcoming). From Social Justice to Access Justice in Private Law: The European Challenge. EUI Working Paper.

Micklitz, H.-W. 2010b (forthcoming). The visible hand of European regulatory private law – The transformation of European private law from autonomy to functionalism in competition and regulation, in *Yearbook of European Law 2009*, edited by P. Eeckhout and T. Tridimas. Oxford: Oxford University Press.

Micklitz, H.-W. and Cafaggi, F. 2010. *European Private Law After the Common Frame of Reference*. Cheltenham: Edward Elgar Publishing Ltd.

Micklitz, H.-W. and Reich, N. 2009. Crónica de una muerte anunciada: The Commission proposal for a 'Directive on Consumer Rights'. *Common Market Law Review*, 46:2, 471–519.

Micklitz, H.-W., Reich, N. and Weatherill, S. 2004. EU Treaty revision and consumer protection. *Journal of Consumer Policy*, 27:4, 367–99.

Moravcsik, A. 1993. Preferences and power in the European Community: A liberal intergovernmental approach. *Journal of Common Market Studies*, 31:4, 473–524.

Möslein, F. and Riesenhuber, K. 2009. Contract governance – A draft research agenda. *European Review of Contract Law*, 5:3, 248–89.

Münch, R. 2008. *Die Konstruktion der Europäischen Gesellschaft – Zur Dialektik transnationaler Integration und nationaler Desintegration*. Frankfurt am Main and New York: Campus.

Münch, R. 2010 (forthcoming). *European Governmentability. The Liberal Drift of Multilevel Governance*. London: Routledge.

Nickel, R. 2001. Handlungsaufträge zur Bekämpfung von ethnischen Diskriminierungen in der neuen Gleichbehandlungsrichtlinie 2000/43/EG. *Neue Juristische Wochenschrift*, 37, 2668–72.

Poiares Maduro, M. 1998. *We the Court – The European Court of Justice & the European Economic Constitution*. Oxford and Portland: Hart Publishing.

Poiares Maduro, M. 2003. Europe and the Constitution: What if this is as good as it gets? in *European Constitutionalism – Beyond the State*, edited by J.H.H. Weiler and M. Wind. Cambridge: Cambridge University Press, 74–102.

Reich, N. 1994. The 'November Revolution' of the European Court of Justice: Keck, Meng and Audi revisited. *Common Market Law Review*, 31, 459–92.

Reich, N. 2008. Gemeinschaftliche Verkehrsfreiheiten versus Nationales Arbeitskampfrecht. *Europäische Zeitschrift für Wirtschaftsrecht*, 18:13, 391–6.

Reich, N. 2010 (forthcoming). How proportionate is the proportionality principle in the internal market case law of the ECJ, in *The European Court of Justice and the Autonomy of the Member States*, edited by B. de Witte and H.-W. Micklitz. Antwerp and Oxford: Intersentia.

Rödl, F. 2009. Europäische Arbeitsverfassung, in *Europäisches Verfassungsrecht*, 2nd edition, edited by A. Bogdandy and J. Bast. Berlin: Springer, 855–903.

Rodotá, S. 2006. The Civil Code within the European constitutional process, in *The Politics of a European Civil Code*, edited by M.W. Hesselink. The Hague: Kluwer Law International, 115–24.

Rott, P. 2009. Cross-border collective damage actions in the EU, in *New Frontiers of Consumer Law*, edited by F. Cafaggi and H.-W. Micklitz. Mortsel: Intersentia.

Rott, P. and Terryn, E. 2009. The proposal for a Directive on Consumer Rights. *Zeitschrift für Europäisches Privatrecht*, 3, 456–88.

Säcker, F.-J. 2004. Europäische Diskriminierungsverbote und deutsches Zivilrecht. *Kritische Gedanken zur Ergänzung des BGB durch Antidiskriminierungsvorschriften, BB – Special*, 59:6, 16–19.

Salais, R. 2006. Reforming the European social policy and the politics of indicators, in *Unwrapping the European Social Model*, edited by M. Jepsen and A. Serrano. Bristol: Policy Press, 189–212.

Saumier, G. 2009. Transborder litigation and international private law: The view from Canada, in *New Frontiers of Consumer Law*, edited by F. Cafaggi and H.-W. Micklitz. Mortsel: Intersentia, 361–77.

Scharpf, F. 1999. *Governing in Europe: Effective and Democratic*. Oxford: Oxford University Press.

Scharpf, F. 2002. The European social model: Coping with the challenges of diversity. *Journal of Common Market Studies*, 40:4, 645–70.

Scharpf, F. 2008. Der einzige Weg ist, dem EuGH nicht zu folgen. *Die Mitbestimmung*, 7/8, 19–23.

Scharpf, F. 2009a. Legitimacy in the multilevel European polity. *European Political Science Review*, 1:2, 173–204.

Scharpf, F. 2009b. The only solution is to refuse to comply with ECJ rulings. *Social Europe Journal*, 4:1, 16–21.

Schepel, H. and Wesseling, R. 1997. The legal community: Judges, lawyers and clerks in the writing of Europe. *European Law Journal*, 3:2, 165–88.

Schulte-Nölke, H. 2009. *The Potential Impact of the Consumer Rights' Directive on the Member States' Contract Law*. Available at: <http://www.europarl.europa.eu/studies> (accessed 2 March 2010).

Schulze, R. 2008. *Common Frame of Reference and Existing EC Contract Law*. Münich: Sellier European Law Publishers.

Schwensfeier, H.R. 2009. *Individual's Access to Justice Under Community Law*. LL.D. Dissertation, University of Groningen.

Slepcevic, R. 2009a. The judicial enforcement of EU law through national courts: Possibilities and limits. *Journal of European Public Policy*, 16:3, 378–94.

Slepcevic, R. 2009b. On the Strategic Use of the Preliminary Reference Procedure, Plausible Assumptions v. Empirical Reality, EUI Working Papers, Max Weber Programme, 2009/24.

Smits, J. 2010. The Draft Common Frame of Reference: How to improve it? in *European Private Law after the Common Frame of Reference*, edited by H.-W. Micklitz and F. Cafaggi. Cheltenham: Edward Elgar Publishing, Ch. 5.

Social Justice Study Group. 2004. Social justice in European contract law: A manifesto. *European Law Journal* 10:6, 653–74.

Somek, A. 2005. Catholic concordance, exploring the context of European anti-discrimination law and policy. *Journal of Transnational Law and Contemporary Problems*, 14, 959–1006.

Stadler, A. 2009. Die grenzüberschreitende Durchsetzbarkeit von Sammelklagen, in *Auf dem Wege zu einer europäischen Sammelklage*, edited by M. Caspar, A. Janssen, P. Pohlmann and R. Schulze. Münich: Sellier European Law Publishers, 149–68.

Tonner, K. and Tamm, M. 2009. Der Vorschlag einer Richtlinie über Rechte der Verbraucher und seine Auswirkungen auf das nationale Verbraucherrecht, *Juristen Zeitung*, 64:6, 277–90.

Walker, N. 2007. Post-constituent constitutionalism: The case of the European Union, in *Constituent Power and Constitutional Form*, edited by N. Walker and M. Loughlin. Oxford: Oxford University Press, 247–68.

Weatherill, S. 2006. European private law and the constitutional dimension, in *The Institutional Framework of European Private Law*, edited by F. Cafaggi. Oxford: Oxford University Press, 79–106.

Weiler, J.H.H. 1995. European democracy and its critique. *West European Politics*, 18:3, 4–39.

Weiler, J.H.H. 1999. *The Constitution of Europe*. 1999. Cambridge: Cambridge University Press.

Whittaker, S. 2009. A framework of principles for European contract law. *The Law Quarterly Review*, 125, 616–47.

Wilhelmsson, T. 2004. Varieties of welfarism in European contract law. *European Law Journal*, 10:6, 712–33.

Wilhelmsson, T. 2007. Introduction: Harmonisation and national cultures, in *Private Law and the Many Cultures of Europe*, edited by T. Wilhelmsson, E. Paunio and A. Pohjolainen. Alphen aan den Rijn: Kluwer Law International, 3–20.

Wilhelmsson, T., Paunio, E. and Pohjolainen, A. 2007. *Private Law and the Many Cultures of Europe*. Alphen aan den Rijn: Kluwer Law International.

Wunder, A. 2008. The Usage of Solidarity in the Jurisdiction of the ECJ: Symbolism or a European Legal Concept? LL.M. Thesis, Florence: EUI.

PART III
Aspects of the Political Constitution

Chapter 7
Multilevel Constitutionalism: Looking Beyond the German Debate

Neil Walker

Two Conceptions of Multilevel Constitutionalism

Multilevel constitutionalism has both a narrow and a broad reference. Narrowly, it refers to a particular school of thinking about contemporary constitutional developments centred on the work of the German scholar Ingolf Pernice and his associates. This approach emerged in the mid to late 1990s in response to the dominant *Staatsrecht* tradition in German public law and as an alternative way of conceiving of constitutional authority in the face of the exponential growth of the supranational European Union. It was an approach that sparked significant interest both within and beyond the German context, resonating closely with the emerging intellectual and political project to endow the EU with a more or less formal constitutional status. However, as the term 'multilevel constitutionalism' became more familiar within legal academic discourse, it no longer remained confined to its original *problématique*, or even to its German and European domicile. Instead, it gradually came to be adopted as a label, or at least as an initial point of reference, for any position that maintained that constitutional ideas, institutions, norms and practices could apply in settings beyond the state.[1]

The main purpose of the present chapter is to examine this more expansive notion of multilevel constitutionalism – or multilevel constitutionalism *senso lato*. In so doing, the chapter seeks to confront the most basic questions of principle about the present and future of constitutionalism in an age of intense globalization of economic, cultural, political and legal circuits of power. First, the threshold question: is it possible even to conceive of constitutionalism as something that ranges beyond the state while remaining relevant at the level of the state, and so as applicable at multiple sites of authority simultaneously? Secondly, to the extent that it is possible, what form does the proper constitutional expression of this new

1 To take but two examples of the diffusion of multilevel constitutionalism, both Jürgen Habermas and Ernst-Ulrich Petersmann from their quite different philosophical and normative starting points are content to use the label to endorse their in-principle support for transnational constitutionalism. See, for example, Habermas 2006: 115–93 and Petersmann 2006.

'post-national constellation'[2] take? In particular, where lie the outer boundaries of the post-national constitutional constellation, and what kind of juridical entities in what kind of relations *inter se* describe its internal structure?

However, before posing these broad questions something should be said about multilevel constitutionalism *senso stricto*, and this for a number of reasons. First, the contribution of Pernice and his associates has been influential in its own terms, and not simply as the source of a popular label. Secondly, in concentrating on the European supranational arena, this body of work has focused upon the domain of legal and political development supplying the initial, the most insistent and the most sustained contemporary challenge to the idea that constitutionalism should be confined to the state. Thirdly, in the terms and in the tone of the initial debate between the defenders and opponents of multilevel constitutionalism, much of the sense of deep division that has come to characterize the broader debate on the future of constitutionalism in the age of globalization can be seen. And fourthly, the circumstances leading to the coining of the multilevel conceptual currency may well have encouraged a certain narrowness of emphasis both in the original choice of terminology and its subsequent pattern of deployment, so raising an alert to the difficulty of capturing under the sign of multilevel constitutionalism all that might profitably be said about the post-national constitutional constellation.

The German Debate

In 1995 Ingolf Pernice proposed the idea of *Verfassungsverbund* to encapsulate the constitutional novelty of the EU.[3] In so doing, he drew an explicit contrast between his position and that of the German Constitutional Court in its famous *Maastricht Urteil* of 1993.[4] In a judgment widely interpreted then and now as a reassertion of the sovereign authority of the state and as a warning against any future demonstration of the expansionist ambition expressed by the EU in the Treaty of Maastricht, the Court chose to characterize the new supranational configuration in more modest state-derivative terms, as a *Staatenverbund*.[5] All candidate English renditions of the two key terms in the German debate are clumsy and lacking in nuance, and these translation problems exacerbate what is already a difficult exercise in conceptualization. Whereas *Staatenverbund* refers, roughly speaking, to a compound of states, *Verfassungsverbund* seeks to capture the same sense of a composite arrangement, but one whose genetic code is constitutional rather than statal. Yet in replacing 'state' with 'constitution' like is not really being replaced with like. Whereas 'state' is clearly a nominal category, 'constitution' is

---

2 See Habermas 2001.

3 At a conference in Lausanne. See Pernice 1995: 261*ff*; 1996; 2001: 163.

4 See BVerfGE89, 155; or *Brunner* v *European Union Treaty* [1994] 1 CMLR 57.

5 A term previously used in an extrajudicial context by Paul Kirchhof, the judge rapporteur of the Maastricht decision. See Kirchhof 1993: para. 69.

ambiguously poised between the nominal and the adjectival. It follows that it is unclear whether *Verfassungsverbund* is better translated as a single constitutional compound (or as a composite constitution) or as a system of compound (or composite) constitutions. The French translation of the German original preferred by Pernice, *constitution composée*,[6] opts for the singular, whereas the term employed by Pernice to disseminate his ideas in the Anglophone world – that of 'multilevel constitutionalism' itself[7] – consolidates the ambiguity by focusing on the abstract quality of constitutional*ism* rather than on a concrete constitutional entity or entities.

However, this is a doubt that Pernice's theoretical enterprise can accommodate with reasonable comfort. For his deeper message is that once 'constitution' rather than 'state' is understood to be the governing regulatory category, the question of how many specific such 'constitutional' units or entities exist is of less moment. Whereas 'state' as a particularizing category suggests singularity and mutual exclusivity of public authority, 'constitutional' as a universalizing category suggests continuity and complementarity of public authority. Pernice's detailed formulations of multilevel constitutionalism underline the fuzziness of boundaries by stressing the centrality of an interactive process of establishing, organizing, sharing and limiting powers.[8] The multilevel constitution is citizen-centred – including a strong focus on individual rights – rather than polity-centred. In so far as it does individuate the polities or 'levels' of the overall configuration, it does not understand their relations in hierarchical terms. Rather, sovereignty is pooled, so that at the level both of cultural identity and of institutional function and loyalty the relations between the state and the supranational platforms are not to be regarded in either/or zero-sum terms, but rather as an interlocking, overlapping and positive-sum whole.

As already intimated, the theory of multilevel constitutionalism *senso stricto* stands as a significant formative influence and background frame for the idea of multilevel constitutionalism *senso lato*. Pernice's theory has been highly influential, especially in the German-speaking academic world, in the development of understandings of the constitutional structure of the European juridical space as a complex and inclusive unity.[9] This influence also acquires a practical edge. In drawing so heavily on the existing pattern of interlocking national and supranational public authority in making its own particular variant of the constitutional argument,

---

6 Pernice and Mayer 2000.

7 First at a conference in Bristol, England, in 1998, see Pernice 1998. See also, Pernice 1999, 2002.

8 See, for example, Pernice 1999.

9 For other conceptions of the EU as a complex unity, see, for example, Bogdandy 2000; Curtin and Dekker 1999, 2002. As is made quite explicit in the work of Pernice (1998, 1999, 2002), Bogdandy (2000) and others, the idea of a complex, internally differentiated constitutional unity owes much to a historical understanding of federalism as a template of decentralized political organization possessing a resilient quality of internal order without necessarily being state-based. See, more broadly, Beaud 2007 and Avbelj 2009.

the multilevel constitutionalist mindset has contributed to the case for viewing the EU in constitutional terms *whether or not* its constitutional status should ever come to be recognized and dignified in the form of a 'Big-C'[10] documentary constitution.[11] Such a generous approach to constitutional branding has in turn established a sharp and lasting break with the kind of constitutional nationalism reflected in the *Staatenverbund* approach, and in so doing has supplied a typically stark context of disputation in the argument over whether constitutionalism can and should spread beyond the state.[12]

Yet if state-centred constitutionalism clearly marks the inner boundary of Pernice's multilevel constitutionalism, its terms and context of application also suggests something about its outer limits. To some at least, the idea of 'levels' continues to imply a notion of hierarchy – of higher and lower – rather than simply one of dispersed parts, and this hint of subservience to 'the higher level' can reinforce the anxiety not only of the defenders of state constitutionalism but also of all who are wary of conceiving of supranational or transnational constitutionalism in 'top-down' regional or global terms.[13] What is more, the notion of a unity, however dispersed and complex, evoked by the idea of a single-cloth constitutional*ism*, speaks to a degree of harmony between the state and non-statal parts that may not be endorsed by more 'pluralist'[14] visions of the relations between different constitutional sites. And finally, the focus of the theory of multilevel constitutionalism *senso stricto* on the European Union, which, on the one hand, stands as a kind of advance challenge to the constitutional hegemony of the state, but on the other, is relatively 'state-like' in many of its own constitutional features, leaves it with little to say about those other forms of transnational constitutionalism – actual or potential – that lack the authoritative scope, institutional intensity, and breadth and depth of cultural identification of the European regional model.

The Wider Debate and the Politics of Constitutional Definition

For much of the modern age of constitutionalism inaugurated by the French and American revolutions, the kind of position struck by Ingolf Pernice and his associates would simply have been unimaginable. The modern state, understood as the key unit within the global framework of authority, was for long the undisputed

10 See, for example, Walker 2006.

11 For example, Pernice has recently argued that, notwithstanding the failure of the 2004 Constitutional Treaty, the explicitly non-constitutional Treaty of Lisbon that has taken its place should be viewed as an example of multilevel constitutionalism in action. See Pernice 2009.

12 For a historically sensitive overview of the German debate, see Murkens 2007.

13 On the authoritarian dangers implicit in international or transnational constitutionalism, see Koskenniemi 2007.

14 See, for example, Walker 2002.

domicile of constitutionalism and the guarantor of its relevance. It was only in the late twentieth century, when the configuration of economic, political and cultural forces that produced the state-centred global framework of authority was no longer so securely in place, that the idea of multilevel constitutionalism *senso lato* – as concerned with the very possibility of constitutionalism beyond the state – could gain any traction in Europe or elsewhere. Like 'multi-level governance',[15] its even better-known sister concept in political science, the advent of multilevel constitutionalism is a product first and foremost of objective changes in the socio-political world rather than of innovation in the world of ideas. Yet for all that it is events-driven, the emergent debate over multilevel constitutionalism *senso lato* has proved to be at once highly charged and extremely fragmented. If we begin by investigating why this is the case and look at how disagreement and disengagement have tended to manifest themselves, this will clear the ground for an examination of what is most fundamentally at stake between the proponents and opponents of multilevel constitutionalism.

An initial survey of the debate over multilevel constitutionalism *senso lato* reveals an exaggerated version of a familiar problem. As is common when dealing with social and political concepts that register both at the 'object' level of everyday use and at the 'observer' level of theoretical inquiry, the answers that many analysts seek or expect when addressing the prospects of constitutionalism seem often to be anticipated in their stipulation of the definitional preliminaries. However, just because so much uncertainty surrounds a conceptual leap of such audacious proportions as is contemplated in taking constitutionalism beyond the state, the absence of agreement over definitional preliminaries is *uncommonly* pronounced and conspicuous in the instant case. In turn, this fractured beginning leads to an unusually sharp polarization of theoretical positions. In effect, one is faced with an irony of overproduction. On the one hand, in academic circles at least, the unsettling of old taken-for-granted certainties about the place of constitutionalism within the global scheme means that never has discussion of law and politics so frequently, so explicitly and so self-consciously occurred within a constitutional register. Likewise, never has the constitutional idea been so insistently reasserted in its old state setting or so vigorously sponsored in new non-state settings. On the other hand, just because the stakes are so high and the value of the currency so volatile, never has discussion of constitutionalism cultivated such little common ground.[16] Scant cross-fertilization occurs from the different points of departure, and what exchange does take place often appears to be the dialogue of the deaf.

This is not intended as a partisan point. Those who want or expect constitutionalism to travel to sites and levels of operation beyond its traditional state domicile are as likely to load the conceptual dice in favour of their preferred conclusion as those who start from the prejudice that no such

15 See Marks, Hooghe and Blank 1996.

16 See, for example, Walker 2002.

mobility is possible or desirable. What is more, each side tends to encourage the other in its conceptual myopia.

On the part of advocates of constitutionalism in multiple sites and contexts beyond the state, a whole series of conceptual starting points is encountered that are in danger of treating constitutionalism in superficial terms – as too easily detached from its statist moorings. This is most evident in the case of what are best described as *nominal* definitions of constitutionalism. Here, constitutionalism is deployed merely as an affirmative label for whatever concept, institution, or attitude of governance, wherever situated, that its sponsor endorses or considers pivotal to the regulatory regime in question, whether human rights protection, anti-discrimination measures, or even just a commitment to 'the Rule of Law' is being talked about. The purpose here is ideological: to clothe the feature(s) of governance to which one is committed or to which one attributes central significance with the additional gravitas of affirmation in a powerful and familiar symbolic register, or to deny such affirmation to other approaches that lack the favoured feature(s) or even oppose the priority given to them. Implicit in this ideological agenda stands the conviction, or at least the unexamined premise, that simply nothing privileges the relationship between the state and constitutionalism, so that nothing of special value stands to be lost in the move beyond that relationship. In sum, the point of the nominalist position is precisely *not to argue* the case for mobility of the constitutional idea beyond the state but, by treating constitutionalism as a floating signifier, to elevate the case to the exalted position of the unarguably correct. Yet one must be careful not to be too critical of nominalist positions. Good arguments are often made for this or that aspect of governance from within a nominalist position; it is just that these arguments are not enhanced by the use of constitutional language. As will be discussed below, nominalism often shades into formalism or materialism, and indeed formal or material borrowing from the state tradition may be the inarticulate premise underlying the nominalist position. Moreover, nominalism may connect to the vital 'placeholding' function of constitutionalism, in that through its insistence on a constitutional register it speaks not only to a desire to obtain ideological advantage for one's position, but also to an awareness of how much remains at stake in the very idea of a political framing of social arrangements.[17]

A second deracinated version of constitutionalism concentrates on *formal* features. Unlike nominalism, here the state, as the undisputed source of the modern constitutional idea, retains some influence over the destination meaning, if much attenuated. The formalist approach suggests that the very manner in which – the form through which – the political world may be understood and organized from a juridical perspective may borrow from or be inspired by the state constitutional template. This is most obviously the case with regard to the idea of a constitutive juridical instrument, whether or not specifically so-called 'Constitutional' (as

17 For just one example of a writer who uses the language of transnational constitutionalism in this loose but provocative way, see Joerges 2001.

in the case of the abortive EU constitutional text of 2004),[18] that is so familiar from state public law. In the context of non-state legal and institutional orders, instruments may be found that are similarly formally constitutive in one or more of various senses; whether with reference to their norm-generative or foundational quality, their assertion of entrenched status, their precedence over other system norms, or their claim to provide an encompassing framework for and measure of the limits of the 'body politic' that they create or recognize.[19] And even where such generative, entrenched, trumping, embracing and delimiting features of a legal and institutional order are independent of a self-styled documentary Constitution, or indeed of a single and unrivalled constitutive instrument of any sort, as has been seen in the case of the advocates of WTO constitutionalism,[20] or of the constitutionalization of the international order,[21] or of the various 'civic' or 'societal' constitutions such as the *lex mercatoria* of the international economy or the *lex digitalis* of the Internet,[22] the mere emergence of some combination of these formal features may still be enough for the juridical initiative in question to be deemed constitutional in kind.

A third form of constitutionalism beyond the state, and the one to which the approach sponsored under multilevel constitutionalism *senso stricto* is closest in conception,[23] concentrates not on formal matters but on the manifestation of a family resemblance between certain *material* features of state constitutionalism and the new transnational legal outgrowth. Aspects of transnational law are deemed to be constitutional not, or not only, because they appear on the commentator's approved list, as with nominalism, but because the mechanisms or concepts in question – from general structural formulae such as separation of powers and institutional balance to more specific principles such as subsidiarity or proportionality – were long ago nurtured in the state constitutional context and, indeed, have often been self-consciously received into transnational law from these state sources.[24] However,

18 Treaty Establishing a Constitution for Europe, 16 December 2004, OJ 2004/ C310, 1–474.

19 For a concise statement of the formalist position, see Stone Sweet 2009.

20 See, for example, Cass 2005 and Petersmann 2000.

21 See, for example, Wet 2006. For an approach which, unusually, seeks to locate the constitutionalization of the international order in documentary terms – in the form of the UN Charter – see Fassbender 1998.

22 See, for example, Teubner 2004; and Teubner and Fischer-Lescano 2004.

23 One must be careful not to overstate this. While this is certainly where much of its practical emphasis lies, multilevel constitutionalism *senso stricto*, as set out in the work of Pernice (1998, 1999, 2002), is by no means only concerned with the incidence and development of material constitutional norms beyond the state. In addition, it is concerned with the variety of formal centres of legal authority, and indeed with the 'federal' co-existence of different levels of political community and identity (see Bogdandy 2000; Curtin and Dekker 1999, 2002; Beaud 2007; and Avbelj 2009).

24 On the migration of particular constitutional concepts from national to transnational level, see Walker 2007a.

as is the case with formalism, the connection between the non-state version and the state original from the materialist perspective is a tenuous one. It is dependent upon analogy, and in some cases conscious imitation. How deep the analogy runs and what is lost – or gained – in translation from one context to another is rarely the subject of sustained analysis.[25]

If one turns, now, to those who would oppose the movement of constitutionalism beyond the state and reject any prospect of multilevel constitutionalism *senso lato*, again they range from the primitive to the more sophisticated. Most basically, and more commonly within everyday 'object' discourse than in academic 'observer' discourse, a position exists that holds that the category of constitution is *necessarily* restricted to the state. That position is the negative image of nominalism, and just as impervious to counter-suggestion. Whereas nominalism holds to or more often simply assumes the solipsistic idea that all meaning is constructed without extra-linguistic check or constraint, *essentialism* holds to or more often simply assumes the opposite. It maintains that meaning is fixed and invariable in its correspondence with some extra-linguistic reality, and so it follows that it is simply *meaningless* to conceive of constitutionalism beyond the fixed and invariable limits of the state.

Beyond essentialism there are at least two positions – or rather a continuum of possibilities framed by two positions – that treat the idea of the constitution as deeply embedded in the state. One position is *culturalist* in nature. It holds the idea of a constitution to be hollow, or at least deficient, in the absence of certain attributes, including the idea of a democratically self-constituting and self-constituted 'people' possessing comprehensive powers of self-determination and self-legislation. These attributes, so the claim goes, are ultimately contingent upon certain prior or emergent socio-cultural facts concerning identity, solidarity and allegiance, absent which any self-styled constitutional project is fated to be either a dead letter or a much more modest affair. Since only the modern state has known such a socio-cultural formation, and since even if the modern state is no longer so robust in these terms that it still constitutes a standing impediment to the development of similar cultural formations at non-state sites, no real prospect can exist of a full constitutionalism beyond the state.[26]

A second position runs even deeper than the culturalist argument, though without succumbing to the semantic sting of state-centred essentialism. This approach may be called *epistemic* in that it focuses on the very idea of the modern state and of the political imaginary associated with the idea of the modern state as embracing 'a scheme of intelligibility … a comprehensive way of seeing, understanding and acting in the world'[27] that is prior to and prerequisite to a full, modern articulation of the idea of constitution. The key insight here, and what distinguishes it from the culturalist position, is that the concept of the modern state, understood as a particular type of relationship between territory, ruling

25 For one attempt, see Walker 2003.

26 See, for example, Grimm 2005.

27 See Loughlin 2009.

authority and people, consists not merely of the expression and fruit of a prior cultural achievement – an accomplishment of national solidarity that supplies the 'battery of power'[28] necessary to run the constitutional machine effectively. More than that, it is a political way of knowing and way of being in the absence of whose emergence the very idea of a constitutional polity is simply unimaginable. Both cases – culturalist and epistemic – strongly convey the message that the modern idea and practice of constitutionalism could not have developed except in the context and through the container of the state, and while this does not, as matter of logical necessity, rule out the possibility of a similar constitutionalism emerging in multiple contexts and through a container other than the state, it certainly stacks the odds against such a development and places a heavy burden on the defenders of post-state constitutionalism to explain just how this is possible.

Constitutionalism and Meta-Politics

This brief examination of nominalist, formalist and materialist positions on the one side of the issue and of essentialist, culturalist and epistemic approaches on the other side of the issue underlines the difficulty in finding common cause in the debate about multilevel constitutionalism *senso lato*. How, if at all, does one move beyond this divide? Such a possibility would seem to depend upon trying to ascertain what is *most* basically at stake – *more* basically than is revealed in the various debate-closing applications of constitutional language – in the various positions, and upon locating some overlapping ground at this more basic level. Clearly, the extreme positions of nominalism and essentialism are distinguished on the one hand by blindness to any argument that would confer any special title to the state and on the other by blindness to any trace of constitutionalism beyond the state. The assumptions and arguments behind this opposition only begin to become articulate in the other, more moderate positions. On the one hand, the formalists and the materialists suggest that something of value may be retained and adapted from the state tradition when one relocates to post-state contexts. In the case of formalism, the key to translation, so to speak, is abstraction, whereas in the case of substantivism the key is disaggregation. In the former case, the very idea of a cohesive legal and institutional order is seen as the basis of certain constitutional virtues in new contexts as much as in old, whereas in the latter the implication is that one can pick some features out of the state constitutional mix, such as a Charter of Rights or a system of inter-institutional checks and balances, and these features will remain of significant value despite being deprived of either the fuller legal framework or the deeper socio-cultural context of the state. On the other hand, the culturalist and epistemic arguments see the same glass as half-empty rather than half-full. For them, the new is an inadequate pastiche of the old rather than a contextually appropriate adaptation. The post-state constitution is a machine that,

28 Canovan 1996: 80.

in the culturalist critique, is deprived of the crude social energy to power itself sufficiently or, in the epistemic critique, lacks the intelligent background software necessary to understand and activate its own operating procedures.

In the final analysis, if one is to overcome this opposition one must look beyond the reductive commitments and self-vindicating judgments of even the more thoughtful of the state-centred and multilevel positions. It must be asked whether something more general is at issue that is capable of being acknowledged within both mindsets, and which can therefore serve as a common point from which to investigate their differences. Therefore, what is needed in methodological terms is a way of treating constitutionalism that is alert to this possibility; a split perspective capable of identifying common ground at one level while at another level continuing to acknowledge difference *in terms of* that common ground. Such a split perspective can be supplied, it is submitted, by recasting the debate in functional terms; no longer as a one-dimensional contest over diverse and rival conceptions of the ends of constitutionalism understood as ends that either are or are not exclusively associated with the state, but as a debate over diverse and rival conceptions of the constitutional means necessary to ends that would themselves be capable of commanding general agreement across state-centred and multilevel positions.

But in order to be genuinely inclusive and not simply to impose an artificial consensus, any such definition of ends must proceed at a very high level of abstraction. At this rarified level, what implicitly unites the two mindsets is a sense, corroborated both by the etymology of the constitutional idea and by its range of applications prior to the age of the modern state, that constitutionalism serves a deep and abiding function in human affairs, namely the meta-political function of shaping the domain of politics broadly conceived – of literally 'constituting' the body politic.[29] More expansively, constitutionalism in this deepest meta-political sense may be understood as referring to that species of practical reasoning which, in the name of some defensible locus of common interest, concerns itself with the organization and regulation of those spheres of collective decision-making deemed relevant to the common interest in a manner that is adequately informed by the common interest. Furthermore, if one is to avoid simply repeating the familiar definitional impasse at this more general level, the meta-political sense of the 'common interest' underpinning the collective decision-making capacities as understood in each of its three key registers – authoritative (in whose name?), jurisdictional (covering which collective decision-making capacities?) and purposive (to what end, and how?) – must, in addition, be acknowledged as possessing an open, and indeed a reflexive quality. Therefore, one cannot either stipulate in advance or treat as permanently resolved what are the appropriate sites for pursuit of the common interest, or what are the appropriate terms of engagement between these sites, or what kinds of things fall within the remit of the common interest, or what is the proper relationship between individual and

29 See, for example, Maddox 1982. See also Walker 2008b.

collective goods or preferences in the identification and pursuit of the common interest. All of these are matters themselves apt for decision in accordance with the common interest, understood as located at the very deepest level of political self-understanding and self-inquiry, and so as necessarily possessing a self-challenging and self-amending quality. Accordingly, if, as is suggested, constitutionalism is equated with the deepest sense of meta-political inquiry, one cannot simply decide *a priori* to equate the common interest with the national or state interest, and so corroborate an initial theoretical preference for state constitutionalism. Equally, one cannot simply assume that post-state sites are as appropriate as are states as authoritative sources of the common interest, as jurisdictional containers of the common interest, or as forums and institutional mechanisms for specifying the common interest, and thus simply wish away the state legacy in favour of a multilevel perspective.

Instead, in order to advance the inquiry and find a point of contentious engagement between the two mindsets, one must turn to a second level of inquiry – to the question of adequacy of means. If the common interest conceived of as the ultimate end of the constitutional project sounds at a level of abstraction – and of perpetual contestability – that does not necessarily or even presumptively discriminate between state and post-state sites, does something about the appropriateness of the means nevertheless pull in one direction rather than another? Is something about the constitutional method available in and supported by the state context more adequate to pursuit of the common interest than is any constitutional method available in and supported by post-state contexts?[30] To answer that question one must first ask what, if anything, is distinctive to the constitutional method that has been available in and supported by the state. Then one must inquire whether that method, or any constitutional method or combination of methods that is the instrumental equivalent of the state constitutional method, may also be available or be made available in multiple sites beyond the state.

Holistic Constitutionalism

The modern state does indeed possess a distinctive constitutional method, best understood as possessing a holistic quality. In a nutshell, the holistic method is a method of constitutional articulation and engagement in which the authority and meaning of the various parts are understood and treated as dependent on

---

30 Note that this challenge, as well as querying the force of the formalist and materialist arguments in favour of post-state constitutionalism, also brings back in many of the concerns of the culturalist and epistemic critics of post-state constitutionalism. However, it does so in terms that, by more clearly specifying the distinction between (state) means and (constitutional) ends, are less at risk of reducing the connection between state and constitution to a tautology.

the integrity of the whole.[31] As will be seen, this holistic feature is no isolated thread, but something that affords texture to the various different aspects of state constitutionalism.

However, to appreciate this something more must first be said about the constitutional concept itself. In so doing, one is no longer concerned, as in the previous section, with constitutionalism in the abstract – as a theoretical concept for making sense of and evaluating the social world, but with constitutionalism in the concrete – as an 'object' already at use 'in' the social world, and in the social world of the state in particular. Considered as such an 'object' concept, state constitutionalism can be viewed both diachronically and synchronically. Diachronically, state constitutionalism in the modern age describes a particular high point of accumulation of various distinct layers of situated 'constitutional' practice that have operated separately or in different combinations in the past. These layers are juridical, politico-institutional, popular and societal.[32] Synchronically, state constitutionalism operates in terms of its own particular formulation of these layers and of their relationship with one another. In other words, constitutionalism in (state) practice behaves as a 'cluster concept',[33] associated simultaneously with a number of different but themselves interrelated definitive criteria.

In each of its four layers – or, if you like, in different parts of the cluster – constitutionalism can be observed operating holistically, offering an encompassing frame for the 'constitutive' representation[34] and regulation of each of the particular dimensions of social 'reality' with which it is concerned. What is more, in the constellation of connections made under the sign of modern state constitutionalism between each of these layers, a further 'frame of frames,' or 'holism of holisms' can also be discerned. Each of the holistic frames of state constitutionalism will now be looked at more closely, first separately, and then in combination.

To begin with, the juridical frame refers to an idea of self-contained legal order, complete with rules of self-production, self-organization, self-extension, self-interpretation, self-amendment, and self-discipline, all of which combine to affirm the autonomous existence and comprehensive authority of the legal order against other internal and external normative forces. The politico-institutional frame refers to a system of institutional specification and differentiation of the sphere of the public and the political. Whereas the idea of autonomous legal order long predates modernity and the modern state, the idea of a secular, specialized

31 See more generally, Walker 2010. For an insightful but rather different treatment of holism, treated not as the basic *organizing method* of modern political life, as in the present case, but as a descriptor of the key *ontological unit* in the ordering of political society (and so considered as equivalent to a fundamentally *pre-modern* idea of indivisible community, and contrasted with modern individualism), see Bogdandy and Dellavalle 2009.

32 See Walker 2008b; and with specific reference to the EU, see Walker 2007b: 59.

33 Connolly 1993: 14.

34 On the ways in which acts of representation of a legal object are routinely (re)constitutive of that legal object, see, for example, Lindahl 2003.

and institutionally defined and delimited political realm, free from deference to particular interests or to any idea of transcendental order, is a key emergent feature of modernity. It is marked by a double move away from pre-modern forms of authority, involving both drawing a general distinction between public and private spheres of influence domains and integration of the public into a single and comprehensive political domain. What is more, the creation and sustenance of this singular political domain, and indeed consolidation of the autonomous legal order, depend upon 'the structural coupling'[35] and mutual support of the two self-contained spheres of the legal and the political.

For its part, the popular frame refers to the dimension of 'we the people', and so to the idea of the specialized and integrated public institutional realm being underpinned not just by the autonomy of the political but also by its democratic self-constitution and self-authorship. Finally, the societal frame refers to the idea that the constitution pertains to a particular 'society', self-understood and self-identified as such. Here the framing work of the constitution is mostly symbolic rather than normative. The constitution depends for its normative effectiveness as a design for a reasonably cooperative and commonly committed form of common living on the plausibility of the very idea of an integrated society – whether the emphasis is on the thin 'political society' of the state or the thicker 'cultural society' of the nation – that its very production and perseverance *as* a constitution seeks to announce and promote.

If one looks more closely at the points of interconnection between the various frames, one can begin to appreciate how a broader 'holism of constitutional holisms' emerges under the template of the modern state. At the juridical and politico-institutional levels, the constitutional order (sometimes in conjunction with self-styled 'organic laws') typically places a mix of *structural* (politico-institutional level) and *substantive* (juridical level) requirements on public actors, which may be either specific functional institutions (e.g. industry-specific regulators) or generic government organs – parliament, executive and judiciary. The structural requirements are both internal and external. They are concerned with the internal governance system of the institution in question – decision-making procedures, representational rules, internal review and accountability rules, and so on, as well as with the situation of the institution in question within a wider institutional complex – including all the classic checks associated with ideas of horizontal separation of powers, of federated vertical division of authorities, and of institutional balance more generally. The substantive requirements include, in positive and constitutive vein, jurisdiction or mandate rules which specify the public purposes of the institutions in question and the boundaries of these purposes, as well as, in negative vein, certain conduct-constraining rules that may take the form of general individual rights catalogues or other more detailed rules which are likewise concerned with trans-sectoral standards (e.g. freedom of information rules, anti-corruption rules.)

---

35 Luhmann 1993.

A number of points may be made about co-articulating these different types of rules. First is the dependence of the substantive rules on the structural rules. The structural rules provide a general framework of orientation, coordination, and sanction that undergird the norm-specific guidelines contained in the substantive rules. Secondly, given their various boundary-setting and transversal qualities, the substantive rules associated with a particular constitutionally recognized function presuppose and are themselves supported and rendered more effective by their situation in a legal order that ranges more broadly than the particular functional specialism in question. That broader framework constrains and informs both by locating issues of the *vires* of particular institutions in a wider context of empowered institutions and by bringing general standards of the 'right' to bear in qualifying the pursuit of the particular 'good'. Thirdly, the content of both the substantive and the structural rules is inscribed in a basic constitutional code that is relatively insulated from the particular institutions that are subject to these very substantive and structural rules. In particular, the combination of the autonomous rules of production of constitutional norms and their settled quality (perhaps entrenched in 'eternity' clauses or protected against simple majoritarian amendment rules, or at least subject to amendment provisions not within the gift of the affected institution itself), provides a form of protection against narrow forms of self-norming. Fourthly, the constitutional code is not only insulated from particular interests, but, more positively, it is receptive at points of origin, amendment and continuing interpretation to notions of common interest informed, one the one hand, by the idea of the constitution as a form of popular self-authorization over the totality of public affairs for a territory, and on the other, by the necessary discipline of ensuring widespread cooperation and compliance within the ambient society.

In summary, this combination of structural primacy, institution-transcending substantive rules, insulation of rules of constitutional norm production and maintenance from control by the institutions affected by these norms, and the openness of the same rules to broader forms of public influence and discipline, provide the key ingredients of a holistic method of constitutionalism. The parts are supported by the whole both within and across the various different frames. Particular sector-specific rules and institutions alike depend for their meaning and authority on their location within broader regulatory and institutional orders, which broader orders are informed by a similarly wide-reaching and holistic conception of the singular public as both the source and the receptive environment of constitutional authority.

Constitutionalism Beyond the State: Multilevel or Multi-Actor?

If one looks to levels and sites of authority beyond the state, what scope is there for application of the holistic constitutional method? And where it is not available, how else, if at all, might constitutionalism's deep meta-political concern with the source, extent and manner of pursuit of matters of common interest be met?

Clearly, some forms of post-state regimes or polities seem to fit quite well on the 'scale' of constitutionalism considered as a layered set of holistic frames. The recent debate about adopting a documentary Constitution for the EU, to return to the best-known and most mature example of a multilevel constitutional pattern, eventually crystallized as one about how an entity whose 'thin' credentials as a self-standing juridical and politico-institutional order are unarguable[36] might also be re-imagined and reconstructed in 'thick' terms as a popular and indeed 'political-societal' constitution – one with its own democratically sensitive self-constituting authority and its 'own' transnational society as an object of reference.[37] In other words, the EU clearly already possessed holistic constitutional qualities in certain layers, so that the outstanding question concerned whether this could be extended across all the layers of modern constitutional practice. Once the supporters of the project were no longer satisfied with the documentary constitutional process as an exercise in self-congratulatory consolidation of its 'thin' (juridical and politico-institutional) credentials, or at least once they were no longer permitted by their opponents to treat the question so complacently, the 'thin' versus 'thick' question came more clearly into focus in the constitutional debate. That this ultimately led to the idea of a European Constitutional Treaty being voted down in the key French and Dutch referenda in 2005 neither undermines the relevance of the wider discussion nor, indeed, precludes its being revisited at some future point.[38]

In other cases, such as the WTO or the UN, the debate over the nature and limits of constitutional holism is very much more confined to the 'thin' legal and politico-institutional registers, with no pretence of and little ambition towards a popular constituent power or dedicated 'society' at the relevant sites.[39] However, even here no doubt exists about the applicability of a holistic method, even if to a truncated conception of constitutionalism. Indeed, it is precisely the well-established quality of a modest constitutional holism in these more limited regimes as much as in the hybrid regime of the EU that feeds much of the argument for post-state constitutionalism within a multilevel constellation, with both formalist and materialist approaches trading in their different ways on the holistic qualities of the juridical and institutional layers.

However, another type of case stands more clearly detached from the tradition of state constitutionalism. Here one refers to the various other autonomy-assertive transnational societal actors exhibiting normative authority and institutional identity who increasingly claim or are deemed to possess constitutional standing,[40] whether in the field of Internet (e.g. ICANN) or transnational commercial regulation (e.g. Lex Mercatoria) or the regulation of sports (e.g. International Olympic Committee, World Anti-Doping Agency). In this context, one finds

36 See, for example, Weiler 1999: Ch. 1.

37 See, for example, Walker 2008b, 2007b.

38 See, for example, Walker 2008a; Dehousse 2005; and Magnette 2006.

39 See Cass 2005; Petersmann 2000; Wet 2006; and Fassbender 1998.

40 See, for example, Teubner 2004.

a much more comprehensive move away from the holistic method, and so an even starker confrontation of the question of whether and how the broader meta-political end of regulating common affairs in accordance with considerations of the common interest can survive the erosion of the state-originated holistic constitutional method. Here, too, one begins to strain against the limits of the 'multilevel' metaphor itself. If the language of levels suggests a constellation of stable, relatively self-contained, and reasonably 'state-like' sites or platforms, the introduction of non-holistically embedded transnational societal agents suggests instead a network of fluid, intermeshing nodes of influence. And in so far as the constitutional language remains at all appropriate – a question to which a return will be made in the final section below – the transnational domain is perhaps more aptly conceived of as a 'multi-actor constitutionalism'[41] rather than as a multilevel configuration.

But in what precise sense do the new transnational societal actors represent a move away from the holistic method? If one looks first to the juridical and political-institutional layers, the idea of holistic self-containment fits ill with the combination of site-specific self-regulation and diverse external regulation which tend to be found in these sectors. While typically a dense network of structural and substantive rules exists, on will not find the same holistic framework for their co-articulation. Internally, structural rules may be found in autonomous enterprise or organizational laws. Externally, different legislative, executive and judicial bodies at national, international and supranational level will stand in various structural relationships with the actors. Substantively, again, the same complex mixture of self-regulation and uncoordinated external regulation through, for example, horizontal application of human rights rules and the general regimes of international standards bodies (e.g. Codex Alimentarius, International Standards Organization) will be found. What is lacking in either case is any idea of an integrated and comprehensive legal and institutional design external to the sector in question.

Equally, the idea of the holistic self-constitution of a popular 'subject' or of a societal 'object' does not translate easily to the domain of the new transnational societal actors. In either case – popular and societal – the wider and deeper embeddedness associated with state constitutionalism is lost in so far as no sense exists of an integrated and generic 'public' context which stands beyond the special institution in question but within which the special institution is fully incorporated. So while a significant degree of domain-specific self-authorship may exist, it neither is identical to nor delegated from any more integrated and generic public. Equally, a 'society' may be constituted in the sense of either or both a particular epistemic community or community of practice associated with

41 This is a less common term, but see, for example, National Research Council, 2002, *Global Networks and Local Values* (Washington: Computer Science and Telecommunication Board): Ch. 8.

the domain in question, but that too is neither identical to nor a subset of any integrated and generic 'public society'.[42]

It follows from this that none of the connecting elements – the 'holism of holisms' – of state constitutionalism can be guaranteed. In the first place, given the diversity of their pedigree (both as separate sets, and, even more so, when considered together), the relationship between the set of structural rules and the set of substantive rules lacks the coherence of the state model. So the structural rules cannot provide the functions of orientation, coordination, and constraint *vis-à-vis* the substantive rules in the 'close fit' manner that characterizes their relationship within the holistic state constitution. Secondly, no commonly bound general constitutional context is available to provide the transversal controls upon and wider jurisdictional context for sector-specific substantive rules. Because the transnational societal actor is not located within a wider complex of international societal actors, each subject to the same transversal rules and the same broader jurisdictional frame, the kinds of constraint and direction that a state constitution can provide by ensuring common negative standards and providing for the mutual coordination of different jurisdictional horizons cannot apply in the same way. Finally, the absence of any broader, singular and autonomously conceived transnational constitutional frame as an appropriate point of common reference both reflects and highlights the absence of any integrated and generic sense of the transnational public as the subject and object of any such regulatory field.[43]

Beyond Constitutionalism?

So the new transnational societal constitutionalism, such as it is, is clearly not simply the occurrence of a more 'thinly' layered version of state constitutionalism at other levels with the thicker popular and societal frame absent – as in the EU and in other less well-developed cases – but a constitutionalism that is reconfigured in each of its framing aspects. The idea of a holistic constitution is lacking in each of the four registers. What one has instead is a complex mix of discrete

42 One should, of course, bear in mind Teubner's (2004) qualification that the 'society' of the state constitutional imaginary was always in an important sense a partial vision. It was first and foremost a 'political society' – it was about the mutual self-constitution of law and politics and not necessarily concerned with other social sectors or sub-systems (economics, culture, and so on). But even if one allows this important point of social epistemology, one still has to take seriously the distinctively 'totalizing' ambition contained in the claim of modern political society to constitute a generic and integrated public sphere, and also recognize the powerful historical synergy between this ambition and the development of a deeper 'cultural' nationalism.

43 On the effect of the decline of holistic constitutionalism on the overall global regulatory field, rather than on the pattern of regulation within particular sectors, see Walker 2008c.

self-constitution and diffuse external constitution across all four registers – legal, politico-institutional, popular and societal.[44]

To what extent, if at all, can this new non-holistic constitutional method nevertheless be conceived of as concerned with, and as effectively engaged in, the same meta-political function as holistic state constitutionalism; namely, the reflexive consideration of the proper locus, jurisdiction, and content of the common interest in matters concerning the organization and regulation of collective decision-making? On the face of it, absent the anchorage for a working conception of the common interest provided by the coincidence of at least some, if not all, of the four holistic frames in a single 'level' under the same territorial coordinates, any prospect of a meaningful investment in these meta-political questions of the common interest would seem distinctly unpromising Yet, for at least three reasons, one should remain slow to dismiss the possibility of a non-holistic constitutionalism beyond the state.

In the first place, the question arises of the viability of other possible constitutional worlds. What are the alternatives, and so what can and what should one compare the new non-holistic candidates for constitutional status with? The most telling comparator for current trends towards decisively non-holistic forms of constitutionalism is not, as often seems to be assumed by the advocates of state constitutionalism, the *past* of state constitutionalism, but the form and circumstances of its *present* incarnation. The high-point of the holistic state constitutional method is long gone. In acknowledging this, it must also be appreciated that much of what is new in transnational regulatory development, whether in the form of hybrid structures such as the EU or WTO or through the more radical forms of societal constitutionalism, is the result not of inadvertent drift or of so many grabs for power devoid of any public justification, but instead is in some part at least a response to the growing inadequacy of the holistic state model in the face of the emergence of collective action and coordination problems that simply do not coincide with the political boundaries of the state. The new world even of the familiar and deeply embedded category of state constitutionalism, it follows, is not the same as the old. The new state constitutionalism may remain holistic in the sense that in each of the four framing registers it continues to emphasize the importance of the integrity of the whole and the interdependence of its parts, but this holism is qualified to the extent that it can no longer aspire to an all-embracing quality. Rather, state

44 One should also distinguish non-holistic societal constitutionalism from the kind of post-national constitutionalism favoured by writers like Jim Tully (1995, 2007). For him and others, the main focus of criticism remains the state form, not from the perspective of a functional differentiation which makes the holistic state constitution inadequate to the range and distribution of *collective practices* but rather from the perspective of a cultural differentiation (first nations, gendered identities, and so on) which makes the holistic state constitution inadequate to the range and distribution of *collective identities*. Accordingly, his version of non-state constitutionalism is about the re-articulation of a much greater diversity of holistic identities than the state form allows rather than the transcendence of the very idea of holistic constitutionalism.

constitutionalism itself becomes an 'open' or 'relational' constitutionalism,[45] concerned to engage in accordance with a necessarily non-holistic logic with the very hybrid polities and non-holistic spheres of governance that have been the focus of attention, and with which the norms, institutions, *demoi* and societal 'objects' of the state constitutional order overlap. In short, by their emergence the non-holistic constitutional forms serve to indicate, and through their regulatory penetration they serve to reinforce, the inadequacy of the very model of holistic state constitutionalism with which, ironically enough, they are often unfavourably compared. And to the extent that a point of comparison remains between old and new constitutional constellations, it is a matter of more or less emphasis upon a now heavily qualified state constitutional holism rather than a stark either/or choice between holism and its opposite.

In the second place, the question arises of (meta-) political morality and prudence. Such important differences of emphasis as do remain between more or less holistic venues, and the choices associated with these, are not necessarily beyond evaluation in terms that are found constitutionally meaningful. Rather, one remains capable of articulating at least some elements of the common language that would allow one to assess the relative merits and demerits of the holistic and non-holistic approaches to meta-politics, and to do so in such a way that suggests that the more holistic solution is not always the better or more 'constitutionally' appropriate.

Holistic constitutionalism, even in qualified form, can lay claim to many political virtues: to the formal equality and calculability dividends that may accrue to a legal order with a single all-embracing centre; to reliable juridical transmission of the (democratically formed) political will; to coordinated and mutually vigilant forms of institutional balance; to popular collective self-determination; and to a sense of societal solidarity necessary to make that collective self-determination effective. But such a model also demonstrates instability at either edge of its precarious accomplishment. On the one side, just because of its all-embracing reach and its exhaustion of the available mechanism of political influence and restraint, holistic constitutionalism is peculiarly prone to capture by powerful special interests and ideologies in any or all of its framing registers. On the other side, the same propensity to stretch across and absorb the entirety of the political sphere may mean that holistic constitutionalism attracts certain disabling tendencies, including a tendency towards inter-institutional stasis and gridlock and towards a thinly spread culture of common commitment. That is to say, comprehensive self-containment of the political sphere may always have been the major strength of holistic constitutionalism, but it also speaks to its irreducible vulnerability and ineradicable sources of danger.

This double-edged concern illustrates and so points towards certain perennial preoccupations over the best mode of accommodation between certain contrasting but balancing virtues associated with identification and pursuit of the common

45 See, for example, Walker 2003.

interest in constitutional arrangements – between attachment and detachment, the special and the general, the particular and the universal, the passionate and the constraining. Holism in the container of the state seeks ever more regulatory distance and abstraction (in substance, in structure and in pedigree) and ever more investment in a broader scheme of political commitments as a guide to and means of avoiding concentration of power in particular institutions, all the while courting the opposite dangers of more expansive forms of political partiality or dilution of the capacity for effective mobilization of political authority.

These moral and prudential concerns are not foreign to the new non-holistic constitutionalism of transnational societal actors. Rather, it is simply the case that its institutional logic is such that these concerns present themselves in inverse form. The problem for non-holistic constitutionalism is neither the corruption and capture nor the impotence of the regulatory whole, but precisely the same dangers of oversteering and understeering under the opposite condition of the *absence* of any such regulatory whole. And the key design puzzle in addressing these dangers of oversteering and understeering concerns the appropriate mode of articulating the internal and external elements within the legal and politico-institutional structure (in the first two framing layers), bearing in mind the fundamental irreducibility of the 'constituency' and 'own society' of the relevant community of practice to some integrated and generic notion of the public (in the third and fourth framing layers). It is quite understandable, then, that so much of contemporary transnational 'constitutional' thinking is concerned to develop 'substantive' and 'structural' rules in a manner that seeks to compensate or substitute both for the myopically self-interested tendencies (oversteering) and for the absence of effective leverage over external factors of influence (understeering) that accompany the lack of embedding of narrow self-regulatory spheres in a wider, holistic constitutional framework. So, for example, one finds an increasing emphasis on the language of universal human rights,[46] on the widespread franchising of general regulatory standards,[47] and on the promulgation and internalization of codes of corporate responsibility[48] as ways, primarily, of correcting for the sectoral self-interest of particular transnational societal actors, but also of encouraging or facilitating the greater mutual coherence of their regimes. On the structural side, too, a number of trends are seen that have the same double purpose and effect of addressing the dangers of oversteering and understeering. This can be observed, for instance, in attempts to develop new forms of general discipline as well as to trace new ways of joining up connected regulatory concerns through initiatives such as elaborating general principles of global administrative law,[49] replicating and

46 See, for example, Petersmann 2000.

47 See, for example, Schepel 2005.

48 See, for example, McBarnet 2007.

49 See, for example, Kingsbury, Krisch and Stewart 2005.

refining new modes of governance[50] and 'rolling out' local or sector-specific forms of democratic experimentation and problem-solving.[51]

Admittedly, in all of this the similarities and continuities in the meta-political concern with the common interest in organizing and regulating collective decision-making between past and present – and so between more or less holistic constitutional forms – operate at a high level of abstraction, require careful translation and certainly do not admit of any easy general conclusions. Still, something is resiliently recognizable at stake between old and new understandings of these deep questions of regulation which may merit the continued use of constitutional language as an analytical and evaluative tool for both.

This brings the debate, finally, to a third consideration, namely the practical question of the use-value of constitutionalism once it is stretched not only beyond the state but also beyond the holistic method, and, arguably too, beyond the limits of appropriate deployment of the metaphor of 'levels'. It is one thing to contend on the rarified level of theoretical inquiry that a connection can be traced between the old and the new, and to be reminded that in terms of viable political possibilities the difference is no longer one of kind but of degree. If, however, below that rarified theoretical level, constitutionalism is in little actual use as a common vernacular extending across the two contexts, and if what use exists has instead the divisive and mutually alienating consequences discussed in the opening section, then what is gained by retaining the constitutional idea for the emerging realm of transnational societal actors? Moreover, this note of scepticism is deeply underscored if the key underlying reason for the scarcity of an inclusive use-language of constitutionalism in the post-state, post-holistic regulatory context is considered. This has to do with lack of the additional, inclusively reflexive 'fifth layer' of constitutionalism within the non-holistic picture, namely the 'frame of frames' or 'holism of holisms'. Absent the coincidence of the other four frames, not only, as already noted, is it objectively the case that constitutionalism is deprived of the single anchorage of a convergence of sites and frames of common interest. At the intersubjective level, too, participants will lack the common 'we' perspective and point of commitment from which to address all questions of the common interest. Instead, it must be accepted, in a post-holistic context, that questions of the common interest in collective decision-making are simply not questions that, at the deepest level of political self-interrogation, it can be envisaged that all interested constituencies affected will address comprehensively *in* common.

Does this not, at last, provide the decisive argument against the value of retaining the language of constitutionalism in the non-holistic transnational context? It is contended that it does not. The explicit adoption of constitutional language in non-holistic settings may remain largely restricted to theoretical and other elite discourse. But the trend, however hesitant and uneven, is towards wider use, and, as the example of the intermediate cases of the EU, WTO, and so on

50 See, for example, Búrca and Scott 2006.

51 See, for example, Sabel and Zeitlin 2008.

show, recent precedents do exist for largely theoretical discourses of post-state constitutionalism gradually to 'catch on' at deeper social and political levels. Much more important is what the resilience and resurgence of constitutional language, however patchy on the ground, might signify. Even – indeed especially – where, as compared to the holistic constitutional tradition, the central issues of non-holistic forms of regulation present themselves in such different ways and are offered a quite distinctive range of regulatory solutions, constitutional language retains a crucial longstop function as a kind of 'placeholder'[52] for certain abiding concerns. These concerns are, quite simply, that unless the meta-political framing of politics can be addressed in a manner that remains wedded to ideas of the common interest, however difficult this may be to conceive and however far the distance travelled from the most familiar and perhaps most conducive framework for such a task, something of great and irreplaceable value will have been lost from the resources of common living.

There is a final irony here. It is precisely because the language of constitutionalism, considered as a normative technology, finds it ever more complex and difficult to address the problems of communal living it poses in and for a post-state world, that it becomes all the more important to retain the language of constitutionalism, considered as a symbolic legacy, as an insistent reminder of what and how much is at stake. The day that constitutionalism's inability – perhaps even an expansively conceived *multilevel* constitutionalism's inability – to provide stock answers to its abiding questions becomes a settled reason no longer even to ask these questions is the day that constitutionalism's historical paradigm will truly have been exhausted.

References

Avbelj, M. 2009. Theory of the European Bund. PhD Thesis. Florence: EUI.

Beaud, O. 2007. *Théorie de la Fédération*. Paris: Presses Universitaire de France.

Bogdandy, A. von. 2000. The European Union as a supranational federation: A conceptual attempt in the light of the Treaty of Amsterdam. *Columbia Journal of European Law*, 6, 27–54.

Bogdandy, A. von and Dellavalle, S. 2009. Universalism renewed: Habermas' theory of international order in light of competing paradigms. *German Law Journal*, 10: January, 5–30.

Búrca, G. de and Scott, J. 2006. *Law and New Governance in the EU and the US*. Oxford: Hart.

Canovan, M. 1996. *Nationhood and Political Theory*. Cheltenham: Edward Elgar.

52 The reference is to Koskenniemi (2007), who has made a similar point about the contemporary fate of international law.

Cass, D. 2005. *The Constitutionalization of the World Trade Organization*. Oxford: Oxford University Press.
Connolly, W.E. 1993. *The Terms of Political Discourse*. 3rd edition. Oxford: Blackwell.
Curtin, D. and Dekker, I. 1999. The EU as a 'layered' international organisation: Institutional unity in disguise, in *The Evolution of EU Law*, edited by P. Craig and G. de Búrca. Oxford: Oxford University Press, 83–136.
Curtin, D. and Dekker, I. 2002. The constitutional structure of the European Union: Some reflections on vertical unity-in-diversity, in *Convergence and Divergence in European Public Law*, edited by P. Beaumont, C. Lyons and N. Walker. Oxford: Hart, 59–78.
Dehousse, R. 2005. *La Fin de L'Europe*. Paris: Flammarion.
Fassbender, B. 1998. The United Nations Charter as the constitution of the international community. *Columbia Journal of International Law*, 36, 529–619.
Grimm, D. 2005. The constitution in the process of denationalization. *Constellations*, 12, 447–63.
Habermas, J. 2001. *The Postnational Constellation*. Cambridge: Polity.
Habermas, J. 2006. *The Divided West*. Cambridge: Polity.
Joerges, C. 2001. 'Good Governance' in the European Internal Market. An Essay in Honour of Claus-Dieter Ehlermann. EUI Working Papers, RSC 2001/29.
Kingsbury, B., Krisch, N. and Stewart, R.B. 2005. The emergence of global administrative law. *Law & Contemporary Problems*, 68:3, 15–61.
Kirchhof, P. 1993. § 183. Der deutsche Staat im Prozeß der europäischen Integration, in *Handbuch des Staatsrechts der Bundesrepublik Deutschland, Band VII*, edited by J. Isensee and P. Kirchhof. Heidelberg: C.F. Müller, 855–87.
Koskenniemi, M. 2007. The fate of public international law: Between technique and politics. *Modern Law Review*, 70:1, 15–19.
Lindahl, H. 2003. Sovereignty and representation in the European Union, in *Sovereignty in Transition*, edited by N. Walker. Oxford: Hart, 87–114.
Loughlin, M. 2009. In defence of *Staatslehre*. *Der Staat*, 48, 1–28.
Luhmann, N. 1993. *Das Recht der Gesellschaft*. Frankfurt: Suhrkamp.
Maddox, G. 1982. A note on the meaning of 'constitution'. *The American Political Science Review*, 76, 805–9.
Magnette, P. 2006. *Au Nom de Peuples: Le Malentendu Constitutionnel Européen*. Brussels: CERF.
Marks, G., Hooghe, L. and Blank, K. 1996. European integration since the 1980s: State-centric versus multi-level governance. *Journal of Common Market Studies*, 34, 343–78.
McBarnet, D.J. 2007. Corporate social responsibility: Beyond law, through law, for law: The new corporate accountability, in *The New Corporate Accountability: Corporate Social Responsibility and the Law*, edited by D. McBarnet, A. Voiculescu and T. Campbell. Cambridge: Cambridge University Press, 9–58.

Murkens, J. 2007. The future of *Staatsrecht*: Dominance, demise or demystification? *Modern Law Review*, 70, 731–58.

Pernice, I. 1995. Bestandssicherung der Verfassungen: Verfassungsrechtliche Mechanismen zur Wahrung der Verfassungsordnung, in *L'espace constitutionnel européen = Der europäische Verfassungsraum = The European constitutional area*, edited by R. Bieber and P. Widmer. Zürich: Schulthess, 225–64.

Pernice, I. 1996. Die Dritte Gewalt im europäischen Verfassungsverbund. *Europarecht*, 27, 27–43.

Pernice, I. 1998. Constitutional law implications for a state participating in a process of regional integration. German constitution and multilevel constitutionalism, in *German Reports on Public Law. Presented to the XV. International Congress on Comparative Law 26 July to 1 August 1998*, edited by E. Riedel. Baden-Baden: Nomos, 40–66.

Pernice, I. 1999. Multilevel constitutionalism and the Treaty of Amsterdam: European constitution-making revisited? *Common Market Law Review*, 36, 703–50.

Pernice, I. 2001. Europäisches und nationales Verfassungsrecht. *Veröffentlichungen der Vereinigung der Deutschen Staatsrechtslehrer*, 60, 148–93.

Pernice, I. 2002. Multilevel constitutionalism in the European Union. *European Law Review*, 27, 511–29.

Pernice, I. 2009. The Treaty of Lisbon: Multilevel constitutionalism in action. *Columbia Journal of European Law*, 15:3, 349–407.

Pernice, I. and Mayer, F.C. 2000. De la constitution composée de l'Europe. *Revue Trimestrielle de Droit Européen*, 623–47.

Petersmann, E.-U. 2000. The WTO constitution and human rights. *Journal of International Economic Law*, 3, 19–25.

Petersmann, E.-U. 2006. Multilevel trade governance in the WTO requires multilevel constitutionalism, in *Constitutionalism, Multilevel Trade Governance and Social Regulation*, edited by C. Joerges and E.-U. Petersmann. Oxford: Hart, 5–58.

Sabel, C.F. and Zeitlin, J. 2008. Learning from difference: The new architecture of experimentalist governance in the EU. *European Law Journal*, 14, 271–327.

Schepel, H. 2005. *The Constitution of Private Governance – Product Standards in the Regulation of Integrating Markets*. Oxford: Hart.

Stone Sweet, A. 2009. Constitutionalism, legal pluralism and international regimes. *Indiana Journal of Global Legal Studies*, 16:2, 621–45.

Teubner, G. 2004. Societal constitutionalism: Alternatives to state-centred constitutional theory? in *Transnational Governance and Constitutionalism*, edited by C. Joerges, I.-J. Sand and G. Teubner. Oxford: Hart, 3–28.

Teubner, G. and Fischer-Lescano, A. 2004. Regime-collisions: The vain search for legal unity in the fragmentation of global law. *Michigan Journal of International* Law, 25:4, 999–1046.

Tully, J. 1995. *Strange Multiplicity: Constitutionalism in an Age of Diversity*. Cambridge: Cambridge University Press.

Tully, J. 2007. The imperialism of modern constitutional democracy, in *The Paradox of Constitutionalism: Constituent Power and Constitutional Form*, edited by M. Loughlin and N. Walker. Oxford: Oxford University Press, 315–38.

Walker, N. 2002. The idea of constitutional pluralism. *Modern Law Review*, 65, 317–59.

Walker, N. 2003. Postnational constitutionalism and the problem of translation, in *European Constitutionalism Beyond the State*, edited by J. Weiler and M. Wind. Cambridge: Cambridge University Press, 27–54.

Walker, N. 2006. Big 'C' or small 'c'? *European Law Journal*, 12, 12–14.

Walker, N. 2007a. The migration of constitutional ideas and the migration of *the* constitutional idea, in *The Migration of Constitutional Ideas*, edited by S. Choudhry. Cambridge: Cambridge University Press, 316–44.

Walker, N. 2007b. European constitutionalism in the state constitutional tradition, in *Current Legal Problems 2006*, edited by J. Holder, C. O'Cinneide and C. Campbell-Holt, Oxford: Oxford University Press, 51–89.

Walker, N. 2008a. Not the European Constitution. *Maastricht Journal of European and Comparative Law*, 15:1, 135–41.

Walker, N. 2008b. Taking constitutionalism beyond the state. *Political Studies*, 56, 519–43.

Walker, N. 2008c. Beyond boundary disputes and basic grids: Mapping the global disorder of normative orders. *International Journal of Constitutional Law*, 6, 373–96.

Walker, N. 2010. Out of place and out of time: Law's fading co-ordinates. *Edinburgh Law Review*, 14:1, 13–46.

Weiler, J.H.H. 1999. *The Constitution of Europe*. Cambridge: Cambridge University Press.

Wet, E. de. 2006. The international constitutional order. *International and Comparative Law Quarterly*, 55, 51–76.

Chapter 8
European Constitutionalism and the Democratic Design of European Governance: Rethinking Directly Deliberative Polyarchy and Reflexive Constitutionalism

Stijn Smismans

Introduction

Since the Convention drafting the Constitutional Treaty explicitly introduced the concept of constitution in the European vocabulary, the debate on European constitutionalism has strongly intensified. The debate has been mainly on the political constitution of the European Union, the central concern being how power is exercised, and how that power could be democratically organized within the Union. As suggested at the start of this book,[1] this illustrates an evolution in the constitutional dimension of the European Union, where the originally predominantly economic constitution set out in the Rome Treaty has by now become a political constitution. However, intensified debate on European constitutionalism over the last decade has also been limited in scope, focusing in particular on voting and decision-making powers of the main Community institutions in European legislative measures, combined with a symbolic playing with constitutional language in a (failed) bid to gain legitimacy with European citizens, relying on a normative framework for democratic governance that even at the national level fails to live up to the complexity of modern governance. Much of the complexity of European governance, and the democratic concerns it entails, failed to appear on the radar of the Constitutional Treaty debate. This was surely the case for the political debate, but equally the academic debate on European constitutionalism has ignored much of the reality of European governance. Therefore, this chapter will place governance at the centre of European constitutionalism.

The chapter is structured in four sections. First the shortcomings of both the political and the academic debate on European constitutionalism in its relation to European governance will be illustrated. Subsequently, the potential and limits

1 See especially the contributions of Tuori and Sand in this volume.

of directly deliberative polyarchy (DDP), as developed by Charles Sabel and co-authors,[2] to address these shortcomings, will be looked at. Unlike most of the debate on European constitutionalism, which has tended to develop in abstract terms, DDP has made more effort to take into account the complexity, diversity and practice of European governance. However, using the European Employment Strategy (EES) as an empirical example, the main shortcomings of DDP as a normative democratic framework for European governance are also identified. Its ultimate claim to legitimacy based on direct citizen deliberation stands so far from the practice of European governance that one can wonder whether the model can ever be used as a guiding framework. Moreover, Sabel and co-authors' belief in spontaneous bottom-up participatory processes underestimates the problems for intersystem communication as identified by systems theory. Therefore, in the following section rethinking DDP is suggested. Taking systems theory as a starting point and using reflexivity as a normative device in addition to deliberation, reflexive deliberative polyarchy (RDP) is proposed as a normative framework for European governance.

Unlike DDP, RDP takes the problems of direct citizen deliberation and intersystem communication as a starting point. Aware of the difficulties in realizing direct citizen deliberation and of the tendency for governance to occur through auto-referential deliberation by functional actors, procedural mechanisms should encourage interaction between different communicative structures. If the numbers of citizens that can be involved in deliberation over policy-making will always be limited, encouraging reflexive interaction between different intermediaries who would normally tend to closure within the proper language and network of specialization may be a useful device to avoid governance in the defence of singular interests. It will be illustrated that current European governance practices can be guided by this normative framework, using the example of European employment policy.

However, encouraging procedurally reflexive processes is as such not enough to guarantee democratic governance. In the last part of the chapter it will be argued how reflexivity in a horizontal polyarchic system needs to interlink with fundamental substantive norms set by representative institutions. Polyarchy in RDP should not only be understood with reference to dispersion of power, as the authors of DDP tend to do, but should also be understood in the traditional sense of the word as developed by Robert Dahl. This also implies rethinking reflexive constitutionalism by bringing in the question of substantive norms. The need for substantive norms engenders the question of the relationship between the EU's multiple constitutions, such as the economic and the social constitutions. RDP can therefore not merely be a procedural design, but needs to ensure a reflexive relationship between substantive values set out at the constitutional level in a democratic way.

2 See Cohen and Sabel 1997; Gerstenberg and Sabel 2002; Cohen and Sabel 2003; and Sabel and Zeitlin 2008.

Rethinking European Constitutionalism: Taking Governance Seriously

From the Laeken Declaration (2001) through the Constitutional Treaty to the Lisbon Treaty, the constitutional debate has focused on what can be called 'traditional EC constitutionalism', including emphasis on functional limitation, concentration on the formal institutional power structure, and definition of rights as a constraint on EU power.[3] Much of the complexity of governance in Europe's multi-level polity has remained out of the debate, such as the relation between public and private authority, involvement of private actors in policy-making, the role of networked governance involving national administrations, and use of modes of governance that do not correspond to the hierarchical command–control assumption underlying the regulatory Community method.

This does not imply that these issues have not been debated at all at the European level. In fact, in 2001 the Commission White Paper on European Governance engendered an intensive debate on European governance in an attempt to reform governance practices without having to wait for treaty reform. This has led to a rather schizophrenic debate over the last decade,[4] with on the one hand the Constitutional debate taking a very restrictive and traditional perspective on constitutional issues, ignoring many governance issues, and on the other hand the White Paper debate dealing with governance issues as if they had no constitutional dimension. Yet questions such as use of self-regulation, or creation of independent regulatory agencies such as debated in the context of the White Paper, are definitely questions of constitutional design. Vice versa, in the constitutional debate many of the major questions of design of European governance have remained largely out of the picture. A good example is the Lisbon Strategy and its main procedural instrument, namely the open method of coordination (OMC). The Lisbon Strategy, making the EU the 'most competitive and knowledge-based economy by 2010', has been said to be 'the most high-profile initiative of the European Union in the first decade of the 2000s',[5] and has indeed absorbed much energy of many policy-makers at both the European and the national level. However, this extensive process of coordinating national policies in many policy areas through soft benchmarking has happened entirely outside the existing constitutional framework. Moreover, it has hardly figured in the constitutional debate.[6]

The schizophrenic nature of the constitutionalism/governance debate is not limited to the political discussion. The academic debate has followed a similar split track, with the governance debate attracting above all the attention of political

3 See Búrca 2003.

4 For the implications of this two-track debate on the issue of vertical and horizontal decentralism, see Smismans 2004.

5 Rodrigues 2003; and Begg 2007.

6 The Lisbon Strategy and OMC were finally discussed in a working group of the Convention, but only at a late stage in the process and without real impact on the text of the Constitutional Treaty and Lisbon Treaty.

scientists, and the constitutional debate balancing between legal comments on particular provisions and broader considerations from constitutional theory. The main academic constitutionalist debate in relation to the EU has been in terms of 'constitutional pluralism', which mainly focused on the relationship between the legal orders of the EU and its member states, and the resulting 'constitutional dialogue' between the Court of Justice and national constitutional courts. Although some authors such as Neil Walker have opened the 'constitutional pluralism' concept to refer to 'a species of normative order which is to be found in networks or in forms of private, hybrid, or pluri-political ordering which are not institutionally nested and polity-centred in the same way as the traditional state constitutional order',[7] the debate has remained largely theoretical without linking in with the detail of European governance practices. The same can be said regarding the debate on 'reflexive constitutionalism', which mainly stresses in abstract terms the need for revisability of constitutional norms through a permanent process of deliberation, without, however, analysing or proposing detailed governance mechanisms through which this would emerge. According to James Tully,

> the orientation of practical philosophy should not be to reaching final agreements on universal principles or procedures, but to ensuring that constitutional democracies are always open to the democratic freedom of calling into question and presenting reasons for the renegotiation of the prevailing rules of law, principles of justice and practices of deliberation.[8]

Such permanent constitutional contestation implies that 'the study of practices of democratic deliberation could not be restricted to constitutional essentials and constitutional referenda or to the genres of adversarial reasoning in the traditional legal and political institutions', but requires study of 'the practices of freedom in any practice of governance in which those subject to, or affected by it, seek to reignite the embers of public autonomy and have an effective say over how their conduct is governed'.[9]

Yet Tully himself does not provide such detailed analysis of governance practices. In the context of the EU, Rainer Schmalz-Bruns pleads for reflexive constitutionalism which needs to include hierarchical forms of self-intervention but again does not point to elements of current European governance practice on which this could be built.[10] James Bohman, who argues for reflexive constitutionalism to be based on a form of deliberative, polyarchic federalism, goes slightly further by briefly referring to the open method of coordination.[11] However, overall a wide gap remains to be bridged between the normative reflections set out in EU

7 Walker 2002: 325.

8 Tully 2002: 218.

9 Tully 2002: 219.

10 See Schmalz-Bruns 2005: 76–81.

11 See Bohman 2005.

constitutional theory and the empirical reality of European governance. Amongst theories for constitutional and democratic design in the EU, DDP seems to come closest to bridging that gap.

Directly Deliberative Polyarchy as a Normative Framework for the Political Constitution: Potential and Limits

Co-writing with changing partners, over the last decade Sabel[12] has developed the suggestion that DDP may be used as a normative framework for European governance.

Arguably, DDP does not articulate *in abstracto* a set of normative principles to deduce their institutional conclusions, but tries 'to imagine what democracy could be' from the vantage point of the possibilities suggested by current governance structures, in this case those of the EU.[13] The strength of DDP is that it combines a normative proposal with an attempt to take the empirical reality and complexity of European governance seriously. This is not to legitimate *post factum* the reality of European governance, but to provide a normative framework that has sufficient anchors in reality to make the normative proposal plausible as guidance for institutional design. Yet it will be argued that the authors of DDP have been too optimistic in reading the reality of European governance in conformity with their model, to the point where one can doubt the usefulness of DDP as a guiding model.

DDP is a democratic ideal based on the idea that

> local-, or more exactly, lower-level actors (nation state or national peak organizations of various kinds; regions, provinces or sub-national associations within these, and so on down to the level of whatever kind of neighbourhood the problem in question makes relevant) are granted autonomy to experiment with solutions of their own devising within broadly defined areas of public policy. In return they furnish central or higher-level units with rich information regarding their goals as well as the progress they are making towards achieving them, and agree to respect in their actions framework rights of democratic procedure.[14]

The system is 'directly-deliberative' since 'citizens must examine their own choices in the light of the relevant deliberations and experiences of others'[15] – in contrast to other discursive ideas of democracy involving deliberation at a distance by an administrative or political elite. The system is 'polyarchic' due to the permanent

12 See Cohen and Sabel 1997; Gerstenberg and Sabel 2002; and Sabel and Zeitlin 2008.

13 Cohen and Sabel 1997: 317.

14 Gerstenberg and Sabel 2002: 291.

15 Cohen and Sabel 1997: 314.

disequilibrium created by the grant of substantial powers of initiative to lower-level units.[16]

Cohen and Sabel have built DDP on Dahl's concept of polyarchy, namely it 'refers to systems in which virtually all adults have rights of suffrage, political expression, association, and office-holding, as well as access to diverse sources of information; in which elected officials control public policy; and citizens choose those officials through free and fair elections'.[17] For Dahl, democracy may be defined as rule by multiple minority oppositions, that is, depending on the particular decision being taken, different groups have access and power to control the decision-making outcome due to a competition in an 'open contest for electoral support'.[18] Yet, while explicitly building on Dahl's concept of polyarchy, DDP uses the concept mainly to refer to the decentralized dispersion of power, remaining silent on how this permanent disequilibrium of powers of lower-level units would relate to traditional representative institutions under Dahl's interpretation of the concept.[19] Therefore, the democratic claims of DDP are mainly akin to ideas of participatory democracy[20] and deliberative democracy in its focus on direct participation and deliberation in terms of rational argument.[21] DDP aims at decentralization 'down to the level of whatever kind of neighbourhood the problem in question makes relevant',[22] and postulates as a normative ideal 'direct participation by and reason-giving between and among free and equal citizens'.[23] In terms of participative membership, DDP takes as 'the basic standard ... that directly-deliberative arenas are to be open to providers and parties affected by the extent and manner of provision. (In the case of schools, for example, parents, teachers, and residents of community served by the school)'.[24] 'There is a presumption in favour of equal membership for affected parties – open meetings, with equal rights to participate in discussion and decision-making for all affected parties', although Cohen and Sabel add that 'rights to participate might also be awarded to organizations with special knowledge that is essential to the problem

16 Gerstenberg and Sabel 2002: 292.

17 Dahl 1989 as quoted by Cohen and Sabel 1997: 318.

18 Dahl 1956 as quoted by Held 1987: 193.

19 Magnette (2006), for instance, criticizes DDP for not having worked out the relationship between direct deliberative forms of participation and representative forms of democracy. See also further below.

20 See Pateman 1970.

21 Also Schmalz-Bruns (2006: 72) criticizes DDP for overtaxing the link that exists between a deliberative account of democracy and participatory politics, in that it appears to be built 'on the presumption that a deliberative perspective should necessarily and unequivocally favour a single democratic form – that of participatory democracy'.

22 Gerstenberg and Sabel 2002: 291.

23 Cohen and Sabel 1999: 1.

24 Cohen and Sabel 1999: 15.

area in question ... or who are able to articulate a point of view in ways that foster deliberation among alternative solutions'.[25]

Now, precisely on this crucial aspect of 'direct deliberateness' or the decentralized participatory dimension of DDP, European governance is miles away from the normative claims of DDP, to the extent that one can question whether this normative model can be used as a framework for the EU. The claim by the authors of DDP that their normative framework is modelled from the vantage point of the possibilities suggested by current governance structures[26] appears far-fetched. This will be illustrated this using the example of the European Employment Strategy (EES), which is part of the broader Lisbon Strategy, and which has been repeatedly proposed by the authors of DDP as an illustration of their model.

Much of the features of the EES, with the OMC as a central policy tool, seem, at least in their design, to conform with the ideal of DDP. Instead of centralized European binding regulation, the OMC leaves policy-making power at the decentralized level of the member states, and within them encouraging further decentralized policy-making, within the framework of policy options suggested by European guidelines. The knowledge that results from different solutions experienced in the member states is then pooled at the European level through the assessment of National Action Plans (NAP) or annual reporting on National Reform Programmes (NRP). The periodicity of that process allows for exchange of best practice and revision of benchmarks. So far, so good, in terms of DDP.

However, while the EES realizes a level of decentralized learning combined with pooling of information and exchange of best practice at a higher level, it does not seem to come anywhere close to the 'deliberate-directness'[27] Cohen and Sabel plead for in the abstract formulation of their model. According to the Lisbon Summit, the OMC procedure is characterized by '[a] fully decentralized approach [that] will be applied in line with the principle of subsidiarity in which the Union, the Member States, the regional and local levels, as well as the social partners and civil society, will be actively involved, using variable forms of partnership'.[28] However, the decentralized participation that would guarantee the EES to be bottom-up polyarchic and directly deliberative is scarce both in the way the EES was originally conceived and institutionalized, and in its actual working. The EES does not provide a (comprehensive) framework for an employment policy that would function bottom-up at the initiative of multiple local units (polyarchy) that ensure direct citizen deliberation. The treaty provisions on the employment guidelines procedure read (mainly) as a coordination of national policies, providing no strong institutional requirements for decentralized involvement below the level of the national administrations. The employment guidelines themselves

25 Cohen and Sabel 1999: 15.

26 See Cohen and Sabel 1997: 317.

27 Cohen and Sabel 1999: 6.

28 Presidency Conclusions, Lisbon Extraordinary European Council, 23–24 March 2000, para. 38.

have propagated a discourse on a fully decentralized approach in implementing employment policies of different intensity over the years. Through annual reporting and assessment it soon became clear that realizing decentralized involvement in drafting and implementing NAPs was one of the most problematic parts of the OMC procedure. References to decentralized participation increased at the end of the first phase of the EES (1997–2002),[29] including explicit references to the role of the social partners in particular. However, with the 'simplification' of the EES in its second phase (2003–2004), explicit references to the social partners were also reduced. This tendency has been confirmed in the third phase of the EES, with the renewed Lisbon Strategy further reducing explicit references to the social partners. The renewed Lisbon Strategy provides for integrated guidelines bringing together both the employment guidelines and the macro-economic policy guidelines. A horizontal objective no longer exists for involvement of social partners or a detailed good governance and partnership provision. References to decentralized participation are limited to a general introductory statement suggesting that member states 'should establish a broad partnership for change by fully involving parliamentary bodies and stakeholders, including those at regional and local levels and civil society organizations. European and national social partners should play a central role.' Only one guideline includes a reference to the social partners, namely to their role in wage bargaining to ensure employment-friendly labour cost developments (Guideline 22). Therefore, if one looks at the guidelines since 1997, when the EES was enshrined in the EC Treaty, decentralized involvement has mainly been limited to vaguely phrased statements that the relevant actors in the field of employment at national, regional and local level have important contributions to make. Only with regard to the social partners – as opposed to other civil society organizations or regional and local authorities – had some more detailed provisions been included by the end of the first phase.

Looking at *de facto* participation in the EES, nothing could support the argument that it is a process of deliberative governance starting bottom-up from the smallest local unit possible. While data about participation in the EES show a diverse picture according to the member states,[30] what is being dealt with in the best of cases is a neo-corporatist style involvement of social partners rather than a bottom-up learning process of direct deliberative participation by all those affected by it. The social partners are consulted (to diverse degrees according to the member states) regarding drafting NAPs or NRPs but only at the national level and without evidence of participatory processes below that level. Even in countries where tripartite structures have been set up in relation to the EES, the process does not seem to have generated new initiatives from the social partners or new national strategies towards unemployment.[31] Seen from the bottom up, civil society actors

29 Three phases in the development of the EES can be historically distinguished, following changes in its governance practice. See Armstrong and Kilpatrick 2007.

30 See Homs et al. 2005.

31 See Goetschy 2003: 67.

are not aware enough of the OMC process to mobilize on it, or they may feel that they are not gaining much from contributing to NAPs which are seen more as a description of government policy than as an actual plan of future action.[32]

In a study on new forms of governance in European industrial relations co-authored for the European Foundation for Living and Working Conditions, the result of about 50 interviews with social partners and researchers in the field showed that the Lisbon strategy and the OMC have not been 'appropriated' by the social partners, except for the European-level elite dealing with these aspects.[33] Hence, reality stands far from the ideal of DDP based on direct deliberative participation in a locally decentralized context.

The EES can be described as a process of experience-driven revising of framework provisions, as suggested by the authors[34] of DDP, but this mode of governance appears to contain very little that would bring it anywhere close to the direct participatory dimension which the normative claims of DDP are focused on. The misfit between reality and the normative ideal appears so strong that one can question whether the latter can ever provide real normative guidance for the former. It will therefore be suggested in the next section that DDP needs rethinking by taking reflexivity seriously.

Rethinking Directly Deliberative Polyarchy: Taking Reflexivity Seriously

In recent literature on (new modes of) European governance, the concept of 'reflexivity' appears with increasing frequency.[35] However, in most cases reflexivity is looked at from an analytical perspective, describing governance practices as reflexive. When reflexivity is presented as a normatively desirable feature, this is mainly done in the context of models of deliberative democracy, such as DDP, which tend to conflate deliberation and reflexivity. The argument here is to take reflexivity seriously from a normative perspective, distinguishing between deliberation and reflexivity. The chapter will first go back to reflexive law theory to identify both an analytical and normative dimension to reflexivity. It will subsequently identify how this differs from DDP, and will therefore propose reflexive deliberative polyarchy (RDP) as a normative model. Relying again on the empirical example of the European Employment Strategy (EES), it will be shown how RDP can be used as a normative framework for European governance.

32 See Jacobsson and Vifell 2004: 23.

33 See Léonard, Erne, Marginson and Smismans 2007: 70.

34 See Sabel and Zeitlin 2008.

35 See Sand 1998: 271–93; Schutter and Deakin 2005: 279–343; Eriksen 2005a; Meer, Visser and Wilthagen 2005: 347–65; Rogowski 2007; and Diamond 2004: 305–32.

The analytical and normative dimension in reflexive law theory

According to the Oxford English Dictionary 'reflexive' means 'that which turns back upon, or takes account of, itself or a person's self, esp. methods that take into consideration the effect of the personality or presence of the researcher on the investigation'. Applied to policy-making, the concept of reflexivity has above all been developed in legal theory. Gunther Teubner has proposed the concept of reflexive law to refer to a new evolutionary stage of law, in which law realizes its systemic limits with respect to regulation of other social systems[36] and 'becomes a system for the coordination of action within and between semi-autonomous social subsystems'.[37] Reflexive law theory has built on the premise of systems theory, and of Niklas Luhmann's theory of autopoiesis in particular,[38] that modern differentiated society is characterized by the 'horizontal' emergence of social subsystems such as the legal, economic, scientific, political and religious subsystems. Each subsystem is self-generating and self-referential; they are normatively closed in that they recognize no norms other than those which they produce as being valid.[39] As a consequence, no one system can declare its world view as the only view and as binding on all others. This has important consequences for the role of law, which is supposed to ensure integration in society. Instead of providing top-down substantive regulatory programmes, reflexive law would enable subsystems to be self-regulatory without damaging the other subsystems. Law is reflexive in that it is aware of its own limits in defining substantive norms on a general basis.

Reflexive law theory is not a democratic theory but a theory about the nature of law and its place in society. The starting point is analytical, identifying in the self-referentiality of subsystems the problems of law in regulating other subsystems; and identifying in the increased differentiation of society the origin for the development of reflexive law as a next step in the evolution of law. Yet the step from reflexive law theory as an analytical description of the nature and evolution of law in society, to suggesting how law *should* be structured in order to be effective, is a very small one. Teubner explicitly defends the dual character of the idea of reflexive law as both analytic and normative, namely as an empirical analysis and normative evaluation of the current position of law in a functionally differentiated society, and the operative consequences of this finding.[40] Obviously,

36 Rogowski 2001: 181.

37 Teubner 1983: 242.

38 Luhmann 1995 (original from 1982); 2004 (original from 1984); and 1993.

39 The catchphrase in autopoietic theory states that subsystems are 'operatively closed' but 'cognitively open' (Teubner 1993: 15), i.e., although characterized by organized processes of communication and action independent from other social communications and actions, not entirely isolated from other subsystems. Yet, the influence of one system on another can only be understood by the latter through translation into the proper language of that system, i.e., 'making order from noise'. Hence, '[t]he system can only deal with its own internal construct of the environment' (Teubner 1993: 74).

40 Teubner 1993: 69.

the normative concern of how law should be structured in order to be *effective* does not imply a democratic concern. In particular, since reflexive law theory became increasingly built on the premises of autopoiesis,[41] the focus has been on the operational closure of subsystems and the problems this creates for the effectiveness of law. The index of subjects of Teubner's 'Law as an autopoietic system' mentions neither democracy nor participation, and the core chapter of the book defining the features of reflexive law in social regulation reads as a search for greater effectiveness of law (by overcoming the limits of command-control regulation) and not as a search for more democratic, participatory, legitimate governance.[42] Yet the earlier Teubner had linked the concept of reflexive law to discursive democracy. 'Reflection within social subsystems', it was argued, 'is possible only insofar as processes of democratization create discursive structures within these subsystems'.[43] It is the role of reflexive law to 'act at the subsystem-specific level to install, correct, and redefine democratic self-regulatory mechanisms'.[44] However, the normative implications and democratizing potential of reflexive law have never been developed comprehensively.[45]

If freed from an over-rigid interpretation of autopoiesis, reflexive law theory can provide a normative conception of reflexivity that fits with democratic theory in a dual way. First, at a minimum level reflexivity means acknowledgment by the (legal) subsystem of its self-referential character. From here it follows that reflexivity also implies acknowledgement by the legal system of its limits in regulating other subsystems and therefore favours more decentralized systems of norm-definition. Freed from the strait-jacket of autopoiesis, reflexivity can have the broader meaning of taking into account contextuality. Reflexive law abstains from uniform substantive interventions but encourages governance mechanisms that allow the taking into account of contextuality and decentralized experience and knowledge. This normative dimension of reflexivity strikes a chord with democratic claims based on subsidiarity and participatory politics as suggested by DDP. Several EU law scholars have pointed to this normative dimension of

41 The theory of autopoiesis as presented by Luhmann has never claimed to provide any way to 'a better society' (see King 2001: 126). Eric Orts (2001: 173) opposes 'the more politically optimistic Habermas, who seems to retain a faith that an enlightened political state informed by democratic discourse and deliberation can successfully "steer" the economic and other social systems' to autopoietic theorists like Luhmann and Teubner who are 'less sanguine about the possibilities of modern democratic politics'.

42 In passing, Teubner (1993: 95) mentions that 'one could couple the granting of privileges to associations with the regulation of their internal order; for instance, one could introduce limited liability, but only in cases where particular social forms and structures are accepted'.

43 Teubner 1983: 273.

44 Teubner 1983: 275.

45 For a comparable criticism on reflexive law theory, see Julia Black (1996: 49) arguing that democratizing social subsystems has been the stated underlying aim of reflexive law which, however, has not been developed.

reflexivity in EU law-making processes. Simon Deakin, for instance, uses the concept of 'reflexive harmonisation', to describe EU regulation by way of directives that preserve space for autonomous governance at lower levels of government.[46]

Second, reflexivity can have an additional normative dimension if one takes as a starting point and focus the insight of limited intersystem communication but stepping back from an over-rigid interpretation of autopoiesis. Awareness of the tendency of subsystems to cognitive closure can be taken as a starting point to conceive the role of law as creating intersystem interaction, which cannot be taken to be a natural process. Reflexive law encourages subsystems to take into account their effects on other subsystems, that is, despite (a certain level of) self-referentiality of subsystems, interconnections between them can be encouraged through law.[47] In the words of the earlier Teubner, the aim of reflexive law is 're-introducing the consequences of actions of social subsystems into their own reflection structure'.[48] Such intersystem interaction is desirable from a normative democratic perspective since it requires policy actors to be 'other regarding' and makes decision-making in the defence of particular interests more difficult. This system-focused awareness of reflexivity can provide additional normative guidance to the model of DDP. It implies the normative encouraging of horizontal interaction among systems which will later be referred to as horizontal reflexivity, in addition to DDP's focus on decentralized actor-centred deliberation.

Rethinking DDP: About reflexivity and deliberation

It is not the place here to repeat the intensive debate on deliberative democracy that has dominated democratic theory since the 1990s.[49] It is enough to quote the definition given by Jon Elster, who defines deliberative democracy as 'collective decision making with the participation of all who will be affected by the decision or their representatives', and which is based on 'arguments offered *by* and *to* participants who are committed to the values of rationality and impartiality'.[50] The concept of deliberation is actor-centred as it refers to interaction between

46 Deakin 1999: 231. Other examples are: Barnard, Deakin and Hobbs 2005; Schutter 2005.

47 The autopoietic interpretation of reflexive law theory stresses the self-referentiality and closure of subsystems. The 'cognitive openness' of subsystems is sought in processes such as 'an hypercycle' or 'structural coupling' (Teubner 1993). Yet, the final verdict (Teubner 1993: 97) is that 'despite all "Reflexivity", law is still a closed autopoietic system operating in a world of closed autopoietic systems. It is impossible to break down the barriers which result from this double closure'. However, reflexive law theory (see, e.g., Orts 2001: 175) has not stuck to this strong autopoietic reading – or mechanisms of hypercycle or structural coupling – giving a more 'optimistic' and normative interpretation to the potential of reflexivity and reflexive law in encouraging interrelations between subsystems.

48 Teubner 1983: 257.

49 See Saward 2000: 5.

50 Elster 1998: 8.

individuals. Yet deliberative politics also presume elements of reflexivity. It presumes reflexivity on the part of the individual, who revises their own position in deliberative interaction with others. As Erik Oddvar Eriksen puts it: 'deliberative politics is seen as a *reflexively organized learning process* – as a problem-solving procedure that brings in knowledge and relevant normative perspectives and qualifies (or validates) them in order to establish mutual understanding and agreement'.[51] The 'organized' character of this learning process implies a second dimension of reflexivity, namely in the sense of revisability of norms as the outcome of permanent processes of deliberation, in particular in relation to revisability of the constitutional norms of the game, mainly referred to as 'reflexive constitutionalism'. However, when stated in such general terms, the risk is to conflate 'deliberative politics' with 'reflexive politics' as the reflexive design is simply the one that would ensure deliberation. There is no particular added normative value in the concept of reflexivity as such.

The same can be said of DDP: while, compared to other writings on deliberative democracy, it does make the effort to look at the empirics of decentralized dispersed governance mechanisms, it does not overcome the tendency to conflate deliberation and reflexivity. DDP tends to glorify the 'spontaneous' bottom-up processes of experimentation, providing little guidance on how these processes would be structured by an overarching (revisable) constitutional design or constitutional principles, and in this way still tends to conflate 'deliberative politics' with 'reflexive politics', that is, the reflexive system seems more the outcome of a spontaneous nearly anarchic bottom-up process of deliberation, rather than a crafted institutional design which, taking into account the problems of intersystem communication, would encourage such interaction and deliberation. DDP does not start from the perspective of systems theory that considers interaction among systems as particularly difficult. Contrasting DDP to systems theory, Gerstenberg and Sabel argue that:

> local knowledge is neither tacit nor fully and self-referentially systematic. Co-ordination among local collaborators is necessary because of the diversity of their views and possible because … the exploration of the ambiguities internal to each shades into exchange with the others. But as local co-ordination yields new ambiguities of its own, there is both need and possibility for inter-local exchange through a new centre that frames discussion and re-frames it as results permit.[52]

However, evidence of governance practices, in particular in the context of the EU, shows that the heterogeneity of participants within local units emerges far less spontaneously than DDP seems to suggest.[53] Moreover, a new centre at a higher level that allows inter-local exchange may indeed provide opportunity to

51 Eriksen 2005b: 17.

52 Gerstenberg and Sabel 2002: 340.

53 See Cohen and Sabel 1997: 333.

reframe discussion, but the (partial) self-referentiality of subsystems implies that it is more likely for such higher-level centres to be created within rather than across subsystems. As the example of the EES shows, European governance tends to occur through auto-referential deliberation between functional actors structured by the language of each subsystem, rather than as a bottom-up process based on citizen participation and a rather spontaneous process of cross-system interaction.

Therefore, taking the system-theoretic interpretation of reflexivity seriously, reflexivity can provide an additional normative guide. Reflexivity is not simply a multiplication of deliberative processes. While deliberation encourages rational argumentation by those concerned, reflexivity creates awareness that deliberation tends naturally to evolve among functional actors within subsystems and that therefore procedural mechanisms are needed to provide intersystem interaction. RDP therefore aims to act as a normative guide to pay particular attention to the problem of horizontal interconnections, that is, it requires horizontal reflexivity in addition to deliberation.

From DDP to RDP (reflexive deliberative polyarchy)

As follows from the analysis above, DDP suffers from two main shortcomings as a normative framework for European governance. Firstly, empirical evidence shows that it is unlikely that European governance practice would come anywhere near the ultimate normative claim of DDP based on decentralized deliberation that goes as far as direct citizen participation. Secondly, DDP underestimates the difficulties of intersystem communication, assuming too easily that deliberative processes would spontaneously include encompassing arguments and not be hindered by the different languages of subsystems.

The authors of DDP themselves appear to be increasingly aware of the huge gap between their normative model and the practice of European governance in relation to the criterion of direct citizen deliberation. In 2002, Sabel and Cohen explicitly acknowledged that it remains an open question to what extent the OMC ensures deliberation beyond the technical elite into civil society. They even no longer placed OMC within a framework of '*directly* deliberative polyarchy' but in one of 'deliberative polyarchy', adding that 'the democratization of deliberative polyarchy remains a project, whose precise institutional commitments have not yet been fixed'.[54] In the most recent article by Sabel and Zeitlin (2008) 'experimentalism' is the key word, and the reality described is indeed mainly one of reflexive decentralized experiencing with pooling of information at a higher level, though without much evidence of direct citizen deliberation. However, the authors remain ambiguous on their normative claims since at the start of their article they argue that DDP and experimentalism will be used interchangeably,[55] thus evoking all the normative expectations with which the concept of DDP had been identified

54 Cohen and Sabel 2003: 369.

55 See Sabel and Zeitlin 2008: 277.

in earlier work. Yet, as far as they develop arguments on democratic accountability in the most recent article, this is not about direct citizen participation, but their focus is on peer review. Now, it is in the nature of peer review that peers speak the same language and act within the same cognitive framework. How can this be sufficient in terms of democratic accountability? How does deliberation of these functional actors relate to other actors and the general interest?

It is here that reflexivity may provide normative guidance to redefine the ideal of DDP to RDP: RDP starts from the tendency for self-referentiality of subsystems. It builds on awareness of the difficulties in realizing direct citizen deliberation and the tendency to cognitive closure of subsystems of functional actors (and thus the problem of peer review as not taking into account contextuality and other discourses). Therefore, RDP aims at providing procedures that encourage interaction among subsystems and taking into account contextuality. RDP retains the normative desirability of decentralized deliberation by all those concerned, but as far as direct citizen deliberation cannot be realized, reflexivity in terms of encouraging horizontal system interaction can help to prevent policy actors from acting in favour of single interests.

Applied to European governance, this means that, aware of the difficulties in realizing direct citizen deliberation and of the tendency that governance occurs through auto-referential deliberation by functional actors, procedural mechanisms should encourage interaction between different communicative structures. If the numbers of citizens that can be involved in deliberation over policy-making will always be limited, encouraging reflexive interaction between different intermediaries who would normally tend to closure within the proper language and network of specialization may be a useful device to avoid governance in defence of particular interests.

This is not to say that such horizontal reflexivity can entirely compensate for the weakness of direct bottom-up citizen deliberation. As will be argued in the last section, horizontal reflexivity needs to be placed within an institutional framework of polyarchy in the traditional Dahl sense of the word, and a reflexive constitutional design that provides a balance of substantive values resulting from democratic procedures. Yet, before that, it will be shown that current European governance practice shows elements of horizontal reflexivity, which makes RDP a more useful normative model than DDP.

Horizontal reflexivity in practice: The example of the EES

The analysis above makes clear that the EES and the Lisbon Strategy do not provide the decentralized direct deliberation that DDP aims at, and there is nothing to suggest that this would be the case in any foreseeable future. However, RDP also allows us to identify another feature of the EES, namely its awareness that employment policy is based on several subsystems between which communication is not spontaneous but should be encouraged. The EES encourages at several levels 'reflexivity' understood as the horizontal taking into account of other subsystems, which should improve policy efficiency but equally ensures that decision-making cannot be based on the single narrative of one subsystem. Not sticking to a strong autopoietic reading, there is a belief that formal organizations or policy sectors can constitute subsystems with a considerable level of communicative and organizational self-referentiality.[56]

The EES has increasingly encouraged reflexivity in the sense of horizontal subsystem interaction at several levels. A first level of horizontal reflexivity can be identified within the OMC of employment itself. The OMC procedure in the employment field provides for a cyclical process involving political representatives in the European Council and the Council, and administrative support from the Commission and the national ministries dealing with employment. A central place in this process is taken by the Employment Committee (EMCO), which has an advisory capacity, and which is composed of two representatives from each member state and from the Commission. The predecessor of EMCO, namely the Employment and Labour Market Committee, was originally closed to external actors and the Committee had mainly an administrative function, preparing the work for the Labour and Social Affairs Council.[57] However, this closed self-referential administrative community was opened up in 2000, with EMCO providing for a reflexive process that integrates scientific and expert knowledge into politico-administrative decision-making.[58] This happens in particular through the 'indicators' working group (IWG) working under the auspices of EMCO. The IWG consists of technical experts from ministries, statistical agencies, or other organizations,[59] and may call upon other external 'specialists'. Its task is to develop, revise and improve a set of common indicators used to assess overall employment, performance, policy progress and results, and to provide technical advice for selection of benchmarks and quantitative targets to support the employment guidelines. The OMC reporting and benchmarking process is thus not simply the result of a politico-administrative community but is based on a reflexive process between the politico-administrative and scientific/technical communities.

A second and more prominent level of horizontal reflexivity occurs with the Lisbon Strategy's increasing encouragement of interaction between the different OMC processes in separate policy sectors. Initially, different OMC procedures had been set up; each with its own policy cycle, proper actors, proper language and normative framework. Yet one can notice increasing encouragement of reflexivity in terms of taking into account what would normally fall out of the self-referential frame. The Lisbon European Council (March 2000) itself had aimed at better articulation between employment and other policy fields, including macroeconomics, structural economic reforms, social protection, education and

56 On the difficulty in defining 'systems' within autopoietic and reflexive law theory, see Witteveen 1992: 59; Vlies 1992: 177; and Wilthagen 1994: 348.

57 See Porte 2008: 81.

58 See Porte 2008: 108.

59 See Jacobsson and Vifell 2004.

training, and implementation of new technologies. Yet Lisbon has not been particularly effective in organizing reflection in operational terms – creating additional OMC procedures without clear coordination among them. The Barcelona Council (March 2002) therefore urged streamlining of the various policy coordination processes at EU level. As a result, policy coordination processes, and in particular the employment OMC and the OMC on Broad Economic Policy Guidelines (BEPG), have been streamlined following a Communication of the European Commission,[60] and focusing around the annual Spring European Council. The synchronization of the start of the BEPG and employment guidelines processes by the Commission's simultaneous presentation of its input for both instruments and their subsequent discussion in relevant bodies is aimed to increase coordination. The relaunch of the Lisbon Strategy in 2005 has strengthened this streamlined process by bringing the employment and economic guidelines together in a set of integrated guidelines, including an integrated reporting system at the national level. The synchronization of policy cycles of different OMCs constitutes a procedural encouragement for reflection as these different policy instruments are now discussed (partially) by the same institutions at the same moment. This coordination of different policy sectors and subsystems (that is, self-referential communicative social spheres) can be welcomed, in particular in relation to tackling the complex problem of unemployment.

Horizontal reflexivity occurs not only *within* the OMC procedure itself or *between* different OMC processes. The Lisbon Strategy increasingly also aims at encouraging interaction between other policy processes that otherwise tend to develop in separate self-referential communities. An example of this is the relationship between the OMC on employment and the activities of the social partners. Although involvement of the social partners at national level in drafting and implementing NAPs was from the start encouraged by the EES, European industrial relations have mainly functioned as a separate subsystem affecting employment independently from the OMC on employment. However, increasing efforts have been made to coordinate the autonomous activities of the social partners and employment initiatives under the EES. Since 2001 the European social partners are invited to contribute to the EES. Moreover, in the Lisbon Strategy their involvement has been institutionalized by an annual tripartite summit bringing together social partners and governments on the eve of the Spring European Council.[61] Since 2002, European cross-sectoral social partners have adopted three annual working programmes in which they set out their autonomous initiatives for the coming years.[62] While autonomous programmes, they have been drafted

60 Communication from the Commission on Streamlining the Annual Economic and Employment Policy Coordination Cycles (COM(2002) 487 final).

61 Watt 2004: 129.

62 For development of an autonomous social dialogue at European level, see Smismans 2007.

explicitly in the light of the objectives set by the Lisbon Strategy and indicating how they would contribute to the set objectives.

A similar pattern can be seen in the relationship between the EES and structural funds policy. The decentralized approach of the EES was meant to involve regional and local actors in drafting and implementing NAPs and NRPs, but sub-national authorities have considered the opportunities to be involved as 'largely insufficient'.[63] Yet, while the EU is limited in its capacity to impose on member states 'vertical decentralisation' and deliberation by regional and local authorities in the OMC employment procedure, it has increasingly sought to encourage horizontal reflexivity between the OMC on employment and the structural funds. The structural funds, and in particular the European Social Fund, aim to contribute financial support to employment initiatives at regional and local level. Structural Funds and the OMC on employment have tended to develop separately, based on different policy cycles, and handled by different administrations at both European and (sub-)national level.[64] Yet the new Structural Funds and Social Fund Regulations require member state initiatives to be 'consistent with and contribute to the EES' and to commit part of their received funds explicitly to objectives set by the EES and Lisbon Strategy.[65]

RDP and polyarchy in the traditional sense

The analysis above illustrates how one can identify an increasing amount of processes of horizontal reflexivity in the EES. As direct citizen deliberation in the EES is difficult to realize, such horizontal reflexivity may at least contribute to avoiding the occurrence of decision-making in the defence of the single interests of one particular subsystem. However, horizontal reflexivity cannot entirely compensate for the shortcomings of direct citizen deliberation and cannot as such guarantee democratic decision-making.

Paul Magnette has rightly criticized DDP for not acknowledging the potential of representative democracy – as opposed to direct participatory processes – in fostering civic equality and civic education.[66] In a comparable way, Schmalz-Bruns

63 Committee of the Regions – Lisbon Monitoring Platform Analysis, Horizon 2010: Local and Regional Authorities for Growth and Jobs, CdR 365/2006fin-Report EN/o: 2. See also Commission Communication on Strengthening the local dimension of the European Employment Strategy (COM(2001) 629 final).

64 Hartwig 2002.

65 Regulation 1081/2006 on the European Social Fund and repealing Regulation (EC) No. 1784/1999, OJ L 210, 31 July 2006: 12–18; and Regulation (EC) No. 1828/2006 setting out rules for the implementation of Council Regulation (EC) No. 1083/2006 laying down general provisions on the European Regional Development Fund, the European Social Fund and the Cohesion Fund and of Regulation (EC) No. 1080/2006 of the European Parliament and of the Council on the European Regional Development Fund, OJ L 371, 27 December 2006: 1–163.

66 See Magnette 2006.

criticizes DDP for underestimating the normative force of the claim of a *demos* and the idea of an encompassing general public of citizens, and therefore being unable to account for how the principles of democratic equality and solidarity would be realized.[67] Although horizontal reflexivity helps to steer decision-making towards the general rather than the singular interest, it still faces similar problems in terms of civic and democratic equality, civic education, and solidarity. RDP as a normative framework therefore needs to take into account the role of representative institutions and polyarchy in the traditional Dahl sense of the word. In particular, representative institutions have an important role to play in formulating substantive values into law through democratic procedures. Without such substantive values set out in democratic legislative procedures, reflexive processes are likely to be dominated by the language of subsystems that do not rely on democratic and participatory processes.

Rethinking Reflexive Constitutionalism: Taking Substantive Norms Seriously

There is a risk in the debate on deliberative democracy and reflexive constitutionalism of thinking about constitutional design in purely procedural terms, as if such design could be neutral in substantive terms. The reflexive law paradigm may appear to strengthen that perspective as far as it would refrain from setting substantive norms and stressing law's role in providing the procedural framework to allow self-regulation by other subsystems.

However, such a perspective involves two problems. Firstly, no single constitution is neutral in substantive terms. The European Constitution in particular is well known to be primarily an economic constitution, with a neoliberal bias. Thinking normatively about ensuring bottom-up reflexive processes without reflecting on the substantive values of the constitutional design in which such processes have to operate is unlikely to deliver democratic governance. Reflexive constitutionalism as a constitutional design of bottom-up deliberative processes should thus go hand in hand with horizontal reflexivity on Europe's multiple constitutions, such as the economic and the social.

Secondly, it is questionable whether a neutral constitutional design is normatively desirable. Or to put it differently, it would be wrong to define the role of law as simply providing procedural mechanisms, to allow self-regulation by other subsystems, without providing itself for the definition of substantive values. Law has traditionally had a role in translating societal norms into substantive legal norms. As in no other subsystem, this process has been linked to democratic procedures. In reducing law to a procedural role, the definition of substantive norms will be left to subsystems that do not guarantee democratic processes. Law, therefore, has to set substantive norms, through legislative or constitutional

67 See Schmalz-Bruns 2005: 65 and 72.

standards following democratic procedures, in order to avoid reflexive processes ending up with the subordination of policy-making to the dominant rationale of subsystems which are not based on democratic procedures.

The need for substantive norms does not have to stand in contrast with reflexive law theory. Even in its autopoietic interpretation, reflexive law is not emptied of all debate on substantive norms, as it necessitates at least democratic norms in guiding procedural organization. In a broader interpretation, reflexive law encourages reflexivity on the particular nature of law as translating societal norms into legal ones. Based on system theory, reflexive law acknowledges the particular nature of law as a subsystem with its own rationality and communicative structure. While the legal subsystem may be operatively closed, it is cognitively open. Whatever may be the way in which ethical or social values or political maxims are translated into the legal system (and into legal constructs), the legal system would not have reason to exist if entirely cognitively closed. On the other hand, it is acknowledged that too much cognitive openness may place at risk the survival of the legal subsystem as 'colonized' by another one.[68] One should thus find a balance between, on the one hand, avoiding colonization of legal rationality by other value systems (and, therefore, plead for a certain restraint on trying to regulate by law in detail all aspects of contemporary differentiated society), and on the other hand avoiding total cognitive closure of the legal system by emptying it entirely of substantive values, in which case law would become entirely procedural and self-referentially closed, and, therefore, bypassed by other subsystems such as economic or statistical in setting objectives and substantive values in society and politics.[69]

Therefore, while reflexive law and RDP can encourage reflexive processes based on deliberation within subsystems and horizontal reflexivity between them, it also recognizes that law should provide for substantive values through democratic procedures, hence avoiding the domination of governance by subsystems which are not based on democratic processes.

This can again be illustrated by the dynamics of European governance in the EES. Looking at the language of the OMC guidelines and the suggestions it makes to the member states, one finds a policy discourse focusing on policy objectives related to a variety of different policy instruments but in which the language of rights, and the definition of substantive norms by (command-control) regulation, is almost entirely absent. As a consequence, horizontal reflexivity between OMC processes may create subordination of some policy sectors to others or colonization of certain subsystems by others. Thus it has been argued that the

68 The risk of endangering the formal rationality of law through the infusion into law of other value systems had already been identified by Max Weber, and is a key topic of legal theory (see Teubner 1983: 243).

69 Even Teubner (1993: 67) in his autopoietic period states that 'substantive legal norms remain indispensable. It is only that the process of their production and justification has to give way to a "socially adequate" proceduralization'.

OMC, as a strategy for reincarnation of the European welfare state, is subservient to the ideologies, path-dependencies, and structures of economic and monetary union, as institutionalized in the BEPGs.[70] The Lisbon process, centred around a discourse of economic growth and competitiveness rather than around social citizenship and encouragement of coordination of social and economic policies, has resulted not so much in economic policy being sensitive to social concerns, but to colonization of the welfare state by the economic policy-making process.[71] As the risk arises that coordination of the BEPGS and the EGs procedures leads to subordination of the latter to the former, interlinking of employment and social policy tends to subordinate social policy objectives and instruments to the objectives of employment policy, which in its turn is dominantly framed in the language of growth and competitiveness. To avoid such subordination, and to encourage reflection between employment and social policy in a reciprocal way, European social policy should build its own referential frame around social citizenship, rights and quality of jobs. This is only possible by defining substantive norms through democratic procedures.

Hence, encouraging horizontal reflexivity between subsystems may partially compensate for lack of direct citizen deliberation, but this will only contribute to democratic governance in a context of polyarchy in the traditional sense, and where law – in constitutional and legislative norms resulting from democratic procedures – sets substantive boundaries.

Conclusion

Much current European governance practice which raises constitutional questions is not appropriately dealt with in either the political or academic constitutional debate. The Lisbon Strategy, which has set out an extensive European governance mechanism over the last decade, is a good case in point. The example of the EES, as part of the Lisbon Strategy, has been used to rethink the normative framework in relation to European governance. The process started with an analysis of DDP, which has the advantage of looking more closely at current European governance practice than other reflections on European constitutionalism, but has the double disadvantage of being overly optimistic on the possibility for direct citizen deliberation and underestimating the tendency of subsystems towards self-referentiality. Taking reflexivity seriously as a normative device has therefore been suggested. RDP encourages both actor deliberation and horizontal reflexivity between subsystems. Yet reflexivity as such is no guarantee for democratic governance. Polyarchy in the traditional sense of electoral process and parliamentary representation needs to ensure the definition of substantive values in legislative and constitutional norms.

70 See Chalmers and Lodge 2003: 2.

71 See Chalmers and Lodge 2003: 10.

References

Armstrong, K. and Kilpatrick, C. 2007. Law, governance, or new governance? The changing open method of coordination. *Columbia Journal of European Law*, 13:3, 649–78.

Barnard, C., Deakin, S. and Hobbs, R. 2005. Reflexive law, corporate social responsibility and the evolution of labour standards: The case of working time, in *Social Rights and Market Forces: Is the Open Coordination of Employment and Social Policies the Future of Social Europe?* edited by O. de Schutter and S. Deakin. Bruylant: Brussels, 205–44.

Begg, I. 2007. Lisbon II, Two Years On: An Assessment of the Partnership for Growth and Jobs. Speech, 10 July 2007, at CEPS. Available at: <http://www.ceps.be/content/lisbon-ii-two-years-assessment-partnership-growth-and-jobs> (accessed 21 January 2010).

Black, J. 1996. Constitutionalizing self-regulation. *Modern Law Review*, 59:1, 24–55.

Bohman, J. 2005. Reflexive constitution-making and transnational governance, in *Making the European Polity. Reflexive Integration in the EU*, edited by E.O. Eriksen. London: Routledge, 32–58.

Búrca, G. de. 2003. The constitutional challenge of new governance in the European Union. *European Law Review*, 28:6, 814–39.

Chalmers, D. and Lodge, M. 2003. The Open Method of Coordination and the European Welfare State. Discussion Paper ESRC Centre for Analysis of Risk and Regulation, 11: June. Available at: <http://www.lse.ac.uk/collections/CARR/pdf/DPs/Disspaper11.pdf> (accessed 21 January 2010).

Cohen, J. and Sabel, C. 1997. Directly-deliberative polyarchy. *European Law Journal*, 3:4, 313–42.

Cohen J. and Sabel, C. 1999. Directly-deliberative polyarchy. Available at: <http://www2.law.columbia.edu/sabel/papers/DDP.html> (accessed 21 January 2010).

Cohen, J. and Sabel, C. 2003. Sovereignty and solidarity: EU and US, in *Governing Work and Welfare in a New Economy. European and American Experiments*, edited by J. Zeitlin and D.M. Trubek. Oxford: Oxford University Press, 345–75.

Dahl, R. 1956. *A Preface to Democratic Theory*. Chicago: University of Chicago Press.

Dahl, R 1989. *Democracy and its Critics*. New Haven: Yale University Press.

Deakin, S. 1999. Two types of regulatory competition: Competitive federalism versus reflexive harmonisation. A law and economics perspective on *Centros*. *The Cambridge Yearbook of European Legal Studies*, 2, 231–60.

Diamond, A. 2004. Soft harmonisation: The 'open method of coordination' in the European Employment Strategy. *European Public Law*, 10:2, 305–32.

Elster, J. 1998. Introduction, in *Deliberative Democracy*, edited by J. Elster. Cambridge: Cambridge University Press, 8–22.

Eriksen, E.O. 2005a. *Making the European Polity. Reflexive Integration in the EU*. London: Routledge.

Eriksen, E.O. 2005b. Reflexive integration in Europe, in *Making the European Polity. Reflexive Integration in the EU*, edited by E.O. Eriksen. Routledge: London, 9–29.

Gerstenberg, O. and Sabel, C.F. 2002. Directly-deliberative polyarchy: An institutional ideal for Europe? in *Good Governance in Europe's Integrated Market*, edited by C. Joerges and R. Dehousse. Oxford: Oxford University Press, 289–341.

Goetschy, J. 2003. The European Employment Strategy, multi-level governance, and policy coordination: Past, present and future, in *Governing Work and Welfare in a New Economy. European and American Experiments*, edited by J. Zeitlin and D.M. Trubek. Oxford: Oxford University Press, 59–87.

Hartwig, I. 2002. Incremental Synergies or Growing Fragmentation between the Luxembourg Process and EU Cohesion Policy? EIPA Working Paper 2002/W/1. Available at: <http://publications.eipa.eu/en/details/&tid=1711> (accessed 28 June 2010).

Held, D. 1987. *Models of Democracy*. Cambridge: Polity Press.

Homs, O., Kruse, W., Lafoucrière, C. and Tilly, P. 2005. *Contribution des organisations syndicales à l'évaluation des actions menées et de leur impact en termes de stratégie européenne pour l'emploi*. Bruxelles: Confédération Européenne des Syndicats. Available at: <http://www.etuc.org/IMG/pdf/Brochure_FR_def.pdf> (accessed 21 January 2010).

Jacobsson, K. and Vifell, A. 2004. Integration by deliberation? Dynamics of soft regulation in the case of EU employment policy. *Journal of European Social Policy*, 14:4, 355–70.

King, M. 2001. The construction and demolition of the Luhmann heresy, in *Law's New Boundaries. The Consequences of Legal Autopoiesis*, edited by J. Přibáň and D. Nelken. Aldershot: Ashgate, 123–56.

Léonard, E., Erne, R., Marginson, P. and Smismans, S. 2007. New structures, forms and processes of governance in European industrial relations. European Foundation for Living and Working Conditions. Available at: <http://www.eurofound.europa.eu/publications/htmlfiles/ef0694.htm> (accessed 21 January 2010).

Luhmann, N. 1993. *Law as a Social System*. Oxford: Oxford University Press.

Luhmann, N. 1995. *The Differentiation of Society*. New York: Columbia University Press.

Luhmann, N. 2004. *Social Systems*. Stanford: Stanford University Press.

Magnette, P. 2006. Democracy in the European Union: Why and how to combine representation and participation? in *Civil Society and Legitimate European Governance*, edited by S. Smismans. Cheltenham: Edward Elgar, 23–41.

Meer, M. van der, Visser, J. and Wilthagen, T. 2005. Adaptive and reflexive governance: The limits of organized decentralization, *European Journal of Industrial Relations*, 11:3, 347–65.

Orts, E.W. 2001. Autopoiesis and the natural environment, in *Laws New Boundaries. The Consequences of Legal Autopoiesis*, edited by J. Přibáň and D. Nelken. Aldershot: Ashgate, 159–78.

Pateman, C. 1970. *Participation and Democratic Theory*. Cambridge: Cambridge University Press.

Porte, C. de la. 2008. The European Level Development and National Level Influence of the Open Method of Coordination: The Cases of Employment and Social Inclusion. PhD Thesis, EUI, Florence.

Rodrigues, M.J. 2003. *European Policies for a Knowledge Economy*. Northampton, MA: Edward Elgar.

Rogowski, R. 2001. The concept of reflexive labour law: Its theoretical background and possible applications, in *Laws New Boundaries. The Consequences of Legal Autopoiesis*, edited by J. Přibáň and D. Nelken. Aldershot: Ashgate, 179–96.

Rogowski, R. 2007. Flexicurity and reflexive coordination of European social and employment policies, in *Flexicurity and Beyond*, edited by H. Jørgensen and P.K. Madsen. Copenhagen: DJØF Publishing.

Sabel, C.F. and Zeitlin, J. 2008. Learning from difference: The new architecture of experimentalist governance in the EU. *European Law Journal*, 14:3, 271–327.

Sand, I.-J. 1998. Understanding the new forms of governance: Mutually interdependent, reflexive, destabilised and competing institutions. *European Law Journal*, 4:3, 271–93.

Saward, M. 2000. *Democratic Innovation. Deliberation, Representation and Association*. London: Routledge.

Schmalz-Bruns, R. 2005. Reflexive constitution-making and transnational governance, in *Making the European Polity. Reflexive Integration in the EU*, edited by E.O. Eriksen. London: Routledge, 59–83.

Schutter, O. de. 2005. The implementation of fundamental rights through the open method of coordination, in *Social Rights and Market Forces: Is the Open Coordination of Employment and Social Policies the Future of Social Europe?*, edited by O. de Schutter and S. Deakin. Bruylant: Brussels, 279–343.

Schutter, O. de and Deakin, S. 2005. *Social Rights and Market Forces: Is the Open Coordination of Employment and Social Policies the Future of Social Europe?* Bruylant: Brussels.

Smismans, S. 2004. Vertical and horizontal decentralism in European governance, in *An Ever More Complex Union*, edited by R. Toniatti, P. Francesco and M. Dani. Baden-Baden: Nomos, 57–82.

Smismans, S. 2007. The European social dialogue between constitutional and labour law. *European Law Review*, 32:3, 341–64.

Teubner, G. 1983. Substantive and reflexive elements in modern law. *Law & Society Review*, 17:2, 242–286.

Teubner, G. 1993. *Law as an Autopoietic System*. Oxford: Blackwell.

Tully, J. 2002. The unfreedom of the moderns in comparison to their ideals of constitutional democracy. *Modern Law Review*, 65:2, 204–28.

Vlies, I.C. van der. 1992. Autopoiese en sociale vernieuwing: een contradictio in terminis? in *Reflecties op reflexief recht*, edited by N.J.H. Huls and H.D. Stout. Zwolle: WEJ Tjeenk Willink.

Walker, N. 2002. The idea of constitutional pluralism. *Modern Law Review*, 65:3, 317–59.

Watt, A. 2004. Reform of the European Employment Strategy after five years: A change of course or merely of presentation? *European Journal of Industrial Relations*, 10:2, 117–37.

Wilthagen, T. 1994. Reflexive rationality in the regulation of occupational safety and health, in *Reflexive Labour Law*, edited by R. Rogowski and T. Wilthagen. Deventer: Kluwer Law, 345–76.

Witteveen, W.J. 1992. Schrijft de wet zichzelf? in *Reflecties op reflexief recht*, edited by N.J.H. Huls and H.D. Stout. Zwolle: WEJ Tjeenk Willink, 59–70.

Chapter 9
Could the Court of Justice Have Done Differently?

Suvi Sankari

Introduction

Once upon a time, not so long ago – in 1968 actually – it was politically correct enough for the Vice-President of the Commission to state that 'it is for capital to go where there is labour and not *vice versa*'.[1] What is more, the 1990 edition of a leading textbook on EU law[2] still stated that even 'the principle of the free movement of workers … is … merely a safety valve'.[3] For a relatively long time after establishing the Communities, working in another member state was mainly perceived as optional to not working at all – a highly welfare state, government-level issue. The contrast with current occupational reality, at least in some sectors, therefore seems drastic. It seems that having worked, or at the very least lived, abroad has become essential in securing a mid- to high-end job, in advancing one's career, or even in demonstrating excellence in any field of scientific research. Moreover, the mobility requirements also apply to the labour market of one's own member state of origin! For many, mobility has thus become a highly personal-level issue writ large.[4]

However, this chapter is not about Union citizens' free movement as such. The development shortly summarized above only forms the context of the highly specific body of Court of Justice case law, the effect and reasoning of which are explored here. That is, the Court of Justice has been credited, or criticized, for bringing about an extraordinary change within the developing field of free movement of persons. The case law at hand is by nature prone to dismay, as it concerns a new EU institution readily christened citizenship, but also as it relates

---

1 Vice-President Levi Sandri as quoted by Kapteyn, Themaat and Gormley (1990: 411) with Bull. EC 11 – 1968: 5 given as the original reference.

2 The term EU law in this chapter is liberally applied also to refer what has been EC law.

3 Kapteyn, Themaat and Gormley 1990: 411.

4 Although all estimates of mobile member state nationals remain low (for example, 0.4 per cent of the population yearly moving to another member state, and 2.5 per cent residing in another member state), the aggregate percentage of once mobile population may be higher, assuming high turnover.

to not one but two legal phenomena described as Pandora's boxes: the principles of free movement (of Union citizens) and non-discrimination (or equality).[5] Moreover, the argued impossibility of direct effect[6] ensuing from the debatably conditional nature of Article 18 EC (before, Article 8A EC, now 21 TFEU) was hotly discussed not only by scholars but by Advocates General (AG) too, even after the *Baumbast*[7] judgment, until finally cemented as having direct effect by the Court of Justice in *Commission v Belgium*.[8] The discussion was of less relevance for those subscribing to the legal order nature of EU law; however, denying direct effect would have been problematic as, if accepted, would the provisions on free movement of goods, for instance, engender direct effect – as there are specific treaty-level limitations to the freedom? All in all, some argued that the way the Court of Justice has brought forth this remarkable change as to free movement of persons is by making new law and going against existing legislation. This criticism against judge-made law, of courts playing politics instead of practising law, is familiar to all. In EU law, such action has most often been discussed as (negative) judicial activism.

The Law in Legal Interpretation

Once more – having already been found guilty in respect of free movement of goods[9] – the Court of Justice stands accused of activism, of going beyond the natural limits of free movement, this time free movement of persons. The discussion on the Court of Justice's proper role and negative judicial activism has already made several unproductive rounds, on both a more abstract and also a particular level. In 1998, Renaud Dehousse had reason to state that although 'much ink has been spilt on judicial activism, no commonly shared definition of this phenomenon exists'.[10] Yet, very much as before, the Court of Justice faces criticism that can summarily be referred to as allegations of unwarranted activism in the area of Union citizens' free movement.[11] Some argue that the actions of the Court of Justice have contradicted the wording and spirit of present or earlier law, going against the intent of the EU legislator. At the very least, such accusations merit an examination of the singled-

5 See Weiler 1999: 333; Somek 1999; and Besson and Utzinger 2007.

6 Traditionally, provisions apt for direct effect are (sufficiently) clear, unconditional and not contingent on implementing measures. See Case 26/62, *Van Gend en Loos*, ECR 1963, 3 (English special edition, 1). For more relaxed views, see for example Chalmers et al. 2006: 368–71; and Prechal 2002.

7 Case C-413/99, *Baumbast and R*, ECR 2002, I-7091.

8 See Case C-408/03, *Commission v Belgium*, ECR 2006, I-2647, para. 34.

9 See, for example, Poiares Maduro 1998: 23.

10 Dehousse 1998: 123.

11 The starting point of the activism debate in the EU context is famously Rasmussen 1986; as to critical commentaries on the case law at hand here, see, for example, Mather 2005; Hailbronner 2005; and Tryfonidou 2009.

out case law from another perspective, namely in terms of legal reasoning and the directives of interpretation applied by the Court of Justice, especially as the criticism focuses on how the Court of Justice has interpreted EU law, that is, the legislative body consisting of primary and secondary provisions. What remains to be seen is: do empirical facts support activism claims as to the case law at hand, or could there plausibly be an alternative rational explanation for the Court's actions?

No single case law study can prove the Court of Justice innocent or guilty as to negative judicial activism. Moreover, all studies phrased in terms of activism come with certain reservations. First of all, activism studies should distinguish between at least two phases in the evolution of the Court of Justice's role (or EU law): a foundational authority-building (activist) period ending about 1990 and a more moderate authority-maintaining period thereafter. This rough division is suggested by Allan Rosas, Joxerramon Bengoetxea, Martin Shapiro and Anthony Arnull.[12] The division also more or less coincides with the EU's geographic enlargement (from 1995 onwards), doubling the number of judges at the Court of Justice, and with the Maastricht Treaty (1993), which those who distinguish phases in the evolution of the Court of Justice's role often regard as urging the Court to interpret law more restrictively thereafter.[13]

Secondly, one inevitably – overtly or, as often is the case, covertly – chooses sides as to one's understanding of the nature of EU law. The understanding here is that EU law is an autonomous legal order and not a form of regular international law.[14] Thirdly, undertaking a study on court behaviour similarly reveals one's background ideology as to what courts should do and how they should do it. Much like Bengoetxea, it is here presumed that all court decisions require an act of interpretation which means that an intellectually honest rational social agent, a court, should openly justify the choices it has made in the interpretative process.[15] The Court of Justice can be perceived as a constitutional court staying true to the very constitution and legal order it was set up to uphold.[16] Thus, the case law on Articles 17 and 18 EC (now Arts 20 and 21 TFEU) may merely suggest the Court is observing the law in its legal interpretation.

There is no universal definition of (negative) judicial activism, and thus observers' opinions differ on when exactly courts impose their views on political power.[17] Especially from a legal point of view, it therefore makes more sense to

12 See Rosas 2005: 338; Bengoetxea 1993: 101; Shapiro 1999: 340–344; and Arnull 2006: 639–644. Somewhat similarly also Rasmussen 1998: 28 and 349–350.

13 See, for example, Arnull 2006: 654.

14 On how this distinction is reflected in the approach to legal reasoning, see Itzcovich 2009: 540–545.

15 See more fundamentally Bengoetxea 1993.

16 As the current Article 19 TEU (ex 220 EC) also states: 'It shall ensure that in the interpretation and application of the Treaties the law is observed.'

17 A limit set for negative activism by Dehousse (1998: 127). The latter-day Rasmussen (1998: 27) defines activism as 'regular judicial policy-making in pursuance

concentrate on the methodology of interpreting law than ambiguous 'activism'. One must concentrate on what is available, since beyond the reasoning in the Court of Justice's judgments it is anyone's guess exactly how the Court reaches agreement on interpretation due to secrecy of deliberations. An educated guess, highly plausible at the very least, is to assume that judicial decision-making of a collegiate court deciding cases in variable compositions does not hinge upon a shared world view, political aims of individual judges, or even consistently rational action by one and the same judge. Referring to his experience with fellow judges at the Court of Justice, Thymen Koopmans suggests: 'a Community-minded view on one point does not imply that the same person has a similar view on a different point'.[18] No doubt there is no objective definition of what constitutes community-mindedness, either. If one assumes deliberations are not mere voting, they are likely to involve discussing general legal arguments arising, at the Court of Justice, from the general rules of interpretation it has assumed, from the 'genetic code' set by the aims of the treaties,[19] and the systemic consistency of interpretation.

Based on the underlying assumptions above, one can ask: in the case law under review here, is the Court merely aiming to uphold the legal fruits of political decision-making by politicians? Is the resistance the case law has met simply born out of a certain unease or frustration in that the political subsystem cannot – not to make simple things too complicated by resorting to Luhmannian/Teubnerian language here – rule supreme or even effectively control the society's legal subsystem? Or is court activism the end product of political inactivity? The legal subsystem in this particular field of law rather heavily affects the social subsystem, if one uses the same taxonomy of subsystems as Kaarlo Tuori, in this volume, applies to constitutions. Although different societal subsystems share impulses and affect each other, their relative closedness towards each other is a fact, which may not be altogether bad. Drawing clear boundaries between politics and law being infeasible, the Court of Justice itself may well be acutely aware of the uneasy position it occupies in the twilight between the two. It may well understand the usual push from the side of politics to leave some decisions for 'the law', although they would more appropriately fall into the sphere of politics. However, what the Court of Justice cannot do is fail to answer preliminary references sent to it by national courts.[20]

Aiming to remain within the field of law, and continuing to invest its authority in the civil law tradition, the Court of Justice pertains to a formalistic,

---

of policy objectives which usurp the rule and policy making powers of other branches of government, specifically if judicial choice-making over a procrasted period of time is at odds with election-day results'.

18 Koopmans 1996: 99.

19 Using the expression 'genetic code' here is inspired by Snell (2008: 623).

20 It must of course also decide other cases, but the case law under review here consists solely of preliminary references, hence the reference only to them.

or even cryptic, approach as to justifying its decisions.[21] It has chosen this way of reasoning, and found it successful in the authority-building of the Court of Justice, or a workable way of a collegiate court to make decisions – or both. It is only reasonable to assume that in answering questions on the interpretation of EU law, the Court of Justice argues over legal interpretation. The directives (or criteria) of interpretation assumed by the Court of Justice have been examined by Bengoetxea.[22] As the results are based on sufficient empiricism, his conclusions can survive the severing of ties to their theoretical foundations within institutional legal positivism or legal argumentation. Moreover, the directives of interpretation coincide greatly with more universal findings on statute interpretation,[23] albeit with the renowned difference that the Court of Justice places little value on legislative intent of a mostly mythical legislator.

Utterly concisely, first-order interpretative criteria documented by Bengoetxea consist of semiotic, systemic(-contextual) and dynamic 'criteria' – in other words 'arguments' as before taking a decision and 'reasons' in judgments that can be studied.[24] The first-order criteria not only follow universal ways of interpretation by courts, but also coincide with the Court of Justice's interpretative credo that EU law must be interpreted according to the spirit (dynamic criteria), the general scheme (systemic-contextual criteria) and the wording (semiotic criteria) of the Treaty.[25] The different categories 'leak' into each other, theoretically and also practically, as observers of case law interpret the wording of reasoning differently. Second-order criteria determine the weight and priority of first-order criteria.[26] According to Bengoetxea, priority between first-order criteria requires preference of systemic-cum-dynamic arguments over others.[27] Moreover, a general second-order criterion for interpreting EU law requires that 'the Community Treaties, as the constitution of the Community are to be interpreted broadly … and its corollary criterion, i.e. that exceptions to fundamental Community principles are to be narrowly interpreted'.[28]

Having framed the role of the Court of Justice as in the above, one can go a long way in analysing case law with just these few plain directives of interpretation. The use of dynamic first-order criteria of interpretation should perhaps set off the alarm bells of activism, as the use of dynamic reasons opens legal reasoning towards non-legal arguments related also to consequences outside law and to policies in

21 For a comparative analysis relativizing the position of the Court of Justice as one between the American Supreme Court and the French Cour de cassation, see Lasser 2004.

22 Bengoetxea 1993.

23 See, for example, a comparative study by MacCormick and Summers (1991) on interpreting statutes.

24 Bengoetxea 1993: 227, 233–62.

25 The often stated criteria of interpretation since Case 26/62, *Van Gend en Loos*, ECR 1963, 3 (English special edition, 1).

26 See Bengoetxea 1993: 228.

27 Bengoetxea 1993: 234.

28 Bengoetxea 1993: 233.

general. However, as the Court of Justice's reasoning remains terse, one must also go beyond it. Observing the development of the field of law in more systemic terms – guided by second-order interpretative criteria – one should be able to understand whether an alternative non-activist way of perceiving the case law could be justified. Also, the noise case law commentaries create is often louder than the Court of Justice's voice, especially as the Court also speaks through silence. Daniel Sarmiento provides an account of how the Court of Justice operates under the contemporary fact of constitutional pluralism, manoeuvring with speaking and staying silent. He categorizes forms of pluralism-facilitating silence as: 'complete' or 'partial silence' by the Court of Justice – the two most interesting categories here – and 'unheard replies' that lack an audience.[29] Sarmiento's account illustrates how attention should be paid to the special nature of preliminary references that are unlike ordinary litigation, allowing the Court of Justice to adapt the question sent to it, and to give a detailed or imaginative answer, or no answer at all: silence. As much as one can agree with Sarmiento's elegant analysis, the other side of the coin would suggest this is not always done just to avoid constitutional conflict, as the silences – unintentionally or not – allow for the Court of Justice to proceed incrementally and attract more references. This enables it to invoke a veritable body of case law on a certain issue while simultaneously boosting its own authority by the influx of cases. Still, one can validly ask whether, in describing what the Court of Justice does, concepts more adequate than politics or activism could be law, silence[30] and self-restraint?

A final reservation relates to the choice of cases to study. In the Union citizenship debate, each scholar has seemed to construct their own unique set of case law. The case law studied here consists of those judgments from 1998 to 2008 that refer to either Article 17 or 18 EC in their operative part – a selection overlapping to a great extent with what the Court of Justice in its digest considers as its Union citizenship case law.

For a More Simple Analysis of Case Law

It is not rare in EU law for something to be too little and too much at the same time. One does not have to read extensively on Union citizenship to understand it is criticized from both directions: it is exclusive rather than inclusive, a meagre set of rights and no duties, meaningful only to those who are mobile, not enough to remedy the democracy and legitimacy deficits of the EU; but it is also an illegitimate incursion into the welfare autonomy of member states, threatening their legitimate national (financial) interests by affecting access to welfare systems based on national solidarity – if not the existence of both welfare systems and nation-states

29 Sarmiento's (2010 forthcoming) work is invaluable in stressing the salience of silence.

30 Sarmiento 2010 (forthcoming).

altogether. Leaving aside more philosophical accounts of the institution, even the jungle of analyses on Union citizenship case law has become too dense to grasp.

Eleanor Spaventa compared the case law on Union citizenship to an impressionist painting instead of a classical still life.[31] She suspected the analyses of this new free movement case law are not seeing the forest for the trees. One could alternatively raise the suspicion: has the forest been there for anyone to see? The handful of cases, in which the partial and total silences in reasoning should have been deafening to scholars, has aroused academic enthusiasm for over-interpretation. Academic overenthusiasm has probably become an incentive among others for the Court of Justice to use as much silence as possible. As silences go unnoticed, scholarly imagination soon fills in the blanks of a developing field of law – only to criticize the Court for having changed its imaginary mind in its ensuing case law. These are some of the reasons why the jungle of analyses on Union citizenship case law has become too dense to grasp.

Hence a more ordinary descriptive normative account of this developing field of law is suggested. The account should take heed of general EU law doctrine and the general methods or directives of interpreting EU law. To adequately take into consideration the context of the case law does not necessarily require a general politico-historical – or philosophical – contextualization, but a more moderate, yet contextual approach internal to law. It should sufficiently take into consideration not only the sporadic development of the case law under review, but also the parallel developments of EU law, here especially in the general field of free movement law. Such a legal positivist account easily becomes overly descriptive. To make it more substantive, or polemic, the case law is approached here by asking: *what could the Court of Justice have done differently (after Maastricht)?* What interpretation other than that made could have served the fundamentals of EU law and its interpretation better?

Free movement in the founding treaties and early years

In a substantively and historically contextual reading of the case law, Article 18 EC (or 8A EC as it first was, now 21 TFEU) can be conceived as a political step towards realizing an aim set for the Communities already in the, literally, founding treaties: free movement of persons, not only workers. However, the new right to free movement is not often analysed in the simple terms of being one of the market freedoms. Most likely this is – looking back – by now considered inelegant, as it is not considered proper to suggest people are like goods, or suggest restricting treaty-based freedom to its natural personal scope, Union citizens.

Nevertheless, both free movement of persons and equality, as prohibition of discrimination on grounds of nationality,[32] can already be found in the original Treaty of Rome. Not only was free movement of persons a part of a subheading of

31 Spaventa 2008.

32 See originally Art. 7(1) EEC (ex 6 EC and 12 EC, now 18 TFEU).

the EEC Treaty under which free movement of workers and the self-employed was established, but according to Article 3 EEC, the Common Market was supposed to be realized through: 'the abolition … of the obstacles to the free movement of persons'. Hence, realizing this aim has been an inseparable part of the genetic code of EU law from its very beginning.

In the formative decades, only those member state nationals who were workers, self-employed or service providers had the treaty-based specific right to free movement. Through interpretation and secondary legislation, service recipients and work-seekers soon followed. As Willem Maas points out, such freedoms did not really distinguish the European Economic Community from any other free market economy.[33] Maas argues that 'freedom of movement represents the core of contemporary EU citizenship' and its genesis should be backdated to the Treaty of Paris 1951 (ECSC).[34] A consensus exists that embryonic Union citizenship was born out of Italy's need to export its surplus agricultural labour, mostly to Belgium, to work alongside Belgians in the coal mines, enjoying generally similar treatment.[35] The treaty Articles on workers and the self-employed included the right not to be discriminated against on grounds of nationality – in addition to the general prohibition of nationality discrimination and some specific secondary law.[36] Unless their right to free movement and residence was denied on the basis of the 'mandatory requirements' applicable to free movement of persons (public policy, public security, public health), these core groups of persons could (and still can) exercise their freedom to move. The Court of Justice's role during this era was to interpret secondary legislation extensively, availing freedom of movement to as many economically active member state nationals as possible.

Setting aside the Commission vice-president's remark on mobile capital and static people in 1968, it might still not be sustainable to claim that, back then, free movement of persons was premised on the idea of allowing only those to move freely who could not burden the economies of host member states. The relevant secondary legislation on workers mentions 'Measures for controlling the balance of the labour market', but does not analyse potential risks to national economies or mention burdening.[37] This is merely logical as only economically active individuals moved freely, and probably most of them did contribute to the host member state's

33 See Maas 2007: 118.

34 Maas 2005: 1010.

35 See Maas 2005: 1012–13.

36 The very detailed secondary legislation (Reg. 1612/68 on freedom of movement for workers within the Community, and Reg. 1408/71 on the application of social security schemes to employed persons, to self-employed persons and to members of their families moving within the Community) on worker's rights caused confusion later on, when the personal scope of free movement was enlarged.

37 Title III of Reg. 1612/68. Also, the 'Coordination Regulation' (1408/71) aims to guarantee migrant workers their social rights and advantages whilst preventing the unjustified overlapping of benefits – remaining silent on any cost–benefit calculation as to burdening the finances of the host member state.

common good, even financially. Without a doubt they also burdened host member states. However, it is highly debatable whether, in any meaningful sense, thinking in quantitative cost–benefit terms on the potential contribution and the offsetting burden had entered the legislative faculties at this stage.

After the Single European Act of 1987, efforts concentrated on furthering the single market. In 1990, new secondary law gave specific new groups of member state nationals, considered economically inactive, the right to free movement.[38] The new groups qualified for using the right only by meeting the (economic) requirements based on the relevant secondary legislation and any right to equal treatment or access to national solidarity they gained was strictly limited within the confines of what the Residence Directives provided for, or what the host member state decided, or was otherwise obliged, to offer them. Although this was a further step on the incremental journey towards fulfilment of free movement of persons, it was also the time when interest in protecting national economies against the burden posed by potentially destitute EU migrants made an entrance as a pivotal issue in the legislative sphere. Since then, the objectives of full-scale free movement of persons and of comprehensive abstinence by individual member states from bearing any ensuing risks or actual costs have remained at variance.

Free movement from Maastricht onwards

Allegedly, the Maastricht Treaty in 1993 – in tandem with shedding the *Economic* from between European and Community – all of a sudden added a new general norm of primary pedigree in declaring that all member state nationals as 'Union citizens' are entitled to free movement.[39] Although born out of member states' unanimous agreement to add the Article, the incompletely theorized agreement – as it were, in Sunsteinian terms – over its meaning meant that mending the relevant secondary legislation remained at a standstill for years. This was the environment in which the Court of Justice had to resolve cases by interpreting law, for the early years of Union citizenship's existence.

Secondary law dating from the pre-Maastricht era remained in force, and had to be interpreted together with the new treaty Article by the Court of Justice, to the effect that the law is observed, so maintaining or creating a systematic whole. The secondary law established a piecemeal structure of rules that determined the outer limits of free movement for the groups of people they concerned. Hence, in the pre-Maastricht sense that they facilitated free movement, they had to be interpreted as encompassingly (extensively) as possible, that is, entitling as many as possible to move freely. From 1993 onwards, however, there was a general right of all Union citizens to free movement. This meant the earlier rules had to be interpreted in a way that would least restrict this *fundamental freedom*. Moreover, not only did the

38 Residence Directives on pensioners (90/365/EC), students (93/96/EC) and a group referred to as, for instance, playboys – the financially self-sufficient (90/364/EC).

39 Wiener (1998) proves this gospel to be untrue, in her thorough political analysis.

law concerning Union citizens' free movement have to form a consistent whole, but it had to reasonably relate to the hierarchy between different groups of people, static or mobile, within the territory of the EU. This is illustrated, for instance, in the Court of Justice repeatedly stating that the Association Agreement with Turkey should not amount to treating those it is applicable to more favourably than member state nationals.[40] The apex of the pyramid – should one wish to put it that way – thus must at least always include Union citizens, especially working ones, perhaps in addition to other groups of people.[41] For instance, the Association Agreement does not provide access to the EU or facilitate free movement within it, but provides for equal treatment and protection against withdrawing the right of residence of both the worker and family members.[42]

Also, what the addition of one glorious Article managed to underline clearly was that one of the overriding pursuits of the EU, the goal of free movement of persons set as long ago as 1957, still remained unattained. Presumably in part due to the somewhat catastrophic early years of Union citizenship, an abundance of critical scholarship not content with the state of affairs followed. It only later turned out that a Union citizen's right to free movement – together with the earlier treaty-based free movement of persons rights – is actually one of the original four market freedoms and not a different, perhaps even more fundamental, fifth category. In the meanwhile, Union citizenship and free movement were dealt with as an amalgamated muddle most closely, maybe, relating to quite philosophical discussions on human dignity and equality. This confusion also contributed to losing sight as to how this freedom should fit into the existing *acquis* on free movement in general. As a further cause for confusion, the Court of Justice clarified its understanding of the relationships between Articles 18, 39, 43 and 49 EC (now 21, 45, 49 and 56 TFEU) in relatively early cases that did not squarely fall within what most often is regarded as its Union citizenship case law by scholars. It stated that the treaty provisions regarding free movement of persons for what are considered economic purposes are specific expressions of the general Article 18 EC.[43]

---

40 See, as a recent case summing up the development, Case C-325/05, *Ismail Derin*, ECR 2007, I-6495, paras 62–9. See also Article 59 of the Additional Protocol (OJ 1973 C 113, 17) to the EEC and Turkey Association Agreement (OJ 1973 C 113, 1): 'In the fields covered by this Protocol Turkey shall not receive more favourable treatment than that which Member States grant to one another pursuant to the Treaty establishing the Community.'

41 For a reconstruction of the new hierarchy and interpretation of norms (both primary and secondary law) on free movement of persons, see AG Geelhoed's opinion in Case C-413/99, *Baumbast and R*, ECR 2002, I-7091, paras 105–18.

42 See in general, and especially on the EC Turkey Association Agreement, Guild (2004: 153–6).

43 The clarification first appeared in the context of the right to establishment and the right to provide services, where Art. 18 EC (now 21 TFEU) was not applied, but, however, was referred to in the reasoning: see Case C-193/94, *Skanavi and Chryssanthakopoulos*, ECR 1996, I-929, para. 22, and Case C-100/01, *Oteiza Olazabal*, ECR 2002, I-10981, para.

It was in this historical, political, and also legal environment, or continuum, that the Court of Justice had to decide the first cases that reached it on Union citizenship, from *Martinez Sala* in 1998 onwards.[44] This phase was brought to an end only with the coming into force of the new all-encompassing Union citizens' Residence Directive 2004/38, with its implementing deadline in 2006, and with the first preliminary references on it being answered by the Court in 2008. It is this intermediate decade before 2008 that produced the most criticized judgments of the Court of Justice in this field, which largely form the case law under review here. This is not to say politically controversial judgments have not appeared since, or elsewhere in the general field of free movement of persons.[45]

Martinez Sala[46] is often considered the Big Bang in the evolution of Union citizenship case law; however, it is not part of the case law that this analysis is built on.[47] Yet there is no doubt that in it, the Court of Justice already exercised an enlarged scope of application of EU law, dipping into both Pandora's boxes referred to above. From the first Union citizenship case onwards, it was clear that the Court of Justice's reasoning concerning the scope of application (material and personal) enlarged the scope of application of EU law – this is by now accepted in all quarters. However, the reasoning to that effect did not include a plain 'you put it up there, now we must see to it that the law is observed'. Instead, the Court of Justice remained relatively silent as to why. Only from *Grzelczyk* onwards did the Court of Justice explain its interpretation of Articles 17 and 18 EC as: 'Union citizenship is destined to be the fundamental status of nationals of the Member States, enabling those who find themselves in the same situation to enjoy the same treatment in law irrespective of their nationality, subject to such exceptions as are expressly provided for.'[48] A more encompassing right to not be discriminated against on grounds of nationality ensued from the larger scope of application of EU law. Compared with the earlier application of the non-discrimination Article (first

26, respectively. In the Union citizenship context, see, for example, Case C-76/05, *Schwarz and Gootjes-Schwarz*, ECR 2007, I-6849, para. 34.

44 Case C-85/96, *Martínez Sala*, ECR 1998, I-2691. However, this case, often considered seminal – and indeed decided by a grand chamber – is not part of the case law material studied here for various reasons.

45 See, for instance, Case C-127/08, *Metock and Others*, ECR 2008, I-6241, causing upset in Denmark especially.

46 Case C-85/96, *Martínez Sala*, ECR 1998, I-2691.

47 In formal terms, the operative part of the judgment makes no mention of either Article 17 or 18 EC and in more substantive terms, the situation giving rise to the preliminary reference was quite particular. That is, a German non-contributory family benefit was denied to Mrs Martínez Sala for not possessing a residence entitlement or permit required by German law, because of German officials' failure either to process her pending application for one or to bring her right of residence to an end.

48 Case C-184/99, *Grzelczyk*, ECR 2001, I-6193, para. 31.

7 EEC, then 6 EC, 12 EC, now 18 TFEU), the existence and application[49] of which preceded Union citizenship, the critics argue, the Court of Justice commenced an unwarranted incursion into the welfare autonomy of the member states, by not striking an adequate balance between free movement and legitimate member state welfare interests.

Let us return to the question: what could the Court of Justice have done differently? Assume the Court of Justice takes seriously its task of ensuring observance of 'the law', and that law has just changed with the addition of a new treaty Article on free movement. Expecting the Court of Justice to give no meaning to the new law – say, for example, by way of accepting the argument that the treaty Article only gave the rights enumerated in the secondary law given before it – under these circumstances seems rather ridiculous. Could it have been logically expected to ignore a new norm of primary EU law? Would one really expect the Court of Justice to conclude in *Martinez Sala*, or *Baumbast*[50] for that matter, that no new rights can be directly derived from new treaty Articles, merely as the intention was to change nothing by changing the Treaty? Not really. The Court of Justice had no choice but to find a reasonable step forward, towards the goal of free movement of persons. Reasonableness being, largely – it is presumed – not a political issue but a question of pertaining to the criteria of interpretation of EU law. The criticism that proceeding on the trajectory towards free movement was really not a legal choice, but a political one, is totally correct if it recognizes this was not a political choice of the Court of Justice.

If one accepts the above view as to interpreting primary law, only the interpretation of secondary legislation remains contested. Briefly put, the most controversial interpretations have concerned interpreting the economic requirements for inactive Union citizens to exercise free movement (comprehensive sickness insurance and having sufficient resources), and the mobile Union citizens' right to equal treatment (relying on national solidarity) or the question concerning the limits of national discretion as to when they have become an unreasonable burden to the host member state. These questions concern the application of both the old Residence Directives and the new Residence Directive 2004/38.

What Did the Court of Justice Do?

The question is not whether Article 18 EC (now 21 TFEU) should be given meaning, but how it should be interpreted together with the relevant secondary legislation

49 See, for instance, Case 42/87, *Commission v Belgium*, ECR 1988, 5445, relying on the treaty Article prohibiting nationality discrimination (7 EEC as it was, now 18 TFEU) in the operative part of the judgment. For a recent example, see Case C-164/07, *Wood*, ECR 2008, I-4143.

50 Case C-85/96, *Martínez Sala*, ECR 1998, I-2691, and C-413/99, *Baumbast and R*, ECR 2002, I-7091.

to form a systemic whole. In fact, the standard formulation on Union citizenship adopted by the Court of Justice could be conceived of as a (substantive) directive of interpretation in itself. It is another way of stating the same as in previous case law; that Union citizenship is a more fundamental status of member state nationals than their economically active – or not – free movement status. What the standard formulation illustrates is the second-order interpretative criterion that 'exceptions to fundamental Community principles are to be narrowly interpreted'.[51] In situations where Union citizens find themselves in another member state, the scope of application of EU law has become a non-issue, but within that scope they are entitled to enjoy the same treatment in law irrespective of their nationality, though 'subject to such exceptions as are expressly provided for'.[52]

In *Baumbast*, for instance, the Court of Justice stated that 'the limitations and conditions which are referred to in Article 18 EC' laid down in the relevant secondary law, and also applicable to residence under five years according to the new Residence Directive 2004/38 'are based on the idea that the exercise of the right of residence of citizens of the Union can be subordinated to the legitimate interests of the Member States'.[53] Whereas the restrictive interpretation of what comprehensive sickness insurance means and the extensive interpretation of the Court of Justice as to what it means to have sufficient resources became relatively clear in *Baumbast* and *Zhu and Chen*, respectively,[54] access to national solidarity and the boundary between reasonable and unreasonable burdening[55] have remained fuzzy.

As already noted above, member states have had difficulties in adapting to the idea that until the right of residence is brought to an end, the Union citizen has the right to rely on Article 12 EC (now 18 TFEU), that is, not to be discriminated against on grounds of nationality – in all situations, including those involving welfare, that do not qualify as express exceptions. As to ending the right of residence, in the words of AG Alber: 'terminating residence as a result of recourse to the social assistance system is … unequal treatment … accepted by Community law and justified on grounds relating to the legitimate interests of the State'.[56] This does not mean that limitations and conditions restricting the general right should not be interpreted restrictively. Thence, in light of the wording of the old Residence

51 Bengoetxea 1993: 233.

52 See any Union citizenship case dealt with by the Court of Justice since the seminal *Grzelczyk* (Case C-184/99, ECR 2001, I-6193, para. 31).

53 Case C-413/99, *Baumbast and R*, ECR 2002, I-7091, para. 90.

54 See Case C-413/99, *Baumbast and R*, ECR 2002, I-7091, paras 90–93, Case C-200/02, *Zhu and Chen*, ECR 2004, I-9925, para. 33, and Case C-408/03, *Commission v Belgium*, ECR 2006, I-2647, paras 38–51, interpreting Directive 90/364, but of general applicability, including Residence Directive 2004/38.

55 For the neither entirely clear nor wholly non-discriminatory guidelines suggested by the Commission, see the Commission Communication on guidance for better transposition and application of Directive 2004/38/EC (COM(2009) 313 final): 8–9.

56 Opinion of AG Alber in Case C-184/99, *Grzelczyk*, ECR 2001, I-6193, para. 110.

Directives' preambles, the restrictive *Grzelczyk* interpretation of the Court of Justice perhaps implies that they never aimed to protect the host member state against an abstract risk of burden. After declaring or proving that one has sufficient resources for the right to reside, the situation may change. This is not enough for the right of residence to be automatically extinguished. Having considered what would be the least restrictive interpretation taking into account the wording of the preambles as to the general right to free movement, the Court of Justice stated: 'beneficiaries of the right of residence must not become an *unreasonable* burden on the public finances of the host Member State. … Directive 93/96, like Directives 90/364 and 90/365, thus accepts a certain degree of financial solidarity between nationals of a host Member State and nationals of other Member States'.[57] This means, together with the requirement that restrictions of a fundamental freedom must always comply with the proportionality principle,[58] that ending the right of residence cannot become the automatic consequence of recourse to the social assistance system.[59]

Reliance on the idea that the right of residence is extinguished automatically is likely a remnant of the practical approach many member states were likely to employ during the times of the old Residence Directives, a system based on relatively short-term residence permits, unlike the new Residence Directive requiring only a registration certificate with no expiry date.[60] Although the Court of Justice has by now made some outer limits of national solidarity clear[61] – for example, that certain groups can still be left totally outside it, according to the Residence Directive[62] – it has taken a long time for member states to adjust to abolishing direct nationality discrimination and to employ a justified and proportionate form of indirect nationality discrimination *vis-à-vis* access to national solidarity. Moreover, many member states are still at a loss as to what constitutes an unreasonable burden. The Commission report on the application of Directive 2004/38 stated in 2008 that '[n]ot one Member State has transposed the Directive effectively and correctly in its entirety' and only two member states had detailed guidelines as to assessing what 'unreasonable burden' means.[63]

57 Case C-184/99, *Grzelczyk*, ECR 2001, I-6193, para. 44. See since, for example, Case C-456/02, *Trojani*, ECR 2004, I-7573, paras 32–3.

58 On this specifically, see Case C-413/99, *Baumbast and R*, ECR 2002, I-7091, para. 91: 'in compliance with the limits imposed by Community law and in accordance with the general principles of that law, in particular the principle of proportionality'.

59 Case C-184/99, *Grzelczyk*, ECR 2001, I-6193, para. 43.

60 See Directive 2004/38, Articles 8 and 14.

61 See, for example, Cases C-138/02, *Collins*, ECR 2004, I-2703, C-224/98, *D'Hoop*, ECR 2002, I-6191, C-209/03, *Bidar*, ECR 2005, I-2119, and Case C-158/07, *Förster*, ECR 2008, I-8507.

62 According to Directive 2004/38, Art. 24(2) host member states are not 'obliged to confer entitlement to social assistance during the first three months of residence'.

63 Commission report on the application of Directive 2004/38/EC on the right of citizens of the Union and their family members to move and reside freely within the territory of the Member States (COM(2008) 840/3): 3 and 6.

In light of how the law is interpreted, the fact that Residence Directive 2004/38 allows host member states to verify – though not systematically – that Union citizens continue to fulfil the conditions of their right to reside seems of little practical use. Some practical difficulties may arise out of member states' obligations, other than under EU law, to guarantee minimum subsistence.[64] True to the spirit of constitutional pluralism often expressed in silence, aspects like these do not prominently feature in the Court of Justice's reasoning. It may seem absurd to use national resources at the same time to deprive an individual of an originally EU law based right to reside and to hand out social assistance on other than EU law grounds, while the question of unreasonable burdening remains debatable, and in any case, as *Shaw* suggests: 'Any procedure for removing those on welfare would be long, cumbersome and costly, and could easily be circumvented by the target obtaining the offer of even part-time below-subsistence-level employment which would be sufficient to qualify her instantly as a "worker" under EC law.'[65] However, administrative efficiency is unlikely to be the most important benchmark for many other issues of a fundamental nature.

As far as extensive interpretation of 'having sufficient resources' and restrictive interpretation of 'comprehensive sickness insurance' go, the Court of Justice has applied its directives of interpretation together with the proportionality principle consistently and, at the very most, demonstrated a similarly active approach as it did with interpreting the law relating to workers and their rights. Hence, although it sticks to its directives of interpretation, those bent on the negative activism argument could criticize the Court of Justice for not curbing its enthusiasm, as expected by those suggesting a divide between its role pre- and post-1990.

Could the Court of Justice have found an earlier point in time for the right to equal treatment (prohibition of nationality discrimination) to expire than that of losing the right of residence, of becoming a certifiably unreasonable burden? Perhaps, had the Court considered it a proportionate consequence also of temporary financial difficulties until receiving a permanent right of residence. The important judgments on this issue were given prior to the passing of the new Residence Directive 2004/38. However, they interpreted the old Directives in a new systematically sound way together with the new treaty Articles, giving 'preference in favour of systemic-cum-dynamic interpretation', that is, to prefer the two first reasons over the wording.[66]

Could the Court of Justice have found a way to allow direct discrimination on grounds of nationality in situations concerning social welfare and falling within the scope of application of EU law? No, it simply could not. What it could have

64 For example, the UN International Covenant on Economic, Social and Cultural Rights, and the European Convention on medical and social assistance. See also Shaw 2000: 81.

65 Shaw 2000: 81. Shaw refers generally to Case 139/85, *Kempf*, ECR 1986, 1035, as to the broad interpretation of worker for purposes of Art. 39 EC (now 45 TFEU).

66 Bengoetxea 1993: 234.

done more than it did, to begin with, is to be more specific about how national and EU interests can be balanced. The Court of Justice has stuck to its directives of interpretation, and often to silence, when its interlocutors could have benefited from hearing that although migrant Union citizens cannot be directly discriminated against on grounds of nationality, indirect discrimination can be allowed if *based on objective considerations independent of the nationality of the person concerned and proportionate to the legitimate aim of the national provisions*.[67]

All paths seem to lead to proportionality review. As performed by the Court of Justice, it does not minutely follow its arguably German model of origin. It is an exercise controlling the suitability, meaning that the measure is suitable to meet the legitimate objective involved, and the necessity of the contested measure, meaning that there are no less restrictive alternative methods for reaching its desired objective. The distinction between these two parts of the review is not often entirely clear in reasoning. It is often argued that the proportionality test – embedded in justifying indirect nationality discrimination, too – is where politics enters the judgments of the Court of Justice.[68] Yet it is exactly in this sense that proportionality review seems disappointing. In practice, at least in the relevant case law, when the Court of Justice finds that a national measure that is indirectly discriminatory on grounds of nationality is not suitable for the purpose it is adopted for, or that another less restrictive measure is available, it will declare the national measure contrary to EU law. How deeply such results affect national policies seems to depend much on the agility of the national legislator in finding an alternative justifiable way to reach, in essence, much the same effects as the earlier law. If a workable alternative for the national measure is not found, the phenomenon of negative integration gains more ground.

As a rule, the Court of Justice does not assess the legitimacy of the objective of a suspect national measure. According to Gareth Davies, legitimacy would be a non-issue anyway as all national legislation presumably has some legitimate aim.[69] The third element of the original German proportionality, called 'small-p proportionality' (weighing and balancing the conflicting principles), still could not help to counterbalance EU interests with national ones in the interpretation of EU law, as it would have to work as an extraordinary reason to save a national measure considered unsuitable or unnecessary, or both. Reconstructing EU law proportionality anew in these terms is highly improbable. Hence the concept of indirect discrimination, the scope of situations it is applied to, and the structure of

67 See also Case C-138/02, *Collins*, ECR 2004, I-2703, para. 72, suggesting that an indirectly discriminatory residence requirement is proportionate when the *criteria are known in advance, means of judicial redress are available, and the required period of residence did not exceed what is necessary*.

68 On the political aspect of both choosing a test and the actual act of balancing, see for example Poiares Maduro 1998: 49–58; and Davies 2003: 90.

69 See Davies 2003: 39.

the discrimination test that follows, remain perhaps more potent than proportionality (alone) in respect of balancing interests or regulatory power.

Importantly, whatever is considered wrong with proportionality review – or the power balance between the interests of the EU and its member states generally – it is still a more general question that should be kept separate from interpretation of Articles 17, 18 and 12 EC (now 20, 21 and 18 TFEU). This chapter began with a reference to how far free movement has come in a short while and how Union citizenship relates to at least two Pandora's boxes (general free movement and equal treatment). The currently contested area of free movement, that is non-discriminatory obstacles or market access, all seem to lead to yet another constant and omnipotent Pandora's box: proportionality.[70] Nevertheless, the political subsystem has now had reasonable time and experience to figure out how law is interpreted, in this field of law also, by the social subsystem of EU law. Moreover, it has had ample possibility to change the law since the Court of Justice started its 'assault on national solidarity', but the political sphere has chosen to bless treaty-level norms again (Lisbon Treaty). No amendments or general changes have been made to the relevant secondary law, Directive 2004/38, the Commission's only minutely watered-down proposition as to consolidating already criticized case law, which the Member States accepted. The ball is effectively, still, in the many political sides of the court.

Concluding Remarks

Arguing that the standard formulation of Union citizenship by the Court of Justice is a directive on interpretation may sound overly simplistic. In part, this is due to the eloquent connotations brought forth by the grand Union citizenship design. What should perhaps have been discussed more honestly as free movement of persons to begin with, is a child of its time: a time when constitutionalism, and later constitutional pluralism, was making an entry and soon flooded the market of the thin layer of legal theoretical EU studies,[71] as the dominating currency.[72] High politics went in tandem from arguing for a single market to a more social Europe to wanting a Constitutional Treaty. Union citizenship was a miracle remedy to cure many deficits of the EU. However, the standard formulation by the Court of Justice as yet another drop of snake oil is not totally without blame.

At first sight, the standard formulation of the Court of Justice on Union citizenship feels like something dynamic, a metaphor, that is, something that enables the interrelationship of the present and the as yet undefined, or releases

70 On using the concept of market access in free movement law, as an example of those against the concept, see Davies 2003: 94–115; and Snell 2010; and for those in favour, see Spaventa 2007: 105–12.

71 See Walker 2005.

72 See Poiares Maduro 2005: 332.

the speculative power of the concept.[73] This is especially true as one begins with exploring the English version of the standard formulation and its interpretations. For instance, Yuri Borgmann-Prebil has suggested the standard formulation is, in Habermasian terms, 'a counterfactual claim that gradually acquires social reality in subsequent case-law'.[74] Yet the conclusion here is that the standard formulation, or Union citizenship for that matter, is not a metaphor or a counterfactual claim. In addition to being a (substantive) directive of interpretation it is actually also a systemic rather than a dynamic goal- or future-oriented argument or reason used by the Court of Justice. Other language versions – those understood by the author in addition to the English – do not share the emphasis, perhaps imaginary even in the English version, on Union citizenship *becoming* ('destined to be' – leaving open now or in the future) anything. They more clearly refer to Union citizenship as being the fundamental status of member state nationals.[75] This is also quite well in line with the case law on the so-called 'specific expressions' of Article 18 EC (now 21 TFEU).

To sum up, what could the Court have done differently? Free movement of persons being one of the general principles of EU law, just like equality, any exceptions to it must be interpreted restrictively. Moreover, everything that limits general principles of EU law must, ultimately, pass a proportionality review.[76] Second, the changed relation of norms (new primary and old secondary law) had to have an effect on their interpretation. As to the relevant secondary law, in *CILFIT*[77] the Court of Justice pronounced that the state of evolution of EU law affects, or should affect, interpretation of relevant provisions.

The reasoning in the relevant case law does not give a very activist image of the Court of Justice. After reviewing it, one can conclude that explicitly dynamic criteria, or reasons, almost never appear in the reasoning, once the standard formulation is omitted from among potential dynamic criteria for the reasons stated above. Only some references to enhancing free movement, to not depriving an EU law-based right of any useful effect (not even the rights of under-age Union citizens), and to how secondary law should be interpreted taking into consideration the aims of the Treaty, can categorically be considered dynamic.[78] Moreover, they are only slightly dynamic in that the reasoning remains strictly legal, referring to respecting

73 See Paasilehto 2002: 33.

74 Borgmann-Prebil 2008: 329–330.

75 See, for instance, the translation into the author's native Finnish of *Grzelczyk* (Case C-184/99, ECR 2001, I-6193, para. 31) claiming Union citizenship by intent is a status of a fundamental nature: 'Unionin kansalaisuus *on tarkoituksensa puolesta* jäsenvaltioiden kansalaisten *perustavaa laatua oleva asema*, jonka nojalla samassa tilanteessa olevat henkilöt voivat saada osakseen saman oikeudellisen kohtelun kansalaisuudestaan riippumatta, jollei tätä koskevista nimenomaisesti määrätyistä poikkeuksista muuta johdu.'

76 For a very recent and rather acrid reminder of this by a grand chamber, see Case C-135/08, *Rottmann*, judgment of 2 March 2010, n.y.r.

77 See Case 283/81, *Srl CILFIT*, ECR 1982, 3415, para. 20.

78 Case C-200/02, *Zhu and Chen*, ECR 2004, I-9925, para. 20.

the treaties and giving full effect to EU law, not to extra-legal factors. Hence, the reasoning can be described as mostly systemic, although it more often than not concentrates on the wording. Taking the exact wording of, especially, secondary legislation as the starting point, the Court of Justice finds an interpretation of it that is least restrictive of primary law rights. The reasoning would seem to reflect the changed *telos* of free movement of persons law.

References

Arnull, A. 2006. *The European Union and its Court of Justice*. 2nd edition. Oxford: Oxford University Press.

Bengoetxea, J. 1993. *The Legal Reasoning of the European Court of Justice: Towards a European Jurisprudence*. Oxford: Clarendon Press.

Besson, S. and Utzinger, A. 2007. Introduction: Future challenges of European citizenship – Facing a wide-open Pandora's Box. *European Law Journal*, 13:5, 573–90.

Borgmann-Prebil, Y. 2008. The rule of reason in European citizenship. *European Law Journal*, 14:3, 328–50.

Chalmers, D., Hadjiemmanuil, C., Monti, G. and Tomkins, A. 2006. *European Union Law: Text and Materials*. Cambridge: Cambridge University Press.

Davies, G. 2003. *Nationality Discrimination in the European Internal Market*. The Hague: Kluwer Law International.

Dehousse, R. 1998. *The European Court of Justice: The Politics of Judicial Integration*. London: Macmillan.

Guild, E. 2004. *The Legal Elements of European Identity: EU Citizenship and Migration Law*. The Hague: Kluwer Law International.

Hailbronner, K. 2005. Union citizenship and access to social benefits. *Common Market Law Review*, 42:5, 1245–67.

Itzcovich, G. 2009. The interpretation of Community law by the European Court of Justice. *German Law Journal*, 10:5, 537–60.

Kapteyn, P.J.G., VerLoren van Themaat, P. and Gormley, L.W. 1990. *Introduction to the Law of the European Communities After the Coming into Force of the Single European Act*. 2nd edition. Deventer: Kluwer Law and Taxation.

Koopmans, T. 1996. Judicial decision-making, in *Legal Reasoning and Judicial Interpretation of European Law: Essays in Honour of Lord Mackenzie-Stuart*, edited by A.I.L. Campbell and M. Voyatzi. London: Trenton Publishing, 93–104.

Lasser, M. de S.-O.-l'E. 2004. *Judicial Deliberations: A Comparative Analysis of Judicial Transparency and Legitimacy*. Oxford: Oxford University Press.

Maas, W. 2005. The genesis of European rights. *Journal of Common Market Studies*, 43:5, 1009–25.

Maas, W. 2007. *Creating European Citizens*. Lanham: Rowman & Littlefield Publishers, Inc.

MacCormick, N. and Summers, R.S. 1991. *Interpreting Statutes: A Comparative Study*. Aldershot: Dartmouth.

Mather, J. 2005. The Court of Justice and the Union citizen. *European Law Journal*, 11:6, 722–43.

Paasilehto, S. 2002. *Constellations. A New Approach to Legal Cultures and European Integration of Private Law*. Helsinki: S. Paasilehto.

Poiares Maduro, M. 1998. *We the Court: The European Court of Justice and the European Economic Constitution: A Critical Reading of Article 30 of the EC Treaty*. Oxford: Hart Publishing.

Poiares Maduro, M. 2005. The importance of being called a constitution: Constitutional authority and the authority of constitutionalism. *International Journal of Constitutional Law*, 3:2–3, 332–56.

Prechal, S. 2002. Direct effect reconsidered, redefined and rejected, in *Direct Effect: Rethinking a Classic of EC Legal Doctrine*, edited by J.M. Prinssen and A. Schrauwen. Groningen: Europa Law Publishing, 17–41.

Rasmussen, H. 1986. *On Law and Policy in the European Court of Justice: A Comparative Study in Judicial Policymaking*. Dordrecht and Boston, MA: Nijhoff.

Rasmussen, H. 1998. *The European Court of Justice*. Copenhagen: GadJura.

Rosas, A. 2005. Tolknings- och tillämpningsproblem i mötet mellan Nordisk och Internationell juridisk metod, in *Forhandlingerne ved det 37. nordiske Juristmøde i Reykjavík 18.–20. august 2005. Bind 1*, edited by Mads Bryde Andersen. Reykjavik: Den islandske Styrelse, 317–45.

Sarmiento, D. 2010 (forthcoming). The silent lamb and the deaf wolves, in *Constitutional Pluralism in the European Union and Beyond*, edited by M. Avbelj and J. Komárek. Oxford: Oxford University Press.

Shapiro, M. 1999. The European Court of Justice, in *The Evolution of EU Law*, edited by P. Craig and G. de Búrca. Oxford and New York: Oxford University Press, 321–47.

Shaw, J. 2000. The problem of membership in European Union citizenship, in *The European Union and its Order: The Legal Theory of European Integration*, edited by Z. Bankowski and A. Scott. Oxford: Blackwell, 65–89.

Snell, J. 2008. 'European Constitutional Settlement', an ever closer Union, and the Treaty of Lisbon: Democracy or relevance? *European Law Review*, 33, 619–42.

Snell, J. 2010. The notion of market access: A concept or a slogan? *Common Market Law Review*, 47:2, 437–72.

Somek, A. 1999. A constitution for antidiscrimination: Exploring the vanguard moment of Community law. *European Law Journal*, 5:3, 243–71.

Spaventa, E. 2007. *Free Movement of Persons in the European Union: Barriers to Movement in their Constitutional Context*. The Hague: Kluwer Law International.

Spaventa, E. 2008. Seeing the wood despite the trees? On the scope of Union citizenship and its constitutional effects. *Common Market Law Review*, 45, 13–45.

Tryfonidou, A. 2009. In search of the aim of the EC free movement of persons provisions: Has the Court of Justice missed the point? *Common Market Law Review*, 46, 1591–620.

Walker, N. 2005. Legal theory and the European Union: A 25th anniversary essay. *Oxford Journal of Legal Studies*, 25:4, 581–601.

Weiler, J.H.H. 1999. *The Constitution of Europe. 'Do the New Clothes Have an Emperor?' and Other Essays on European Integration*. Cambridge: Cambridge University Press.

Wiener, A. 1998. *'European' Citizenship Practice. Building Institutions of a Non-State*. Boulder: Westview.

PART IV
Aspects of the Social Constitution

Chapter 10
Social Constitution in Historical Perspective: Hugo Sinzheimer in the Weimar Context

Sakari Hänninen

Many Constitutions

It is possible to trace a social undercurrent back to the original plan of action of the European Economic Community. The Lisbon Summit was a climax on this route. The social dimension to the EU was there articulated as its social model beside the economic, political and juridical dimensions. The different dimensions and their interrelations can be also articulated in constitutional terms. In this mode one could speak about the many constitutions of Europe. Kaarlo Tuori stresses the possibility that in the future one might also speak about the social constitution as another constitutional dimension of the EU.[1]

A claim was made (at the Stockholm European Council 2001) that 'Lisbon [extraordinary European Council] has successfully integrated economic and social matters.'[2] This claim could with certainty be challenged on the ground that the social dimension was not exactly coordinated with but rather subsumed under the internal market project. In these circumstances, it may be altogether problematic to talk about a social constitution of the EU. It might be claimed that this constitutional aspect is almost entirely overshadowed by the economic constitution. However, the validity of such a claim is, again, thoroughly dependent on what is meant by a social constitution.

In this chapter, the aim is not to evaluate or analyse the degree of social constitutionality of the EU but to try to make sense of the possible idea of a social constitution against the background of the Weimar Republic. This chapter will specifically examine the thinking of Hugo Sinzheimer, who – with his former students Franz L. Neumann and Ernst Fraenkel – has been characterized as the pioneer of *Sozialverfassung* (the social constitution).[3]

---

1 See Tuori's contribution in this volume.

2 Presidency Conclusions, Stockholm European Council 23–24 March 2001, para. 50.

3 See Joerges 2004.

Constitutional Validity

The nature and quality of social law and social constitution should be defined in relation to other aspects of a constitution, especially in relation to economic constitution. Without this specification, social constitution faces the danger of remaining an empty concept. It might, though, be claimed that what is written in the constitution need not yet specify the relationship between different aspects of the constitution. The reason for this 'paradox' could be seen to reside in the fact that behind the written constitution can lie a 'real' constitution referring to the interpretative commitments which link together rules from different domains of society. In order to be able to proceed to this problem space – unorthodox from the jurisprudential standpoint – one should first ask what it means when social rights are written into the constitution.

Avi Ben-Bassat and Momi Dahan have studied the relationships between written constitutional commitment to social rights, the size of government and redistribution policy, using a data collection of 68 constitutions.[4] If the commitment to social rights in the constitution is seen to make it social, then their study amounts to a concrete study of the functioning of social constitutions. In order to rank these 68 constitutions according to their constitutional commitment to social rights, they applied a fivefold classification of social rights:

> 1) the right to live in dignity or the right to social security (insurance for pension, survivors, disability, unemployment, accident, minimum income and sickness); 2) the right to education (primary and secondary education); 3) the right to health; 4) the right to housing; 5) protection of workers' rights (minimum wage, the right to maternity leave, a limit on hours of work and rest, paid leave and higher wage rate for extra work).[5]

When the degree of constitutional commitment to these social rights is ranked on a scale from 0 to 3, indices of those 68 countries can be counted by reading the constitutional texts. Having read and analysed the constitutional texts – by no means an unproblematic exercise – Ben-Bassat and Dahan provide us with some surprising results. According to the summary index of social rights in the constitution (in the case of the UK, the Human Rights Act), Portugal (2.45) is in the lead, followed by three Latin American countries (Nicaragua 2.25; Brazil 2.13; Mexico 1.97). Poland (1.91) is fourth in line followed again by three Latin American countries (Paraguay 1.71; Panama 1.71; Uruguay 1.58). Finland stands in 13th place, while Denmark (0.43) and Sweden (0.42) lag way behind. Norway (0.0) belongs to the group of countries whose constitutions make no mention of social rights. Not only the United States (0.0), Canada (0.0) and the United Kingdom (0.0), but also Germany (0.0) belong to this group. It should be added

4 See Ben-Bassat and Dahan 2008.

5 Ben-Bassat and Dahan 2008: 105–6.

that if the written constitutional right to social security were regarded as a sign of the modern welfare state, then the top-ranking countries would include, in this order, Brazil (3.0), Finland (2.14), Switzerland (2.14) and Portugal (2.0).[6]

Ben-Bassat and Dahan not only provide us with these astonishing figures but, as public policy experts, seek to make some sense of them. The authors look for explanations in three directions involving social rights: endurance of the constitution, legal sources and legal traditions, and religious beliefs. The significance of the endurance of the constitution is easy to understand just by looking at the constitutional genealogies of the Nordic countries: the Constitution of Finland was amended in 1995 with special reference to social rights, the Constitution of Sweden dates back to 1974, the Constitution of Denmark to 1953, while the Constitution of Norway was laid down as long ago as 1814. These and similar differences should naturally be given much more attention in the analysis than the authors indeed pay.

Ben-Bassat and Dahan draw the overall conclusion that countries classified as having French civil law have a much higher constitutional commitment to social rights than common law countries, which actually do not express such a commitment at all. The reason seems quite obvious: in the common law tradition, the constitution (written or unwritten) is meant to protect citizens from the power of government, while in the civil law tradition (especially after the codifications of the nineteenth century) the constitution gives more power to the government to run the life of its citizens. Ben-Bassat and Dahan conceive it to be somewhat surprising to find that French civil law countries have, on average, a higher constitutional commitment to social rights than countries with a socialist tradition. They aptly perceive that this is due to the fact that the top 10 (or even 20) are disproportionately populated by Latin American countries, and test how sensitive the results are to the inclusion of a dummy variable for these countries. The test shows that, after this kind of reordering, countries with a past socialist tradition have the highest constitutional commitment to social rights. Besides these observations, the authors process the data to further find that poor countries tend, on average, to a higher constitutional commitment to social rights. The authors end with two more conclusions: the older the constitution, the less committed it is to social rights; and countries with a higher share of population with Catholic and Muslim beliefs tend to a higher constitutional commitment to social rights compared with Protestant countries.[7]

Ben-Bassat and Dahan's study is – in spite of interpretative difficulties – interesting to read from the point of view of constitutional validity, which is the true topic of the study. This topic refers to the relationship between expressed constitutional commitment to social rights and actual government expenditure and policy outcomes. Applying an econometric model, they test the validity of three possible hypotheses (Hypothesis 1: The constitutional text is meaningful;

6 Ben-Bassat and Dahan 2008: 107–8.

7 See Ben-Bassat and Dahan 2008: 108–12.

Hypothesis 2: The cheap talk hypothesis; Hypothesis 3: The propaganda hypothesis). The conclusions are somewhat mixed but still revealing. Ben-Bassat and Dahan find that the summary index of constitutional commitment to social rights has no significant effect on the size of government. Besides, a constitutional commitment to social rights does not have a significant impact on social spending. A constitutional commitment to social security is, however, positively connected to the share of transfer payments in GDP, even though this commitment has no effect on the index of inequality as a policy outcome. The results regarding education and health are, in fact, even more consistent with the cheap talk hypothesis due to negative connections (the Latin American case especially).[8]

Hugo Sinzheimer in Context

Even if open to various interpretations as a constitutional reading, Ben Bassat and Dahan's study makes it clear that writing social rights into the constitution is not necessarily an effective way of guaranteeing social security and welfare of citizens. This kind of insight has been a crucial motive for those thinkers who have pioneered the sociology of law, which examines the real functioning of legal institutions in a specific society behind the formal normative order of law. These thinkers include Karl Marx and Max Weber, who were credited accordingly by Hugo Sinzheimer,[9] the pioneer of social law. However, as far as the genesis of social constitution is concerned, Sinzheimer was much more directly influenced by other Germans – or even non-Germans like the Webbs (Beatrice and Sydney)[10] – than directly by Marx or Weber. Mention should be made, first of all, of Ferdinand Lassalle. Otto Kahn-Freund, a former student of Hugo Sinzheimer, recalled that the influence of the state-socialist Lassalle on the German Social Democratic Party by far exceeded that of Karl Marx, who named Lassalle one of the 'German ideologists'.[11] Sinzheimer emphasized that Lassalle made it absolutely clear that the actual, or factual, power relations in a society were truly constitutive or determinative of the legal relations and practices in a country, and ultimately specified how they really worked.[12] In other words, Lassalle argued that in order to properly understand the operation of law and legal institutions, one had to penetrate the legal reality (*Rechtswirklichkeit*) which stands behind the formally valid normative order.

Many other prominent legal thinkers in Germany worked in Lassalle's direction – without necessarily agreeing with his arguments and conclusions –

8 See Ben-Bassat and Dahan 2008: 112–18.

9 See Sinzheimer 1976b: 188–206.

10 See Blanke 2005: 17.

11 See Kahn-Freund 1981: 201.

12 See Sinzheimer and Fraenkel 1968: 229 – references to this book always refer to the writings of Sinzheimer.

and significantly influenced Sinzheimer and his understanding of social law and social constitution. In a shorthand fashion, it could be claimed that the idea of social constitution, as originally innovated by Sinzheimer, is the outcome of a series of transformations in legal style of reasoning and legal culture which took place in Germany from the mid-nineteenth century, culminating in social law. In other words, social law grew out of labour law (*Arbeitsrecht*), which was already pioneered by a social understanding of law. This social understanding of law is interrelated but not identical to the sociology of law, and more directly linked with legal science leading to labour law.

Otto von Gierke was a foundational figure for Sinzheimer's thinking on labour law. Sinzheimer emphasizes that, even in 1868 (*Die Deutsche Genossenschaftsrecht* [The German Law of Associations]) Gierke made us look, in the context of labour relations, beyond the narrow horizon of individuals and private law by pointing out that the capitalist enterprise is also an organization of domination (*Herrschaftsverband*).[13] When Sinzheimer later points out that social law manifests a turning point in the development of law, by definitely leaving behind the Roman civil law tradition, and eloquently states that 'die Dämmerung der alten privatrechtlichen Götter ist angebrochen und die Morgenröte eines neuen sozialen Rechtszeitalters zieht herauf',[14] he is above all referring to Gierke's influence. In fact, it was Gierke who first made the distinction between the individual law and the social law and used the word 'social' to refer to relationships between persons, not as individuals but as members of more organic wholes (*Verbandsganze*).[15] Sinzheimer makes the point that Gierke's struggle against the individualism of the Roman private law tradition led him to a social conception of law.[16] Another person who departed from the Roman private law tradition, thereby contributing to a social understanding of law, and also sociology of law, was Rudolf von Jhering. Jhering's idea that 'rights are legally protected interests' also later penetrated social law and had an impact on Sinzheimer's thinking.[17]

It was not Gierke but Lorenz von Stein who, for the first time (1876), used the phrase 'labour law' (*Arbeitsrecht*) in his treatise 'Gegenwart und Zukunft der Rechts- und Staatswissenschaft in Deutschland' ('The Present and Future of Jurisprudence and State Theory in Germany'). Sinzheimer emphasizes that Stein's real significance (for social law) cannot be reduced to just adopting a historical perspective on law but in making clear that living forces stand behind the law so that labour law must be understood in the sense of 'class law' ('*Klassenrecht*').[18]

13 See Sinzheimer 1927: 217; Kahn-Freund 1981: 78.

14 Sinzheimer and Fraenkel 1968: 149. Author's translation: 'the twilight of the old private law gods has begun and the dawn of a new age of social rights is rising'.

15 See Gierke 1895: 26.

16 See Sinzheimer 1976a: 403.

17 See Kahn-Freund 1981: 96.

18 Lassalle 1993. See also Sinzheimer and Fraenkel 1968: 258, 318; and Sinzheimer 1976b: 156, 160–61.

In other words, Stein already pointed out that for a social understanding of law it is necessary to penetrate the legal reality, which was a leading motive throughout Sinzheimer's writings from early on. However, more pertinent to Sinzheimer's approach to social law than Stein's writings (even his *Verwaltungslehre* [Theory of Public Administration]), was the discussion on labour law at the turn of the twentieth century, in which a real quest for the social facts behind the law (*Rechtstatsachenforschung*) was emphasized and initiated first of all by Philip Lotmar.[19] In this quest, though not in many other respects, Sinzheimer agreed with Lotmar completely.[20] Quite similarly to Lotmar, Sinzheimer participated, but not uncritically, in the positive effort to introduce sociology concretely into law – as initiated especially by Eugen Ehrlich in the first decade of the twentieth century.[21] As far as sociology of law was concerned, Sinzheimer mentions as his most important trend-setters Ehrlich (descriptive sociology of law), Anton Menger (analytic sociology of law) and Karl Renner (constructive sociology of law).[22] All of these can also be seen as proceeding in the direction opened up by Lassalle. Therefore, it is opportune to take up his point of departure for a more systematic treatment of Sinzheimer's views on social law and social constitution.

In contrast to Marx, Lassalle gave due merit to representative democracy, even though by coining the term 'night-watchman state' he cast a critical eye on the violent kernel of the liberalist state of formal equality.[23] Another distinction was made by Lassalle in his presentation in Berlin (16 April 1862) *Űber Verfassungswesen* ('On Constitutional Studies'), which is especially relevant in trying to capture the meaning of social constitution as it was originally perceived by Hugo Sinzheimer: a distinction between what Lassalle called a 'juridical constitution' and a 'real constitution'.[24] Lassalle himself spoke in the 1860s – facing the 1871 Imperial Constitution – about the catastrophe of constitutionalism and characterized it as '*Scheinkonstitutionalismus*' ('sham constitutionialism'), which should be set aside to look instead at reality as it is.[25] In a similar fashion one should look at the reality of the tensions, conflicts, contradictions and challenges behind the Weimar Constitution in order to pass judgement on the force and real significance of this constitution.

19 See Coutu 2006–2007: 169–85.

20 See Blanke 2005: 26.

21 See Blanke 2005: 28–9.

22 See Sinzheimer and Fraenkel 1968: 331.

23 See Lassalle 1993.

24 See Sinzheimer and Fraenkel 1968: 124; and Lassalle 1993.

25 See Sinzheimer and Fraenkel 1968: 232–3.

Kirchheimer on the Weimar Constitution

If the sheer number of social rights mentioned in a constitution could make it a social constitution, then the Weimar Constitution might be judged a kind of prototype for a social constitution. However, in the Weimar Constitution social rights were challenged by numerous other basic rights. The rights section in the Weimar Constitution of 11 August 1919 consisted of 57 articles, each of which detailed one or more specific rights. Social rights were written in the second, fourth and fifth chapters which addressed 'Life within a Community', 'Education and School' and 'The Economy'. Neither the 'father' of this constitution, Hugo Preuss, nor Max Weber wanted this development to happen, but opposed it.[26] The subset of rights in the Weimar Constitution actually covered all aspects of German life and encompassed a wide range of right-bearers from the individual to the family and community, from public institutions like schools and churches to economic institutions and the welfare of the whole nation.[27]

As far as the introduction of social rights in the Constitution was concerned, the active role of the social-liberal parliamentarian Frederik Naumann was significant as he both attacked the 'old-liberal rights' as thoroughly insufficient or even outdated and sought also to present an alternative to socialism.[28] However, if the Weimar Constitution is read as a socially influential labour constitution (*Arbeitsverfassung*), then the contribution of Hugo Sinzheimer was decisive. There is, though, no reason to overstate the role of any one person, not even Preuss or Hans Kelsen, in the Weimar constitutionalization process, since the final form of the Constitution was very much the result of the influence and pressure yielded by different political parties and pressure groups. Otto Kirchheimer, in his short pamphlet 'Weimar – and what then?', first published in 1930, sums up neatly what became the problem:

> All claims to a constitutional anchoring were given satisfaction, including those of agricultural, business and commercial middle classes (*Mittelstand*). And since all wanted to be anchored down, there was not much left to do for the force which supposedly dominated the Constitution, socialism, but to let itself be anchored down. The Weimar system of basic rights, which is often inexactly labelled a compromise, consisted in reality of this row of anchors … [such concessions characteristic of a compromise] … were no part of the basic rights arrangement of the Weimar Constitution.[29]

His pamphlet is an important critical survey of the Weimar Constitution, which actually was written out as a kind of critique of critiques and, therefore, a kind of

26 See Caldwell 1997: 73.
27 See Caldwell 1997: 74.
28 See Kirchheimer 1969: 52.
29 Kirchheimer 1969: 53.

attempt to rescue the rational kernel of the Weimar Constitution. This text could thus be read as answering above all Carl Schmitt and Hermann Heller who – from altogether different perspectives – had launched heavy assaults on the Weimar Constitution, ultimately due to its claimed tendency to incur fragmentation, indecision, even chaos. However, in spite of his outspoken disagreement with his former teachers, Schmitt and Heller, Kirchheimer still seems to have advanced especially in the shadow of Schmitt. The problem with Kirchheimer's appraisal is not the critical characterization of the Weimar Constitution as a kind of manifestation of the principle of plenitude but the biased standpoint. Kirchheimer's verdict on the Weimar Constitution is based on a number of problematic assumptions which make his political analysis highly questionable.

First of all, Kirchheimer's starting point lies in Rosa Luxemburg's claim that any extant constitutional legislation can only be the product of revolution. This argument reflects Kirchheimer's pessimistic appraisal of lost opportunities for a 'real socialist democracy'.[30] Drafting and radically amending constitutions need not, though, be connected with revolutions but can well be conceived to take place in the reformist climate of political democracy. Kirchheimer cannot agree with this conclusion since he challenges the promise of representative political democracy, especially when it is applied in terms of the majority principle.

From Kirchheimer's perspective, political democracy is a kind of tautology. The crucial issue addresses the relationship between the procedure of authoritative decision-making and justification and the social fabric of society. Kirchheimer claims that:

> [T]he principle of majority rule is comprehensible only with reference to that social homogeneity which incorporates the principle of a democratic value community in our time ... majority decision means only the application of a tested technique for settling differences over which means are technically the best ones for achieving the principles which are adhered to by all. The less agreement there is about the preconditions and the social principles of the society, the more the ruthless-application of the majority principle tends to transform it into a technique of oppression, with the general will becoming a phantom.[31]

Kirchheimer's point about the significance of shared social principles of society or interpretative value commitments of a community for democracy is well made, as is his insistence that the procedure for making and justifying decisions is crucially conditioned by these social forces and patterns and their distribution. Kirchheimer is also right in emphasizing that 'since the nineteenth century the decisive problems of democracy have been social in character, even though some, like that of the United States and the nineteenth century constitutions, do not recognize the

30 See Kirchheimer 1969: 73.
31 Kirchheimer 1969: 40–41.

problem of social democracy'.[32] The real problem is linked with Kirchheimer's warning about the possibility that the majority principle turns into a technique of oppression so that the general will becomes a phantom. Even though there are circumstances – due to the condition of social forces and interpretative and other commitments of the community – in which this danger can be real, this critique of representative democracy, which it is, is not well argued. It would be much more to the point to claim that the idea, or ideal, of unanimous decision carries with it this danger just because it may lean on the general will or sovereign will as a counterfactual fiction.

The Weimar lesson, though, made it quite clear that the relationship between these autonomous collective subjects, and the automatic compulsory normative effects of their agreements, in relation to the democratic decision-making bodies of the state, was by no means unproblematic. Here, Franz L. Neumann's comment on the Weimar effect is illuminating:

> The history of the Weimar Constitution shows that the conception of a social contract is not a mere methodological device for the justification of the state, but even sometimes a historical reality. It is strange that nobody ever observed that the Weimar constitution was in fact the work of various social contracts concluded between various groups of society.[33]

The reason for Kirchheimer's critical standpoint about the Weimar Constitution is crucially linked with his verdict of the shortcomings of representative democracy as he saw it:

> But herein lies the basic and irreparable error of this constitution: it did not come to a decision; it fell prey to the misconception that the principles of democracy alone constitute the principles of a specific social or ideational order; it forgot that democracy cannot do more than articulate already existing conditions. What a democracy can do is to give external expression to an existing social order and to represent it meaningfully.[34]

Kirchheimer's conclusion about the indecisiveness of the Weimar Constitution sounds even more Schmittian than Weberian. Even if it anticipated events to come (Hindenburg's emergency decrees in the early 1930s) it is astonishingly cynical about the reformist potentialities of democracy, which surely are not confined to articulating existing conditions. In spite of all this, and the fact that Kirchheimer at least partly leans on his teacher Carl Schmitt's ideas about 'compromise on a dilatory formula' in the *Verfassunglehre* ('Constitutional Theory'),[35] he presented

32 Kirchheimer 1969: 38–9.
33 Neumann 1986: 269–70.
34 Kirchheimer 1969: 72.
35 Kirchheimer 1969: 53.

a useful reading of the shortcomings and perplexities of the Weimar Constitution which are truly relevant in the context of the social constitution.

Kirchheimer's critical survey of the Weimar Constitution, 'Weimar – and what then?', was both joined and partly challenged by Franz L. Neumann who wrote a text, *Erst einmal Weimar* ('Weimar to begin with').[36] While Kirchheimer at the time still belonged to the militant left wing of the SPD, Neumann rather supported the reformists of the party who were more willing to emphasize the significance of political democracy, especially when it was seen to peacefully extend and deepen into social democracy. For this reason the social dimension of the Weimar Constitution was emphasized as the 'social rule of law' and as directly connected with political democracy. It was clear to Neumann – as it was to his teacher Hugo Sinzheimer – that one can speak truthfully of a social constitution only if it is supported by political democracy and supplemented by industrial democracy. Therefore, if one treated political democracy only instrumentally as a strategic or tactical means to other ends, the outspoken adherence to social constitution would be cheap or empty talk.

Sinzheimer on the Weimar Constitution

The great innovator of the social constitution, Hugo Sinzheimer, did not overlook the pitfalls, complications and weaknesses of the Weimar Constitution but still regarded it as a great constitutional leap forward in Germany, especially thanking for this the leading and democratic role of Hugo Preuss.[37] It is well known that, besides taking part in the Constitutional Committee of the National Assembly, Sinzheimer was personally responsible for drafting the significant §165 of the Weimar Constitution which introduced the council system into the Constitution. Connected directly with the labour constitution (*Arbeitsverfassung*), the promise of the social constitution embedded in the Weimar Constitution was evidently another reason motivating Sinzheimer to appreciate this document. Even if he challenged Hans Kelsen's liberal-formalist defence of the Weimar Constitution (as *Grundnorm* [the basic norm]), he was altogether more critical of Carl Schmitt's value-nihilist decisionism.[38] In this respect, Kirchheimer's critical survey of the Weimar Constitution could also be juxtaposed with Sinzheimer's style of reasoning. This reading not only offers relevant counterarguments to Kirchheimer's critique but also introduces the crucial dimensions or domains in which the topic of social constitution was fashioned by Sinzheimer.

In spite of his socialist inclination(s), Sinzheimer did not consider the drafting of the Constitution to be a revolutionary founding act but situated it in the frame of the evolution of society. He displaced Marxism as 'theology of development'

36 See Neumann 1930.
37 See Sinzheimer and Fraenkel 1968: 40.
38 See Sinzheimer and Fraenkel 1968: 356.

(*Theologie der Entwicklung*)[39] with a variant of ethical socialism especially inspired by the neo-Kantian philosophical thinking prevalent in Marburg. In this context the influence of Rudolf Stammler, whom he also praised for his critique of historical materialism,[40] was decisive for Sinzheimer's (earlier) legal and constitutional thinking.[41] This influence is explicit in his emphasis that the development of society can also be affected by law, just as law – and the legal system – should be constantly developed to meet the new needs and demands of changed circumstances. For this reason, Sinzheimer also concluded that not all formally valid law is effective since it does not necessarily meet with the concrete life of the people.[42] For him, it is this concrete social reality or legal reality (*Rechtswirklichkeit*) which forms the basis of legal transformations (*Rechtsveränderungen*).[43] Sinzheimer thought (in line with Stammler and Renner) that the force of law and social functions of legal institutions should be crucial topics of legal analysis. It was from this perspective that he conceived the significance of the Weimar Constitution, too.

Hugo Sinzheimer was also more than aware that 'no constitution has ever been written and unanimously accepted by the full membership of a community'.[44] For him the counterfactual idea of a founding social contract, a revolutionary constitutional act, a unanimous decision or a general will was a dangerous fiction, the aim of which was to distort reality and attention to it. He did not think that either the functioning of political democracy or its constitution was definitely dependent on the social homogeneity of the citizenship or population. In fact such an assumption would have violated the working principles of political democracy and its constitution whose task it was to regulate conflicts and differences of values. Since Sinzheimer's starting point was acknowledgement of a plurality of norm-generating communities and sources of law, he situated the (legally binding) norm-giving faculty of the state in proper perspective. He considered differences of values and political divisions to be a fact of reality which found expression in the relationship between forces.

Sinzheimer was specifically concerned about the true nature of the relationship between forces in Weimar Germany, since he emphasized that the fate of legal constructs always depends on the factual relationship between forces in society, especially on economic relationships.[45] Sinzheimer naturally assessed the fate of the Weimar Constitution in relation to dominant forces which he evidently identified with property (capital) and labour. Of course, he underscored that in the present circumstances of capitalism there was an imbalance of forces in favour of capital. For this reason an economic constitution (*Wirtschaftsverfassung*) was needed to

39 Sinzheimer 1976b: 272.

40 See Sinzheimer 1976b: 274.

41 See Sinzheimer 1976b: 219–44.

42 See Sinzheimer 1976b: 6.

43 See Sinzheimer 1976b: 119.

44 Mueller 2002: 134.

45 Sinzheimer and Fraenkel 1968: 383.

adjust this imbalance in favour of labour,[46] which was exactly what he himself tried to accomplish in the Weimar Constitution. This attempt also explains why Sinzheimer wanted – with regard to labour and property – to replace the fictions of invisible hand and general will with the existence of the 'whole hand' (*die Existenz der gesamten Hand*) and the common will (*einen gemeinsamen Willen*).[47] This kind of 'associative move' or even a kind of 'will-to-community' might be partly explained by the 'organistic influence' of Gierke and Jhering. In any case, such a communal ethos, also evident in his identification of the constitutional or republican spirit with the spirit of unity (*Einheitsgeist*),[48] certainly qualifies but does not disclaim Sinzheimer's adherence to pluralism.[49]

Even though in Sinzheimer's constitutional design the political and juridical constitution was to be supplemented by the economic and labour constitution, where the main actors would be autonomous social forces such as occupational groups and associations, and where the norms of these autonomous social forces were significant, these collective subjects would be subordinated to the democratic state. In relation to the democratic state they could act in a kind of consultative role. Sinzheimer always emphasized that the ultimate decision-making bodies in society should be the democratic political institutions, above all Parliament. He certainly did not think that all democracy can do is to articulate pre-existing conditions, but rather emphasized that democratic politics always reads the present from the point of view of the future too.[50] Democracy exists in action. Therefore, he did not think that democracy only refers to the ordering activity but is ultimately concerned with human character and conduct (*Haltung*). For this reason, one can talk about a democratic way of life (*ein demokratischer Lebenstil*).[51]

Sinzheimer was a consistent democrat who pointed out that while political democracy is the breath of life (*Lebensluft*) for many people, for example in the Anglo-Saxon countries, it still poses a theoretical problem for the German people who still have to fight for the principle and value of democracy.[52] Sinzheimer emphasized that due to the history of authoritative schooling (*obrigkeitlicher Erziehung*) the German people certainly cannot turn into democrats overnight.[53] Sinzheimer concluded in 1930, some 10 years from the drafting of the Weimar Constitution (1919), that the Germans were not yet a political nation and had yet to become one, which was only possible by way of democratic self-government.[54] Therefore, one still had to be patient and cautious in criticizing the Weimar

46 See Dukes 2008: 343.
47 See Sinzheimer 1927: 209–11.
48 Sinzheimer and Fraenkel 1968: 87.
49 See Knorre 1991: 127–54.
50 See Sinzheimer and Fraenkel 1968: 124.
51 Sinzheimer and Fraenkel 1968: 205.
52 See Sinzheimer and Fraenkel 1968: 151.
53 See Sinzheimer and Fraenkel 1968: 40.
54 See Sinzheimer and Fraenkel 1968: 279.

Constitution, since one cannot expect it to yield quick and easy results. Sinzheimer was, above all, critical of Carl Schmitt's political and legal doctrine which he considered to be the opposite of the democratic legal thinking also exemplified by the Weimar Constitution.[55]

If Sinzheimer considered Schmitt to be *the* opponent among the main critics of the Weimar Constitution, then Herman Heller perhaps came closest to some of his own conclusions. Sinzheimer gave credit to Heller for his critique of Kelsen's purely formalist conception of both democracy and the legal ordering by the state, a purely formal legitimation of the Weimar Constitution. He thought that this bore the danger of losing contact with reality and the sense of justice of the people. Heller argued that Kelsen's attempt to make of the state an exhaustively rational and legal structure must fail, since it leads to circular reasoning.[56] Sinzheimer agreed with Heller that there was material content besides positive form and procedure to political democracy and '*Rechtsstaat*' ('constitutional state').[57] However, he concluded that Heller, in his critique of the dominant positivist ideology, recognized the problem but could not solve it. Heller could not specify how the constitutionally supported democratic political form could be so substantiated that it could achieve political unity, credibility and legitimacy.[58] If this statement of Sinzheimer is read in the context of Heller's critique of the Weimar Constitution, it then becomes clear how subtle but also pertinent and significant their differences in outlook were.

In criticizing the Weimar Constitution, Hermann Heller was also alert to the deep social divisions and tensions which he considered to be a threat to the functioning of the democratic political regime. However, he did admit that tensions and contradictions are constant elements of constitutionalism, which are connected with the conventions of a particular society. In order to cope with this threat, Heller argued that the liberal *Rechtsstaat* could and should be transformed into a social *Rechtsstaat*, a 'social rule of law', which would strengthen social homogeneity and unity by promoting equality.[59] Since Heller presumed that this transformation could only succeed if it were based on general ethical principles of law (*Rechtsgrundsätze*) embedded in culture – in a similar fashion as constitutional law was rooted in values[60] – Heller himself could be claimed to argue in circles. This seems to have been Sinzheimer's conclusion in spite of Heller's emphasis on the democratic process of collective judgements about morality being constitutive of the moral quality of the legal order.[61] Figuring out how Sinzheimer perceived this argument to be inadequate or wanting provides a crucial clue to his own

55 See Sinzheimer and Fraenkel 1968: 354.
56 See Dyzenhaus 2000: 26, 31.
57 See Sinzheimer and Fraenkel 1968: 356.
58 See Sinzheimer and Fraenkel 1968: 245.
59 See Caldwell 2000: 136–53.
60 See Dyzenhaus 2000: 34; Caldwell 2000: 143.
61 See Dyzenhaus 2000: 46.

conception of the social constitution. The answer was also Sinzheimer's response to the challenge that, in circumstances of international economy and growing complexity, the state was unable to resolve all the problems on the agenda.[62]

Sinzheimer does not find it sufficient or even possible that a transformation of the liberal *Rechtsstaat* into a social *Rechtsstaat* would solve the problem of political democracy in need of substance and supporters. The solution must be sought from the involvement and participation of human beings who, in this way, develop into democratic citizens with genuine social rights.[63] For this reason the social substance of democracy and social rights of citizens cannot just be guaranteed by state warrant, as in the form of a state constitution (*Staatsverfassung*).[64] Sinzheimer perfectly well understood that writing basic rights into the constitution – as exemplified by the Weimar Constitution – can open the way to state interventionism.[65] However, state interventionism as such is no guarantee that social rights and social equality of citizens are realized in practice. It all depends on the relationship between forces and struggles between different classes and groups of people in society.

Sinzheimer argues that democracy has to be extended to the economy (industrial democracy) and society at large (social democracy) which reciprocally makes it possible to develop genuine social and labour law and outline a practically effective social constitution. Sinzheimer calls this the task of fighting for the social self-determination (*soziale Selbstbestimmung*) of human beings in general and workers in particular. This task is parallel to 'the problem of human beings in law',[66] which is ultimately a question of being- and becoming-in-society: the 'I–You relationship' ('*Das Ich-und-Du Verhältnis*').[67] However, Sinzheimer did not think that social self-determination and state interventionism are mutually exclusive, as was understood by Georges Gurvitch, who, in line with French syndicalist pluralism (Saint-Simon, Proudhon), focused on the constitutive role of community for social law.[68] Sinzheimer emphasized that besides the contractual effect, collective agreements also possessed a normative part,[69] which was a sign of the plurality of norm-generating communities and sources of law. However, this recognition could well be combined with a positive vision of state interventionism supported by social rights as norms of the social state.

62 See Sinzheimer 1976b: 75.

63 See Sinzheimer and Fraenkel 1968: 156–157, 205, 274, and 279.

64 See Sinzheimer and Fraenkel 1968: 156–157, and 358.

65 See Caldwell 2000: 137.

66 Sinzheimer 1933:6. Author's translation from: 'das Problem des Menchen im Recht'.

67 Sinzheimer1948: 7–44.

68 See Sinzheimer 1976b: 164–187.

69 Sinzheimer 1977; Neal 1984.

Hugo Sinzheimer on Social Constitution

Sinzheimer even spoke about many constitutions, in fact, about multiple constitutions. He talked about 'political constitution' (*politische Verfassung*),[70] 'national constitution' (*Reichsverfassung*[71]), 'state constitution' (*Staatsverfassung*),[72] 'democratic constitution' (*demokratische Verfassung*)[73] and 'estate constitution' (*Ständeverfassung*),[74] but also about 'labour constitution' (*Arbeitsverfassung*),[75] 'economic constitution' (*Wirtschaftsverfassung*),[76] 'works constitution' (*Betriebsverfassung*),[77] 'finance constitution' (*Finanzverfassung*)[78] and 'council constitution' (*Räteverfassung*).[79] However, in his major writings he did not use the term 'social constitution' (*Sozialverfassung*), but rather talked about 'societal constitution' (*Gesellschaftsverfassung*).[80] This choice of terminology is not accidental. The crucial point is that the 'social constitution' as 'societal constitution' is clearly distinct from 'state constitution', even if the two are closely connected. Sinzheimer's basic idea is that neither the state administration (*Staatsverwaltung*) – even in the form of social *Rechtsstaat* – nor the private economy are able to make the most out of human potential for spontaneous activity (*Selbsttätigkeit*). For this reason a 'societal constitution' beneath a 'state constitution' is highly significant in organizing spontaneous human activity, but it is only possible by carefully finding out how the organs of 'societal constitution' (such as councils) can be coordinated with the organs of state.[81] For this reason, the relationship between society and state was the basic question in Sinzheimer's legal and political theory, which never approached state and law as detached from the play of social forces.[82]

The meaning and significance of 'social constitution' as 'societal constitution' in Sinzheimer's work cannot be truly understood without paying attention to what he meant by the 'social'. For Sinzheimer the 'social' was more or less identical with that which is for humans real, factual in an existential sense,[83] one could add 'ideally real'.[84] It is noteworthy that Sinzheimer talked about basic social rights

70 Sinzheimer and Fraenkel 1968: 274.
71 Sinzheimer and Fraenkel 1968: 39, 43 and 193; and Sinzheimer 1976a: 350.
72 Sinzheimer 1976a: 321, 350.
73 Sinzheimer and Fraenkel 1968, 274.
74 Sinzheimer 1976a: 136.
75 Sinzheimer 1927: 207–13; and 1976a: 95.
76 Sinzheimer 1976a: 105, 221, 341 and 350.
77 Sinzheimer and Fraenkel 1968: 189.
78 Sinzheimer and Fraenkel 1968: 189.
79 Sinzheimer 1976a: 345.
80 Sinzheimer 1976a: 357–9.
81 See Sinzheimer 1976a: 357–8.
82 See Sinzheimer 1976b: 71–2, 81–2 and 116.
83 Sinzheimer 1976a: 58, 312 and 442.
84 See Sinzheimer 1976b: 135–6; and Blanke 2005: 32–42.

as 'existential rights' (*Existenzrechte*).[85] Such a conception of the 'social' and the 'societal' was naturally inspired by neo-Kantian and phenomenological ideas which profoundly revised his rather Marxian points of departure. It is no wonder then that he conceptually operated with an arsenal of terms derived from the root 'social' referring basically to 'social reality, relations, forms and determinations of human beings'[86] or to 'social conceptions of reality' (*Erfassung* as well as *Verfassung*, that is, conceiving and constituting).[87]

This way of understanding the 'social' as the 'societal', makes it clear that 'social constitution' as 'societal constitution' cannot have as its domain only a particular field of law (such as labour law or social security law) but penetrates law's empire, thus challenging traditional disciplinary divisions and transforming law systematically as a legal system. The principal task of the 'social constitution' as 'societal constitution' is to help in organizing the 'social order' (*Sozialordnung*),[88] 'social system of order' (*Soziales System der Ordnung*)[89] or 'compulsory social order' (*Soziale Zwangsordnung*)[90] in the most human manner as 'social order among persons' (*Soziale Personenordnung*).[91] This aims at a socially self-determined societal order (*Soziale Selbstbestimmung*)[92] of all producers (workers included) and consumers as citizens. In this manner Sinzheimer also laid the foundations for the concept of collective self-determination.[93] In the frame of the social constitution, the socially self-determined societal order can and must be coordinated with the rights-ensuring activity of the social *Rechtsstaat*, which is only possible in a truly democratic society.

The most direct way to understand what was ultimately at stake in Sinzheimer's approach to social law and social constitution is to proceed from the point of view of labour law, which Sinzheimer developed in pioneering fashion. Sinzheimer's former student, Otto Kahn-Freund, in his retrospective portrayal, *Hugo Sinzheimer 1875–1945*, outlined outstandingly what Sinzheimer was up to in his treatment of labour law:

> Society covers the unequal treatment of human beings (*Menschen*) with the veil of equality of persons (*Personen*) … Sinzheimer's task was to unmask the "persons" … It was Sinzheimer's aspiration to show the way from the law of contract to the law of labour, from the treatment of the worker as a "person", abstractly equal to the employer, to his treatment as a human being, concretely

85 Sinzheimer 1976a: 113, 125.
86 Sinzheimer 1927: 60, 67; 1976a, 272; and 1976b: 50, 88–9,184.
87 Sinzheimer 1976a: 403.
88 Sinzheimer 1976a: 111; and 1976b: 180.
89 Sinzheimer 1976a: 173.
90 Sinzheimer 1976a: 408.
91 Sinzheimer 1927: 61.
92 Sinzheimer 1976a: 224, 247, 263, 405; and 1976b: 125.
93 See Coutu 2006–2007.

> dependent in his existence. The law had previously focused on the equal rights of all persons before the law, it was now to concern itself with the concrete conditions under which individuals had to exist … the law, which had previously ignored the dependency of the working human being, will now recognize it as the norm. The extra-legal fact of human existential dependency will now become a legal fact, the person will now become a living being, the law will no longer take as its starting point the abstract freedom of the person, but the concrete dependency of the individual, not the postulated "will", but the empirically established "condition" of the human being.[94]

In his aspiration, Sinzheimer evidently echoes Marx but follows Gierke, who had already abandoned the Roman law idea of contracting – as merely a private contract law matter – and referred to the employment relationship as one of subordination so that the capitalist enterprise could be conceived of as an organization of domination, which Sinzheimer also later contrasted with cooperatives (*Genossenschaftsverband*).[95] In his legal analysis of the collective agreement, but also in his critical sociology of law, Sinzheimer seeks to link the two moments or elements of exchange and of subordination.[96] In so doing, he actually has an eye on the capital–labour relationship, which reveals that it is not naked individuals *in abstracto* who here confront each other legally, but individuals positioned as interest-bearing, collective subjects. In his *Grundzüge des Arbeitsrecht* ('Features of Labour Law') Sinzheimer specifies that in this game of forces the participants are not individual persons but personifications of societal events (*Personifikation gesellschaftlichen Vorgänge*).[97] Sinzheimer further argues that legal science should reach beyond the 'commodity order' towards the 'human order' and, therefore, recognize and unveil the fact that abstractions such as commodity, property, contract, legal person, for example, also cover real contradictions, oppositions, tensions, domination and dependencies between human groups and classes.[98]

Even though Sinzheimer principally focused on labour law and specifically labour constitution, he did work towards a more encompassing economic law and economic constitution.[99] In this way the social(ized) person-order between employers and employees was generalized. In fact, societal constitution could be perceived as an even more comprehensive mode of legal ordering of the social (*rechtlichen Bestimmung des Sozialen*) in order to reach a factual human order challenging the idea of social order supposed to be guaranteed by the hypothetical contract. In his *Grundzüge* Sinzheimer writes:

---

94 Kahn-Freund 1981: 102–3.

95 See Sinzheimer 1976a: 402–7; Kahn-Freund 1981: 78.

96 Kahn-Freund 1981: 91–2.

97 Sinzheimer 1927: 9.

98 See Sinzheimer and Fraenkel 1968: 84, also Kahn-Freund 1981: 102.

99 See Sinzheimer and Fraenkel 1968: 148.

> Wir nennen die Ordnung, die so den Menschen in seiner sozialen Existenz zur Geltung bringt soziale Personenordnung. Sie tritt im Ganzen des Rechts mit eigenen Prinzipien neben die Güter- und Eigentumsordnung, indem sie den Menschen selbst in seinem gesellschaftlichen Sein und Wirken erfasst und dafür besondere Rechtsformen aufstellt. Sie begründet ein eigenes rechtliches Reich, in dem die zentrierende Kraft nicht das Eigentum sondern der Mensch ist. Wir sehen diese neue Ordnung in fortschreitender Entwicklung sich erheben. Einst war Mensch, der nicht ein 'Freier' war, Sache. Durch die Rechtsgleichheit wurde er Person. Die neue Ordnung macht ihm zum Menschen.[100]

To take into consideration the concrete social conditions under which individuals live and have to exist interdependently definitely meant that one could no longer be satisfied with a purely formal analysis of law as normative order. This was Sinzheimer's definite point of departure, which was also reinforced by the influence of the *Freirechtsschule* ('German School of Legal Realism') on his thinking. Sinzheimer did not, though, underestimate the significance of technically and logically correct reasoning about legal norms and normative order. On the contrary, he always emphasized that 'Der Jurist muss juristisch denken können'.[101] This goal was, however, not the only objective of legal education or the only referent of legal practice. Sinzheimer emphasized that a distinction should be made between 'positive law' (*geltendes Recht*) or 'normative law' (*normatives Recht*) and 'law in action' (*wirkendes Recht*) or 'legal reality' (*Rechtswirklickeit*) and even distinguished both of them from 'just law' (*richtiges Recht*) or 'ideal law' (*ideales Recht*).[102] He concludes that law comprises all these modes as a whole.[103] Accordingly, he thought that legal education has to be suited to technical or logical, practical and philosophical tasks.[104] These distinctions can be compared with the different approaches of positive law, sociology of law and philosophy of law,[105] but they have nothing to do – in Sinzheimer's own words – with Carl Schmitt's

100 Sinzheimer 1927: 61. Author's translation: 'We call order what humans bring to their social existence for the validity of social order among persons. In general, it shadows law with its own principles in addition to the movable and immovable property order, by seizing humans in their social being and makeup and sets in place a special form of law. It justifies its own legal realm, in which the centre of gravity is not property but humans. We see this new order arising in progressive development. Once humans who were not 'freemen' were things. Through equality of rights they became persons. The new order turns them into humans.'

101 Sinzheimer and Fraenkel 1968: 85. Author's translation: 'The legal scholar must be capable of legal thinking.'

102 See Sinzheimer 1976b: 86–107.

103 See Sinzheimer 1976b: 87.

104 See Sinzheimer and Fraenkel 1968: 85.

105 See Kahn-Freund 1981: 97.

triad in his '*drei Arten des rechtswissenschaftlichen Denkens*'.[106] Sinzheimer concludes that, all in all, this means that 'Der Jurist versteht das Recht innerlich erst dann, wenn er die sozialen Tendenzen einer Zeit im Ganzen erfasst und in der Rechtsordnung den Ausdruck geistiger, sozialer und wirtschaftlicher Tendenzen zu finden weiss'.[107]

Sinzheimer argued retrospectively in 1935 – after emigrating to Holland – that the problem of the present state of the world of law (*die Welt des Rechts*) is the one-sidedness of normativism, characteristic, for example, of legal positivism. By elevating one part of law – formal or normative law – to stand for law as such, normativism neglects those constitutive forces which are operative in the ideals of law and in the reality of legal practices. It is precisely Sinzheimer's critique of normativism that provides the key to the political rationality of the social constitution as societal constitution. The crucial point of the critique of normativism is this: 'Er hat die verkehrte Vorstellung geweckt, das Problem des Rechts sei nur die logisch geordnete Rechtsordnung und nicht das Problem des Im-Gleichewicht-Halten und stets erneut Ins-Gleichgewicht-Bringen der wirklichen Kräfte, die zusammen das Recht bilden.'[108]

Since Sinzheimer thought that an imbalance of power between property and labour in favour of property was a basic characteristic of capitalism, he concluded that a constitutional arrangement was necessary to correct this imbalance.[109] It is not only the task of a labour constitution or economic constitution, but that of the societal constitution to promote this balance since achieving equilibrium (*Ins-Gleichgwicht-Bringen*) can be properly done only by acting in the entire field of forces, that is, integrally in society. Sinzheimer certainly did not believe those ideologists who argued that one (the unions) cannot challenge the laws of the market. On the contrary, he argued that the onto-theological idol of harmony associated with the functioning of the capitalist market economy was a myth which had to be challenged. In fact, Sinzheimer argued in 1928 that due to the collapse of free play of market forces (or '*freie Spiel der Kräfte*') a new regulator – in place of automatic self-regulation of the market – had to be found for the economic system to run properly.[110] Even if Sinzheimer considered the role of the state as crucial in regulating the economy,[111] he certainly did not want to overload the state with problems and tasks which were beyond its powers. He actually considered

106 Sinzheimer 1976b: 87. Author's translation: 'three kinds of jurisprudential thinking'.

107 Sinzheimer and Fraenkel 1968: 85. Author's translation: 'The lawyer understands the law internally when he grasps current overall social tendencies and can identify the expression of mental, social and economic tendencies in the legal order.'

108 Sinzheimer 1976b: 87. Author's translation: 'It brought about a misconception that the problem of law is only the logically arranged legal order and not the problem of achieving and maintaining equilibrium of the real forces which together form the law.'

109 See Dukes 2008: 343.

110 See Sinzheimer and Fraenkel 1968: 150, 162.

111 See Sinzheimer and Fraenkel 1968: 162.

the development towards the 'total state' to be truly dangerous.[112] In other words, Sinzheimer's own remedy to the system-specific instability of capitalism connected with the liberal individualism of the commodity order was to promote a human order supported by both a just legal order (*Rechtsordunung*) ruled by the state and a social order (*Sozialordunung*) of autonomous collective agents. For this reason, he also emphasized that the constitution is a unity between the legal order and the social order.[113]

The basic principle of balancing and ordering in the social constitution is solidarity.[114] Hugo Sinzheimer is explicit in that social law is unequal law. Social law privileges the weak against the strong, it challenges the abstract and purely formal idea of equality (before the law), which reproduces inequalities in the real world and, therefore, can function as a backbone for the strong and wealthy.[115] These are two of those characteristics which François Ewald also attached to the concept of social law.[116] Ewald does not make any reference to Sinzheimer since his analysis concerns the French example. Nevertheless, practically all of Ewald's points about social law were already articulated by Sinzheimer. Sinzheimer also thought that social law is a completely new way of thinking about law and that it penetrates and transforms the whole set of legal fields. He understood that social law brings social conflict between groups of people with opposing interests under the law by emphasizing the question of 'who has rights' rather than 'who is right'. He also emphasized that the basic issue of social law is balancing or counterweighting, which challenges the counterfactual assumptions of hypothetical contractualism. Social law is based on factual solidarity contracts between interested parties, which make it possible to promote social reforms politically. He understood that society as a whole could only be represented by a democratically elected Parliament but he saw that democracy should be constitutionally extended to society as a whole, including the economy. This was the specific task of the societal constitution, as well as that of economic and labour constitutions.

Hugo Sinzheimer was certainly a creative thinker, but can he be characterized as an innovating ideologist in Quentin Skinner's sense?[117] In order to give a definitely positive answer to this question, Sinzheimer should have been able to 'show that a number of existing and favourable evaluative-descriptive terms can somehow be applied to his apparently untoward actions'.[118] Sinzheimer was quite obviously so much ahead of his time that he could not perform this trick outstandingly enough. He realized this himself well before he had to emigrate from Germany. But would the conclusion be different if one thought about his innovations and suggestions,

112 See Sinzheimer and Fraenkel 1968: 358.
113 See Sinzheimer and Fraenkel 1968: 35.
114 See Sinzheimer 1976a: 310, 314–15.
115 See Sinzheimer and Fraenkel 1968: 195–6.
116 See Ewald 1986: 45, 61.
117 See Skinner 1974.
118 Skinner 1974: 294.

such as the societal constitution and the democratic community of Pan-Europe[119] from the perspective of more recent times, against the background of welfare state development and European integration? In spite of all this (modification in the evaluation–description of the present), Sinzheimer is altogether too radical and critical a thinker to be reconcilable to the cultural logic of capitalism and its commodity-order as an ideologist.

References

Ben-Bassat, A. and Dahan M. 2008. Social rights in the constitution and in practice. *Journal of Comparative Economics*, 36, 103–19.

Blanke, S. 2005. *Soziales Recht oder Kollektive Privatautonomie? Hugo Sinzheimer im Kontext nach 1900*. Tübingen: Mohr Siebeck.

Caldwell, P.C. 1997. *Popular Sovereignty and the Crisis of German Constitutional Law. The Theory & Practice of Weimar Constitutionalism*. Durham, NC and London: Duke University Press.

Caldwell, P.C. 2000. Is a '*Social Rechtsstaat*' possible? The Weimar roots of a Bonn controversy, in *From Liberalism to Fascism*, edited by P.C. Caldwell and W.E. Scheuermann. Boston, MA: Humanities Press.

Coutu, M. 2006–2007. Labour law, legal pluralism and state sovereignty. *Canadian Labour & Employment Law Journal*, 13:2, 169–86.

Dukes, R. 2008. Constitutionalizing employment relations: Sinzheimer, Kahn-Freund and the role of labour law. *Journal of Law and Society*, 35:3, 341–63.

Dyzenhaus, D. 2000. The gorgon head of power: Heller and Kelsen on the rule of law, in *From Liberalism to* Fascism, edited by P.C. Caldwell and W.E. Scheuermann. Boston, MA: Humanities Press.

Ewald, F. 1986. A concept of social law, in *Dilemmas of Law in the Welfare State*, edited by G. Teubner. New York: Walter de Gruyter, 40–75.

Gierke, O. von. 1895. *Deutsches Privatrecht, Bd. 1: Allgemeiner Teil und Personenrecht*. Leipzig: Duncker & Humblot.

Joerges, C. 2004. What is Left of the European Economic Constitution? A Melancholic Eulogy. EUI Working Paper Law, No. 2004/13. Badia Fiesolana.

Kahn-Freund, O. 1981. *Labour Law and Politics in the Weimar Republic*. Oxford: Basil Blackwell.

Kirchheimer, O. 1969. Weimar – and what then? An analysis of a constitution, in *Politics, Law, and Social Change. Selected Essays of Otto Kirchheimer*, edited by F.S. Burin and K.L. Shell. New York and London: Columbia University Press, 33–74.

Knorre, S. 1991. *Soziale Selbstbestimmung und individuelle Verantwortung. Hugo Sinzheimer (1875–1945). Eine politische Biographie*. Frankfurt am Main, Bern, New York und Paris: Peter Lang.

119 See Sinzheimer 1976a: 221–5; and 1968: 26–32.

Lassalle, F. 1993. *Über Verfassungswesen*. Rede am 16. April 1862 in Berlin. EVA Reden; Bd. 8. Hamburg: Europäische Verlagsanstalt.

Mueller, D.C. 2002. The importance of uncertainty in a two-stage theory of constitutions, in *Method and Morals in Constitutional Economics. Essays in Honor of James M. Buchanan*, edited by G. Brennan, H. Kliemt and R.D. Tollison. Berlin, Heidelberg and New York: Springer.

Neal, A.C. 1984. Employment protection laws: The Swedish model. *The International and Comparative Law Quarterly*, 33, 634–62.

Neumann, F.L. 1930. Die soziale Bedeutung der Grundrechte in der Weimarer Verfassung. *Die Arbeit*, 569–82.

Neumann, F.L. 1986. *The Rule of Law. Political Theory and the Legal System in Modern Society*. Leamington Spa, Heidelberg and Dover, NH: Berg Publishers.

Sinzheimer, H. 1927. *Grundzüge des Arbeitsrechts*. 2nd edition. Jena: Verlag von Gustav Fischer.

Sinzheimer, H. 1933. *Das Problem des Menschen im Recht*. Groningen-Batavia: P. Noordhoff N.V.

Sinzheimer, H. 1948. *Theorie der Gesetzgebung. Die Idee der Evolution im Recht*. Haarlem: H.D. Tjeenk Willink & Zoon N.V.

Sinzheimer, H. 1976a. *Arbeitsrecht und Rechtssoziologie. Gesammelte Aufsätze und Reden. Band 1*. Frankfurt – Köln: Europäische Verlagsanstalt.

Sinzheimer, H. 1976b. *Arbeitsrecht und Rechtssoziologie. Gesammelte Aufsätze und Reden. Band 2*. Frankfurt – Köln: Europäische Verlagsanstalt.

Sinzheimer, H. 1977. *Der Korporative Arbeitsnormenvertrag. Eine privatrechtliche Untersuchung (2. Bde, I (1907), II (1908)). 2 unveränderte Aufl*. Berlin: Duncker & Humblot.

Sinzheimer, H. and Fraenkel, E. 1968. *Die Justiz in der Weimarer Republik. Eine Chronik*. Berlin: Neuwied und Luchterhand.

Skinner, Q. 1974. Some problems in the analysis of political thought and action. *Political Theory*, 2, 277–303.

Chapter 11
Social Rights and Market Freedom in the European Constitution: A Reappraisal

Stefano Giubboni

Introduction

In 1956, during negotiations for the Treaty of Rome, the prime minister of France, the socialist Guy Mollet, strongly supported in his initiative by the employers' organizations of his country, fought determinedly for the harmonization of national social policies. Social harmonization, including the sensitive issue of financing social security systems, was posited as a precondition for the market integration of future member states in the new Community. The opposing vision maintained by, above all, Germany, rejected preliminary harmonization and advocated leaving national social systems to harmonize spontaneously, at least in the medium term, as an almost certain and automatic consequence of the integration process. This follow-on model of social rights had already been accepted, with marginal corrections, in the report adopted by the group of ILO experts led by Bertil Ohlin, one of the leading scholars of international economy of that period. And above all this theory was incorporated in what has been effectively defined as the 'White Paper' of the Treaty of Rome:[1] the Spaak Report.[2]

Fritz Sharpf begins one of his most famous studies on the relationship between the so-called 'European social model' and the EC integration process by asking the provocative 'counterfactual question' of what would have happened if the Treaty of Rome had adopted Mollet's approach. As Scharpf observes, during the mid-1950s the welfare states of Europe 'were still rudimentary in quantitative terms, and structurally much more similar than they became in the following decades'.[3] Given the relative homogeneity of the welfare structures of the six founding member states around the Bismarck model of an employment-based and corporatist welfare

1 Davies 1992, 319.

2 Monnet 1976, 474, emphasizes '*le mérite politique de ce document considérable*'. The Spaak Report, as it is commonly called, is the Rapport des chefs de délégation aux Ministres des Affaires Etrangères (Report of the Heads of Delegation to the Ministers of Foreign Affairs) of 21 April 1956, prepared by Paul-Henry Spaak.

3 Scharpf 2002, 646.

state, although harmonization would have been politically challenging, it 'would not have been hopeless'.[4]

This chapter will not further question the reasons behind the 'road not taken', between 1956 and 1957, by the (former) European Economic Community.[5] Instead, the starting point will be the original 'system-decision'[6] to separate creation of the common market from construction of a corresponding supranational sphere of welfare policies and the long-term consequences of this constitutional choice will be investigated. It will be argued that the original decision not to have a European welfare state structure has framed the Community's intervention in social policy as a matter of 'governing the differences'[7] between national systems while constructing the common market. Indeed, it is argued that the main purpose of Community intervention in the social field is also its main challenge – to bring together the different national models of welfare along with parallel construction of the common market. In other words, it has become more difficult to reconcile the different traditions of national labour law and social security, which are central to the substantive democratic legitimacy of the member states, with the needs of a common market built upon the constitutionalization of common competition law and the unfolding of supranational economic freedoms.

The Original Constitutional Compromise and Ordo-Liberal Conceptions

The original absence of significant social competences in the founding treaties is consistent with the choice outlined above, lucidly defined by Scharpf as the 'political decoupling of economic integration and social-protection issues'.[8] The Paris and Rome treaties, despite the objective lack of supranational social competences, did not ignore social issues, but tried to position them, using different institutional devices, to accommodate two distinct needs. On the one hand stood the need to functionalize new supranational institutions to build a common market, relying on the freedom of movement of factors of production (including work) and on free enterprise and competition. On the other hand stood the need to ensure full respect for the sovereignty of member states in the sphere of social and redistribution policies, a sphere considered entirely reserved for national democratic political processes and institutions, and thus removed from the range of competences given to the newborn Communities.

All the founding member states incorporate the normative foundations of the welfare state into their constitutions. The 1948 Italian Constitution offers an example

4 Scharpf 2002, 646.

5 For an in-depth analysis of these issues see Giubboni 2006a.

6 This expression is typical of the language of the German ordo-liberal school, which had readapted it from the famous Schmittian taxonomy. *Cf.* Gerber 1994.

7 Torchia 2006.

8 Scharpf 2002, 646.

of particularly explicit incorporation. It sets out a social model characterized by an extensive and detailed catalogue of fundamental social rights. Attention to social issues was then reduced in the original founding treaties, recognizing full freedom of action for member states in the sphere of social and labour policies. These were indeed pursued and developed at national level, with the extraordinary intensity that marks the so-called 'golden age' of European welfare states,[9] in fulfilment of those post-war constitutional promises of social emancipation and liberation from deprivation. On that basis, after the devastation of the Second World War, a new and inclusive idea of democratic citizenship was established.

It has been suggested that the theoretical model offered by the German ordo-liberal school supports this original division of competences – as a type of foundational division of labour between the Community and its member states, in which the former was allocated the functional task of progressive pooling of markets and economies, and the latter the edification of social citizenship on the premise of public policies of full employment. In fact, many similarities exist between the ordo-liberal requirements and the foundations of the European Economic Community in 1957. First of all, the then highly influential ordo-liberal conceptions are undeniably consistent with the deep *raison d'être* of the division of competence between the Community and the national level as inscribed in the text of the Treaty of Rome and 'the decoupling of the social dimension from the institutionalization of the Europeanised system of undistorted competition'.[10] As Christian Joerges has observed,

> in the ordo-liberal account, the Community acquired a legitimacy of its own by interpreting its pertinent provisions as prescribing a law-based order committed to guaranteeing economic freedoms and protecting competition by supranational institutions. This legitimacy was independent of the state's democratic constitutional institutions. By the same token, it imposed limits upon the Community: discretionary economic policies seemed illegitimate and unlawful.[11]

The idea was precisely that of a system built on two separate processes: the first, at the supranational level, consisted of the route towards uniform integration propelled by the binding force of the higher law of the European Community that implemented an economic rationality around the principles of freedom of movement of factors of production and non-distorted competition. The second process involved anchoring redistributive social policies at the national level. Composition of social policies was to be decided democratically by member state electorates inevitably diversifying national preferences and traditions, and

9 Ferrera 2005a.
10 Joerges 2004, 471.
11 Joerges 2004, 471.

building constellations of interests as different as the 'worlds' of welfare states in Europe.[12] To summarize with Joerges,

> Europe was constituted as a dual polity. Its economic constitution was un-political in the sense that it was not subjected to political interventions. This was its constitutional-supranational *raison d'être*. Social policy was treated as a categorically distinct subject. It was the domain of political legislation and, thus, had to remain national. The social embedness [*sic*] of the market could, and should, be accomplished by the Member States in differentiated ways – and, for a decade or so, the balance seemed stable.[13]

The almost quintessential translation of this constitutional bifurcation can be found in the sophisticated system of EEC social security coordination implemented for the first time with Regulation No. 3/1958. The coordination technique was chosen not just to guarantee free movement of workers. Admittedly, the immediate reason for coordinating social security systems was to enable effective exercise of this freedom. However, a deeper reason exists for the primacy and the durability of social security coordination. The coordination technique reflected the basic choices made and the balance struck by the treaties regarding the relationship between supranational institutions and member state social systems. Indeed, it allowed the preservation of regulatory state monopoly in a sector central to the legitimacy of the nation-state, at the same time ensuring the opening of national systems to the functional requirements of economic integration. Therefore, the strategic option to coordinate national social security legal regimes, while ensuring gradual liberalization of movement of labour, reflected, more deeply, the founding constitutional decoupling of the national social dimension from the institutionalization of the common market around the fundamental economic freedoms and undistorted competition.

The Community was essentially devoid of significant social policy competences, and the narrow confines in which the EEC Treaty conferred powers undoubtedly reflect the Community's conception as 'mere compensation for the socially undesirable effects of economic integration'.[14] But in this original setting, lack of competence was not the result of a lack of social concern on the part of the EEC founding fathers; on the contrary, it was structured so as to preserve the necessary normative autonomy of the reborn national democratic welfare state under the new international economic context. As has been observed,

> when it was launched in the 1950s, the project of European integration did not intend to challenge the institutional foundations of national social contracts. Quite the contrary, the Founding Fathers and most of the relevant national elites

12 Esping-Andersen 1990.

13 Joerges 2004, 471–2.

14 Mechi 2003, 79.

> conceived of European integration as a project capable of creating and sustaining a virtuous cycle between open economies and out-ward looking economic policies on the one hand and closed welfare states and in-ward looking social policy on the other.[15]

Indeed, the coordination of national social security schemes achieved a level of openness that was necessary for controlled liberalization of the movement of labour, without undermining the social sovereignty of the member states. The idea that building a strong national social dimension and consolidating the European common market were two separate tracks fully agreed with the theoretical model of legitimacy of the newborn Community offered by the ordo-liberal school.

The Brief Season of Upward Harmonization

It is well known that the EEC began to acquire its own (slight) body of social policies, in spite of the absence of a specific and autonomous legal base in the Rome Treaty, in the wake of the first social action plan approved at the Paris summit in 1974. It is noteworthy that the beginnings of European social policies, or at least of some harmonization of national labour laws, occurred, not only many years after entry into force of the Treaty of Rome, but also long after the historical development of labour and social security legislation of the member states. These 'Social Europe' beginnings coincide with the decline of the post-war 'glorious' expansive cycle of the welfare state in all member states. A new phase of crisis and restructuring began.

Beyond the apparent paradox of this time lag, the season of the 'grand Directives' of harmonization of the mid-1970s which Massimo D'Antona defined as 'functionalist'[16] does not seem inconsistent with the constitutional premise underlying the original structure of the treaties, although it marks a first separation from the purity of theoretical ordo-liberal paradigms. The consistency of these normative premises with the Directives on enterprise crisis[17] seems undeniable to the extent that, if 'the basis for social harmonization policies exclusively oriented

15 Ferrera 2005b, 3.

16 Distinguishing it from the 'cohesive' one, which aims at promotion of common social values, separated from the logic underlying the operation of the integrated market, see D'Antona 1996, 22.

17 The Directives from 1975 to 1980 are: Council Directive 75/129/EEC of 17 February 1975 on the approximation of the laws of the Member States relating to collective redundancies (OJ L 48, 22.2.1975, 29–30); Council Directive 77/187/EEC of 14 February 1977 on the approximation of the laws of the Member States relating to the safeguarding of employees' rights in the event of transfers of undertakings, businesses or parts of businesses (OJ L 61, 5.3.1977, 26–8); and Council Directive 80/987/EEC of 20 October 1980 on the approximation of the laws of the Member States relating to the protection of employees in the event of the insolvency of their employer (OJ L 283, 28.10.1980, 23–7).

towards a non-distorting competition in the market is created',[18] then such policies will aim to protect national labour law systems from deregulatory pressures potentially prompted by economic crisis, in other words from the risk of social dumping. These Directives express the purpose of the Community's social policy as imagined in the founding Treaty: protection of national systems from the threat of social dumping and of downward competition of the standards of protection for workers.[19] This aim is both ancillary to and instrumental in the correct functioning of the common market, but that is at once congruous with the priority need to preserve the social sovereignty of the member states by managing the competition process within the Community.

Missing suitable bases (or, rather, operating within the narrow functional limits drawn by the EEC Treaty), upward legal harmonization was nevertheless pursued 'with innovative audacity and imagination'.[20] However, the fragility of the harmonizing consensus was soon exposed thanks to the variables and contingencies and growing difficulties of political compromise between member states. Despite undeniable success in prompting upward harmonization even in areas of great importance to national labour law systems, the golden age of social policy directives declines in a brief turn of time.

The relaunch of the European integration process, designed in the Delors White Paper of 1985 on the internal market, also symbolically marks a turning point in building the common market. Mutual recognition and minimum harmonization stand at the core of the new ambitious re-regulatory programme as envisaged in the White Paper and towards which the Single European Act directed the new regulatory machinery. Gaining new (limited) legal basis meant that social policy was no longer purely ancillary to establishment of the common market. Social objectives were refocused towards minimal intervention compatible with an integration process geared towards 'regulatory minimalism'.[21] Other forms of supranational intervention gradually assume prevalence, including a new generation of less invasive, post-regulatory mechanisms aimed at political coordination or convergence instead of at normative standardization.[22] As D'Antona had warned, in this process harmonization is seen as a process of governed differentiation.[23]

18 Sciarra 2009, 9.
19 See Barnard 2007, 109.
20 Treu 2004, 33.
21 Simitis and Lyon-Caen 1996, 8–9.
22 See Szyszczak 2001.
23 See D'Antona 2000.

From Upward Harmonization to Regulatory Competition among National Social Systems

It has already been noted that in the original balance struck by the treaties the 'economic constitution' and 'social constitution' belong to two fundamentally distinct spheres, with the former, at least in its supranational projections, the domain of Community law, and the latter the domain of national legal orders. In this configuration, no European social deficit occurs. Despite the almost complete lack of social competence of the Community, no such deficit existed in the first phase of the integration process mainly because the social dimension was completely realized within the spheres of the constitutions and of the democratic political processes of the member states. The social concerns of the common market and of the Community are, in fact, rooted entirely within the national constitutions and the democratic institutions of the member states, including the original social autonomy recognized for trade unions.

The European social deficit, as conceptualized in the early 1980s, originated in the unsettling of this equilibrium, notably from marked contrast between the failure of expansion of Community social competence and the increased impact of the principles of the economic constitution upon national legislatures, 'infiltrating'[24] virtually all areas of national social policies and amplifying the potential for negative integration. If the position of the epigones of the ordo-liberal school is considered, the unsettling of the original constitutional equilibrium is caused mainly by undue expansion of Community competences in spheres of *political* action, such as industrial or social policy. Unstoppable after the Maastricht Treaty, these political forays have exceeded the legitimacy resources available to the supranational institutions.[25]

But here it is proposed that the most important tipping point of the imbalance lies in the increasingly pervasive penetration of the limitations imposed by EC competition and market law – the backbone of the economic constitution of the Community – directly into the sphere of public policy and particularly national labour and social security laws.[26] This is and will remain the most critical point of intersection between Community law and national legal orders in striking a new balance between market freedoms and protection of social rights within European constitutional space.

For our purposes, the epicentre of the rift in the original constitutional compromise lies in the case law of the Court of Justice on the relationship between national labour and social security laws and the principles of the Community economic constitution. This case law covers *inter alia* the rules regarding competition *sensu stricto* and, especially recently, the rules regarding fundamental

24 As Lyon-Caen 1992, 313, wrote in an article that became famous.

25 See Streit and Mussler 1995.

26 See, among the first comprehensive surveys, Davies (1995), and most recently the masterful summary by Lord Wedderburn of Charlton (2007).

economic freedoms (of movement of goods and especially of services). The constitutional asymmetry between the principles governing construction of the European market and autonomy of national social systems springs from the new dynamics of regulatory competition in the domain of labour law triggered by case law on free movement of services.

The institutionalization of mutual recognition as the operational principle of free movement of goods within the internal market fed into the new dynamics of regulatory competition from which the national systems of labour law and social security remained at first immune. Following early uncertainty, attempts to use Article 28 EC (now 36 TFEU) to question the legitimacy of barriers to importation of goods deriving from indistinctly applicable labour law rules, such as those on the prohibition of Sunday work, have been subverted by the Court of Justice.[27] Free movement of goods and labour law rules indeed operate on quite distinct and distant spheres of interaction within the internal market. However, the situation changes radically in the case of freedom to provide services: every time that an enterprise established in another member state rightly makes use of its employees by posting them temporarily in the territory of the state in which the service is destined, the protective labour laws of the latter can create indistinctly applicable barriers with regard to Article 49 EC (now 56 TFEU). Therefore, the logic of competition between legal orders fully enters the domains of national labour laws[28] only through the ban on non-discriminatory obstacles, effectively extending the principle of mutual recognition in the field of free movement of services.[29] The unstoppable spillover of free provision of services had already reached national systems of labour law. In *Rush Portuguesa*[30] the Court of Justice had considered the mobility of workers temporarily posted abroad by an employer providing services to be governed by the principles enshrined in Article 49 EC (now 56 TFEU). In this way, intra-Community posting of workers was detached from the scope of Article 39 EC (now 45 TFEU), which until then had always been regarded as the general rule for all instances of free movement of workers.[31] The Court had thus made clear that, in such cases, the principles developed in interpreting Article 49 EC (now 56 TFEU) should be taken into account.

In a highly controversial passage from the ruling, in declaring the illegitimacy of the obligation of prior authorization required by France, the Court was careful

27 See Poiares Maduro 2001.

28 *Cf.* Carabelli 2007.

29 Definitively sanctioned by the leading case *Säger* of 1991, see Case C-76/90, *Säger v Dennemeyer & Co. Ltd*, ECR 1991, I-4221.

30 Case C-113/89, *Rush Portuguesa Lda v Office National d'Immigration*, ECR 1990, I-1417.

31 See Lo Faro 2008a. For the sake of precision, *Rush Portuguesa* established that the derogation from Article 39 EC, then 48 EC, did not apply because of non-access to the host labour market, but did not specifically disapply Art. 39 EC; the ECJ only did so explicitly in Joint Cases C-49–50/98, C-52–54/98 and C-68–71/98, *Finalarte Sociedade de Construção Civil and others* ECR 2001, I-7831. See Verschueren 2008.

to reassure host member states that they could continue to apply their (higher) legal or collective standards of labour protection. The Court recognized – although ambiguously – the legitimacy of the need to preserve an area of 'social sovereignty' in member states when determining conditions of employment which were also applicable to workers temporarily posted in their territory for provision of a service, compatibly with the principles of Article 49 EC (now 56 TFEU). This is a very significant passage: implicitly,[32] the Court recognizes that protection from social dumping, which was the original ratio of the social policy of harmonization, becomes in the new context a potential justification for national protective (and 'protectionist') labour law rules and a possible obstacle to free intra-Community provision of a service.

The original perspective is therefore *in nuce* completely reversed. Protection against the risks of social dumping is no longer the trigger for a process of upward harmonization of national standards of protection, the generalization of higher levels of protection being unthinkable in an enlarging Europe.[33] In the new context, it is a reason for justifying the legitimacy of more favourable national measures for the posted worker, although under the constraint of the necessity/proportionality test of Article 49 EC (now 56 TFEU).

This is a groundbreaking decision filled with inherent tensions and possibly irreducible elements of contradiction.[34] The desire to protect the national labour market from the entrance of lower standards of protection from the country of origin of the service provider, which could otherwise prove deregulatory and destructuring to the legal autonomy of the host member state, must be squared with an aversion to obstacles to service provision. However, as will be better seen shortly, the whole construction of the 'Posting Directive' 96/71/EC,[35] laboriously built on the precarious balance of concerns envisaged by *Rush Portuguesa*, focuses on social protection of workers temporarily posted in other member states. Deciding the appropriate balance of interests in the context of protecting posted foreign workers highlights the inevitable tension between possibilities for social dumping and defence of economic and legal conditions applied to the national

32 The Court of Justice would subsequently make explicit this innovative conceptual passage; see Cases C-60/03, *Wolff & Müller GmbH & Co. KG*, ECR 2004 I-9553, para. 41; C-244/04, *Commission v Germany* ECR 2006, I-885, para. 61; and especially the (in)famous Cases C-341/05, *Laval un Partneri Ltd v Svenska Byggnadsarbetareförbundet* ECR 2007, I-11767, para. 103 and C-438/05, *International Transport Workers' Federation v Viking Line ABP*, ECR 2007, I-10779, para. 77. See Barnard 2008.

33 Even in a relatively small enlarged Europe, including Spain and Portugal, which *Rush Portuguesa* referred to, and *a fortiori* today in the European Union of 27 member states.

34 See Orlandini 2008. See also the classic analysis by Davies 1997.

35 Directive 96/71/EC of the European Parliament and of the Council of 16 December 1996 concerning the posting of workers in the framework of the provision of services, OJ L 18, 21.1.1997, 1–6.

workforce.[36] The many disputes originating within Directive 96/71/EC show how the interests of service providers – and their employees who may seek to exploit the competitive advantage arising from the lower cost of labour in the countries of origin, in order to find temporary employment opportunities in the country of provision of the service – often stand in contrast with the workforce of host member states.

It is no wonder, then, that the rules concerning posting of workers in the intra-Community provision of services has become the testing ground, both in symbolic and practical terms, for the sealing capability of the labour law systems of member states against the pervasive and deregulatory ban on non-discriminatory obstacles to cross-border service provision. This is a new, decisive testing ground for the possibility of rebalancing the asymmetrical relationship between EC economic freedoms and national constitutional social rights stemming from their 'decoupled' origins.

The Paradigmatic Case of Posting of Workers in the Framework of Transnational Provision of Services

Given its roots in compromise and its consequent limited scope, Directive 96/71/EC does not contain even partially harmonizing rules on the labour laws of the member states; it does not dictate standards of substantive protection in favour of employees involved in the three types of posting that the Directive itself defines as its material scope. This is limited to coordinating the systems of labour law of the member states, determining to what extent legislation (or collective bargaining[37]) of the host member state shall[38] or may[39] be applied. In this sense Directive 96/71/EC is a special instrument of private international law as it helps to provide a solution to the problem of determining which legislation is applicable in cases of posting, because it integrates the provisions of the Rome Convention on the law applicable to contractual obligations.[40]

Article 3(1) of Directive 96/71/EC establishes the minimum level of protection that the host member state must ensure to workers temporarily posted in its territory, regardless of which law applies to the employment relationship. The list of terms and conditions of employment that form this minimum level of mandatory protection includes the rules laid down by laws, regulations, administrative provisions, or collective agreements declared universally applicable and

36 See Reich 2008, 139.

37 See Art. 3(8) of Directive 96/71/EC.

38 See Art. 3(1) of Directive 96/71/EC.

39 See Art. 3(10) of Directive 96/71/EC.

40 See also Regulation No. 593/2008 of the European Parliament and of the Council, of 17 June 2008, on the law applicable to contractual obligations (Rome I), OJ L 177, 4.7.2008, 6–16.

concerning: maximum work periods and minimum rest periods, minimal duration of paid annual holidays, minimum rates of pay (including overtime), conditions of hiring out workers (particularly supply of workers by temp. agencies), health and safety, protective measures for pregnant women, children and young people, equality of treatment between men and women, and other provisions relating to the prohibition of discrimination.

A much more ambiguous provision, however, reflects all the ambivalence, if not contradiction, of Directive 96/71/EC, which oscillates between promotion of freedom to provide services in the common market (although in a context of fair competition) and protection of national systems of labour law. Article 3(10) allows member states, in compliance with the Treaty and on the basis of equality of treatment, to impose on undertakings the observance of terms and conditions of employment on matters other than those contemplated in the first paragraph of the same Article, 'in the case of public policy provisions', and terms and conditions of employment laid down in collective agreements or in arbitration awards concerning activities other than those relating to the building sector covered in the Annex to Directive 96/71/EC. This is one of the most problematic and elusive provisions of the Directive[41] and it is no coincidence that the many interpretative disputes in which the Court of Justice was and is involved relate to the demarcation of its limits. The case law on the matter clearly indicates the orientation of the Court. Among the various options for interpretation enabled by the Directive's open and deliberately ambiguous wording, the Court has definitely chosen the most liberal ones, or rather those most likely to use Community legislation as a powerful vehicle for liberalizing service provisions in the internal market, beyond what direct interpretation of Article 49 EC (now 56 TFEU) would, in all probability, have enabled.[42]

Particularly with its latest ruling,[43] the Court has adopted a 'minimalist' interpretation of Directive 96/71/EC, considering it an instrument almost exclusively devoted to promoting negative integration in the services market in the absence of adequate countermeasures to prevent wage-dumping.[44] The focal point of this restrictive interpretation can be found in the combined provisions of paragraphs 1, 7 and 10 of Article 3 of Directive 96/71/EC, in reference to which the core of *minimum protection* defined by the employment regulations of the host state ends up setting the *maximum standard* of protection legitimately applicable to posted workers during transnational provision of services.[45] These standards

41 See Syrpis and Novitz 2008.

42 As pointed out by Carabelli 2007.

43 In addition to the famous and already mentioned *Viking* and *Laval* cases, see the recent decisions in Case C-346/06, *Dirk Rüffert v Land Niedersachsen*, ECR 2008, I-1989 and C-319/06, *Commission v Luxembourg*, ECR 2008, I-4323.

44 See also Deakin 2008; Veneziani 2008.

45 In this sense, Malmberg and Sigeman (2008, 1140) state that 'the Directive does not only provide *a floor* of protection that the host States must extend to posted workers.

must, therefore, be identified in minimum levels of protection defined by host state legislation in the matters listed in Article 3(1) and in any subsequent provision of public policy identified by the state according to Article 3(10). On the back of this liberalizing approach, Directive 96/71/EC was, in essence, 'transformed from a model based on minimum protection for cross-border posting of employees towards a model based on maximum protection'.[46]

This 'liberal reading'[47] of its core provisions clashes with the original intent of the Community legislature and is far from being automatically imposed by the wording of Article 3 of Directive 96/71/EC. A proper systematic reading of the relevant provisions, coherent with the *ratio* of the Directive, had been persuasively proposed in Advocate General Bot's Opinion presented in *Rüffert*, according to which it was made clear that all member states in which the service is carried out, in accordance with Article 3(7), are allowed 'to improve, for the matters referred to in Article 3(1) of the Directive, the level of social protection which [they] wish to guarantee to workers employed in [their] territory and which [they] can therefore apply to workers posted there'.[48] Such a provision can therefore be read in the sense of allowing the host member state to apply reinforced, enhanced national protection to the extent permitted by Article 49 EC (now 56 TFEU).

No less questionable is the reading that the Court accepts of Article 3(10) of Directive 96/71/EC. Even after the broadest glimpses offered by *Commission v Luxembourg*, the minimal and very restricted role that the Court assigns to collective bargaining in determining the contents of minimum standards of protection is controversial. In the legalistic reading of the Court, the Directive ends up becoming a formidable vehicle for deregulatory competition in central areas of national systems of labour law. The wage-setting function of the collective agreement, constitutionally protected in Germany as the core expression of *Tarifautonomie*, is to a large extent being questioned. The judges in Luxembourg adopt an interpretation that dramatically reduces the role played by collective autonomy, almost annulling it at localized and decentralized levels.

In the *Rüffert* judgment the unfavourable attitude towards mechanisms of supporting the collective agreement, other than those strictly provided for by Directive 96/71/EC, is brought to bear on forms of protection that fully belong to the classic instruments of labour law and that are closely related to its founding mission as an essential barrier against the commoditization of human labour.[49] The Court peremptorily ruled in *Rüffert* that Directive 96/71/EC, interpreted in the light of Article 49 EC (now 56 TFEU), precludes adoption by a member state (in this

---

It also establishes *a ceiling* of employment conditions that the host States are allowed to extend to posted workers'.

46 Van Den Eeckhout 2008, 115.

47 Reich 2008, 156.

48 See the opinion of AG Bot in Case C-346/06, *Dirk Rüffert v Land Niedersachsen*, ECR 2008, I-1989, para. 83.

49 Case C-346/06, *Dirk Rüffert v Land Niedersachsen*, ECR 2008, I-1989.

case, Germany) of a legislative measure that requires the contracting authorities to designate as contractors for public works only those undertakings whose tenders included an agreement to pay their employees at least the minimum remuneration prescribed by collective agreements in force at the place where those services are performed. National legislators are therefore warned: rules such as that of Land Niedersachsen, or the not dissimilar rule set out in Article 36 of the Italian *Statuto dei lavoratori*, risk being deemed incompatible with the requirements of regulatory restraint imposed by the new interpretative approach to free movement of services.

No less problematic is the weak relevance accorded by the Court in *Viking* and *Laval* to rights to industrial action that impact on the exercise of fundamental economic freedoms guaranteed by Articles 43 and 49 EC (now 49 and 56 TFEU). It has been rightly said that, in *Viking* and *Laval*, 'the right of collective action is largely anaesthetized'[50] in confrontation with EC fundamental market freedoms. *Viking* and *Laval* assert a set of inherent preferences that clash not only with the new set of values recognized in the Lisbon Treaty and in the annexed Charter of Fundamental Rights of the European Union, but also with the Court's own inspiring commitment to the centrality of social and solidarity values in the context of Union citizenship.

Social Rights and Market Freedom in the Enlarged European Union: Searching for a New Balance

Several commentators have suggested[51] that such a vigorous erosion via negative integration of the sphere of autonomy and contractual freedom of social partners, which is the very collective foundation of national labour laws, is likely to exacerbate the European social and democratic deficit. This corrodes the already scarce resources of input-oriented legitimacy of EC institutions without giving effective answers in terms of political output and output-oriented legitimacy.[52] This surge towards an absolute and unrestrained assertion of supranational market freedoms also appears to contrast with the expansion of social goals and with the same social vision of the Union that has been emerging since the European constitutional Treaty and that has been to some extent strengthened by the Lisbon reform.[53] It also contrasts with the Court's gradual case law development of a concept of European cross-border social solidarity upon the cornerstone of Union citizenship and the principle of equal treatment undertaken among member state

50 Corti 2008, 250.
51 See Supiot 2008 and Joerges 2007.
52 See Scharpf 1999.
53 See Bronzini 2008.

nationals.[54] This notion outlines a common European *status civitatis*, an inclusive concept of substantive equality and of transnational social citizenship which overcomes the functional logic of the market. Despite all concerns about this judicial superimposition of a 'sentiment of solidarity on an unsuspecting population',[55] the importance of this case law is undeniable. A new idea of transnational social solidarity is emerging, which is reflexive, bound not to the productive process nor to the labour market, but to the elective place of residence in the EU and societal integration within the host member state.

Undeniably, some contradictory trends are taking place, even inside the wider body of the case law of the Court of Justice. For example in recent years, though not without fluctuations, the Court has proved very sensitive to affirmation of certain fundamental work-based guarantees in favour of workers employed in non-standard (especially fixed-term) employment contracts and rigorous application of the principle of non-discrimination and equal treatment in the context of worker protection. Even the case law on the principles of the economic constitution is not reducible to a strictly market-oriented logic.

It is the fluidity, and in some ways also the essential ambiguity of ongoing processes at European and national level, that suggests that the just criticism of Court of Justice case law on freedom to provide services should not lead to reactions invoking forms of unduly national closure aimed at erecting protective barriers to preserve total 'immunity' of national social models from the European market integration process. Critical reactions[56] which deny *tout court* that the Court of Justice has the legitimacy to mediate between national social constitutional traditions and EC constitutional principles are not convincing. Similarly unconvincing are proposals for total legislative immunization of national systems of industrial relations from processes of supranational economic integration. It is well known that among the various initiatives undertaken by the European trade union movement to respond to the *Viking* and *Laval* rulings features a proposal for treaty reform introducing a special clause for immunity or exemption of collective rights from the scope of EC economic freedoms.[57] But the proposition of complete 'immunization' is a view which, regardless of any sceptical evaluation about its political or institutional feasibility, is not obviously desirable. It seems to depend on an attempt to restore the separation of functions between economic and social spheres reminiscent of the same ordo-liberal conception, albeit from a reversed point of view.

However, the history of construction of the integrated market demonstrates that this separation no longer holds, or at least, is no longer appropriate given the depth reached today by the European integration process. A well-governed

54 See Case C-184/99, *Rudy Grzelczyk v Centre Public d'aide sociale d'Ottignies-Louvain-la-Neuve*, ECR 2001, I-6193, and Giubboni 2008.

55 Barnard 2007, 129.

56 See Ballestrero 2008.

57 See Gottardi 2008, 576.

confrontation with the rules of the market, a certain degree of controlled openness to competition, has been shown to benefit reform of national social protection systems. Social partners, in the guise of 'private governance', also form part of these processes, so one must agree with Silvana Sciarra that this vital sphere of social autonomy 'does not protect itself through a system of immunization from market rules; it is strengthened in the assiduous interaction with such rules and it can also emerge from these contexts with new and more extensive tasks'.[58] The different traditions of national social models are therefore not defended by erecting barriers to and immunity from EC market freedoms, rather by building a more balanced system of interdependence between social values and economic integration.

However, effective answers, adequate to meet the new challenges, need to be elaborated. The post-regulatory techniques of the open method of coordination (OMC), which firmly occupy the centre of the European social agenda since the Lisbon summit of 2000,[59] seem clearly inadequate. If the main problem after enlargement is that of governing increased socio-economic differences to avoid the dangers of deregulatory regime competition and wage-dumping, then OMC cannot provide the solution. The goal of setting minimum standards of employment protection as a sound and effective antidote against social-levelling-down spirals lies well beyond the reach of this soft law technique. Rather, different hard law coordination mechanisms should be reinforced in an attempt to strengthen the minimum mandatory protection of workers engaged in transnational provision of services. In this context, and from a constitutional point of view, it is essential that one goes back to rethinking the matter in terms of a true balance between fundamental social rights and values and economic freedoms.

Concluding Remarks

(a) If the EC economic constitution of the new millennium is not to be based on the legitimization of social dumping, the area in which coordination must be strengthened is that offered by Directive 96/71/EC on the posting of workers. In fact, the Directive – as it stands – could provide more appropriate responses if a departure was made from the strongly liberal but weakly founded interpretation used by the Court of Justice in *Viking*, *Laval*, *Rüffert* and *Commission v Luxembourg*. If the more nuanced and articulate solutions argued by the Advocates General in the *Viking*, *Laval* and *Rüffert* cases had been accepted by the Court, they would have largely defused the acute problems the Directive now poses to national systems of labour law and industrial relations.

58 Sciarra 2008, 263.

59 For a recent summary, largely based on a (not entirely convincing) positive evaluation of this new form of Community governance, see Sabel and Zeitlin 2008.

But it may be that Directive 96/71/EC itself should be amended in key parts. It has been persuasively argued that the choice to permit extension of the nucleus of minimum mandatory protections listed in Article 3(1) only in the case of public policy provisions is not actually imposed by general principles of free movement of services, but represented a political option. This choice was initially conceived as capable of embracing the *magna pars* of domestic labour laws and eventually became, in Court of Justice case law, a vehicle to compress the regulatory autonomy of national legislators and trade unions in host countries. If this legislative limitation to public policy provisions were dispensed with, member states could benefit from the more extensive and flexible principles developed by the Court of Justice regarding the objective justification of non-discriminatory obstacles to provision of services under Article 49 EC (now 56 TFEU), according to the general proportionality assessment. Such principles could thus prevent the disproportionate protectionist application of national labour standards and could offer resistance to the temptation to bring temporarily posted workers under the principle of full equality of treatment with national workers. Flexible modulation of the proportionality test would, however, allow application of minimum standards of protection higher than those currently allowed by the Court of Justice on the basis of Article 3(10) of Directive 96/71/EC, and so more effectively prevent social dumping.

On a theoretical level, a suitable ground for justifying such pragmatic suggestions may be found in Joerges' reconceptualization of Community law, such as in 'First Order Conflict of Laws'.[60] The basic idea that supports the proposal was effectively summed up by its author: the constitutional function of European law 'is to give voice to "foreign" concerns', meaning, 'first of all, that Member States mutually "recognise" their laws (that they are prepared to "apply" foreign law), that they tolerate legal differences and refrain from insisting on their *lex fori* and domestic interests'. At the same time, the 'discipline imposed on a Member State's political autonomy must be limited. The principle and its limitations can be discovered and best studied in the jurisprudence of the ECJ pertaining to Article 28 [ex 30]'. As Joerges further notes, 'This jurisprudence has repeatedly documented how mediation between differences in regulatory policies and the diverse interests of the concerned jurisdictions can be accomplished', especially after the *Keck* reform.

(b) Clearly connected to the above proposal is the equally constitutionally relevant issue of an effective balance between fundamental social rights and economic freedoms. As mentioned, the panorama offered by the case law of the Court of Justice does not lend itself to linear and unambiguous reconstructions. However, it is indisputable that the Judges in Luxembourg have given gravely 'elusive'[61] answers, to put it mildly, on questions concerning the fault line producing the

60 Joerges 2007: 14–15.
61 Poiares Maduro 1999.

strongest asymmetry, while a proper constitutional balance demands more clarity. *Viking* and *Laval* have essentially rendered void of content the right to strike and industrial action recognized by the constitutions of Finland and Sweden. The only fundamental right to be recognized in the two judgments is, in fact, economic freedom, respectively of establishment and provision of services. Collective action with cross-border effects is reduced to a strictly limited exception to transnational market freedoms. The direct horizontal effect of the two economic freedoms – an objectively strong innovation of the two judgments – gives European undertakings a potentially formidable weapon of 'containment' of the effects (and the 'viability') of collective action and industrial conflict at the Community level. This further unbalances the equilibrium of power between the social actors, which is already unfavourable for trade unions.

The debate on the relationship between economic freedoms and fundamental rights truly deserves to be rethought *funditus* in view of the Treaty of Lisbon's formal assignment of the same legal force of the treaties to the European Union Charter of Fundamental Rights. In a sharp deconstructive criticism of the discourse of the Court of Justice, Eleanor Spaventa has rightly drawn attention to the necessity of challenging the very conceptual premises which guide the judges in Luxembourg. The use of the same terminology for, and the presumed conceptual equivalence between, economic freedoms and fundamental rights must be discussed again *in limine*. 'The use of the same terminology, that of fundamental rights, to identify two radically different types of rights is ... debatable; it suggests a homogeneity which is not conceptually sound'.[62] It is indeed based on this 'fallacious premise' that, with a clear conceptual inversion, in *Viking* and *Laval* the Court converted the fundamental social rights at issue 'from individual rights to a "legitimate interest", to public policy reasons'.[63] This transformed the treaty rights into

> a vehicle to impose upon member states a restrictive approach to fundamental rights, so that the margin of appreciation is transformed into an instrument, however debatable, which acknowledges some pluralism in our understanding of the precise content of fundamental rights; into a useful tool to enforce the primacy of treaty rights.[64]

The order of the Court of Justice's discourse should simply be reversed: thus the Court in *Viking* and *Laval* should have asked itself *not* whether the collective rights in question would have been able to justify a restriction in freedom of movement, but rather whether freedom of movement could be interpreted in terms able to ensure respect for fundamental (social) rights.[65] Perhaps a rereading of horizontal clauses of the EU Charter of Fundamental Rights, as suggested by Spaventa within

62 Spaventa 2009, 355.
63 Spaventa 2009, 357.
64 Spaventa 2009, 357.
65 See Bercusson 2007, 303.

this different perspective, could further positively support the coherence of this deconstructive and reconstructive proposal.

(c) The fundamental (social) rights discourse, though necessary, is, however, insufficient to correct and rebalance the asymmetry that has arisen. Coherent social policies are needed. This is probably the most difficult part of the proposal that is being argued. And yet, neither is it possible to contemplate only the open method of coordination, nor is it realistic to think of large-scale revitalization of the hard law classic Community method centred on directives providing for social harmonization, albeit minimal and gradual. Space here is lacking to argue thoroughly that the first soft law instrument is insufficient and the second is, in fact, at best, unlikely.[66] Instead new forms of political or collective intervention must be addressed which are not confined to the essentially procedural dimension of the open method of coordination but are directed towards establishing, albeit in a flexible and appropriately differentiated way, the minimum substantive social standards necessary to manage the growing socio-economic differences within the EU while avoiding social dumping. In the repertoire of theoretical proposals to this end made in recent years, two seem worthy of summary at the conclusion of this chapter.

The aim of the first proposal – owed to Fritz Scharpf[67] – is to combine the experimental governance of OMC with the use of special framework directives. These should be designed to establish minimum standards with due regard to the different degrees of development of different welfare state regimes and different, embedded traditions of social solidarity throughout Europe. The proposal has the merit of determining, by way of hard law, the acceptable rate of differentiation on the basis of effective standards of protection which may not, however, be uniformly imposed on the 27 different member states.

The second proposal – made to the European Commission by a prestigious group of experts coordinated by Edoardo Ales[68] – aims to introduce a sound EC legal framework promoting and supporting a transnational process of collective bargaining. The aim is to promote cross-border collective standardization of minimum terms and conditions of employment. To this end, the most appropriate instrument suggested would be a Directive establishing an optional legal framework for the European transnational collective bargaining process based on Article 94 EC (now 115 TFEU), within which such agreements can be concluded. Referring to the example of paradigmatic asymmetry taken into consideration above, it has been rightly suggested that one of the first targets of transnational collective bargaining should be to set minimum wage levels to be observed by

66 See Giubboni 2006b.

67 Scharpf 2002.

68 See Ales et al. 2006.

cross-border companies, thus integrating the provisions of Directive 96/71/EC with the necessary material standards of social protection for posted workers.[69]

After the 2004 enlargement, rebalancing the economic and social objectives of the European Union has become an increasingly delicate and complex exercise of essential strategic relevance for the very legitimacy of the whole European project. Rebalancing must be carefully pursued with an appropriate mix of judicial and political approaches and responses.[70] While the Court of Justice is asked to develop a true human rights discourse, respecting the constitutional balance of interests and overcoming the fallacies of a strict pro-market-integration approach,[71] the European legislature and the member states cannot avoid taking the necessary *political* steps. *Viking* and *Laval* have marked, even symbolically, a turning point in this respect: new answers are needed to rebalance the social and the economic at the EU level, and all the (social, political and institutional) actors involved collectively bear this crucial responsibility.

References

Ales, E., Engblom, S., Jaspers, T., Laulom, S., Sciarra, S., Sobczak, A. and Valdés Dal-Ré, F. 2006. *Transnational Collective Bargaining: Past, Present and Future (Final report)*. Brussels: European Commission.

Azoulai, L. 2008. The Court of Justice and the social market economy: The emergence of an ideal and the conditions for its realization. *Common Market Law Review*, 45:5, 1335–55.

Ballestrero, M.V. 2008. Le sentenze Viking e Laval: la Corte di giustizia 'bilancia' il diritto di sciopero. *Lavoro e Diritto*, 371–92.

Barnard, C. 2007. Social policy revisited in the light of the constitutional debate, in *The Fundamentals of EU Law Revisited. Assessing the Impact of the Constitutional Debate*, edited by C. Barnard. Oxford: Oxford University Press, 109–51.

Barnard, C. 2008. *Viking* and *Laval*: An introduction. *Cambridge Yearbook of European Legal Studies*, 10, 463–92.

Bercusson, B. 2007. The trade union movement and the European Union: The judgment day. *European Law Journal*, 13:3, 279–308.

Bronzini, G. 2008. Il modello sociale europeo, in *Le nuove istituzioni europee: Commento al Trattato di Lisbona*, edited by F. Bassanini and G. Tiberi. Bologna: Il Mulino, 109–24.

Carabelli, U. 2007. Una sfida determinante per il futuro dei diritti sociali in Europa: la tutela dei lavoratori di fronte alla libertà di prestazione di servizi nella CE. *Rivista giuridica del lavoro e della previdenza sociale*, 58:1:1, 33–134.

69 See Lo Faro 2008b.

70 See Syrpis and Novitz 2008.

71 See Azoulai 2008.

Corti, M. 2008. Le decisioni ITF e Laval della Corte di giustizia: un passo avanti e due indietro nell'Europa sociale. *Rivista Italiana di Diritto del Lavoro*, 249–300.

D'Antona, M. 1996. Sistema giuridico comunitario, in *Dizionario di diritto del lavoro comunitario*, edited by A. Baylos Grau, B. Caruso, M. D'Antona and S. Sciarra. Bologna: Monduzzi Editore.

D'Antona, M. 2000. Armonizzazione del diritto del lavoro e federalismo nell'Unione europea, in *Opere: Scritti sul metodo e sulla evoluzione del diritto del lavoro – Scritti sul diritto del lavoro comparato e comunitario, vol. I*, edited by B. Caruso and S. Sciarra. Milan: Giuffrè, 325–50.

Davies, P. 1992. The emergence of European labour law, in *Legal Intervention in Industrial Relations: Gains and Losses*, edited by W. McCarthy. Oxford: Blackwell, 313*ff* (Ch. 10).

Davies, P. 1995. Market integration and social policy in the Court of Justice. *Industrial Law Journal*, 49–77.

Davies, P. 1997. Posted Workers Directive: Single market or protection of national labour law systems? *Common Market Law Review*, 571–602.

Deakin, S. 2008. Regulatory competition after *Laval*. *Cambridge Yearbook of European Legal Studies*, 10, 2007–2008, 581–610.

Esping-Andersen, G. 1990. *The Three Worlds of Welfare Capitalism*. Cambridge: Polity Press.

Ferrera, M. 2005a. *The Boundaries of Welfare. European Integration and the New Spatial Politics of Social Protection*. Oxford: Oxford University Press.

Ferrera, M. 2005b. The European Union and National Welfare States. Friends, not Foes: But What Kind of Friendship? URGE Working Paper 4/2005. Available at: <www.urge.it>.

Gerber, D. J. 1994. Constitutionalizing the economy: German neo-liberalism, competition law and the 'new' Europe. *American Journal of Comparative Law*, 42, 25–84.

Giubboni, S. 2006a. *Social Rights and Market Freedom in the European Constitution. A Labour Law Perspective*. Cambridge: Cambridge University Press.

Giubboni, S. 2006b. La costituzionalizzazione 'asimmetrica' dell'Europa sociale, in *Nuove forme di regolazione: il metodo aperto di coordinamento delle politiche sociali*, edited by M. Barbera. Milan: Giuffrè, 367–75.

Giubboni, S. 2008. A Certain Degree of Solidarity. Free Movement of Persons and Access to Social Protection in the Case-Law of the European Court of Justice, URGE Working Paper 3/2008. Available at: <www.urge.it>.

Gottardi, D. 2008. Diritti sindacali e libertà economiche al Parlamento europeo. I nodi del coordinamento sistematico. *Lavoro e Diritto*, 555–78.

Joerges, J. 2004. What is left of the European economic constitution? A melancholic eulogy. *European Law Review*, 30, 461–89.

Joerges, C. 2007. Democracy and European Integration: A Legacy of Tensions, Re-conceptualisation and Recent True Conflicts, EUI Working Papers Law

2007/25. Available at: <http://cadmus.eui.eu/dspace/bitstream/1814/7081/1/LAW-2007-25.pdf>.

Lo Faro, A. 2008a. Diritti sociali e libertà economiche del mercato interno: considerazioni minime in margine ai casi Laval e Viking. *Lavoro e Diritto*, 63–96.

Lo Faro, A. 2008b. Is a Decent Wage Part of a Decent Job? Answers from an Enlarged Europe, WP C.S.D.L.E. 'Massimo D'Antona', Int-64/2008. Available at: <http://www.lex.unict.it/eurolabor/default.htm>.

Lyon-Caen, G. 1992. L'infiltration du Droit du travail par le Droit de la concurrence. *Droit Ouvrier*, 313*ff.*

Malmberg, J. and Sigeman, T. 2008. Industrial actions and the EU economic freedom: The autonomous collective bargaining model curtailed by the European Court of Justice. *Common Market Law Review*, 45, 1115–46.

Mechi, L. 2003. La costruzione dei diritti sociali nell'Europa a sei (1950–1972). *Memoria e Ricerca*, 69–81.

Monnet, J. 1976. *Mémoires*. Paris: Fayard.

Orlandini, G. 2008. Trade union rights and market freedoms: The European Court of Justice sets out the rules. *Comparative Labor Law & Policy Journal*, 29:4, 573–603.

Poiares Maduro, M. 1999. Striking the elusive balance between economic freedom and social rights in the EU, in *The EU and Human Rights*, edited by P. Alston. Oxford: Oxford University Press, 449–72.

Poiares Maduro, M. 2001. Never on Sunday – What has (EU) law got to do with it? in *Labour Law in the Courts. National Judges and the European Court of Justice*, edited by S. Sciarra. Oxford: Hart Publishing, 273–90.

Reich, N. 2008. Free movement vs. social rights in an enlarged Union – the *Laval* and *Viking* cases before the ECJ. *German Law Journal*, 9:2, 125–61.

Sabel, C.F. and Zeitlin, J. 2008. Learning from difference: The new architecture of experimentalist governance in the EU. *European Law Journal*, 14:3, 271–327.

Scharpf, F.W. 1999. *Governing in Europe: Effective and Democratic?* Oxford: Oxford University Press.

Scharpf, F.W. 2002. The European social model: Coping with the challenges of diversity. *Journal of Common Market Studies*, 40, 645–70.

Sciarra, S. 2008. Viking e Laval: diritti collettivi e mercato nel recente dibattito europeo. *Lavoro e Diritto*, 245–72.

Sciarra, S. 2009. Diritto del lavoro e diritto sociale europeo. Un'analisi delle fonti, in *Il lavoro subordinato, vol. V*, edited by S. Sciarra and B. Caruso, in *Trattato di diritto privato dell'Unione europea*. Turin: Giappichelli, 1–34.

Simitis, S. and Lyon-Caen, A. 1996. Community labour law: A critical introduction to its history, in *European Labour Law. Principles and Perspectives. Liber Amicorum Lord Wedderburn*, edited by P. Davies, A. Lyon-Caen, S. Sciarra and S. Simitis. Oxford: Clarendon Press, 1–22.

Spaventa, E. 2009. Federalisation versus centralisation: Tensions in fundamental rights discourse in the EU, in *50 Years of the European Treaties*, edited by M. Dougan and S. Currie. Oxford: Hart Publishing, 343–64.

Streit, E. and Mussler, W. 1995. The economic constitution of the European Community: From Rome to Maastricht. *European Law Journal*, 1:1, 5–30.

Supiot, A. 2008. L'Europe gagnée par l'économie communiste du marché. *Le Monde*, 24 January.

Syrpis, P. and Novitz, T. 2008. Economic and social rights in conflict: Political and judicial approaches to their reconciliation. *European Law Review*, 33:3, 411–26.

Szyszczak, E. 2001. The new paradigm for social policy: A virtuous circle? *Common Market Law Review*, 38:5, 1125–70.

Torchia, L. 2006. *Il governo delle differenze. Il principio di equivalenza nell'ordinamento europeo*. Bologna: Il Mulino.

Treu, T. 2004. Le regole sociali europee: quali innovazioni? *Europa e Diritto Privato*, 33–52.

Van Den Eeckhout, V. 2008. Promoting human rights within the Union: The role of European private international law. *European Law Journal*, 14:1, 105–27.

Veneziani, B. 2008. La Corte di giustizia e il trauma del cavallo di Troia, in *Scritti in onore di Edoardo Ghera, vol. II*. Bari: Cacucci, 1281–94.

Verschueren, H. 2008. Cross-border workers in the European internal market: Trojan horses for member states' labour and social security law? *International Journal of Comparative Labour Law and Industrial Relations*, 24:2, 167–99.

Wedderburn of Charlton, Lord. 2007. Labour law 2008: 40 years on. *Industrial Law Journal*, 36, 397–424.

Chapter 12
Constitutional Issues in European Health Policy and Practice

Meri Koivusalo

Introduction

Health policies within Europe are not at the core of Treaty of Lisbon, nor has health been prominent in previous European treaties. However, in spite of this and as a result of a lack of clear boundaries, governance on health policies has increasingly become part of an evolving process within the European Union. In this process, competence allocation between the EU and the member states with respect to health policies and organization of health systems has become a particular area of contestation, frequently raising constitutional aspects of policy-making and practice. In practice, a large share of issues pertains to the politics of market-making, market-limiting, regulation, and standard-setting, where member states and the Commission are at odds. In some other areas, policy differences tend to reflect more particular national or industry interests or vulnerability in relation to organizing and financing national health systems.

While health policy issues, such as member state cooperation with respect to social security and occupational health and safety, have been part of Community considerations and treaty provisions since the Treaty of Rome,[1] the definition of health policies and organization and financing of health systems have remained tasks for member states. Although member state obligations with respect to health systems remain recognized, the real issues apply to regulation and powers, namely competence to regulate and govern overall policy choices in the area. The issues of crucial importance are thus competence basis and the right to regulate.

If one traces the European debates and focuses more on the context of regulatory powers and decision-making – of how and on what basis health system governance is undertaken – a more consistent policy process within the EU can be discerned.

1 Art. 118 EEC from 1957 states: 'Without prejudice to the other provisions of this Treaty and in conformity with its general objectives, it shall be the aim of the Commission to promote close collaboration between Member States in the social field, particularly in matters relating to employment, labour legislation and working conditions, occupational and continuation training, social security, protection against occupational accidents and diseases, industrial hygiene, the law as to trade unions, and collective bargaining between employers and workers.'

While constitutional issues play a role in this development, the politics of different actors influence the extent and the ways in which it has taken place. Negotiation, interpretation and use of treaties, as well as use of Court of Justice decisions thus form part of a broader political space, ways and means of the European integration process that not only guide it, but are influenced and shaped by the politics of this process as well. This chapter first traces the background and context of the current situation in health. Then the focus shifts to some key areas of concern: constitutional policy-making and policy content issues that have become more evident as European policies on health have been unfolding, including the basis and context of governance of national health systems.

Health and European Union Policies

The relationship between health and European policies long remained nominal. Clearly, it can be assumed that the founding fathers in Rome or later in Maastricht would not have assumed that health services would become part of the broader agenda, although reference to occupational health was made in Rome, and to a high level of health protection in the Maastricht Treaty. In the broader context of public services, reference to services of general economic interest was made in 1957. However, the role and relevance of health services as part of services of general interest became an issue only later, as a result of Commission focus on the matter in the late 1990s and early 2000s.

Health policies and social security systems are also affected by broader EU priorities and policy emphases. In many ways, emphasis on market freedoms by the Court of Justice also complements overall focus on budgetary limits, services trade, innovation policies, and emphasis on competitiveness, articulated within more formal European policies in the Lisbon strategy context. As part of this broader process, health and social security systems have increasingly been considered in the context of the need for modernization and reform. Thus health policies are and remain affected by policies implemented and prioritized as part of broader EU policies and policy priorities.

Incremental changes and decisions on the health policy front as well as the creeping nature of European involvement have implied that it has been possible to tolerate and accommodate further integration, even in spite of negative implications for health systems, alongside redefinition of European influence. In part, this has been enabled by delays in understanding the scope of implications within national health ministries, focusing on strictly legal aspects in comparison to the consequences of these changes on policies and available regulatory policy space at national level, the tendency to use positive language with emphasis on 'patients' rights', modernization, and focus on overall benefits from cross-border arrangements. For example, as political decision-makers willingly engage in assessing the limited consequences of expected actual cross-border movement of European citizens, the broader framework, legitimacy, and longer-term consequences of actions concerning shifts in competence and governance tend to receive less focus and attention amongst policy-makers.

While health services can be defined as an area where European influence is expanding, Commission engagement in health has not always been swift or easy. In the 1990s, member states and public health activists sought to engage with the Commission on matters concerning public health and health promotion. However, Commission interest remained low – as shown by experiences from early years and lengthy negotiation with respect to tobacco control measures.

Early Years: Strengthening Public Health Considerations and Action on Tobacco

European focus, and in particular action on tobacco, was part of the early emphasis on public health policies even before explicit competence on public health at European level. Boessen and Maarse have noted that it took over 10 years of negotiating before the EU adopted policy measures that could address the issue, which is important to note in comparison to the swift Commission action on health services later on.[2] Even though the aim of Directive 98/43[3] was to ban tobacco advertising, it was based on what is currently known as Article 114(1) TFEU,[4] the principal object of which is to ensure the establishment and functioning of the internal market. The contested choice of legal basis was partly due to the fact that it took until 1993 before the Community was given legal competence in the field of public health, although this had already been sought in 1989.[5] This was also the first time in the history of the EU that a European legislative Act was struck down by the Court of Justice on the ground that the EU was acting outside its jurisdictional boundaries.[6]

Strengthening of the public health voice in the EU was on the agenda in the 1990s by default and as result of public health-related problems leading to a need to focus on how to ensure high levels of health protection in all policies. This led to the strengthening of public health provisions as part of negotiations on the Amsterdam Treaty. However, in terms of health systems and health governance, Article 152 EC excluded health services and their financing, reserving this as an

2 See Boessen and Maarse 2008.

3 Directive 98/43/EC of the European Parliament and of the Council of 6 July 1998 on the approximation of the laws, regulations and administrative provisions of the Member States relating to the advertising and sponsorship of tobacco products, OJ L 213, 30 July 1998: 9–12.

4 Before the Lisbon Treaty known as Article 95 EC, and at the time of bringing the action 100a(1) EC.

5 See Boessen and Maarse 2008.

6 See Kumm 2006, referring to the so called 'Tobacco Advertising' case, i.e., Case C-376/98, *Federal Republic of Germany v European Parliament and Council of the European Union*, ECR 2000, I-8419.

area within member state competence.[7] While the EU was given the green light on taking care of public health concerns, the case was effectively closed with respect to health services. The willingness of member states to allow expansion of EU work on public health can be seen in part as the result of policies 'by default', as public health-related crises and lack of focus on health protection had also become a problem for free movement of goods within Europe. Council conclusions on health also actively sought that the Commission would initiate work on health in other policies, including health impact assessment.[8] However, in spite of these efforts, only limited action took place in practice. The constitutional obligations of focusing on health implications of activities in other policies or ensuring a high level of health protection has gained relatively little enthusiasm within the Commission and its work, although it was raised to the political agenda again in the 2000s in the context of health in all policy approaches.[9]

Court of Justice Decisions on Health: From Rights to Access to Compliance by All

The focus of EU policies remained rather solidly on public health until two landmark decisions by the Court of Justice in the late 1990s – *Kohll* and *Decker*[10] – opened scope for further engagement with health systems within Europe. However, it seems that in practice initial standards were raised in the 1980s[11] and in an early 1990s case concerning access to medical termination of pregnancy

7 Art. 152(5) EC stated that: 'Community action in the field of public health shall fully respect the responsibilities of the Member States for the organisation and delivery of health services and medical care. In particular, measures referred to in paragraph 4(a) shall not affect national provisions on the donation or medical use of organs and blood.' In practice this has traditionally been interpreted as limiting Commission competence in the area to public health and not including health services.

8 Council Conclusions on Health in All Policies (HiAP), Brussels 30 November–1 December 2006, documents several previous Council resolutions on the matter dating back to the early 1990s as well as referring to 'the long-dated commitment of the Council to intersectoral health policies expressed in several Council Resolutions and Conclusions'. Available at: <http://www.consilium.europa.eu/uedocs/cms_Data/docs/pressdata/en/lsa/91929.pdf>.

9 See Ståhl et al. 2006; and Council Conclusions on Health in All Policies (HiAP), Brussels 30 November–1 December 2006.

10 Since Cases C-158/96, *Kohll*, ECR 1998 I-1931 and C-120/95, *Decker*, ECR 1998, I-1831, the case law on health and health services has been developing with follow-up cases, including: C-368/98, *Vanbraekel*, ECR 2001, I-53631; C-385/99, *Müller-Fauré*, ECR 2003, I-4509; C-157/99, *Geraets-Smits v Peerbooms*, ECR 2001, I-5473; C-145/03, *Keller*, ECR 2005, I-2529; and C-372/04, *Watts*, ECR 2006, I-4325.

11 The earliest cases referred to are Joined Cases 286/82 and 26/83, *Luisi and Carbone*, ECR 1984, 377, which held that medical activities fall within the scope of Art. 60 EC.

in other member states, as well as the right to distribute information on these services.[12] The implications of *Kohll*[13] and *Decker*[14] were initially considered less extensive as well as more focused on social security systems operating on the basis of social and health insurance. However, subsequent Court of Justice decisions further confirmed its approach and, with the landmark case of *Watts*, made it clear that freedom to provide services also affected all health systems within Europe.[15]

Coordination of social security systems had traditionally been dealt with in the context of Regulation 1408/71, but Court of Justice decisions have in practice enabled further expansion of EU competence in health services. Notably, in many member states this is where the 'real health policy power and resources' reside. Thus the Commission expanded its influence to health services, where there are substantially more resources and power, rather than tinkering with public health and seeking to influence policies in other sectors. Public health policies have traditionally been managed with fewer resources and less prestige. Furthermore, engaging actively with policies in other sectors was likely to be more difficult with more prominent Directorates, and in policy areas where taking health considerations into account would have interfered with or been in conflict with policies and policy priorities that would otherwise have been adopted. While it can be asked why the Commission has been keen on moving further and more swiftly in respect of health services on the basis of Court of Justice decisions than in some other areas, it is also necessary to consider why the Court of Justice itself chose to emphasize individual rights over other necessities of governance within national health systems.

Newdick has brought up a number of difficulties with the Court of Justice approach to health care, pointing out firstly that the terminology used may have two consequences in terms of making national authorities less able to manage the consequences of financial constraint than seems to have been assumed by the Court and secondly, the likelihood of inconsistent results from national courts.[16] This is in line with how the Court of Justice has prioritized individual rights over governance of health systems and created a market in health care, as emphasized

12 Case C-159/90, *Grogan and others*, ECR 1991, I-4685, made it clear that medical termination of pregnancy constitutes a service within the meaning of Art. 60 EC.

13 Case C-158/96, *Kohll*, ECR 1998 I-1931.

14 Case C-120/95, *Decker*, ECR 1998, I-1831.

15 Case C-372/04, *Watts*, ECR 2006, I-4325. Kaczorowska (2006: 351) states in terms of the influence of Court of Justice decisions on the change in balance: 'The judgement in Kohll constitutes a very dramatic example of the long-term development of the jurisprudence of the European Community. When in 1971 the Member States agreed to adopt Regulation 1408 they did not foresee that by doing so they would eventually, depending upon the manner in which they organise their social security and healthcare funds, be forced to surrender dominion over their national health schemes. The above raises the issue whether or not it is acceptable for the Court of Justice to interpret secondary legislation in the light of EC law.'

16 See Newdick 2006.

by Hatzopoulos.[17] In light of an increasing number of new and very expensive treatments for cancer and rare disease groups, concerns over financial sustainability are not merely a theoretical matter for member states. Furthermore, political pressures towards individualization and portability of insurance are not separable from requirements to enable free movement within internal markets, yet these would have substantial implications as to how and on what basis national health systems are organised and financed as well as to what extent cross-subsidization takes place within these systems.

One of the potentially worrying recent cases in this area is that of *Stamatelaki*,[18] where the Court of Justice concluded that Article 49 EC (now 56 TFEU) precludes member state legislation from excluding all reimbursement by a national social security institution of costs occasioned by treatment of persons insured with it in private hospitals in another member state. This is also reflected in the Commission proposal for a Patients' Rights Directive,[19] which follows the Court of Justice decision to not distinguish between public and private hospital service providers. However, this has different implications for residence-based national health services than for other types of health service organization. Residence-based provision of care functions differently from care based on reimbursement of costs. In countries where care is residence-based, funds spent on reimbursement for care in other member states are implicitly additional to the costs of maintaining services for those who use them at home. Furthermore, if patients have the right to seek private care in another member state and be reimbursed from public funds of the home state, it is difficult to deny that this cannot be done within the home state. When a decision not to distinguish between public and private health care is accompanied by limited support for concerns over financial consequences, it may as well be considered a political statement in support of the market.

In legitimating creation of health care markets, the relevance of Court of Justice decisions emphasizing rights of individuals over national interests in health systems organization and financing needs to be recognized. Enabling patient choice and mobility at European level is likely to increase rather than decrease inequalities in access to health care. While the long-term effects of such prioritization on the sustainability of health care financing remain unknown, due grounds exist to expect that enhancing individual choice and health care markets is likely to increase overall costs of care as well as to increase inequities in access to care.

17 See Hatzopoulos 2002.

18 Case C-444/05, *Stamatelaki*, ECR 2007, I-3185.

19 Commission proposal for a directive of the European Parliament and of the Council on the application of patients' rights in cross-border healthcare (COM(2008) 414 final).

Constitution Negotiation and Constitutionalism as Part of Making and Limiting Markets

Key Court of Justice decisions[20] on health and health care have been swiftly followed by the Commission focusing on creating policy space for EU-level action and expanding its own role in the field. This has also been reflected in further Lisbon Treaty negotiations, where aspects of health services were brought in as part of health provisions. However, as part of treaty negotiations, some of the tension remained in spite of worries over cross-border care and expansion of EU competence. This was also the case in the field of external and trade policies as limits for EU competence in negotiation of agreements in health services were sought by member states both in the Nice and Lisbon treaties. On the other hand, focus on and a basis for legitimate action for health was sought as part of the Lisbon Treaty negotiations. The practice of the open method of coordination (OMC) in the field of health care was brought in as part of the Public Health Article.[21] While Article 168 TFEU is still entitled 'public health', it now has additions and omissions broadening the scope for health services, as will be discussed below. The shift from 'public health' to 'health' was also realized as part of active Commission policies, as emphasis on an EU 'public health' strategy was changed to focusing on 'health' strategy, initiated by a reflection process in 2004 and resulting in the White Paper 'Together for health' adopted in 2007.[22]

Services of general interest were part of the Lisbon Treaty negotiations and foreseen by some proponents as means of enhancing the EU social agenda and restricting the influence of internal market considerations. The first reference to services of general economic interest was made in the Treaty of Rome,[23] in the narrower context of undertakings, but the issue has also been tackled more recently at European level in a Commission Green Paper, a White Paper, and a communication on services of general interest.[24] The importance of defining services of general interest has gained focus and emphasis since then as, in particular, non-governmental organizations have sought exclusion from implementation of internal market regulations on the basis of claims of services of general interest. However, on the basis of the definition used, it is made clear that in practice internal market rules apply to services of general economic interest where potential markets exist,

20 See e.g. Case C-158/96, *Kohll*, ECR 1998, I-1931; Case C-120/95, *Decker*, ECR 1998, I-1831; Case C-372/04, *Watts*, ECR 2006, I-4325.

21 Article 168(2) TFEU effectively represents this inclusion.

22 Commission White Paper on Together for Health: A Strategic Approach for the EU 2008–2013 (COM(2007) 630 final).

23 See the original Rome Treaty of 1957, Art. 90 EEC.

24 See Commission Green Paper of 21 May 2003 on services of general interest (COM(2003) 270 final), White Paper of 12 May 2004 on services of general interest (COM(2004) 374 final), and Communication on Services of general interest, including social services of general interest: a new European commitment (COM(2007) 725 final).

including contracting-out public services. This explicit emphasis was brought up in the context of the White Paper.[25]

The use and battle of definitions concerning services of general interest and general economic interest can be seen as part of a broader context of market-making and market-limiting efforts by various actors. It could be argued that preservation of the emphasis on services of general economic interest as a key category is part of Commission's market-making activity in effectively defining that all outsourced services or contracted-out services fall within the sphere of internal market rules and regulations. The articulation on services of general interest became clearer in the context of the Services Directive and also needs to be seen against the background of the respective provisions of the Constitutional Treaty. However, rather than providing further clarification, the Lisbon Treaty protocol and provisions on services of general interest remain weak in terms of market-limiting impacts, with the most important limitation of treaty provisions covering only non-economic services of general interest.

While the Directorate-General for Employment (DG Employment) has sought to clarify and mediate, the Commission interpretation seems to be quite solidly grounded in the basically generic emphasis of services of general interest as a residual category of services for which no commercial provider interests or markets exist. While there might be sense in taking into account crucial issues with respect to the nature and role of services of general economic interest as the broader and more likely category, the actual provisions do not seem to lend much more support than warm embracing of values and the important role of these services.

Trade in Services and Emerging Concerns in External Aspects of European Policies

The Treaty of Nice first engaged with institutional changes aiming to enable the EU to function more effectively, in particular in the area of trade negotiations. However, health-related issues and concerns were raised in this context due to

25 See Commission White Paper of 12 May 2004 on services of general interest (COM(2004) 374 final): 16–17, stating: 'While in principle the definition of the missions and objectives of social and health services is a competence of the Member States, Community rules may have an impact on the instruments for their delivery and financing. A clear recognition of the distinction between missions and instruments should help to create more clarity with a view to the modernisation of these services in a context of evolving user needs while preserving their specific nature in terms of the particular requirements of, amongst others, solidarity, voluntary service and the inclusion of vulnerable groups of people. Clarifying this distinction will in particular assist Member States which use market-based systems to deliver social and health services to anticipate the possible impact of EU competition law on them. It will of course remain a matter of political choice for Member States whether to use such systems or to provide services directly via tax funded state agencies.'

the emerging broader context of global trade negotiations on services, including health, social and educational services. Member states' concerns applied to the ways in which liberalization of services could be further enhanced through trade agreements without due process or capacity of member states to have a say on at what pace and to what extent they wished their health services to be governed by global or bilateral trade-related agreements.

Particular aspects of Lisbon Treaty negotiations focused on scope for articulation on health, social and educational services as an area of shared competence in trade negotiations as defined in the Treaty of Nice.[26] This had more relevance for some member states than others as some, such as Finland and Sweden, had not bound their health services as part of multilateral trade agreements, such as the General Agreement on Trade in Services, and it was not in the interests of their health ministries to do so either. This is also an example of a case where sectoral policy interests can strongly differ from overall policy priorities as trade and foreign policies were actively supporting more effective coordination and negotiation capacities in the field.

While the Treaty of Nice was a far-reaching compromise between effectiveness of trade negotiations and national sovereignty, it was still insufficient for trade policy proponents. In the Lisbon Treaty this carve-out was further narrowed – in spite of active engagement by several health ministries – to a so-called 'emergency break' limitation, reducing shared competence to requirements for unanimity in negotiating and concluding trade agreements with third countries in the field of trade in social, education and health services, where these agreements risk seriously disturbing the national organization of such services and prejudicing the responsibility of member states to deliver them.[27] Valid concerns exist over how international trade agreements may affect or limit national policy space for regulation and cost-containment within health systems, yet policy priorities of weaker ministries easily become undermined by stronger and more prominent national interests in foreign and trade policies. While international legal analysis and advice would suggest careful and thorough consideration of how, to what extent, and whether health services are included as part of multilateral trade agreements,[28] policy developments within the EU and negotiations on treaty provisions have led more towards undermining this approach. This is a particular concern with respect

---

26 This issue was more explicitly analysed by the Court of Justice only recently in Opinion 1/08, of 30 November 2009, n.y.r., where the Grand Chamber of the Court addressed shared competence (see paras 134–52).

27 Art. 207 TFEU in fact uses almost the same wording as the rather limited recognition of this in Case C-120/95, *Decker*, ECR 1998, I-1831, para. 39: 'It must be recalled that aims of a purely economic nature cannot justify a barrier to the fundamental principle of the free movement of goods. However, it cannot be excluded that the risk of seriously undermining the financial balance of the social security system may constitute an overriding reason in the general interest capable of justifying a barrier of that kind.'

28 See Luff 2003; Fidler, Correa, and Aginam 2003.

to health services, whose organization and nature differ across member states and the implications of trade are not similar in each member state.

Expanding and Negotiating Scope for Health Services in European Union Competence

The European Commission and proponents of health care markets utilize Court of Justice judgments and even Advocate General's Opinions on health services as a basis for expanding Commission competence on health, irrespective of member state criticism over lacking treaty provisions. As part of this process, a high-level group was established to articulate the matter.[29] The need to address long-term sustainability of financing health care was also emerging in the context of using OMC as a means to enhance this. Similar aspects to those that could be raised in the context of services of general interest can again be brought up with respect to the roles and responsibilities of the Commission and member states as to what is sought from OMC. Expansion of the role and relevance of Commission activity in ensuring that member states respect rules laid down in the Treaty in defining, organizing, and financing health care, becomes evident in articulating the Commission's future role.[30]

DG Employment is formally responsible for social policies, which include matters concerning services of general interest and social security. However, the interest of DG SANCO (Directorate-General for Health and Consumer Affairs) in expanding its scope of action can also be seen as part of the desire to engage with the 'weightier politics' of health services issues within national health systems. Health and social security systems operate under considerable budgets and cover substantial economic interests and activity, where European regulatory presence and interest could enable a stronger role and relevance for the Directorate-General responsible for health within the Commission in ensuring that relevant treaty requirements are taken fully on board within member states. The role and aim for enhanced European action would thus not be to counteract policies otherwise

29 See Report of the High Level Committee on health: The internal market and health services, of 17 December 2001. Available at: <http://ec.europa.eu/health/ph_overview/Documents/key06_en.pdf>.

30 The Commission Communication on Modernising social protection for the development of high-quality, accessible and sustainable health care and long-term care: support for national strategies using the 'open method of cooperation' (COM (2004) 304 final): 11, clearly articulates that: 'Responsibility for the organisation and funding of the health care and elderly care sector rests primarily with the Member States, which are bound, *when exercising this responsibility, to respect the freedoms defined and the rules laid down in the Treaty*. The added value of the "open method of coordination" is therefore in the identification of challenges common to all and in support for the Member States' reforms' (emphasis added).

directed by the Court of Justice, but to ensure that member states comply with the requirements of fundamental freedoms and internal market legislation in the area.

Considering that health is an area where treaty provisions have explicitly excluded focus on health services, it has not been one that was easy to expand. On the other hand, treaty provisions can always be changed. This is what took place in the Lisbon Treaty negotiations that aimed to both limit internal market influence on health services, on the one hand, as well as to enhance the Commission's role in the area, on the other. Initial proposals were made, for example by Finland, to specifically exclude health services from the sphere of the internal market as part of treaty provisions to clarify the matter. However, that did not materialize. This aspect is claimed to remain reflected in Article 168(7) TFEU, which states that 'Union action shall respect the responsibilities of the Member States for the definition of their health policy and for the organisation and delivery of health services', and now addresses all Union action. However, in hindsight it is more likely that this merely provides words of comfort for member states which sought this change. Article 168 TFEU is unlikely to be amongst the first considered in the context of the internal market.[31] It was not possible to move this reference closer to the internal market treaty provisions in the Lisbon Treaty negotiations. While at best not much was gained, at worst changes in the Public Health Article may have created further room for Commission action in health services – especially including measures to ensure that national health systems comply with internal market regulations – which initially was one of the problems sought to be addressed through this change. Accommodating the OMC process initiated in the area of health reflected proposals to strengthen EU competence on health to include health services, and a reference was added to Article 168(2) TFEU that the EU will 'encourage cooperation between the Member States to improve the complementarity of their health services in cross-border areas'. It could be claimed that the process of OMC was thus also used to legitimate inclusion of health service-related functions in Article 168 TFEU. Finally, negotiations on the Article's last paragraph (i.e., former 152(5) EC, now 168(7) TFEU) also reflected member state concerns over governance of their health systems. The paragraph was argued to provide the explicit definition that: 'The responsibilities of the Member States shall include the management of health services and medical care and the allocation of the resources assigned to them.' While it is likely that member states assumed this part of the Article would guarantee that governance of health systems falls solely within their competence, the wording merely mentions management

31 The issue reportedly gained positive ground within ministries of health in several member states. However, it is unclear to what extent this aim survived further in negotiations, due to other more pressing priorities and potential lack of national support even in member states which otherwise seemed more open to the issue (e.g. Finland, Sweden and the United Kingdom). This information is based on the author closely following processes during the negotiation phase of the Draft Constitutional Treaty.

of health services and allocation of resources assigned to them, still in practice leaving scope for an EU role in regulating the area.

One of the more contested areas of negotiations was the inclusion of health competence in technology assessment and regulatory oversight on pharmaceutical products, which gained some ground in the treaty process, enabling establishment of a health mandate in pharmaceutical policies. The inclusion of technology assessment in pharmaceuticals and action on alcohol policies was promoted by some member states. However, the wording of Article 168(4)c TFEU on medicines remains contextualized in terms of 'setting high standards of quality and safety for medicinal products and devices for medicinal use', which still falls short of the aims of establishing explicit scope for economic assessment or assessment against existing treatments as part of technology assessment, although it may have paved the way for strengthening health governance in pharmaceutical policies within the EU. In the EU policy division, pharmaceutical policies have been part of industrial policies, with strongly demarcated divisive policy lines between health and industrial policy proponents and also within the Commission. As part of EU policies, a potential constitutional and political gain for health was that in 2009 pharmaceutical policies were shifted under DG SANCO, closer to health governance.

A particular constitutional issue as to evolving EU competence thus relates to the ways in which different aspects of health policy issues and priorities were included or not included in the Lisbon Treaty. As to health, the Lisbon Treaty does not just draw together previous treaty provisions. Further, where treaty negotiations did not bring forth the proposed changes, they were to be complemented as part of other measures in Commission proposals. The active approach of DG SANCO in expanding the treaty base and focus on health services was associated with its weak position within the Commission as a whole. In this context, the active stance of DG Internal Market on matters concerning health services had both positive and negative implications for the role and presence of DG SANCO on health. Moreover, if a choice had to be made between DG Internal Market and DG SANCO, it is prudent to assume that member states would choose DG SANCO.

Internal Markets and Health Services

In health, one of the most contentious areas of disagreement relates to the realization of treaty provisions on the four freedoms, as well to the extent to which health services form part of internal markets. Court of Justice decisions were actively used by the Commission as a basis for its proposals when health services were included as part of the 'Services Directive'[32] proposal and health was swiftly included as part of internal markets. The extent to which this was done irrespective of or in support

32 Directive 2006/123/EC of the European Parliament and of the Council of 12 December 2006 on services in the internal market, OJ L 376, 27 December 2006: 36–68.

of policies and processes enhanced by DG SANCO remains unclear. However, a tendency exists to interpret this as an example of Commission expansion of action in one area extending to another without appropriate consideration for the actual substance of matters involved.[33]

The timing of the Services Directive was of importance as it made more explicit some concerns with respect to Lisbon Treaty negotiations. Furthermore, health services were a particular area where views differed between health ministries and the Commission. Inclusion of health services in the Directive was by no means an accident or something the Commission was forced to do. It was a political choice. The exclusion of health services from the Services Directive was also a political choice. This was further emphasized and confirmed by the Council of Ministers statement on common values, which emerged as a reaction largely against inclusion of health services as ordinary market commodities to be regulated in the context of internal markets.[34]

As health services were excluded from the initial Services Directive, the task of preparing guidance to regulate the area was shifted to DG SANCO. This covered health and consumer issues but in practice ignored DG Employment and Social Affairs, which to a large extent dealt with issues on services of general interest that represented an alternative avenue. However, any expectations of excluding protection of health services from internal market influence were demolished when the subsequent Commission communication and proposal on efficient cross-border health care – later renamed on application of patients' rights – prepared by DG SANCO was first leaked and then submitted in summer 2008.[35] While the proposal for a Directive initially referred to common values, this was in practice used merely as an introductory reference. In contrast to stated values, the Commission proposal chose to emphasize the right to choose health services as well as to use Article 95 EC as the legal basis of the proposal. Using a treaty Article focusing on the functioning of the internal market can be understood in the context of the Commission aiming to include health services as part of stronger Union competence than public health. However, in the context of division of work and competence between the EU and member states, it raises further uncertainties. While in the initial case on tobacco and the internal market, Article 95 EC (now 114 TFEU) was used to enhance health priorities within the EU, this was no longer the case in the context of the proposal on health services, where the aim was more to put health services into the context of internal markets. In this light, it is

33 See, e.g., Greer 2009.

34 See Council conclusions on common values and principles in European Union Health Systems. Council of the European Union, Luxembourg 1–2 June 2006 (OJ C 146, 22 June 2006: 1–3).

35 Commission proposal for a directive of the European Parliament and of the Council on the application of patients' rights in cross-border healthcare (COM(2008) 414 final).

unsurprising that the Commission proposal met with criticism by the European Parliament and most recently by the Council and some member states as well.[36]

The shift of this proposal to DG SANCO may have given it the best of both worlds in terms of power and possibilities of establishing a stronger treaty basis of competence: internal market provisions. On the other hand, ejecting health from the Services Directive implied that, irrespective of the treaty basis, the main oversight and responsibilities were likely to fall to DG SANCO, responsible for health. Member states would also be more willing to support the role of DG SANCO. However, these hopes may be well intended but unrealistic as in many ways this allegiance to the internal market has confirmed the role of DG SANCO as making member state policies comply with internal market regulations, rather than as a channel for member state needs and a 'proponent for health policies' and for taking into account health considerations in all Union policies. The political contentiousness of the proposed Patient's Rights Directive is reflected not only in its change of name but also in that it was first published late and as part of a broader 'social package' in summer 2008, which could also be seen as a means to limit its potential impact on adoption of the Lisbon Treaty.[37]

Public Procurement, Competition and Services Regulation

One example of the new dynamics between Court of Justice decisions and European processes is the area of government procurement, where again the Commission has swiftly provided for interpretative aid for Court decisions.[38] Traditionally, the scope of application of Directives on government procurement has excluded low-

36 The Council of the European Union. Employment, Social Policy, Health and Consumer Affairs. Brussels 30 November–1 December 2009 (document 16611/09): 13, states that 'despite substantial progress, the Council did not reach political agreement on a draft directive concerning the application of patients' rights in cross-border healthcare. The discussions at the Council meeting focused mainly on the reimbursement of costs with regard to non-contractual healthcare providers. The search for a compromise was featured by the intention to fully respect the case-law of the European Court of Justice while preserving Member States' rights to organise their health care system. The incoming Spanish Presidency committed to continue the work and to try to reach an agreement.'

37 The Directive's earlier leaked versions had a different title to the final version. Views and perspectives about the delay were presented, for example, in EU-related news with a reference that 'one of the reasons put forward for holding up the proposal concerns the fears that it could be considered as the "second Bolkenstein Directive". This could come at a politically sensitive time for the EU in the run-up to the ratification of the Lisbon Treaty and jeopardize – yet again – the EU's institutional reform'. See EurActiv.com, January 28 2008: Confusion surrounds EU's health services directive. Available at: <http://www.euractiv.com/en/health/confusion-surrounds-eu-health-services-directive/article-169882>.

38 See the Commission Interpretative Communication, of 23 June 2006, on Community law applicable to contract awards not or not fully subject to the provisions of the Public Procurement Directives.

priced purchases and particular sectors or services on a classificatory basis. This has implied that health services in many countries are not considered as services falling under public procurement provisions. However, some recent case law has changed this in terms of emphasizing that 'although certain contracts are excluded from the scope of the Community directives in the field of public procurement, the contracting authorities which conclude them are nevertheless bound to comply with the fundamental rules of the Treaty'[39] as in the *Vestergaard* case, and also highlighted by the Commission's interpretative communication.[40]

While not necessarily requiring equal measures in terms of tendering, this has in practice implied political room to manoeuvre for those willing to cover health services within public procurement law and to treat health services increasingly as another area of public service and procurement. For example, the government procurement law in Finland was amended to comply with expected Court of Justice case law and thus included health services even at an early stage to anticipate required changes. Other aspects of similar considerations, for example with respect to state aid, have been discussed in the context of their implications for municipal or local government activities.

A number of Court of Justice cases centre on government procurement with different implications for health systems depending on their organization and financing. However, in relation to organization and financing of health services, the requirement to follow the 'fundamental rules of the Treaty' could become disturbing if these mature to policy approaches requiring that where commercial interests are involved in providing services, the services should be contracted-out through a process of tendering. Generally speaking, it is not necessarily beneficial or more efficient for health systems to become dependent on commercial provision or that provision of health services is considered mostly in the context of commercial activities and interests from a health systems and health policy priorities point of view, in particular if health systems are based on the common values articulated in the Council Statement.

Life after the Lisbon Treaty and Efforts to Expand External Competence in Health

As a result of the Lisbon Treaty negotiations, a significant change is expected by way of more 'common' external policies. While the treaty provisions formally limit EU competence to internal issues, this is already an area of contestation and negotiation between the EU and its member states. It is also problematic in relation to partial or limited competences as expressed, for example, in relation to cross-

39 Case C-59/00, *Vestergaard*, ECR 2001, I-9505, para. 20.

40 See the Commission Interpretative Communication, of 23 June 2006, on Community law applicable to contract awards not or not fully subject to the provisions of the Public Procurement Directives: 3.

border care. While the proposed Patients' Rights Directive and the competence definition in that context are likely to focus *de jure* on the narrower area of cross-border care, the shift and competence creep in *de facto* policies could well be larger. A new communication on global health and the EU is also under preparation by the Commission and can be expected to pave the way towards a stronger EU role in international health matters.[41]

Global normative and regulatory policies in health policies have been traditionally defined on the basis of member state coordination and cooperation, rather than strong involvement by the Commission in substantive matters. This is for two reasons. First, the Union has not been a member of the World Health Organization, nor has it had the necessary substantive knowledge, focus and competence in the area of health. Second, policy priorities differ across countries and, as to health, the Commission stands have at times more prominently represented European industrial policy interests than those of health policy. For example, while global health is now promoted by DG Development, the role of DG Development in more substantive areas of health has remained weak and development-related views on health can differ from health ministry views on international health-related standard setting issues that are also governed by the WHO. The basis for decisions is of importance for EU decision-making within international organizations as even if policies were decided from a 'common European Union car', the member states may not always be convinced that health or development policies will occupy the driving seat in respective normative decisions in international organizations. This is an issue particularly in problematic regulatory matters, where substantial conflicts of interest can be foreseen between European economic and industrial policies and those on health.

While the Commission has been active in treaty negotiations concerning tobacco and international health regulations, this role has always been explicitly granted by member states. It is in this context that member states have now started to read carefully what is implied by common foreign and security policies and how treaty provisions can or should be interpreted.

Health in the European Union: Recognition of Rights to Health or Governance by Stealth?

It would be fair to articulate that health issues are not perceived as that important in the EU. For instance, Commissioners responsible for health have frequently come from small or new member states; recent consecutive choices of representatives were from Cyprus and Malta. Expansion of EU competence – i.e., the role of the Commission – has been promoted as a better choice in comparison to having

---

41 See Commission issues paper, of 14 October 2009: EU role in Global Health. Available at: <http://ec.europa.eu/development/icenter/files/europa_only/EU_role_global_health_issue_paper_en.pdf>.

the Court of Justice 'in the driving seat'. The choice of the Court of Justice to focus strongly on treaty provisions and freedoms with little understanding of their implications for national health systems has further enabled this articulation and expansion of the Commission's health competence as one of 'lesser evil'. However, in terms of actual substantive policies, there is little to indicate that expansion of EU competence on health has benefited member state health systems. Conversely, further regulatory engagement at EU level seems also to have created problems of its own as it creates scope for regulatory action, while member states bear the financial consequences.

The Commission's active role in widening the scope of competence contributes to current shifts. A large share of changes is also based on judicial activism, which has defined the starting point for analysis, strengthening the dominance of internal market-based needs and priorities in health policies. However, as a result, 'creeping' governance through different avenues has also created more common ground for more concerted European cooperation in terms of joint opposition by member states on the basis of health concerns, perhaps so far best articulated in the context of the Council statement on values.

While the creeping impact of EU governance and pressures towards commercialization and compliance with treaty provisions have become a kind of integration by 'stealth' of health services, expansion of the EU role and focus in the field of public health and health promotion is lagging, although it is considered, if not promoted, more favourably by member states in issues such as technology assessment, addressing health inequalities and tackling health in other policies. Without further attention to crucial substance issues in health policy, European policies have potential to hinder more than help. If the Lisbon Treaty, constitutionalism or the Court of Justice are to gain a more positive role, this will require balancing measures and considerations, which take seriously the context of health policies, health systems and their organization and financing, as well as duly emphasizing the well-being of citizens and regulatory policy space for health. Otherwise the risk is that the current direction is moving more towards undermining health policy priorities rather than supporting them, and by ensuring market freedoms, paving the way merely to commercialization of health care, rather than addressing crucial European health and health policy concerns of member states.

References

Boessen, S. and Maarse, H. 2008. The impact of the treaty basis on health policy legislation in the European Union: A case study on the tobacco advertising directive. *BMC Health Services Research*, 8:77. Available at: <http://www.biomedcentral.com/1472-6963/8/77> (accessed 18 January 2010).

Byrne, D. 2004. *Enabling Good Health for All. A Reflection Process for a New EU Health Strategy*. Brussels: European Commission. Available at: <http://

ec.europa.eu/health/ph_overview/Documents/pub_good_health_en.pdf> (accessed 18 January 2010).

Fidler, D., Correa, C. and Aginam, O. 2003. Draft Legal Review of the General Agreement on Trade in Services (GATS) from a Health Policy Perspective. Globalisation, Trade and Health Working Paper Series. Geneva: WHO. Available at: <http://www.who.int/trade/resource/GATS_Legal_Review_15_12_05.pdf> (accessed 20 January 2010).

Greer, S. 2006. Uninvited Europeanization: Neofunctionalism and the EU in health policy. *European Public Policy*, 13:1, 134–52.

Greer, S. 2009. *The Politics of European Union Health Policies*. Open University Press: Maidenhead.

Hatzopoulos, V. 2002. Killing national health and insurance systems but *healing* patients? The European market for health care services after the judgments of ECJ in *Vanbraekel* and *Peerbooms*. *Common Market Law Review*, 39:4, 683–729.

Kaczorowska, A. 2006. Review of the creation by the European Court of Justice of the right to effective and speedy medical treatment and its outcomes. *European Law Journal*, 12:3, 345–70.

Kumm, M. 2006. Constitutionalising subsidiarity in integrated markets: The case of tobacco regulation in the European Union. *European Law Journal*, 12:4, 503–33.

Luff, D. 2003. Regulation of health services and international trade law, in *Domestic Regulation and Service Trade Liberalisation*, edited by A. Mattoo and P. Sauve. New York: World Bank and Oxford University Press, 191–220.

Newdick, C. 2006. Citizenship, free movement and health care: Cementing individual rights by corroding social solidarity. *Common Market Law Review*, 43:6, 1645–68.

Ståhl, T., Wismar, M., Ollila, E., Lahtinen, E. and Leppo, K. 2006. *Health in all Policies: Prospects and Potentials.* Helsinki: Ministry of Social Affairs and Health.

Index

Tables are indicated by *italic* page numbers. Legal cases are indicated by *italic* headings.

For Product Safety Concerns and Information please contact our EU representative GPSR@taylorandfrancis.com Taylor & Francis Verlag GmbH, Kaufingerstraße 24, 80331 München, Germany

Batch number: 10725973

Printed by Printforce, the Netherlands